Spirit Deep

Studies in Religion and Culture

John D. Barbour and Gary L. Ebersole, Editors

TISHA M. BROOKS

Spirit Deep

RECOVERING THE SACRED IN BLACK WOMEN'S TRAVEL

UNIVERSITY OF VIRGINIA PRESS
Charlottesville and London

University of Virginia Press
© 2023 by the Rector and Visitors of the University of Virginia
All rights reserved
Printed in the United States of America on acid-free paper

First published 2023

1 3 5 7 9 8 6 4 2

Library of Congress Cataloging-in-Publication Data

Names: Brooks, Tisha M., author.
Title: Spirit deep : recovering the sacred in Black women's travel / Tisha M. Brooks.
Description: Charlottesville : University of Virginia Press, 2023. | Series: Studies in religion and culture | Includes bibliographical references and index.
Identifiers: LCCN 2022035686 (print) | LCCN 2022035687 (ebook) | ISBN 9780813948928 (hardcover ; acid-free paper) | ISBN 9780813948935 (paperback ; acid-free paper) | ISBN 9780813948942 (ebook)
Subjects: LCSH: American literature—African American authors—History and criticism. | American literature—Women authors—History and criticism. | Travelers' writings, American—History and criticism. | African American women—Intellectual life. | African American women—Travel. | Spirituality in literature. | Holy, The, in literature. | LCGFT: Literary criticism.
Classification: LCC PS153.B53 B76 2023 (print) | LCC PS153.B53 (ebook) | DDC 810.9/32082—dc23/eng/20221110
LC record available at https://lccn.loc.gov/2022035686
LC ebook record available at https://lccn.loc.gov/2022035687

Cover photo: Woman in dark dress holding a fan, ca. 1890, photographed by Alvan S. Harper in Tallahasee, Florida. (State Archives of Florida, Florida Memory)

*To the women who made me: Tonyia, Rita, Della, and Gertrude.
Your lives and work made possible my own.*

The past is neither inert nor given. The stories we tell about what happened then, the correspondences we discern between today and times past, and the ethical and political stakes of these stories redound in the present.
—Saidiya Hartman, *Lose Your Mother*

Contents

Acknowledgments xi

Introduction 1

ONE   Spirituality and Mobility in Hagar's Narrative 13

TWO   Visionary Movement in Zilpha Elaw's *Memoirs* 39

THREE   Colonial and Missionary Crossings in Amanda Smith's *An Autobiography* 71

FOUR   Searching for Home in Nancy Prince's *A Narrative* 109

FIVE   Mapping Sacred Movement in Julie Dash's *Daughters of the Dust* 147

SIX   Secular Journeys, Sacred Recovery in Saidiya Hartman's *Lose Your Mother* 180

Coda 217

Notes 223

Bibliography 243

Index 259

Acknowledgments

This project has changed a great deal on the journey to becoming a book, and I am grateful for the many people who have supported me along the way, especially Christina Sharpe, Elizabeth Ammons, and Joycelyn Moody, who read my work in the early stages, offered critical feedback, and asked challenging questions. Special thanks also to the late Rev. Charles Rice for helping me chart a path toward becoming a writer, scholar, and professor. Our conversations about this project pushed me to wrestle with the questions I did not have the answer to. I am grateful not only for this critical engagement with my work but also for this mentorship that has transformed my scholarship and teaching.

Thanks to the entire team at the University of Virginia Press. I am grateful to Eric Brandt for his gracious guidance and communication throughout the process and to the series editors, John D. Barbour and Gary L. Ebersole, for seeing the potential in this project and championing the manuscript early on. Many thanks to Kate Epstein, Amber Williams, and to the outside reviewers of the book for taking time to read and provide substantive feedback on the manuscript. I have written an infinitely better book thanks to their recommendations and investment in this project.

Thanks to Southern Illinois University Edwardsville (SIUE) for institutional support in the form of a Seed Grant for Transitional and Exploratory Projects, as well as a sabbatical that enabled me to do the research, writing, and revision necessary to complete this book. Thanks also to the Graduate School, the College of Arts and Sciences and Department of English for helping to subsidize the printing of this book.

Writing a book is hard. Writing a first book is harder. Thankfully, I have the privilege of working with supportive colleagues at SIUE who made the path forward clearer. Many thanks to Howard Rambsy, who was willing to help me chart the journey and provide inestimable guidance along the way. Elizabeth Cali was willing to talk with me about my work and write with me during the difficult seasons—helping me find clarity in the midst of uncertainty. Catherine Seltzer has been a joyous accountability buddy and a constant reminder that I do not write alone. Jessica DeSpain and Helena Gurfinkel answered my questions about book proposals and offered models for navigating the proposal process.

Thanks also to my African American literature students for joining me on this journey. Our critical engagement with the literature and film in this study has enriched my understanding of the women in *Spirit Deep* and has underscored the significance of their lives and journeys in the classroom and beyond.

I am grateful for the support of my Faculty Success Program colleagues: Manu Chander, Helene Lee, and Cassandra Jones. Our regular calls helped sustain me through the marathon process of writing and publishing this book. Many thanks for listening to my frustrations, helping me navigate challenges, and for celebrating every win.

Finally, this journey would not have been possible without the care and support of my family, who have my deepest love and gratitude. To Alex and Avery, my dear ones, for reminding me what truly matters and for graciously understanding the importance of my work. They have been gifts to me on this journey and a profound source of joy along the way. To my partner, Branden, for believing in me and this book even when I doubted and for making sacrifices to ensure that I had everything I needed to reach the finish line. To my grandmother, Rita, for introducing me to travel from a young age, for opening up the world and showing me what's possible. To my parents, Tonyia and Corey, for teaching me the value of a faith-filled life and passing down to me the spiritual resources necessary to sustain hope in the midst of despair. Thanks to this spiritual legacy, I have the privilege of resting in the unending grace and steadfast love of God that has sustained me on my way.

Earlier versions of parts of this book were previously published. Courtesy of Africa Knowledge Project, the article, "Conflicted Journeys: Colonial and Missionary Crossings in Amanda Smith's *An Autobiography*" was originally published in *JENdA: A Journal of Culture and African Women Studies*, Issue 22, 2013: 66–86. *JENdA: A Journal of Culture and African Women*

Studies and can be accessed online at https://www.africaknowledgeproject.org/index.php/jenda/JENdA: *A Journal of Culture and African Women Studies.* The article, "Searching for 'Free Territory' in Saidiya Hartman's *Lose Your Mother*," was originally published in the *Border States* special issue of *The Journal of the Midwest Modern Language Association* 50, no. 2 (Fall 2017): 57–83.

Spirit Deep

Introduction

Zilpha Elaw, Amanda Berry Smith, and Nancy Prince engaged in radical spiritual practices, characterized by an unlikely mobility. As missionaries, tourists, activists, ethnographers, and entrepreneurs at a time when the majority of Black women in America were held captive within the institution of slavery or within white domestic spaces in the "free" North, they traveled domestically and internationally, preaching, prophesying, and lecturing. They also documented their extraordinary lives in spiritual travelogues: Elaw's *Memoirs of the Life, Religious Experience, Ministerial Travels and Labours of Mrs. Zilpha Elaw* (1846), Smith's *An Autobiography: The Story of the Lord's Dealings with Mrs. Amanda Smith* (1893), and Prince's *A Narrative of the Life and Travels of Mrs. Nancy Prince* (1853). These narratives ground this book's exploration of the spiritual knowledge and theological productions evident in Black women's literature. Elaw, Smith, and Prince's narratives also demonstrate an inextricable link between spirituality and travel—an intersection that persists in and through the journeys of twentieth and twenty-first century Black women whose texts reveal the movement of the sacred in unexpected places. Beyond Elaw's, Smith's, and Prince's works, this book draws on the biblical narrative of Hagar (an enslaved Egyptian woman owned by Abraham and Sarah), Julie Dash's twentieth-century film *Daughters of the Dust* (1991), and a twenty-first-century travel narrative by Saidiya Hartman *Lose Your Mother* (2007). This unlikely collection of works exploring spirituality and travel illustrates the new conversations and connections that become visible when we move beyond the traditional boundaries and approaches that delimit the study of travel and of Black women's journeys.

Spirit Deep is a study of crossings and connections. It examines a disparate collection of texts that rarely fit neatly into a single genre. That is, they reflect what some literary scholars refer to as the "hybridity" of African American literature. For example, Smith's and Prince's texts merge the slave narrative, spiritual autobiography, and travel writing genres. Similarly, Hartman's contemporary narrative of slavery blends historical, autobiographical, and travel writing. *Spirit Deep* makes visible these disruptions, the ways in which these texts cross borders and boundaries of genre.

This study also bridges two disciplinary divides. The first is between religious and literary studies; *Spirit Deep* places spiritual texts in conversation with so-called secular ones. Reading through both a theological and literary lens reveals that its subjects' journeys are expressions of their radical spiritual practice. *Spirit Deep* takes seriously the spiritual knowledge and theological contributions of Black women's narratives, claiming theology as the primary shaping force for Black women spiritualists and making visible how the spirit runs deep through all of the texts in this study. The second divide is that within travel writing studies, between coerced and "free" passages. The dominant narrative of Black women within American travel writing studies has positioned Black women as lacking the freedom of the traveler, defined as white and most often male.[1] *Spirit Deep,* however, rejects the singular story of Black women during the nineteenth century as captive bodies held in place by their raced, gendered, and classed status. Rather, it takes seriously Black women's mobility and the ways it complicates the relationship between travel and freedom by showcasing the often spirit-led movements of Black women with varying access to material resources and privilege. As such, it troubles the divide between "free" and coerced movements.

This divide has constrained our understanding of Black women's travel. The statements of one editor as to why her collection of travel writing excluded women of color illustrate this (Morris xxi–xxii). She describes women travelers as having long been "of the upper classes . . . invariably white and privileged" and attributes, regretfully, the lack of "multicultural voices" in the collection to their nonexistence, writing, "the voices we present are those we found." She further explains: "For various reasons, we decided not to include involuntary travel. It would have seemed casual—disrespectful, even—to juxtapose slave narratives . . . and . . . stories of flight and displacement with accounts of deserts crossed, swamps forded, and mountains climbed by choice." This justification does not consider the impact of a narrow definition of travel on the search process: the continued marginalization of Black travel writing and the subsequent mythology that "Black folk don't travel."[2]

Such exclusions also ignore the blurring of boundaries. The narratives I explore here reflect the tenuous link between coerced and "free" movements, rather than a firm divide. They chronicle the journeys of formerly enslaved and free Black women, those who were orphaned, indentured, and even at times homeless but who also became itinerant preachers, entrepreneurs, activists, and academics. *Spirit Deep*, therefore, expands on and contributes to a growing body of work that foregrounds the travel of Black people and, consequently, responds to this historical erasure of their journeys.[3] While previous studies either foreground the travel of Black men or place Black women in comparative analysis with white women or Black men, *Spirit Deep* places the journeys of Black women alone at the center of study. This allows for a deeper engagement with the multiplicity of Black women's journeys across a variety of time periods and genres. *Spirit Deep* also enters into a broader conversation about the theological, literary, and sociopolitical contributions of Black women spiritual autobiographers by drawing from and building on a legacy of literary scholarship on nineteenth-century Black women writers, especially scholars such as Carla Peterson, Joycelyn Moody, Richard Douglass-Chin, and Rosetta Haynes, who have argued for the significance of nineteenth-century Black women spiritualists within African American literary studies.[4] *Spirit Deep* urges us to reconsider these texts by moving Black women's mobility to the forefront of analysis because the fundamental questions that arise from their travel—questions of home, identity, and belonging continue to haunt our communities and landscape.

Moreover, the complexity of Black women's writing—their refusal to embrace singular narratives about travel, about slavery, about Black people in the United States or abroad—demands an expansive approach by scholars.[5] Thus, I employ multiple critical and theoretical perspectives, including womanist theology and the work of Black feminist scholars within the fields of literary, cultural, and Black diaspora studies. I also draw on scholarship focused on slavery, colonization, and migration in order to place Black women's travel in conversation with these larger historical processes and diasporic movements. In providing this broader context for Black women's spiritual journeys, *Spirit Deep* demonstrates how race, gender, class, and Black women's often-tenuous status as Western subjects informs and complicates their mobility.

I agree with literary scholar Joycelyn Moody's claim that "to overlook, to 'read around' the spiritual dimensions present in these books is to neglect an essential and vital aspect of them. . . . Any person who values literature should read spiritual texts *as* spiritual texts because we should not disparage or diminish the full complexity of any text" (xi–xii). Thus, I bring together the work of African American literary scholars who foreground spirituality in their analyses of Black women spiritualists/writers, as well as womanist theologians because of their professed commitment to take the sacred seriously in Black women's lives and writing. Reading the sacred in the works examined here, including "spiritual texts" and so-called secular texts, involves taking seriously what Black women know and how they come to know it.

Likewise, womanism has interdisciplinary roots in the fields of literature and religion; therefore, it complements my goal of bridging the sacred and secular. The term womanist originates in Alice Walker's collection of literary essays, *In Search of Our Mothers' Gardens* (1983). She writes that it includes "outrageous, audacious, courageous or *willful* behavior. Wanting to know more and in greater depth than is considered 'good' for one.... Committed to survival and wholeness of entire people.... *Loves* the Spirit.... Loves struggle. *Loves* the Folk. Loves herself. *Regardless*" (xi). In line with these elements of Walker's longer definition, the womanist praxis that I employ in *Spirit Deep* includes the desire for depth, to go deep, a desire to "know more" that is often viewed as excessive, unruly, disruptive. It includes "tal[k]ing back to the text," a principle in line with both womanist and Black feminist praxis.[6] Hence, I challenge, interrogate, and question texts and inherited traditions, as well as larger systems of oppression and domination that have shaped and continue to shape our world. Talking back resists the erasure, marginalization, and violation of Black women's bodies, lives, and spirits. It is central to the survival of Black people and Black women in particular.

The ongoing assault against Black life has always been physical, psychic, and spiritual.[7] Therefore, survival demands a commitment to wholeness grounded in interdependence. Unlike the traditional Western value of individualism, within this particular cosmology, as Toni Morrison claims in "Rootedness: The Ancestor as Foundation," the survival of the individual is inextricably linked to the survival of the entire community, the collective, the folk, and the ancestors, who "provide a certain kind of wisdom" (Morrison 62). For both Morrison and Walker, knowledge about Black people who came before and who survived in hostile and unlivable places is spiritual and characterized by a "profound rootedness in the real world" (Morrison, "Rootedness" 61). Hence, within a womanist framework, wholeness is expressed not only through the interdependence of all people but is achieved also through embracing the intersection of sacred/secular and the body/spirit.

Bridging the sacred/secular and body/spirit, womanist scholar Katie G. Cannon offers a foundational understanding of womanism as an interpretive framework for theological study. In her book, *Katie's Canon: Womanism and the Soul of the Black Community* (1995), Cannon employs Walker's definition as a methodological framework but also foregrounds Black women's literature as a primary source for unearthing Black women's theological work, as well as their spiritual and cultural legacy. Rather than limiting their search for spiritual knowing to strictly sacred texts, womanists embrace a variety of genres recognizing that the sacred can be found throughout the diversity of Black women's creative productions. Demonstrating a similar commitment to unearthing the ancestral knowledge of Black women, *Spirit Deep* traces the continuities of Hagar's legacy throughout the various texts it considers. In adopting this approach *Spirit Deep* brings together a diversity of stories about what it has meant and continues to mean for Black women to move through the world—making visible the sacred at work in their movements.

If Black women's narratives are "the soil" of a rich spiritual and cultural inheritance, in their reading of such source material, womanist scholars foreground Black embodiment and lived experience in their analysis of how Black women understand and navigate a harsh world. A primary concern of Cannon's womanist praxis is "identify[ing] the critical contestable issues at the center of Black life—issues inscribed on the bodies of Black people" (70). This concern persists throughout womanist scholarship. For womanist scholars, theology is not just a critical reflection on the self and one's relationship to God but it is also a critical reflection outward onto the world and its injustices (Moody 17). Hence, theology is not concerned solely with the spirit, but with the body as well and particularly with what happens to that body in a world shaped by race, class, and gender oppression. This is precisely how Zilpha Elaw, Amanda Smith, and Nancy Prince use theology in their narratives—as a critical framework and lens through which to view the world. Theology shapes not only their perspectives but also their practices—how they act and especially how and even where they move in the world. Therefore, taking the sacred seriously (tending to the theological and spiritual aspects of the text) demands that we place the body "at the center of inquiry," as M. Shawn Copeland attests (ix).

Placing the Black body at the center of analysis necessitates talking about slavery and its afterlife, in particular its attempted destruction of Black bodies through physical and spiritual violence. Though *Spirit Deep* certainly addresses physical violence, the study foregrounds the less visible forms of violation that occur through the inscription of dominant narratives on and the misnaming of Black women's bodies as monstrous, strange, and alien.[8] Within the context of slavery, something I will address further in the chapters that follow, Black female bodies were defined as objects of property, objects of production, objects of reproduction, and objects of sexual violence rather than as subjects.[9] Though this study focuses largely on free Black women, my analysis reveals that these definitions are inscribed on the bodies of Black women regardless of their status as "free." Hence, all of the texts are informed by slavery—bearing witness to the incomplete nature of freedom in the United States, as well as in the various countries and locations Black women journey to. Though *Spirit Deep* takes seriously the fluid and multiple contexts (historical, social, literary, and spiritual) in which Black women move, this study privileges the intersections between and the continuities across the varying texts included. In doing so, I hope to make visible the persistence of Black women's journeys as central to their attempts to "tell a free story" and to demonstrate the role of the sacred in their movements and practices of freedom.[10]

Spirit Deep also bears witness to Black women's knowledge about their lives and journeys that presents an alternative, often discredited, perspective about travel, about spirituality, about Black (female) bodies and Black (female) subjectivity. Kimberley Wallace-Sanders has noted that "When Black women stand at the center of the discussion about the female body, their bodies tell a profoundly different story about historic and contemporary American culture" (5). *Spirit Deep* pushes beyond a single story about Black women and their spiritual journeys because, as so many Black feminist and womanist writers, thinkers, and scholars attest, "To be black in America is no singular thing;. . . . To be a black woman in the Americas is to navigate and negotiate multiple identities and perspectives" (Gafney 2). Rather than produce a singular vision of Black women as traveling subjects, I explore the competing subjectivities at work in their texts that complicate and disrupt the trajectory of their narratives and purposes of their voyages abroad. Consequently, I reveal their journeys to be informed by slavery and freedom, by sacred and secular motivations, privilege and oppression, anti-racism and imperialism. This methodology requires highlighting not only the multiple trajectories for Black women's travel, but also their various expressions of spirituality, and their rich, intersecting, and sometimes-divergent visions for how to reconstruct our present and future world.[11]

In contrast to the dominant definition of Black women's bodies as "not sacred" and as all body (flesh), the varied works in this study reveal the inextricable link between the body and spirit.[12] *Spirit Deep* centers around what I term the *embodied spiritual practices* of Black women. That is, it centers around the link between Black women's spiritual lives and their material reality in bodies marked by race, gender, class, and the violent forces of slavery and colonization. Positioning themselves as subjects who resist the objectification of their bodies, Black women define themselves as "made for freedom" and as "subjects of freedom." I define these practices as sacred and as embodied because the Black body reflects "the enfleshing of created spirit" (Copeland 24). The spirit finds its home in the body and, as Copeland asserts, freedom is achieved through the union of body and spirit. The body is both the vessel through which Black women throughout this study encounter the sacred and a medium through which the sacred moves in and through the world.[13] In opposition to the classification of Black women in the nineteenth century as spectacle, as foreign and as monstrous (i.e., as not sacred), Elaw, Smith, and Prince continually asserted their bodies as sanctified or holy through practices such as preaching, singing, prophesying, and itinerancy. These practices bear witness to the spirit at home and at work in and through their bodies. Dash's film and Hartman's travel narrative reveal the persistent legacies of alienation and violation. Though, in these texts, the spiritual practices of Black women grow and expand beyond any single or formal religious/spiritual framework and include work often deemed secular (filmmaking, historical recovery, academic research and writing), they reflect the continuation of an alternative spiritual legacy.

Building on Katherine McKittrick's theorizing of the Black female body and space, my analysis emphasizes itinerancy. Here I reference both the traditional definition of itinerancy that has its roots in sacred movements (preaching and ministry) and the broader meanings of the term, which can also mean "to travel about" or "to journey from place to place." Given that *Spirit Deep* explores a diversity of Black women's movements and crossings (physical, geographical, and social), I employ the term *itinerant* to indicate Black women (body and spirit) as "on the move." Through it I highlight the significance of free Black women's movements across boundaries and spaces shaped by race, class, and gender, as well as their circum-Atlantic travel as preachers, missionaries, and tourists. I have borrowed the term "circum-Atlantic" from Joseph Roach's text *Cities of the Dead: Circum-Atlantic Performance* (1996), in which he defines the circum-Atlantic world as "a vortex in which commodities and cultural practices changed hands many times. The most revolutionary commodity in this economy was human flesh. . . . The concept of a circum-Atlantic world (as opposed to a transatlantic one) insists on the centrality of the diasporic and genocidal histories of Africa and the Americas, North and South, in the creation of the culture of modernity" (4). I have chosen this term because it invokes, like Paul Gilroy's "black Atlantic," the violent itinerancies of slavery and colonization, which haunt all of the narratives included in *Spirit Deep*. But, more than "black Atlantic," it invokes a sense of circulation, movement—especially nonlinear movement, which is important for describing the nonlinear travel routes that Smith's, Prince's, and Julie Dash's narratives depict.

Through their spiritual itinerancy, transgressive movements and passages, Black women have resisted violently enforced geographies of the slave trade, colonization, and imperialism, as well as the violence of socially constructed spaces, such as the pulpit, the courthouse, the auction block, the slave ship, and the marketplace. The constructed nature of these spaces enables possibilities for reimagining the places Black women inhabit.[14] In this way Black women create alternative spaces and geographies that re-vision Black women as sacred and free.

Chapter Overview

In tension with the academic tendency to align knowledge production solely with thinking, *Spirit Deep* begins with the following premises: a) the sacred is embodied through lived experience, b) spiritual knowledge is gained and accessed through embodiment,[15] and c) the varying texts in the study bear witness to the deep spiritual knowing housed in the bodies of Black women. Given the devastating consequences of slavery and colonization, which sever and divide body and spirit, leading to practices of alienation and captivity rather than of freedom, *Spirit Deep* engages in two forms of recovery:

1) the practice of reclaiming that which has been lost through disciplinary and methodological divides and
2) the process of returning to a state of health and wholeness through the reintegration of body and spirit.

In tracing the sacred across the six chapters that follow, *Spirit Deep* does not only reclaim what has been lost in these various divides. If I have done my job well, my exploration of Black women's journeys will reveal possibilities for a decolonized vision of our present and future world—one that can return us personally and collectively to a state of wholeness and well-being.

The opening chapter centers on an analysis of the spiritual journey of Hagar, whose narrative of captivity, escape, and return appears in the biblical text of Genesis. Although feminist scholars in both religious and literary studies have sought to recover Hagar's theological and literary impact, my analysis of Hagar's text locates her specifically as a spiritual foremother (i.e., ancestor) of nineteenth-century Black women spiritualists. Through an analysis of Hagar's theological and literary contributions, this chapter delineates one possible point of origin for a Black female spiritual legacy at work in African American women's literature and film and foregrounds Black women's movements as inextricably linked to and as key expressions of their spiritual practice. Providing the foundation for the chapters that follow, chapter one reveals the complexity of Black women's spiritual journeys by revealing how Hagar's varied movements demonstrate a practice of freedom that seeks both spiritual and material (embodied) transformation.

Chapter 2's focus on Zilpha Elaw's *Memoirs* (1846), one of the earliest Black female spiritual autobiographies, demonstrates more fully the link between Black women's spiritual narratives and travel writing. I begin my discussion of nineteenth-century Black women spiritualists with Elaw because she was the first to foreground international travel within her text. This chapter builds on and expands beyond the growing body of scholarship on *Memoirs* by considering how Elaw's work of spiritual autobiography contributes to our understanding of nineteenth-century Black women's travel. My analysis demonstrates how, much like Hagar's journeys, Elaw's itinerant movements, her travel to England, and her struggle against slavery and against definitions of Black women as captive bodies reflect and are informed by her visionary encounters with God. This multi-perspective approach foregrounds Elaw's body and embodied practices of itinerant preaching, prophecy, and missionary travel to uncover the discredited knowledge she accessed through her embodied encounters with the divine and reveal the unlikely direction and impact of her spirit-led journeys. As such, this chapter makes visible her theological and literary contributions to spiritual autobiography and positions Elaw within broader conversations about Black mobility and freedom in the United States and abroad.

Like Elaw's *Memoirs*, Amanda Smith's 1893 text expands the bounds of spiritual autobiography by revealing the inextricable link between Black women's spiritual visionary experience and their travel. Chapter 3 foregrounds Smith's blending of the slave narrative form, spiritual autobiography, and travel writing to reveal travel as spiritual work that is liberatory, meaningful, and God-supported. My analysis of Smith's text widens the typical scholarly focus on domesticity as the prime motivator of women's travel. In so doing, I consider both her theological contributions and her engagement with the key political conversations of her day, including colonization, the contested meaning of Africa, and lynching. Embracing the multiplicity and complexity of Smith's text, this chapter locates her movements and her embodied spiritual practice within the broader contexts of slavery, white supremacy, and Western tourism, as well as colonial and missionary travel.

Chapter 4 continues to explore the intersection of slavery, spirituality, and travel. My analysis of Nancy Prince's narrative draws from scholarship that foregrounds Prince's travel and writing as challenging racial injustice within the United States, ultimately questioning whether the United States is a viable home for Black people. This chapter extends beyond current scholarship by exploring the multiple spiritual legacies that inform her activism, which is typically read as secular rather than sacred practice, and by offering an alternative interpretation of Prince's travel to and nine-year stay in Russia. By reading her account through the lens of the sacred and secular, I demonstrate that her experiences there were spiritually transformative and shaped her travel and activism in the United States and Jamaica. Moreover, Prince's engagement with the question of home for African Americans persists through the chapters that follow.

Chapter 5 opens up the spiritual legacy of Black women even further by turning to Julie Dash's 1991 film, *Daughters of the Dust,* which recovers the complex spiritual geographies of Black people throughout the diaspora. This chapter expands our understanding of Black women's travel by revealing the complexity of their diasporic movements and by broadening the conversation about Black women's travel beyond narratives of captivity and traditional travel texts. The film makes visible the intersection between journeys of captivity, migration, and "free" travel. Like Elaw's, Smith's, and Prince's texts, the content of *Daughters* as well as Dash's methods of filming reflect the joint expression of the sacred and secular in the lives and work of Black women. Centering my analysis on both Dash's cinematic practice and the geographies of Black female characters in the film, this chapter situates

Dash's filmmaking and Black women's diasporic movements as expressions of and at times shapers and transformers of Black women's spiritual work. I position *Daughters* as part of Hagar's spiritual and literary legacy, as the film expands beyond a singular focus on Christianity by considering the intersection of Islam and African traditional spirituality with the various diasporic crossings of Black people in Africa, the Caribbean, and in the southern United States. By tracing connections across Hagar's narrative and those of nineteenth-century Black women spiritualists, chapter 5 illustrates the continued significance of these earlier works and opens up a conversation about potential intersections between the nineteenth- and the twentieth-century journeys of Black women.

Chapter 6 shifts from the twentieth- to the twenty-first century with a focus on Saidiya Hartman's 2007 work of travel writing, *Lose Your Mother*. Like Dash's film, Hartman's text is committed to the important work of recovery. Specifically, Hartman seeks to recover the voices and narratives of enslaved people that have been lost to the historical archive and to practices of forgetting. In line with this, current scholarship on Hartman reflects a singular focus on memory and loss. Yet *Lose Your Mother* fully embraces the travel writing genre. In choosing to foreground the inextricable link between slavery and between Western and diasporic travel, *Lose Your Mother* reflects a central theme of slavery. My approach, thus, explores the intersection of slavery, travel, and spirituality in Hartman's work. Although Hartman positions her own travel and recovery work as secular, my analysis reveals the role of the sacred in her journey and in her critical practices. It also places Hartman's travel within a broader conversation about Western travel, slavery, colonization, and the diasporic movements of Black people in the past and present. Most important, Hartman's book enables us to draw a link between the early legacy of Black women spiritualists and travelers from the nineteenth century through the twentieth century and into our contemporary moment. This chapter demonstrates the significance of nineteenth-century Black women's spiritual journeys to understand the complex and persistent movements of Black people throughout the world.

The book's coda reconsiders the central question of what's at stake in recovering the spiritual journeys of Black women travelers. It clarifies the continuities between Elaw, Smith, and Prince and the continued journeys of Black women considered in chapters 5 and 6. If as Saidiya Hartman asserts, slavery's afterlife is an ever-present reality in our world, we must take seriously how that reality continues to haunt Black people's movements in the present. Just as Dash and Hartman's work explores the lasting impact of diasporic legacies of slavery and colonization on Black people's lives in the United States and abroad, the coda reminds us that Black travel continues to reflect those legacies, as do our critical approaches to the study of Black travel writing. Ultimately, in recovering the spiritual geographies and practices of Black women, *Spirit Deep* considers the possibility of developing mobile and critical practices that do not replicate the violence of the past.

As the title of the book suggests, I position my work as a project of recovery—one that engages in recovery work and draws from the recovery practices of other Black women writers—positioning such practices as sacred work. In its commitment to the recovery of Black women's bodies and lives, *Spirit Deep* recognizes that recovering the physical body alone is not enough. As Deborah McDowell notes in her afterword to *Recovering the Black Female Body: Self-Representations by African American Women* (2001), the body is more than flesh. For this reason, McDowell urges that scholars adopt "a view of the body that perceives the reciprocal relation between exterior and interior, between visible and invisible 'matter,' between the outside and the inside body" (309). My own recovery efforts integrate body and spirit by attending to the external material realities and the interior (spiritual) lives of Black women, revealing the intersection of the two in their journeys. Hence, this study offers an expanded understanding of recovery as one in which we must go deep to find the inner workings of the spirit.

· ONE ·

Spirituality and Mobility in Hagar's Narrative

> Cast out this slave woman with her son; for the son of this slave woman shall not inherit along with my son Isaac.
> —Genesis 21:10 (NRSV)

> Now this is an allegory: these women are two covenants. One woman, in fact, is Hagar, from Mount Sinai, bearing children for slavery.... But the other woman [Sarah] corresponds to the Jerusalem above; she is free, and she is our mother.
> —Galatians 4:24, 26 (NRSV)

Hagar's Legacy: Dispossession, Exile and Erasure

Hagar's story in the book of Genesis begins with her enslavement and forced journey from Egypt, her homeland, to the household of Abraham and Sarah, her master and mistress. As an enslaved woman, Hagar is expected to provide physical labor for Sarah and Abraham, as well as sexual and reproductive labor. In response to God's promise that their descendants will number the stars in the sky, Sarah, certain of her own barrenness, uses her power and privilege to bring God's promise to fruition. Commanding Abraham to "go into my slave girl . . . that I may obtain children by her" (Gen. 16:2), Sarah gives Hagar to Abraham to produce an heir.[1] Hagar's status as chattel becomes doubly evident as Sarah's words (go into) position Hagar's body as an always open and always available vessel that can be entered at the behest of the master and mistress—laying claim to Hagar's body and to any children she produces.

At this point in the text only Sarah and Abraham have the privilege of speaking while Hagar's voice is silenced in this moment. The text withholds her response to this violation of her body to meet the varying needs and demands of her owners. However, once Hagar becomes pregnant, she begins to challenge her marginalized status. Perhaps her pregnancy emboldens her as the text bears witness to Hagar's active resistance to Sarah's abusive authority and power. After Sarah physically punishes Hagar for challenging her authority, Hagar disobeys further by running away to the desert—most likely to escape further violence. While there, Hagar has an intense and transformative encounter with God, who, seeing her all alone and with no resources in the wilderness, invites her to tell her story with the question "Hagar, where have you come from and where are you going?" Promising her a future inheritance as the mother of so many descendants "that they cannot be counted" (Gen. 16:10), God commands Hagar to return to Sarah and Abraham's household. In awe that God would see her at all, meet her in a profound place of need, and offer her a future inheritance characterized not by captivity and dispossession but by freedom and fulfillment, Hagar obeys God and returns to Sarah and Abraham.

As a result of her return, Ishmael is born safely and healthy in Sarah and Abraham's household, where she nurses and cares for him alongside Isaac, the son eventually born to Abraham and Sarah. But when Sarah sees her son Isaac playing with Ishmael, she responds with fear and unrestrained power, calling for the exile of "this slave woman with her son" (Gen. 21:10). Denying their full identity and humanity in her refusal to name Hagar and Ishmael, Sarah consigns them to the dessert with little chance of survival. Though Abraham gives Hagar a small amount of water and bread before sending her out, this does not provide nearly enough sustenance to survive a long journey to some more habitable place. In short, Hagar's exile is a death sentence.

Yet once again, God enters into Hagar's place of need, hearing her cries for help and giving her divine sight to find water for herself and for her son. Moreover, God reiterates the divine promise of hope and a future decreed during her earlier escape into the wilderness. But this time, Hagar's journey is defined not by captivity but by freedom. She is now free to mother her son on her own terms and to build a life for herself and her son, which she does through her eventual return to Egypt where she finds him a wife. Further honoring her agency and freedom, God fulfills the promise to protect her son and to make her the "mother of a people."[2]

Notably the biblical story of Hagar in Genesis ends with Hagar's possession of freedom and God's fulfillment of a divine promise—a God-authored inheritance. Yet Sarah and Abraham's exploitation and expulsion of Hagar, as well as Paul's allegorical positioning of Christians in the book of Galatians (4:21–5:1) as Sarah's descendants, not Hagar's, have profoundly shaped Hagar's legacy within American culture (religion, literature, and art). This legacy has been defined by dispossession rather than possession, a legacy of exile rather than homecoming, a legacy of perpetual enslavement with no hope of freedom. Through a critical reading of her story in Genesis, however, I make visible an alternative legacy for Hagar as well as for her spiritual and literary daughters—a legacy of persistent and disruptive movement that challenges this history of alienation and marginalization at the center of Black women's experiences.

In opposition to the legacy of spiritual dispossession and exile that has plagued Hagar, womanist scholars reclaim Hagar's narrative as a significant cultural and spiritual resource for the Black community—a story in which Black women find their own experience reflected.[3] Thus, I begin this study of Black women's spiritual journeys with Hagar because her story forms the foundation of the womanist theological framework that I employ in this book. As an enslaved Egyptian woman, who is also a victim of rape and forced reproductive surrogacy, Hagar speaks to Black women's particular experiences of sexual violence during slavery and after emancipation. Hagar functions both as a symbol of Black women's struggles for liberation and as a theological model whose spiritual practice and encounters with God engender real possibilities for survival, resistance, and agency.

Building on and expanding beyond womanist recoveries of Hagar, this chapter participates in reclamations of her narrative by positioning her as a spiritual *and* literary ancestor of Zilpha Elaw, Amanda Smith, and Nancy Prince. By foregrounding Hagar's mobility, specifically her itinerancy and travel, to her spiritual experience, this chapter expounds a heretofore overlooked aspect of her narrative. In addition to bearing witness to the free and open movement of the spirit and her encounters with the divine, Hagar's narrative describes recurring travel between geographic and social spaces, revealing the complexity of movements that Black women have practiced and been subjected to. As this chapter will lay out, this travel echoes the history of coerced and "free" movements that have shaped the lives of Black women in the Americas.

As Saidiya Hartman asserts in her book *Lose Your Mother,* from which the book's opening epigraph was taken, slavery has an afterlife, and its persistence shaped the realities of African and African-descended women and men in the nineteenth century and into the present. Ending slavery's hold demands that we take seriously the correspondences between the past and the present *and* that we take seriously the stories we tell about slavery in the past, since they impact our present reality in profound ways. This chapter extends this understanding both to slavery in the Americas and biblical slavery, which was often used it to justify, shore up, and even at times structure that more recent institution. In fact, because of her perceived Blackness, Hagar's enslavement specifically served as biblical evidence for Christian pro-slavery advocates' justification of slavery and their claims about the inferiority of African-descended people. Hagar's enslavement and Black women's experience of captivity and dehumanization in the US have significant similarities, even though the transatlantic slave trade and the institution of slavery in the Americas was based on race and has often been defined as harsher than slavery in the Bible. Thus, beginning with Hagar's narrative and her experience of slavery enables us to see the troubling continuities across time and space.

HAGAR'S PECULIAR FAMILIARITY

Not only does Hagar's status as an enslaved African parallel that of many Black women in nineteenth-century America, but the exploitation of her bodily labor, physical and sexual as both handmaid and concubine, mirrors the experiences of both enslaved and free Black women in the US. As such, her experiences seem "peculiarly familiar" to Black women (Weems 1).

First, Hagar's relationship to Sarah and Abraham echoes across the centuries. White slaveholding women and men in the Americas, for instance, possessed and exercised the absolute power to use the bodies of enslaved women as "mistresses, whores, or breeders" (Giddings 43). The dominant definition of Black women as "always willing" and of the enslaved body as existing for the "full enjoyment" of the master provided justification for this nonconsensual sexual and reproductive exploitation (Hartman *Scenes,* 81, 86). In Sarah and Abraham's home, we see a similar hierarchy of power between enslaved woman and master/mistress. Hagar exists for their pleasure and profit. For example, the text states, "Now Sarai, Abram's wife, bore him no children.[4] She had an Egyptian slave girl whose name was Hagar, and Sarai said to Abram, 'You see that the Lord has prevented me from bearing children; go in to my slave girl; it may be that I shall obtain children by her. . . . He went into Hagar and she conceived'" (Gen. 16:1–2, 4). Rodney Sadler Jr. has called attention to the sexual overtones of "go in to my slave girl" and "He went into Hagar."[5] This language reduces Hagar to all flesh, devoid of spirit and therefore personhood. Moreover, the text demonstrates Hagar's body as always open and as always available to meet the needs and demands of the master and mistress.[6] When Hagar subverts Sarah's authority, Sarah appeals to Abraham, who tells her, "Your slave girl is in your power; do to her as you please" (Gen. 16: 6). Abraham's reply as patriarch of the household reaffirms the power structure within the domestic space, which enables Sarah's limitless, unbounded power over Hagar's body—the absolute power of a slave mistress over her property. Although Abraham is the patriarch, Sarah serves as an active participant in the exploitation of Hagar's body, much as white women abused and exploited the bodies of Black women in the southern slavocracy but also in northern domestic spaces as well—a legacy of violence that slave narratives and autobiographical accounts of free Black women, like Zilpha Elaw, Amanda Smith, and Nancy Prince bear witness to.[7]

Womanist readings of Hagar, like my own, that make visible Hagar's experience of sexual violence matter because Hagar's experience is part of a longer legacy of violence that Black diasporic women experience. The matter-of-fact positioning of Hagar within the text of Genesis as always open and available for her masters' desires, a positioning that goes unquestioned by Sarah, Abraham, and the author, demonstrates how biblical slavery, much like slavery in the US, masquerades as fixed and inherent rather than as a socially constructed institution. By foregrounding these intersections in slavery across time period and geography, my reading of Hagar's narrative contributes to womanist and feminist recoveries of Hagar that challenge the elision of rape and sexual violence from our readings of the Bible. It also adds to a growing conversation about the afterlife of biblical slavery by exploring its continuing impact on Black women's spiritual lives, journeys, and literature.[8]

Although biblical slavery was not race-based, the persistent definition of Hagar as *other* likewise resembles North American slavery. The text represents Hagar's enslaved body as different—foreign and alien—through repeated references to her being an Egyptian and a "slave girl" (Gen. 16:1, Gen. 16:3, Gen. 21:9). As only Israelites were part of God's chosen people, her Egyptian origins mark her exclusion from the community and from

God's covenant. Sarah and Abraham's use of the term "my slave girl" or "your slave girl" (Gen. 16:5–6) and "this slave woman" (Gen. 21:10) similarly defines her as property, devoid of identity. But even her name as it is given in the text does not acknowledge an identity: Hagar means "foreign thing" in Hebrew and, ironically given her use as a sexual and procreative object, it is masculine (Gafney 34).

The silencing of Hagar's true Egyptian name mirrors the ongoing silencing, dispossession, and disinheritance that characterized enslavement in the Americas. Stripping her name is as an act of violence and dehumanization—one that mirrors the various practices of cultural stripping that occurred aboard slave ships during the Atlantic slave trade to transform people into things.[9] The crewmen aboard slave ships stripped captives' names as a way to break all ties to family, ancestor, and tribe. Not only is the stripping of Hagar's Egyptian-rooted name an act of violence but her renaming reflects an attempt to remake her in the language and culture of her oppressors and reveals her objectified status. Moreover, Hagar's abject status compounds through the multiple attempts to mark her alienation: "foreign thing," "Egyptian," "slave girl." Clearly, the marker "slave girl" was not enough to communicate Hagar's unique experience of alienation and reflects the dependence of biblical slavery on difference.[10] For this reason, Hagar's naming both marks her vulnerability and enables the violating and brutalizing treatment she receives from Sarah and Abraham. In short, for Hagar and indeed for Black women throughout the diaspora, violence and violation begin first in language.

Bearing witness to the legacy of misnaming as a primary inheritance of Black diasporic women, Hortense Spillers claims in her essay "Mama's Baby, Papa's Maybe: An American Grammar Book," "I am a marked woman, but not everybody knows my name. . . . I describe a locus of confounded identities, a meeting ground of investments and privations in the national treasure of rhetorical wealth. My country needs me, and if I were not here, I would have to be invented" (203). Despite the many "confounded identities" inscribed on Black women (Mammy, Topsy, Jezebel, Sapphire, Black Venus), all of these stereotypical misnamings and misrepresentations reflect the positioning of Black women as "always already known" and their bodies as always available to meet the rhetorical needs of individuals and the nation.[11] In her analysis of the Black Venus figure as the dominant representation of Black women in literature and visual art, Shirley Anne Tate further illustrates the rhetorical labor Black women are made to perform.

She argues that the misnaming of Black women as Black Venus positions Black women as "devoid of agency, a blank canvas to be written on" (7–8). Extending this Black feminist critique to Hagar's narrative, I argue that Hagar's own misnaming in the Genesis text functions similarly—positioning her as "a blank canvas" without agency, assigning to her an array of singular and constricting identities: slave woman, foreigner, stranger.

My reading of Hagar thus foregrounds her status as Egyptian (African) and as Black, following womanist scholars Delores Williams, Renita Weems, and Wilda Gafney. Hagar's identity is complex; she can be read as Egyptian, African, Arab and she is positioned at the intersection of multiple spiritual traditions including Judaism, Christianity, and Islam. I highlight Hagar's Blackness as a way to respond to a legacy of erasure and marginalization of Black women's spiritual experience and critical engagement with biblical narrative. Foregrounding Hagar's Blackness is my critical response to historical literary and artistic appropriations of Hagar that have either whitewashed Hagar or have appropriated and employed her Blackness as a literary device—negatively defining her Blackness in objectifying and dehumanizing ways.

THE LONG MARGINALIZATION OF HAGAR'S NARRATIVE

Womanist theology's reclamation of Hagar questions Black theology's frequent positioning of the Exodus story as the sole narrative of Black people's spiritual legacy.[12] Placing the Exodus story at the center relegates the particularities of Black women's spiritual lives and journeys to the margins. As Williams has argued, Black theology's sole focus on the Exodus story wrongly suggests that Black men and women's experience of oppression has been the same.[13] Despite a shared history of oppression in the US, Black men and women's struggles for freedom have been shaped by the particularities of race, sex, and class oppression, which the Exodus narrative alone cannot fully address. In contrast, Williams identifies an alternate tradition within the Black community that "lifted up from the Bible" Hagar's story—foregrounding the particularities of Black women's experience and agency (1–2). Offering a different representation of Black people's freedom struggle, Hagar's narrative positions the lived experiences of Black women, both their material reality as physical and sexual labor and their spiritual reality as God's people, at the center. Hence, without Hagar's narrative we cannot fully grasp the spiritual complexity of the Black community and its relationship to God. In addition, if we are to understand Black women's religious experience and how it shapes their resistance to multiple forms of oppression, we cannot relegate Hagar's narrative to the margins.

In addition to womanist theology such as Williams's, Jewish feminist theologian Savina Teubal's exegetical work on the biblical text of Hagar expands my reading of the text by locating Hagar within multiple spiritual traditions.[14] Particularly useful is her critique of how Hagar and her narrative have been marginalized to serve the patriarchal needs of Jewish, Christian, and Muslim communities. While Williams focuses specifically on Hagar's relevance to Black Christian women, Teubal calls for reclaiming Hagar as an important spiritual model for women across the Jewish, Christian, and Muslim faith traditions, noting her erasure in all three. As she notes, the biblical text defines Hagar in relationship to her masters, as Sarah's "slave girl" (Gen.16:1) or Abraham's concubine. Although the Qur'an defines Hagar as the mother of the Arab people and includes her sojourn through the wilderness in pilgrimages to Mecca, the text never uses her name; she is only Abraham's wife and Ishmael's mother (Teubal xiv).

Building on feminist and womanist readings of Hagar, I argue that such practices of marginalization ultimately lead to a legacy of disinheritance and dispossession for Hagar—a legacy that has its roots in both the book of Genesis and Galatians. For example, after Sarah gives birth to Isaac, she sees Hagar and her son (Ishmael) as a threat. Hence, despite forcing Hagar to serve as a sexual and reproductive surrogate, Sarah commands Abraham, "Cast out this slave woman with her son; for the son of this slave woman shall not inherit along with my son Isaac" (Gen. 21:10). Sarah's justification for the disinheritance lies in her naming of Hagar as "this slave woman." In short, Sarah's words position slavery as the marker of dispossession—a rhetorical move that Paul repeats in the book of Galatians. In Galatians 4:31, Paul references Hagar without using her name or Sarah's, contrasting the "slave" with the "free woman" and claiming that Christians are the children of the free woman (Sarah) and *not* the slave woman (Hagar).[15] Thus Hagar's status as enslaved once again marks her for dispossession. In this case, Paul's figurative redeployment of Sarah's command to "Drive out the slave and her child" (Gal. 4:30) transforms Hagar's physical exile from Sarah and Abraham's household into a kind of spiritual exile, what I name as a spiritual disinheritance within the Euro-American Christian tradition.

Notably, the impact of Paul's representation of Hagar through allegory persists through Christian theological writings and literary scholarship, further contributing to this legacy of dispossession. As Kimberleigh Jordan has noted, Hagar, when she is mentioned at all in "Euro-American scholarship," often "serves as a literary pawn in the larger, seemingly more important, tale of God's covenant with Abraham" and continues to be cast in disparaging ways as "the slave woman" in the writings of Martin Luther and John Calvin (113, 114). Even literary scholar J. Lee Greene, whose scholarship underscores how Hagar's story was employed by the "slavocracy, its defenders, and its detractors . . . as a structural model to explain analogically the position of . . . blacks . . . in southern society" terms this Genesis narrative the "Abrahamic paradigm," naming only Abraham, Isaac, and Ishmael (84). This appropriation of Hagar by US pro-slavery advocates to justify the enslavement and inferiority of African-descended people builds on and extends from this long-standing marginalization and dispossession of Hagar as spiritual ancestor because of her enslaved status. Within a pro-slavery context, Hagar's exile from Sarah and Abraham's household becomes a marker of physical and spiritual dispossession that justified the exclusion of Black people from the promises of America (citizenship, freedom, and democracy), consigning them instead to perpetual enslavement.

The denial of Hagar as spiritual foremother grounded in a singular focus on Hagar as a captive body, however, fails to consider Hagar's full story in Genesis—her agency (evident through her resistant and persistent movements), her spiritual encounters with God in the wilderness, and her transformation from "slave woman" to free woman as the recipient of a divinely authored promise that would rename her the mother of a people. In opposition to this legacy of marginalization and disinheritance, my own womanist recovery of the text constructs a Hagaric paradigm in which Hagar, rather than Abraham or his sons, becomes the focus of analysis. Moreover, by reading Hagar's narrative through the lens of freedom rather than strictly through the lens of slavery, I offer a fuller and freer telling of Hagar's legacy. A Hagaric paradigm, as this chapter will demonstrate, forms the foundation of Black women spiritualists' theological and literary legacy—repositioning Hagar as a spiritual and literary foremother to the Black women in this study. Such a paradigm shift is imperative to make visible Black women's spiritual journeys and the inextricable link between spirituality, mobility, and freedom at the core of their narratives.

NINETEENTH-CENTURY USES OF HAGAR AT THE MARGINS

Hagar's legacy of spiritual disinheritance and marginalization extends beyond religious traditions to the fields of nineteenth-century American literature and visual art. Nineteenth-century neoclassical painters depicted Hagar as white, much as they did all other figures, which ensured the continued othering of Blackness.[16] Despite the recognition of Hagar as culturally Black, within the neoclassical form it was nearly impossible to represent her Blackness because as Charmaine Nelson explains, neoclassical art "located the privilege[ed] . . . white body as the aesthetic paradigm of beauty" (xxxi). For white southern female novelists, who created an entire tradition of Hagar novels, these depictions, juxtaposed with the Bible's reference to her Egyptian (i.e., African) heritage, gave her a racial ambiguity that they could exploit as a useful rhetorical device. These novels appropriate the biblical figure Hagar to facilitate their proto-feminist critique of patriarchal Victorian values that narrowly circumscribed white women's lives, especially their sexuality.[17]

Hagar's representation and appropriation by nineteenth-century white artists reflected the association of Blackness with illicit sexuality—a definition grounded within the institution of slavery and used to justify rape and forced reproduction for the master's pleasure and profit.[18] In Hagar's narrative her body is desired for its reproductive and sexual uses but it also threatens the patriarchal institution that requires her physical and sexual labor. Hagar's "whitewashing" thus expresses white Americans' paradoxical desire *for* and fear *of* Blackness and Black sexuality that reflected America's *dis-ease* with the presence of Black bodies in the country.[19]

For white female novelists, the racially ambiguous Hagar became a way to resist a patriarchy that defined white women, in contrast to Black women, as pure and lacking sexual desire.[20] As Janet Gabler-Hover writes in her analysis of American cultural representations of Hagar, "Hagar's ethnic complexity—Is she white? Is she black?—provided a tantalizing opportunity for southern [white] women under the thumb of a restrictive patriarchy to reimagine themselves in richer and more admirable identities through their black Hagar heroines. Why Hagar? She was, in her blackness, imagined to have a sexuality outside the permissible boundaries of femininity. . . . Hagar's freer sexuality—her passion—is presented as integral to other freeing and empowering qualities" (8–9). Hagar's Blackness made her an ideal symbol of the sexual freedom that white women desired to access and possess. Possessing sexual desire beyond the bounds of the Victorian ideal of true womanhood, she was figured as the "fallen woman." Gabler-Hover positions southern white women's appropriation of Hagar as "a feminist resistance" to the narrow construction of women's sexuality within Western art. However, their novels end with a "disavowal of their white heroines' ethnic ambiguity once empowerment ha[s] been achieved" (10, 23). This disavowal repeats the erasure of Hagar's Blackness by white visual artists. While white female southern novelists imagine themselves as Black through their Hagar heroines to move beyond the limits of white femininity, they ultimately retreat back into the security of whiteness at the end of their novels. Their continued complicity with the white power structure facilitates its maintenance.

The disavowal of Hagar's Blackness likewise indicated the risk of invoking her sexuality, as transgressing the bounds of true womanhood was stigmatized. The appropriation and representation of Hagar as the "fallen" woman within white women's texts helps explain her absence from nineteenth-century Black women's spiritual narratives. The risk of invoking Hagar would have been even greater for Zilpha Elaw, Amanda Smith, and Nancy Prince, who do not explicitly mention Hagar as a model for their own spiritual practice. When they do reference female biblical figures to justify their own spiritual roles as itinerant preachers or as spiritual leaders, they invoke much "safer" women, such as Deborah, Mary, or Miriam. Unlike white women, who find the hiding of their bodies to be narrowly constricting, Black women suffer from the violence and violation of exposure—revealing as Beverly Guy-Sheftall claims, "[t]here is nothing sacred about Black women's bodies. . . . They are not off-limits, untouchable, or unseeable" (18). Hence, the frequent circulation of Black female bodies throughout the nineteenth century as objects of sale and entertainment, objects to be seen and consumed illustrates the terror that all Black women in the nineteenth century faced, especially those like Elaw, Smith, and Prince, whose itinerant practices placed them before white, and frequently male, audiences and the violating gaze that could reduce the Black woman to some*thing* shameful and monstrous. To invoke Hagar's cultural legacy in America as "fallen," sexually impure and racially tainted, could put them in real danger. Invoking Hagar would also have invoked proslavery supporters' use of Hagar as evidence of the inferiority of Black people.[21]

Black communities, however, claimed Hagar as both spiritual ancestor and as referent for the particularities of Black women's experiences in the

US. As the sole enslaved African woman in the Bible and the first woman to liberate herself from slavery,[22] Hagar's story was referenced in sermons within Black churches, as well as within Black art and literature. As Williams and Gafney have noted, Black folk have often referred to themselves as Hagar's children or as sons and daughters of Hagar.[23] This naming and claiming of Hagar within the Black (Christian) community challenges the dominant cultural legacy of alienation and dispossession that has accrued to Hagar through Euro-American theological, artistic, and literary practices. Elaw, Smith, and Prince would certainly have been familiar with Hagar's story. In my reading of their narratives, I argue that she functions as a kind of absent presence—we can see her legacy in the text even if she is not explicitly mentioned. All of the primary texts in this study bear witness to Hagar's legacy evident in Black women's persistent struggle against misrepresentation and their deployment of embodied spiritual practices that redefine the Black (female) body as sacred and as "made for freedom," through their visionary encounters with the divine, as well as through transgressive and often spirit-led movements that characterize their freedom journeys.

To make this legacy visible, this chapter reclaims Hagar from a history of misappropriation and misrepresentation within the American cultural and political landscape that led to her absence from Black women's spiritual narratives. This recovery work is necessary because marginalization, erasure, and misrepresentation persists for all the women in this study despite their different social, cultural, and geographic contexts. By tracing the continuities between Hagar and the Black women whose journeys I explore in subsequent chapters, I make visible the critical spiritual practices that Black women have employed to challenge this marginalization and misrepresentation—practices that are characterized by a deep spiritual knowing and an always disruptive movement. This recovery effort has three steps: (1) reclaim Hagar's erased Blackness by situating her narrative and experiences within the context of African American history in the nineteenth century; (2) resist Hagar's silencing by doing what Elaw, Smith, and Prince could not publicly do—claim Hagar as a spiritual foremother for these later Black women spiritual itinerants; and (3) recover the sacred at the foundation of Hagar's movements and, therefore, as central to understanding the journeys of nineteenth-century Black women spiritualists. Building on this effort, subsequent chapters will show the continuities between Hagar's spiritual practices and journeys and those evident in the spiritual narratives of Black women into the twentieth century. In doing so, I claim an alternative spiritual legacy for Hagar and her many daughters—one that recognizes and names Black women's inheritance as more than dispossession, loss, and captivity.

Unearthing New Legacies

I seek an alternative legacy for Hagar and for Black women living in the wake of slavery and colonization. Therefore, the remainder of this chapter will foreground Hagar's embodied spiritual practice as expressed through her itinerancy and unruliness. Through my critical reading of the biblical text, I locate and analyze the places where I see a resistance to the persistent, oppressive readings of Hagar's narrative. I am interested in potential ruptures in the text—places that challenge this traditional notion that Hagar is a marginal figure, an appendage to Abraham, or a slave whose inferior status excludes her from possessing any spiritual or cultural legacy.

Expanding beyond womanist and feminist readings of Hagar, my analysis of Hagar's encounter(s) with God explores the possibilities of reading Hagar as an itinerant figure, a wanderer, whose journeying, much like that of nineteenth-century Black women itinerants, is sometimes a method of escape, a form of exile, or a call by God to move. Looking closely at the positioning of Hagar's narrative within the larger dominant biblical account of Sarah and Abraham and her tenuous position within their household, I present Hagar as a disruptive and unruly figure—one whose body, marked as alien and foreign, enables Sarah and Abraham's performance of dominant notions of gender, class, and social tradition, while disrupting such categories as well. Hagar's itinerancy and unruliness form the foundation of a Black female embodied spiritual practice that writers such as Elaw, Smith, and Prince employ as a strategy for resisting the social, economic, and spiritual marginalization they face as Black women.

HAGAR THE TRAVELER: ITINERANCY IN HAGAR'S NARRATIVE

Throughout the nineteenth century, Black women's bodies circulated as property via the Atlantic slave trade, the internal slave trade within the US, and the slave trade in the West Indies, as well as sources of entertainment and scientific curiosity. Against this backdrop of coerced and oppressive movement, I define Black women's itinerancy as a transgressive act because their movements challenged traditional definitions of Black women as captive bodies rather than free. Drawing on Timothy Hall's definition of itinerancy as "the intentional transgression of various types of boundaries" that "made possible a world radically open to the free operation of God's Spirit" (72), I position itinerancy as one core expression of Black women's embodied spiritual practice that enables them to cross race, class, and gender boundaries.

Despite Hagar's status as enslaved and as property within Sarah and Abraham's home, Hagar rejects this status as fixed by engaging in an embodied spiritual practice that I characterize as transgressive and itinerant. Throughout this section, I use the terms "itinerant practice" and "itinerancy" interchangeably to refer to Hagar's physical movement and travel between spaces. However, I find the term "practice" useful at times for emphasizing Hagar's agency and her action. Like many Black women in the Americas, Hagar's initial journey is a coerced one, as she is forced to leave her home of Egypt and travel to Abraham and Sarah's home where she is given a new status as *slave* and foreigner. Yet even this coerced movement, invokes the radically open possibility in her movements later in the narrative. If we read Hagar's narrative through a single lens of captivity, we miss the complexity of her journeys and the transgressive movements and passages she engages in, including journeys of escape, exile, journeys of return and homegoing, as well as journeys in which Hagar is called by God to move. In offering a more expansive reading of Hagar's journeys, this chapter illustrates a much more complex legacy of movement that informs the tradition of Black women's spiritual autobiography and of Black travel writing—revealing the centrality of Black women's spiritual journeys to understanding their travel more broadly.

Building on Katherine McKittrick's theorizing of space and geography, I expand beyond Hall's definition of itinerancy as more than just itinerant preaching.[24] It includes all Black women's travel between and movements across socially defined boundaries and spaces (shaped by race, class, and gender). Although these spaces and boundaries masquerade as fixed, and settled, they are in fact produced. The movement of Black women specifically outside of their "appropriate" places calls attention to the instability of spatial boundaries, thereby disrupting supposedly "natural" identifications of the Black female body as monstrous and alien.[25] Thus their bodily practices become transgressive acts that make the construction of those boundaries visible, thereby undermining their power.

According to the biblical text of Genesis, Hagar is an "Egyptian maidservant," suggesting she has been brought, or rather taken, from her native land of Egypt to become a domestic laborer in Sarah and Abraham's home. Hence, her journey from Egypt into an Israelite household parallels the capture and transportation of Black women from Africa to America—the Middle Passage, as well as the internal slave trade in America and the slave trade between Africa and the West Indies. Despite Hagar's initial forced journey into Sarah and Abraham's home, the biblical text offers a much more complex portrait of her mobility as a key expression of her embodied spiritual practice.

Later in the story, for example, Hagar runs away to the desert to escape Sarah's abuse. This follows Hagar's conception of Ishmael, which the text states led her to treat her mistress with "contempt" (16:4). Although the text is not explicit about Hagar's actions toward Sarah, the word contempt, which also means disobedience, suggests that Hagar undermines Sarah's authority. According to the text, in response "Sarai dealt harshly with her, and [Hagar] ran away from her" into the wilderness (Gen. 16:6–7). This move makes Hagar's itinerant practice visible, and her resistance to Sarah's abuse demonstrates one of the fundamental characteristics of itinerant movement—the transgression of social hierarchies. Hagar's movements in particular transgress the hierarchy between master/mistress and slave. Her running away challenges such hierarchies because it illustrates a refusal to do the bodily labor required of her within the domestic space. Her escape threatens Sarah and Abraham's authority and possession expressed through their attempts to produce an heir through her body. In short, Hagar's itinerancy, her physical movement into the wilderness with her unborn child, places her own claim to her body and to her child's life over that of her masters.

Hagar's itinerancy, her transgressive and unpredictable movement into the wilderness, also opens up radical possibilities for divine encounter. Here in the wilderness, in this space of profound possibility, God finds Hagar and asks her the question, "where have you come from, and where are you going?" (Gen. 16:8).[26] This question suggests that Hagar's movement away from oppressive domestic space engenders a powerful shift in her subjectivity. While earlier in the text Hagar is marginalized and objectified, referred to simply as a possession of Sarah and Abraham, here in the wilderness God's question repositions Hagar as subject who speaks and acts rather than an object. God's question invites Hagar to tell her story, thereby inviting her to move from the margin of the story to the center.

Additionally, God's question marks Hagar as an itinerant figure—someone who has journeyed physically from one place and who will continue to travel to some other place but also as someone whose physical movement leads to a transformative spiritual shift. In fact, God is most concerned with Hagar's journey: the question is not *who* she is but rather *where* she has been. Nevertheless, I would argue that the "who" is tied to the "where." If we want to know who Hagar is, we must find out where she has been. In short, identity is tied to place.[27] Thus, although Hagar's location within the domestic space of Sarah and Abraham's home marks her as enslaved sexual object, her escape into the wilderness opens up possibilities for a more expansive identity beyond that of captive body as she claims agency over her body and over her son—expanding her status as "slavewoman" to that as mother. The divine promise Hagar receives in the wilderness not only re-identifies her as the mother of Ishmael but also the mother of a people including God's pronouncement to "so greatly multiply your offspring that they cannot be counted for multitude"—a promise that mirrors that given to Abraham (Gen. 16:10). Moreover, God's renaming of Hagar in the wilderness facilitates her dramatic transformation from enslaved woman to free woman by the end of the narrative.

Like Hagar, Black women's identity is inextricably linked to the spaces/places their bodies inhabit. While Zilpha Elaw, Amanda Smith, and Nancy Prince were free Black women in the North, they were, like Hagar, exploited for their bodily labor.[28] Significant portions of their narratives, for instance, discuss their experiences as exploited domestic workers in white homes. Within the violating and constrictive space of white households, they are paid subsistence wages for work that literally breaks down their bodies. Fortunately for Elaw, Smith, and Prince, itinerancy becomes a way out of such oppressive labor.

Hagar, like Elaw, Smith, and Prince, receives and obeys God's call to move, despite the unpredictable and seemingly inexplicable nature of the call. After Hagar explains her reasons for running away, God commands her to return to Sarah, claiming, "You are now with child and you will have a son. You shall call him Ishmael [God hears], for the Lord has given heed to your affliction" (Gen. 16:11). Hagar obeys God's command and returns to Sarah and Abraham. While this return to the space of her enslavement seems unjust, Hagar's willingness to go where God leads is another example of her itinerant practice. Furthermore, Hagar is pregnant and alone in the desert without food or water, and her return leads to the healthy birth of her son. Being born in Abraham's household, rather than in the desert, legitimizes Ishmael's birth by proving that, as Elsa Tamez and Delores Williams state, he is Abraham's heir (Williams, *Sisters* 14). Hence, God is not just concerned with Hagar's immediate survival but with her long-term survival and that of Ishmael.

Nonetheless, after Hagar's return, Sarah attempts to deny Hagar and Ishmael access to the inheritance her return should have ensured. Because God gives Sarah a child of her own, Hagar's presence, her body and that of her son, are no longer useful in the household.[29] Their bodies threaten Sarah's power and authority within the domestic space in the form of Isaac's inheritance, and she therefore demands her husband to "Cast out this slave woman with her son" (Gen. 21:10), which leads to another departure. Abraham sends Hagar and her son away with just some bread and a container of water after which "she departed, and wandered about in the wilderness of Beer-sheba" (Gen. 21:14). Both Hagar's exile and her wandering in the desert demonstrate the complexity of Hagar's itinerant practice. Sarah's command ("Cast out this slave woman") and Hagar's responsive action ("she departed, and wandered about") suggests the intersection of coerced/forced and self-initiated movements that have characterized Hagar's earlier travels. Though Sarah commands Hagar's exile, I also read her active leaving as an extension of her earlier escape. Hence, Hagar's journey is characterized not only by exile but also by freedom. The Exodus story echoes this, as Israel leaves in response to Pharaoh's command and finds freedom, but they, too, wander in the wilderness, where God does the transformative interior work necessary to prepare them for freedom.

Although this time Hagar is no longer enslaved, her second journey into the wilderness parallels the first in that she encounters God again. After she runs out of water, Hagar, fearing that Ishmael will die, cries out for help. In response, "the angel of God called to Hagar from heaven, and said to her, 'What troubles you, Hagar? Do not be afraid; for God has heard the voice of the boy where he is. Come, lift up the boy and hold him fast with your hand, for I will make a great nation of him.' Then God opened her eyes and she saw a well of water. She went, and filled the skin with water, and gave the boy a drink" (Gen. 21:17–19). Once again, we see the wilderness as a place of struggle and need but also as a space in which God demonstrates a steadfast commitment to Hagar's and Ishmael's survival. Much as before, God begins with a question that places Hagar at the center and expresses concern for her and her son's material reality. Hagar also receives another call, though quite different from the previous command to *go* and *return* to her mistress. Like other feminist and womanist scholars, I read this God-encounter as powerfully transformative for Hagar, whose agency as mother becomes even further visible.[30] God's reiteration of the earlier promise of a hope and a future for Hagar and Ishmael and God's opening of Hagar's eyes demonstrates her growth and preparation for freedom. Thus, God's directive to Hagar both reinforces Hagar's new status as free but also, through the promise, ensures that her legacy will be one of freedom and not of slavery—an inheritance that the many spiritual and literary misappropriations of Hagar actively silence.

Rather than an exclusion from God's promises, here we see God's deep concern for Hagar's material and spiritual present and future. It reveals that Hagar's radical obedience to and willingness to follow God's journey for her was an expression of her embodied spiritual practice evident through active responses to God's call: *she saw* (the well), *she went* (to it), *she gave* (her son a drink). Hagar's spirit-led movements and practices throughout the text, lead her to escape the oppressive conditions of Sarah and Abraham's household, to survive and gain provision for the future. In stark contrast to Sarah's literal attempts to disinherit Hagar and Ishmael in Genesis and Paul's figurative disinheritance in Galatians, God offers them a promise that echoes the promise given to Abraham—a hope and a future for themselves and for future generations to come.[31]

Hagar's embodied spiritual practice, evident through her wilderness experience and journeys, continues to sustain Black people and Black communities who position Hagar as spiritual ancestor. Echoing Williams, I suggest that the wilderness is not just a physical place (the literal desert that Hagar found herself in with her son Ishmael), but also a spiritual space of struggle where Black women, like Hagar, may find themselves—a place "in the midst of trouble" where they encounter God who can make a way where there is none (108–9). Certainly, this understanding of the wilderness moves beyond physical definitions of the term as an "uninhabited" and "inhospitable" place by invoking the religious understanding of the term, which posits life on earth as one of spiritual struggle in preparation for the next life in heaven. In recovering Hagar's narrative, Black women recognize the inextricable link between our spiritual reality and the material need to ensure life and survival.

The centrality of the wilderness as a site of transformation in which Black women and their broader community seek out spiritual resources to respond to the "death-dealing" realities of Black life persists throughout African American literature. Perhaps one of the clearest examples of the spiritual and literary legacy of the wilderness occurs through the character of Baby Suggs in Toni Morrison's novel *Beloved*. Described as "an unchurched preacher," Baby Suggs's preaching in the Clearing functions as a kind of wilderness experience for the entire Black community proving the wilderness to be not just a place of struggle but also a place of transformation and healing. The narrator describes the Clearing as "a wide-open place cut deep in the woods," where Baby Suggs would take the Black community of Cincinnati, Ohio, for healing (87). In this sacred space, "Baby Suggs, holy, offered up to them her great big heart. . . . She told them that the only grace they could have was the grace they could imagine. That if they could not see it, they would not have it. 'Here,' she said, 'in this here place, we flesh; flesh that weeps and laughs; flesh that dances on bare feet in grass. Love it. Love it hard. Yonder they do not love your flesh. . . . They despise it. . . . *You* got to love it, *you!*'" (87–88). Like Hagar, these men, women, and children experience spiritual transformation in the wilderness that enables them to feel valued not as property but as God's people—worthy of grace and love. The epigraph at the novel's opening further illustrates this: "I will call them my people, which were not my people; and her beloved, which was not beloved" (Romans 9:25). In this verse, Paul references a verse from Hosea to posit that the Gentiles, not just the Israelites, are God's people. In other words, blood lineage is no longer the requirement for consideration as God's chosen. Given this context, I argue that Morrison's epigraph suggests that although white Christians in the US excluded people of African descent from the Christian community because of their race, God looks beyond blood and lineage as prerequisites for beloved community. Hagar's narrative makes a similar argument, as God considers her as one of God's own by offering her a distinct promise to be the mother of a nation and a legacy, not of enslavement but of freedom. Hence, as Morrison argues in *Beloved* and as Hagar's narrative asserts, God welcomes those of African descent—even though, as Baby Suggs states, their "flesh" has been violated and exploited. In Hagar's narrative and in *Beloved*, the wilderness experience is key to this spiritual transformation from enslaved property to people of God. Once again, we see that for Black women, and for the entire Black community as in *Beloved*, spiritual experience is tied to the journey embarked on and the place in which we encounter God.

THE UNRULY, DISRUPTIVE BODY IN HAGAR'S NARRATIVE

Dominant constructions of gender in the Christian tradition and within nineteenth-century American culture have shaped Hagar's representation as a disobedient and disruptive figure, and therefore a problematic model of womanhood. Within the New Testament, for instance, the celebrated ideal woman has "a gentle and quiet spirit" and women "accept the authority of their husbands" (1Peter 3:4). In this letter, the author positions Sarah as the model of ideal womanhood citing her obedience to Abraham as evidence of her worthiness as a wife and as a woman to be emulated.[32] Expounding to Christian women, "You have become her daughters as long as you do what is good" (1 Peter 3:6), here the letter echoes Paul's positioning of Sarah as spiritual mother and ancestor. Thus, to be Sarah's daughter (the daughter of the free woman rather than Hagar the slave woman as Paul notes in Galatians) is to imbibe these qualities of ideal womanhood as well.

Nineteenth-century American culture enforced a similar model of ideal or "true" womanhood and used it to contrast free (white) women with enslaved (Black) women. Hazel Carby explains that within the institution of slavery only privileged white women could be true women—defined as virtuous, chaste, and pure, focused on motherhood and without sexuality (26). As an enslaved woman, Hagar has no access to this model of womanhood that places marriage at the center and rewards obedience to patriarchal authority. Unlike Sarah, Hagar has no husband and is forced to conceive a child outside of marriage. And although being gentle, quiet, and obedient to authority are central characteristics of a true woman, Hagar fails to exercise any of these qualities within the domestic space.

Hagar's troubling of the domestic space begins with the embodied spiritual practices that disrupt her misnaming. Notably, Hagar's misnaming as foreign thing, slave girl, alien, exiled, and as disinherited marks the boundaries of who belongs and who does not.[33] Her misnaming, therefore, describes not only her marginalized status but also reinforces Sarah and Abraham's status as God's chosen, as belonging, as free, as heirs of the promise, as well as patriarch, wife, master, and mistress. Yet Hagar's identity shifts as she changes location. For example, within Sarah and Abraham's household, as we have already seen, Hagar is "the slave girl," "the Egyptian," "foreign thing"—all of which mark her as alien and "out of place" among this chosen people. However, once Hagar enters the wilderness she is no longer a foreigner, an enslaved woman, spoken of with contempt and excluded from the larger community. Her escape disrupts those boundaries that mark her as enslaved and alien. In place of this she becomes someone who God knows and calls by name: "Hagar, slave girl of Sarai, where have you come from and where are you going?" (Gen. 16:8). Of course, this use of the degrading Hebrew name and "slave girl" reference repeats the earlier erasures of her identity. But it also suggests God's recognition of Hagar's lived experience as an enslaved woman. Moreover, in the wilderness, a place of possibility, Hagar becomes someone who God sees and who sees God in return. Once again, Hagar's transgressive practice—her movement outside of Sarah and Abraham's domestic space into the desert—enables this moment of recognition and therefore this moment of transformation for Hagar.

This transformative encounter with God is so powerful for Hagar that she names God: El-roi (meaning "God of seeing" or "God who sees") and the place of encounter: Beer-lahai-roi ("the Well of the Living One who sees me").[34] Hagar's naming, her spiritual practice, is notable for several reasons. First, she is the only woman in the Bible to name God. Second, foregrounding vision and sight in her encounter with the divine, Hagar's naming of God and the well underscores that God sees her. This emphasis on being seen by God and Hagar's subsequent agency in telling an alternative story about her life and journey challenges her marginalized status as an enslaved woman and an Egyptian. In God's eyes, her status does not make her illegible or unknowable. Rather, in contrast to the vulnerability and abuse Hagar faces as an enslaved and foreign woman, Hagar describes God as "a God of seeing . . . who looks after me," linking divine vision with divine care.[35] Thus Hagar's testimony contests the exploitation of women and foreigners informing the broader cultural context of the narrative.

Hagar also sees God, revealing vision and sight as a key expression of her embodied spiritual practice as well. Through seeing God and surviving the experience, Hagar violates the statement in Exodus that "no one shall see God and live."[36] Her seeing also disrupts the many attempts, both in the biblical text and in American literature, religion, and art, to fix Hagar's identity as an object devoid of agency. Hagar clearly recognizes the extraordinary nature of her vision, as she exclaims "Have I really seen God and remained alive" (Gen. 16:13). Notably, Hagar's "I-witness" claim to seeing God and her subsequent naming of the well after her personal encounter with God demonstrates a "subject constituting practice" in which Hagar claims authorship over her body and life.[37] Hagar's "I-witness" claim indicates a transgressive act of "free telling"—the same as that which literary critic

William Andrews describes as the central feature of Black autobiographical practice that sought to redefine Black people as made for freedom in opposition to dominant systems of oppression.[38] Although Hagar's narrative is not autobiography, she exists within a longer tradition and legacy of free telling that includes Elaw's, Smith's, and Prince's autobiographies: expressing freedom as a central theme and goal through a redefining of freedom for the self and declaring oneself as free. Though Hagar does not have the privilege of writing her own story like the autobiographers examined hereafter, her embodied practices of vision and of naming God and the well where her personal encounter with the divine takes place reflect her claims to self-authorship. Moreover, Hagar's embodied practices of vision and naming ensure that her free telling, this alternative story about her spiritual experience, persists in opposition to the many attempts to erase her spiritual legacy.

Hortense Spillers's theorizing of the potential for Black female resistance to domination through visionary practice further illuminates the power of Hagar's narrative. She explains, "The fact of domination *is* alterable only to the extent that the dominated subject recognizes the potential power of its own 'double-consciousness.' The subject is certainly seen, but she also *sees*. It is this return of the gaze that negotiates at every point a space for living, and it is the latter that we must willingly name the counter-power, the counter-mythology" (163). Spillers defines *seeing* as a critically transgressive practice that has the power to alter and disrupt practices of domination. In this act of seeing, Hagar "negotiates . . . a space for living," disrupting attempts to fix her body in place as slave, foreigner, and disinherited. Her vision enables her to access divine resources and challenges the dominant constructions of her body by positioning herself as entitled to freedom. Hagar's transgressive visual practice also disrupts the dominant narratives that have attempted to narrowly define her legacy through literature, theology, and visual art. By re-reading Hagar's narrative through womanist and Black feminist lenses, we make visible the legacy of misnaming imposed on Black diaspora women as well as how they resist that oppressive legacy and construct a new inheritance for Black women through their embodied spiritual practices.

Hagar's naming of God also reflects the transgressive nature of her spiritual practice that produces an alternative knowledge about God rooted in the particularity of her cultural experiences. As Delores Williams has asserted, Hagar's naming is notable because in her encounter with the Israelite God, the God of her master and mistress, she draws on her indigenous

Egyptian and, therefore, African culture in her naming.[39] This transgressive act challenges Hagar's erasure and marginalization within Abraham and Sarah's household but also within theological, literary, and artistic spaces that position Hagar as object and as a "blank canvas" on which an array of identities and meanings can be inscribed. In other words, Hagar's radical decision to bring her experience as an African woman to bear on her visual encounter with and naming of God challenges and disrupts this long legacy of cultural imperialism that positions Hagar and all Black diaspora women as "always already known"—knowable by the singular narratives and identities imposed on them rather than by their own self-knowledge and self-authorship. By bearing witness to Hagar's embodied knowledge as an African-descended Egyptian woman, I join and extend the legacy of womanist and feminist recovery scholarship that calls into question the continued marginalization of Hagar's spiritual and cultural ways of knowing.

The unruly potential of Hagar's body becomes further evident through her continual disruption of Abraham and Sarah's household. Hagar's display of contempt for Sarah and her oppressive control over her body once she becomes pregnant disrupts the power hierarchy within the domestic space. This produces a "harsh" response from Sarah. According to the commentators note for verse 16:6, the words "dealt harshly with her" literally mean "oppressed her," linking Sarah's oppression of Hagar with the Egyptians' oppression of the Israelites (*HarperCollins Study Bible* 25). Given that the oppression of enslaved Israelites in Egypt included forced labor and physical violence as a form of punishment and control, it seems that Sarah's oppression of Hagar involved a similar degradation and brutality. Moreover, the treatment is harsh enough to cause Hagar to run away into the dangers of the desert for the first time.[40] This escape is disruptive not only because it represents the loss of labor but also because her unborn child is Abraham and Sarah's heir and the beginning of the fulfillment of God's promise to make a great nation of their descendants.

After the birth of Sarah's son, Isaac, Hagar and Ishmael's presence disrupts the household—threatening Isaac's inheritance, as well as Sarah's power and authority.[41] In removing Hagar and Ishmael from the household, Sarah and Abraham effectively eliminate their obligation to and responsibility for them as well. Hagar's pregnancy is clearly not of her own choosing. Yet through the exiling of her body (the locus of sexual violence), Hagar is made to bear the burden of and is held culpable for her own violation. The expulsion of Hagar's unruly body also mirrors the much longer legacy of Black diaspora peoples whose bodies have been defined and treated as commodifiable, violable, and expendable. This is part and parcel of her continued representation as the "fallen" woman—a figure so threatening that nineteenth-century white artists, as we have already seen, found it necessary to silence her transgressive potential.

Hagar's embodied spiritual practices underscore and challenge the dominant representation of the Black (female) body as a failed body and therefore a guilty body—one that exceeds the boundaries of respectability and fails to follow the rule of law.

Despite Hagar's disruptive behavior, her unruliness and physical resistance to her earthly masters, Hagar is continually obedient to God, even returning to her harsh mistress. Even in this moment, where we might question God's motivation and interests, Hagar obeys, seemingly without hesitation. While disruptive of every earthly authority, she accepts divine authority unequivocally. Thus it is clear that Hagar's disobedience is a resistant practice that she utilizes under oppressive circumstances to ensure her and her son's survival. Her obedience to God serves the same purpose, reflecting her faith that God is also invested in her survival. And indeed, her obedience to God leads to her survival. This tension between unruliness and obedience exists across the varying texts in this study and reflects a vital element of Black women's spiritual and embodied practice.

If being quiet and obedient to authority is what makes women "true women" and the spiritual daughters of Sarah, then what kind of spiritual legacy does Hagar offer and what might it mean to be Hagar's daughter? I posit that Zilpha Elaw, Amanda Smith, and Nancy Prince are Hagar's daughters, as they practice her spiritual legacy of itinerancy and unruliness. Much like Hagar, Elaw, Smith, and Prince trouble the boundaries of true womanhood. As free Black women, they are able to marry and have households of their own. However, their domestic labor in white homes, like Hagar, and their itinerant spiritual work as preachers, prophetesses, lecturers, and activists in opposition to patriarchal authority exclude them from the definition of a "true woman" and from Sarah's spiritual lineage. Like Hagar, Elaw, Smith, and Prince find themselves in the wilderness, a space of seeming impossibility and struggle yet also a space of transformation. Hagar saw God and lived in the wilderness; her daughters have visionary encounters with the divine in the wilderness as well. Their prophetic readings of the Bible lead them to challenge the assumed patriarchal authority of husbands, church leadership, slaveholders, and white leadership within anti-slavery societies and missionary organizations. By beginning with Hagar's narrative, I have sought to establish a framework to reveal the embodied spiritual practices of Black women as part of a longer legacy of transgressive spiritual practice. Reclaiming Hagar's narrative in this way encourages us to re-see Hagar and her daughters in opposition to a confining and exclusive model of womanhood.

Within this critical context, informed by womanist and Black feminist scholarship, Hagar becomes a righteous woman, "a new kind of woman" in the mold of Julie Dash's "Yellow Mary," a character in the film *Daughters of the Dust,* which I explore more deeply in chapter 6. Yellow Mary, like Hagar, has a disruptive sexual past (including rape, prostitution, and homosexuality) that marks her as a "failed" woman or a "fallen" one. By representing Yellow Mary as a strong woman, "a proud 'oman" who embraces her family even as they ostracize her, Dash rejects the "true woman" ideal as inadequate for expressing the full complexity of Black women's experiences. Through the figures of Yellow Mary and Eula Peazant, another victim of rape, Dash suggests sexual violation is the history of all Black women. True womanhood has always excluded them, and Black women should not judge each other by its standards. Hagar is neither the "fallen" woman that white southern women writers portray her as nor the mother of an inferior race as proslavery supporters suggest. Neither is she the whitewashed figure that nineteenth-century visual artists represent in their sculpture and paintings. Rather, what Hagar's narrative makes evident is that her body—violated and exploited—is sacred. Therefore, as daughters of Hagar, through her spiritual legacy, all Black women, regardless of their status as enslaved, as laborers, or as sexually exploited, can claim access to the sacred.

By sacred, I mean that which is holy, divine, and set apart. However, drawing from M. Jacqui Alexander's definition of the sacred in *Pedagogies of Crossing,* I do not use the term to refer to something single, static, or fixed.[42] Rather the sacred is open, fluid, and ever-changing. It refers to divine power that exceeds limitations of time, space, and geography but that often expresses itself through human embodiment and movement. Because the sacred is fundamentally tied to Black women's journeys, I will show in the following chapters that just as their journeys expand so too does their expression of the sacred become more expansive as well. While in the opening chapters, the sacred appears primarily as an expression of Elaw, Smith, and Prince's Christian faith, this understanding of the sacred expands with Dash's film, *Daughters of the Dust* and Hartman's *Lose Your Mother,* which demonstrate the varying geographies of the sacred including Catholic and Protestant Christianity, as well as Islam and African traditional spiritual practices. In short, the sacred cannot be contained solely within formal religious institutions, as the spirit-led movements of Black women outside of the boundaries of the church reveal the deep working of the spirit in journeys and places often overlooked, marginalized, or named strictly as secular.

Although my reading of Hagar positions slavery at the foundation of Black travel writing, her narrative also expands that foundation to show the complexities of Black women's journeys beyond slavery.[43] Her narrative sheds light on conversations about Black women's journeys, as her movements, at times coerced but also transgressive, complicate the relationship between mobility and freedom. Though principally a narrative about her enslavement, Hagar's text challenges the single story of Black women as captive bodies and, therefore, challenges methodologies that focus solely on their movements as coerced. In contrast, the reading that I have offered here illustrates the multiplicity of Hagar's journeys and of those Black women who carry on her legacy of itinerancy and transgressive movement. Although Hagar's narrative falls outside the boundaries of traditional autobiography, her mobile, visionary, and rhetorical (naming) practices in her narrative bear witness to her attempts, like Elaw, Smith, and Prince, to author an alternative narrative about her life—one that defines her body as sacred and as "made for freedom." In the chapters that follow, we will continue to see Black women engaged in transgressive movements, visionary encounters with the divine, and rhetorical practices through their writing, preaching, and prophesying. The continuity of such resistant practices showcases the continuing spiritual and literary legacy of Hagar—revealing her transgressive movements and unruly behavior as key elements of Black women's embodied spiritual practice.

· TWO ·

Visionary Movement in Zilpha Elaw's *Memoirs*

> One morning, I saw a remarkable vision; I appeared to be in a strange place and conversing with a stranger, ... I there heard the voice of the Almighty, saying, "I have a message for her to go with upon the high seas, and she will go."
> —Zilpha Elaw, *Memoirs*

The distance between Hagar's narrative and Zilpha Elaw appears great. Many centuries as well as geographical and cultural borders separate the two women. Unlike Hagar, Elaw was never enslaved. She was born in the early 1790s to free Black parents in Pennsylvania.[1] Nevertheless, Elaw understood separation from her family and home, as she was orphaned at the age of twelve and indentured to a white Quaker family, Pierson and Rebecca Mitchel, who fed, clothed, and educated her in exchange for her domestic service until the age of 18.[2] Although Elaw was not enslaved, she occupied a similarly uneasy position in the household, noting that "I was sometimes met with severe rebukes from my mistress" often for talking back (58). Though Elaw is cryptic about the "severity" of Mrs. Mitchel's scolding, she, like Hagar, is marked as unruly and punished for disrupting her mistress's authority in the domestic space. Elaw received a solid book education, learning to read and write with great facility, as her 1846 *Memoirs of the Life, Religious Experience, Ministerial Travels and Labours of Mrs. Zilpha Elaw* makes evident. But Elaw notes her spiritual education was lacking. She describes the Mitchels' spiritual life and practice as deeply hidden in the recesses of their minds, and therefore profoundly alienating. The embodied spirituality of Methodism and its externalized and tangible practices of worship thus attracted her. Her memoir reflects an embodied spiritual practice based on her experiences in Methodist churches and communities, characterized primarily by visionary encounters with the divine that inform her preaching, prophesying, and itinerant movements and travel. Despite the obvious differences between them, I locate Elaw's visionary practice as an extension of Hagar's spiritual legacy, grounded in visionary encounters with the divine that are prompted by mobility and that often lead to a divine call to move—one that disrupts all physical and discursive attempts to fix her raced, classed, and gendered body in place whether within white domestic space or within her own home.

The opening epigraph of the chapter illustrates the inextricable link between spiritual vision and mobility. Like Hagar, Elaw's visions are tied to her lived material reality, and her divine encounters reflect God's willingness to enter into that reality. Also like Hagar, Elaw's visions are accompanied by a divine call to move, to go forth. However, Elaw's call also includes the calls to prophesy and to preach, which are inextricably linked to God's command that "she will go."

Unlike the majority of nineteenth-century Black female itinerants, Elaw traveled internationally, from the United States to England, and published her *Memoirs* with a London-based publisher.[3] While Jarena Lee's narrative *The Life and Experience of Jarena Lee* (1836), which chronicles her spiritual journeys across the United States in the first half of the nineteenth century and testifies to the centrality of divine vision, embodiment, and mobility as a sacred call, is generally thought to mark the beginning of Black women's spiritual autobiography, I foreground Elaw as the first international traveler in the genre. Her *Memoirs,* therefore, broadens the audience for Black women's spiritual autobiography beyond the United States by embracing a transatlantic Christian community.[4] Elaw's narrative also offers a longer and much richer portrait of the challenges Black women spiritual itinerants faced during the early nineteenth century, including the risks of traveling through and preaching in the slave states. Despite the notable contributions of her narrative and her achievements as the first Black female Methodist Episcopal preacher during her lifetime, as Kimberly Blockett has noted, Elaw has been forgotten in the historical archive and her *Memoirs* understudied.[5] Thus, I build on scholarship on Black women's spiritual autobiography that tends to focus on Lee by extending the small but growing body of scholarship on Zilpha Elaw, including that of Joycelyn Moody, Richard Douglass-Chin, Rosetta Haynes, and especially Kimberly Blockett. I answer the latter's call for a more sustained analysis of Elaw's life and work. Rather than reproduce a comparative reading between Lee and Elaw, as so much previous scholarship has done, this chapter offers a solo study of Elaw's text that recognizes the distinct hybridity and significance of *Memoirs* by locating it within both the spiritual autobiographical and travel narrative forms and within a broader conversation about Black mobility and freedom. Through my analysis, I show that Elaw's itinerancy and travel, much like Hagar's, are inextricably linked to and shaped by her visionary encounters with the divine.

For both Hagar and Elaw, God enters into the tangible realities of their lives as Black women—a reality defined primarily by a persistent state of vulnerability. For Hagar, this vulnerability was evident in the physical and sexual abuse she experienced in Sarah and Abraham's home but also in the threat of death that she and her son faced in the wilderness. Elaw experiences such vulnerability through her orphaned and indentured status as well as the danger she faces as a lone Black female traveler throughout the United States and abroad. A defining feature of slavery's afterlife, the imperiled condition of Black life persists as a common thread tying together Hagar and Elaw's texts but also Smith, Prince, Dash, and Hartman's works as well—linking their seemingly disparate journeys across centuries, oceans, and national boundaries. Their narratives also bear witness to a legacy of co-creative spiritual practice enabling them to challenge and to survive the lived reality of Black (female) embodiment. Though Elaw is born free in the northern United States, the conditions under which she lives and moves, her experience of indentured servitude as a child and adolescent as well as the dangers she faces as a mobile Black woman with a public ministry, demonstrate the continued vulnerabilities she faces as a Black girl and Black woman. For Elaw, then, visionary movement as the core expression of her embodied spiritual practice *is* her creative and critical response to the vulnerability she faces again and again.

Elaw's text reveals the instability and economic uncertainty of life as a central feature of "freedom" in the North for poor Black people in the nineteenth century. Foregrounding this experience of instability and vulnerability through the death of her mother, followed soon after by the death of her father, *Memoirs* opens with Elaw being orphaned, separated from her siblings, and forced to live as an indentured servant within a white household. Her indentured status further reiterates Elaw's precarity in such a household as she lacks power or authority over her life, is totally dependent on the economic provision of her master and mistress, and, as literary scholars and historians have noted, this economic arrangement exposed Black girls and women to the whims and abuses of the white families they served.[6] Elaw's vulnerability continues as a married woman whose call to preach threatens her husband's status as patriarch within the home. His persistent hostility toward Elaw's preaching demonstrates the risk she faced in obeying God's authority and in placing God's call over her husband's command. The vulnerability that Elaw faces as a Black female preacher only increases when she begins to travel beyond her local community—taking God's message far and wide. The physical danger she faces throughout the United States and the obstacles she faces as a poor Black woman in England signals the unique legacy of travel for Black people and Black women in particular. Elaw's journeys demonstrate, as bell hooks argued more than a century later, that travel for Black people can be characterized as a confrontation with terror.[7] This legacy of terror echoes across Elaw, Smith, and Prince's nineteenth-century narratives and persists through Dash's 1991 film and Saidiya Hartman's 2007 travel text. This experience of terror and vulnerability unites all of the travelers in this study regardless of their status as enslaved or "free," regardless of time period or geographic location—revealing the incomplete nature of freedom for Black diaspora peoples. Foregrounding Elaw's visionary movement as a central feature of her spiritual practice enables us to see the contributions of her narrative to the genre of travel writing, as it makes visible the embodied reality Black travelers face but also the embodied spirituality that enables Elaw to stay on the move in spite of the many dangers.

In her deployment of the body throughout her narrative, Elaw departs from the dominant representational strategies Black women novelists and public intellectuals used in the nineteenth century. Many Black women writers, as Carla Peterson notes, engaged in varied "decorporealizing" techniques, thereby "rendering [the Black body] invisible and privileging the soul or mind instead" (xii). Such strategies included either hiding the body from view, rendering the body abstract, or normalizing the Black female body within socially prescribed definitions of womanhood. In contrast to those writers who hide the body from view, Peterson notes that Black women spiritualists embrace the materiality of the body. While Peterson foregrounds Jarena Lee in her argument about Black female evangelists, I position Elaw's narrative as similarly constructing a "counterdiscourse" about the body—one that "affirm[s] the material reality of the black female body" and in the process "suggests a more successful attempt at reconciling body and spirit" than many Black-authored nineteenth-century texts (xiv). Elaw's attention to the vulnerability of her own body throughout her *Memoirs,* her charting of the risks to a mobile Black (female) body, and her attempts to unite body and spirit also distinguishes her narrative from the traditional spiritual autobiographical form, where many scholars have located her narrative.[8]

Elaw does adhere to several key aspects of the genre. Her epigraph and dedication, for instance, place *Memoirs* firmly within the spiritual autobiographical tradition. The former is from 2 Corinthians 3:5: "Not that we are sufficient of ourselves to think any thing as of ourselves; but our sufficiency is of God." In other words, in keeping with Anne Hunsaker Hawkins's definition of spiritual autobiography, *Memoirs* reflects a turning away from the self "toward[s] the eternal things of God" (19). Elaw's dedication, a message addressed to "the Saints and faithful Brethren in Christ," further points to this persistent elevation of eternity and spiritual concerns, as Elaw expresses her longing for "the eternal developments of elevated holiness, blissful immortality, and transcendent glory" (51). Following in the path of early spiritual autobiography, like John Bunyan's *Pilgrim's Progress* (1678), eighteenth-century Black spiritual autobiographers such as Ukawsaw Gronniosaw and Olaudah Equiano, as well as Lee's *Life and Religious Experience,* Elaw's *Memoirs* focuses on the spiritual experiences of sin and conversion. As Joanne Braxton and Joycelyn Moody have argued, the quest is a central feature of such texts and the difficulties and temptations on the quest as well as its eventual satisfaction provide the narrative structure.[9]

Whereas authors of traditional spiritual narratives attempted to transcend the earthly world and therefore the materiality of the body to demonstrate the primacy of the soul over the body (Hawkins 22), Elaw, like other Black women spiritual autobiographers, complicated the genre by revealing the inextricable link between spirit and body, especially between spiritual and embodied movement. As an international traveler, Elaw's *Memoirs* highlights the link between her interior spiritual journey and her geographical movements abroad—a key intersection that deepens with Smith and Prince's narratives. Through the construction of a hybrid text (spiritual and travel narrative), Elaw effectively moves her body to the foreground and in opposition to the dominant construction of her poor, Black female body as a liability—marked as foreign, strange, and "not sacred." Elaw's visionary practice and movements redefine her body as a divinely empowered, sacred vessel called to travel across the country and across the ocean with the word of

God. Elaw grounds the opening of her spiritual narrative in the body and in a real material reality—revealing a tenuous link between spirit and material.

This tension becomes first apparent through the title: *Memoirs of the Life, Religious Experience, Ministerial Travels and Labours of Mrs. Zilpha Elaw, An American Female of Color; Together with Some Account of the Great Religious Revivals in America [Written by Herself]*. The title suggests that for Elaw, "religious experience" and travel are inextricably linked. Moreover, Elaw ties her travel and work to the particularities of her embodied experience, describing herself as American, female, of color, while also foregrounding her status as married even though her husband died more than two decades before she published her book.[10] Naming herself as married, female, and as African American clearly illustrates her narrative's concern with such materiality and the challenges she must face as a result, including her struggle to break free from her marriage to follow the call to preach and travel internationally. Thus, the title reminds Elaw's audience that she inhabits a real, material body that cannot and will not be elided by a narrative that seeks to focus solely on spiritual things. Rather than deploying a disembodied rhetoric in an attempt to transcend the body like many nineteenth-century Black writers, Elaw takes a different path, employing embodied spiritual practice and rhetoric as a radical resistance to social hierarchies (race, class, gender) and dominant definitions of Black women.[11]

Elaw's dedication further extends her concern for the material body, as she requests from her audience "prayers for my preservation from the perils of the deep, whensoever my path may lie through it; and your continued remembrance of my pilgrim course and ministerial labors, at the throne of grace" (51). While Elaw's reference to her "pilgrim course" invokes the spiritual quest at the center of Puritan spiritual narratives, Elaw specifically seeks prayer for her safety at sea on her intended return journey to the United States. Elaw's concern for the safety, or lack thereof, of her body persists throughout her narrative. For this reason, I read her dedication as in part foreshadowing three central concerns and contributions of her text: (1) defining spiritual experience as a fully embodied practice—grounded in, not set apart from the material world; (2) revealing the inextricable link between travel and terror for Black people, illustrating specifically the imperiled condition/status of Black (female) bodies on the move; and (3) engaging in an embodied rhetoric that both foregrounds the dangers of misrepresentation she faces within the public space *and* challenges that misrepresentation through counternarratives about the Black (female) body.

Elaw expresses a concern with the dangers of misrepresentation through a stark warning to her audience about the newspaper press near the end of her dedication. She admonishes them to "[t]ake heed what you read: as a tree of knowledge, both of good and evil, is the press; it ofttimes teems with rabid poisons, putting darkness for light, and light for darkness; extolling earthly grandeur and honor, spurious valour and heroism; fixing reputation and character on a false basis. . . . Above all, shun an infidel, obscene or disloyal newspaper press, which is the scavenger of slander, and the harlequin of character" (52). Elaw's condemnation of the written word as a potential evil and "poison" grows out of her larger concerns with misrepresentation as a Black woman writer and preacher. Kimberly Blockett's article, "Disrupting Print," provides further context for Elaw's representational concerns, noting that British and American newspapers often represented Black preaching and Black religiosity in stereotypical ways: steeped in dialect, unrefined, and illiterate. Growing out of stereotypical constructions of Black people used to justify slavery, these representations, according to Blockett, conflated Blackness with enslavement and made it impossible for white audiences to recognize a free Black woman preacher, like Elaw, as anything but spectacle (100–101). One critic of Elaw's preaching, for example, compared her to "a dog walking on its hind legs" (Cater 33).

Offering a narrative, as she describes, "written by herself," both enabled Elaw to challenge racist misrepresentations and exposed her to new challenges, such as writing for a predominantly white audience. As William Andrews has noted, Black autobiographers could not assume the trust of their white readers, recognizing that white audiences often doubted the veracity of the Black voice and might meet it with outright hostility, especially in published reviews of their work.[12] Such challenges were far worse for Black female authors, who dared to cross race and gender boundaries by opening up their stories for public consumption. As Frances Smith Foster explains, Black women writers who entered the literary marketplace "were subjected to more criticism, skepticism, and censorship than their peers" (9). Within this context, Elaw's critique is a form of resistance to a press that might publicly malign her and undermine her work as preacher and missionary. As this chapter will show, this critique which begins with comparing the press to the "tree of knowledge" ultimately extends to all human-authored written and spoken language.

In the biblical story (Gen. 3: 1–24), Adam and Eve fall from grace after believing the serpent's lie that along with the knowledge that comes from eating fruit from the tree of good and evil comes power—enough power to make them equal to God. This biblical narrative is about greed and pride as the defect of human nature and, as Elaw claims repeatedly throughout her text, "destructive" to "Christian community" (51). Thus, through her dedication and her *Memoirs*' critique of "human language," Elaw undermines traditional Western epistemology that equates the attainment of language with power. Just as Adam and Eve, in the Genesis story, discovered that the attainment of knowledge does *not* make them greater than God, Elaw argues that any privileging of what she refers to as "human language" is potentially destructive.

Establishing all human language as distrustful is a shrewd rhetorical move for Elaw, who must prove the veracity of her voice to potentially doubting readers. If all human language is impure and cannot be trusted, the words of Black women cannot be inferior to anyone else's. Elaw privileges godly language as pure, a language she can access only through divine visions and voices. As Delores Williams asserts, such visions and voices are central to Black women's spiritual experiences as they challenge the patriarchal, institutional church's claim to be the sole source of knowledge about God.[13] For Elaw, visionary encounters with the divine empower her to move "out of place," thereby disrupting the raced, classed, and gendered boundaries that narrowly define her and seek to confine her body in place.[14] Elaw's continued critique of language sprang from her embodied experience as a poor Black female preacher who both spoken and written language had, as she accuses in her dedication "misrepresent[ed]" and "slander[ed]." Moreover, throughout her *Memoirs,* Elaw narrates the devaluation of her voice by white audiences in scenes where she preaches before slaveholders in the South, residents of all-white or predominantly white towns in New England, and British anti-slavery and Methodist Episcopal leaders, who explicitly challenge her divine call to ministry. Against the continuous representation of the Black female body as foreign, exotic, spectacle, and as property to be bought and sold, Elaw's visionary movements and practice demonstrate an alternative way of knowing that posits the Black female body as sacred vessel in which divine knowledge and power lives and moves.

Visionary Experience and Embodiment

This chapter, then, as the title suggests, focuses on Elaw's vision as a central part of her embodied spiritual practice. Like Hagar, who is able to see new possibilities for her and her son's future through her visionary encounters with God, Elaw gains a new way of seeing herself through divine encounters. These encounters endow Elaw with a sharp critical vision (a critical way of seeing, looking, and gazing at herself and the world around her) that she uses to challenge and transform the often-hostile vision of her audience.[15] Drawing on the work of Delores Williams and Yolanda Pierce, I define visionary encounters, visionary experiences, and spiritual visions as encounters with the divine that include dreams, apparitions, and experiences of seeing God, angels, or Jesus.

Significantly, Black women's visionary experience both propels them into the public arena and sustains their careers as preachers and prophets. Through visionary experience, as Williams argues, "the spirit is nurtured for the work of resistance" (89). Pierce similarly writes, "dreams and visions provided Black women with prophetic intelligence and symbolic guidance" (90). I interpret Elaw's encounters with the divine as an alternative source of knowledge that empowers Elaw's work and directs her movements. They permitted her and other Black women spiritual itinerants to stand boldly before those who were critical of their decision to travel and preach God's word.

God's prophetic call to Elaw also locates her in a lineage of nineteenth-century Black writers and leaders who drew inspiration from and located themselves in relationship to the biblical prophets. Most scholarship on the prophetic roots of Black literature and leadership privileges Black men, including Nat Turner, Frederick Douglass, David Walker, Martin Delany, Booker T. Washington, and W. E. B. Du Bois, with Maria Stewart and Sojourner Truth the lone nineteenth-century female voices whose oratories have been recognized as part of this tradition.[16] As a Black female spiritual autobiography, Elaw's *Memoirs* thus serves to broaden the conversation about Black prophetic writing and leadership.[17] Elaw's spiritual practice, specifically her visionary movement abroad, demonstrates the far reach of Black women's prophetic critique beyond the political context and geographical location of the US.

Two central theological tenets form the foundation of Elaw's visionary practice; the first is an experience of the sacred as embodied. This implies a belief that the body is not separate from the spirit. Rather, for Elaw, like other nineteenth-century Black women spiritualists, the body bears witness to the sacred, making visible God's presence in the world. It is the only site of divine revelation and the primary way that humans connect to and commune with God (Copeland 7–8). This understanding of the body in relationship to the sacred becomes apparent in Elaw's visionary encounter with the divine that ultimately leads to her conversion: "As I was milking the cow and singing, I turned my head, and saw a tall figure approaching, who came and stood by me. He had long hair, which parted in the front and came down on his shoulders; he wore a long white robe down to the feet; and as he stood with open arms and smiled upon me, he disappeared. . . . I was overwhelmed with astonishment at the sight, but the thing was certain and beyond all doubt" (56–57). Elaw's vision begins with her own embodied action: milking, singing, turning her head. Much like Hagar who sees God in the wilderness, Elaw's ability to bear witness to and encounter the sacred happens only through her body. Moreover, God's divine presence enters into Elaw's world through a physical body—a "tall figure" with "long hair," in white robes that extend to his feet and "open arms." Naming this figure as the "wonderful manifestation of my condescending Savior," Elaw's visionary encounter of Jesus testifies to the sacred as embodied (57). This core belief certainly extends from Elaw's incarnational theology (the Word made flesh). In making visible her own poor, Black, and female body throughout her text and specifically in this vision showcasing an embodied Christ who stands by her side with arms open, Elaw reveals the radical nature of her visionary experience grounded in an incarnational faith that links the body of Jesus with the bodies of Black women. Jesus Christ's embodiment, as Copeland explains, his "suffering and his death" resists attempts to forget, elide, or erase the body, in particular "living black bodies" (3). Through his life, death, and resurrection, moreover, Jesus's embodied practice asserts the redeemability of "*all* human bodies" and proves that even those differently marked bodies, deemed monstrous and strange, can be made holy.[18]

After her visionary encounter with Jesus, Elaw exclaims "from that happy hour, my soul was set a glorious liberty; and, like the Ethiopic eunuch, I went on my way rejoicing in the blooming prospects of a better inheritance with the saints in light. This, my dear reader, was the manner of my soul's conversion to God" (57). This invocation of the eunuch from the book of Acts (8:26–39) as metaphorical representation of Elaw's conversion further illustrates her embodied theology and rhetorical practice. The soul's conversion, an interior and virtually invisible process, becomes an embodied transformation, in line with the eunuch's baptism immediately following his conversion (Acts 8:36–39). Baptism serves as an outward, tangible, concrete, and often public display of the soul's conversion, reminding the newly converted and their surrounding witnesses that sacred power is experienced in and through the body and also that the body is the vessel through which we bear witness to our spiritual encounters with God.

The Ethiopian eunuch has a similar visionary sacred encounter and experiences a spiritual conversion expressed in and through the body. Offering one of the clearest expressions of her embodied rhetoric, Elaw's representation of herself after her conversion as the Ethiopian eunuch reflects her celebration of the body's transgressive potential and enables her to navigate the challenges she faces as a Black (female) author writing before a predominantly white audience. The book of Acts depicts the beginnings of the Christian Church and its expansion in the first century following Jesus's crucifixion. This biblical passage, in which the eunuch also seeks out the gospel, has been widely interpreted as a signal that Christianity is open to people of all races and nations.[19] Consequently, it serves as a reminder to Elaw's audience of the important role of those who spring from African descent in the Bible and in the propagation of Christianity. The Ethiopian eunuch's narrative legitimizes Elaw's visionary encounters, providing biblical proof that people of color have access to intimate encounters with the divine and that such encounters are true and authentic, rather than the product of "deceptive imagination" (Elaw 57).

The Ethiopian eunuch's castration, in keeping with Deuteronomy, excludes him from the Jewish community.[20] Eunuchs were both marginalized as less than male and not female at the time and given positions of authority in government. The Ethiopian eunuch, for instance, is described as "a court official of Candace, queen of the Ethiopians, in charge of her entire treasury" (Acts 8:26-39). I argue that all of these qualities of the Ethiopian eunuch, a marginalized figure who disrupts race and gender boundaries and who occupies a position of power, enable Elaw to overcome the representational concerns she has in her narrative.

Richard Douglass-Chin notes the significance of Elaw's self-representation as a eunuch, focusing especially on the eunuch's lack of a phallus. Reflecting on why such a lack might appeal to Elaw, Douglass-Chin asserts that Elaw "rejoices" over the lack of that which patriarchal standards value highly: "[t]hroughout her text, Elaw urges her readers to renounce their love of all those qualities extolled by prevailing white American standards," to recognize as evil "whiteness, riches, and social standing" as a way of "rejecting prevailing notions of power" and thereby becoming "whole" (54–55). The lack of a phallus becomes a stand-in for

Elaw's lack of whiteness, wealth, and social position and facilitates her conversion (Douglass-Chin 55). Through this signification, we see Elaw once again redefining power—not as rooted in worldly standards that privilege race, gender, and class status, but as coming only from Christ, who enables "power in weakness" (Elaw 51). As such, her bold embodiment of the Ethiopian eunuch, a body that thwarts race and gender boundaries, enables her to challenge attempts to devalue and exclude her voice and ministry because of the body she inhabits.

The second foundational principle of Elaw's visionary practice, her belief in sanctification, sustains her transgressive bodily practice as it enables her to redefine her differently marked body as sacred. A key element of Methodist religious practice, sanctification, or holiness typically occurs after conversion. According to Jean Humez, sanctification can be defined as "a kind of redoubling of one's assurance of transformation by grace . . . [a] controversial second blessing [that] signal[s] entrance into a state of Christian perfection, purity, holiness, or perfect love, in which one [feels] permanently beyond the reach of committing further intentional sin" (133). Spread during the Second Great Awakening (1800s-1840s) through the teachings of the Methodist itinerant minister John Wesley, sanctification was a controversial theological stance because it rejected the belief in the body as irrevocably sinful. This division between body and spirit, which Paul gives expression to in his letter to the Galatians (5:16–21 and 6:8), affirms that the soul can be redeemed, while the body must "fall away," because it hinders spiritual growth. Methodism, however, denies this soul/body split, acknowledging the possibility of a purified body.[21]

Sanctification is a central tenet of Black women's theology, as their spiritual narratives evidence, because of the power and authority it provided them. Expounding on the principle of holiness as "the basic source of these women's empowerment," Bettye Collier-Thomas explains that holiness enabled Black women to exceed the limitations of the Church, which refused to endorse women as preachers: "Preaching women who embraced the holiness doctrine asserted that they did not need the Church's sanction, because their ministry was authorized by a power beyond the Church, namely God, who spoke to them through the Holy Spirit" (12). The promise of purity and indwelling of the Holy Spirit through sanctification opened up, for believers, the possibility for women's bodies to become acceptable vessels for God's message to be spread. As Yolanda Pierce claims, "Sanctified believers feel that this process *constantly* purifies them and that their lives, souls, and bodies are set apart for a special purpose" (91). This message of purification was particularly appealing to Black women whose raced and gendered bodies were deemed, as Beverly Guy-Sheftall contends, "not sacred."

Like Hagar, Elaw's body would have been read as spectacle, as foreign, and as useful only for physical and sexual labor—a body certainly unfit to carry God's holy message. Yet, in her *Memoirs* Elaw manipulates her white audiences' positioning of her as a "dark coloured female stranger . . . from afar" (Elaw 92). By appropriating this dominant trope of the Black female body as exotic spectacle, Elaw redefines her body as a vessel of divine knowledge and as the source of an alternative vision that enables her to critique the limited vision of her audience.

Narrating her experience of sanctification during a visionary encounter at a camp meeting she describes as taking place "in the wilderness," Elaw makes a significant claim about the intersection of the body, space, and the Spirit:

> It was at one of these meetings that God was pleased to separate my soul unto Himself, to sanctify me as a vessel designed for honour, made meet for the master's use. Whether I was in the body, or whether I was out of the body, . . . I cannot say; but this I do know, that at the conclusion of a most powerful sermon . . . , I became so overpowered with the presence of God, that I sank down upon the ground, . . . and while I was thus prostrate on the earth, my spirit seemed to ascend up into the clear circle of the sun's disc; . . . I distinctly heard a voice speak unto me, which said, "Now thou art sanctified; and I will show thee what thou must do." (66)

Elaw's description of her visionary encounter illustrates her understanding of the centrality of both the body and the spirit within sanctification. Not only does Elaw's visionary encounter enable her to transcend her body, to rise above her body and beyond the material world, but her narration makes clear that the body is still important. Elaw's inability to distinguish whether she is in the body or out of the body suggests that the boundaries between physical and spiritual reality have been blurred. Moreover, her experience of God's presence physically moves her body, causing her to fall to the ground and prostrate herself before God.

Elaw's characterization of the space she inhabits as a wilderness further reveals the importance of both the spirit and material world and reiterates Williams's definition of the wilderness as both a physical and spiritual space. For Hagar, the wilderness was a real, physical desert that threatened her survival and yet also a spiritual place that facilitated her visionary encounters with God. Similarly, for Elaw this wilderness is the physical location of the camp meeting outside in nature, in an uncultivated wooded space or as Elaw states, a "wildly rural and wooded retreat" as well as a place of spiritual transformation, as the above passage makes evident (65). Elaw's emphasis on the physicality as well as the spirituality of this space becomes apparent in her description of the camp meeting as a place characterized by bodily movement. According to Elaw, "Many precious souls are on these occasions introduced into the liberty of the children of God; . . . the grove is teeming with life and activity . . . the salutations of old friends again meeting in the flesh . . . the concourse of pedestrians, the arrival of horses and carriages of all descriptions" (65). Elaw's emphasis on moving bodies and active flesh suggests that this space of wilderness is both an embodied space and an itinerant space—a space in which the surrounding physical world and the bodily movements of those who inhabit it shape spiritual experience.

In his book on camp-meeting religion during the early nineteenth century, Dickson Bruce confirms a link between the physicality of the wilderness and spiritual experience when he asserts the importance of the physical space of the camp-meeting for creating an atmosphere "proper" to the proceedings (71). He writes that clearing the small trees left "a natural canopy of tree limbs over the site" from the large trees, "emphasiz[ing] the site in contrast to the natural gloom of the forest and . . . creat[ing] a cathedral in the wilderness" (Bruce 71) that made possible "a particular kind of interaction to occur between the individual and the divine" (Bruce 69). Elaw also found that the physicality and materiality of the wilderness were crucial for spiritual encounters and visionary experience. She describes "a light shining round about me as well as within me, above the brightness of the sun; and out of that light, the same identical voice which had spoken to me on my bed of sickness many months before, spoke again to me on the camp ground, and said, 'Now thou knowest the will of God concerning thee; thou must preach the gospel; and thou must travel far and wide'" (82). Describing this voice and vision as "my commission for the work of the ministry," Elaw clarifies the source of the call and her authority to travel and preach as not coming "from mortal man, but from the voice of an invisible and heavenly personage sent from God" (82). Similar to Hagar's encounters with God in the wilderness, Elaw's visions enable her to see or hear God. While previous visions, such as during her conversion, involve a physical figure of God, here Elaw sees only a light but hears a clear voice—one that she recognizes from previous encounters. Notably, God prompts both Hagar and Elaw's encounters seeing them and then issuing particular commands to move. Here Elaw's vision begins with God's verbal call to "[g]o, outside of the tent while I speak with thee" and ends with the command, "thou must preach the gospel; and thou must travel far and wide" (81–82). Elaw's description of her godly encounter foregrounds geography, space, and the body. After explaining that she sits down on the ground, Elaw describes God as entering into the material world—positioning divine light in relationship to the sun and her body as she notes the light "shining round" and "within" her body. She also positions God's voice in relationship to her body, noting that before receiving God's initial command to "Go outside of the tent," Elaw "felt . . . a hand, touch me on the right shoulder" (81). Ultimately, Elaw's visionary encounter confirms the embodied nature of divine revelation as her body becomes the vessel for divine light and divine voice.

This indwelling of God's light and voice is the source of Elaw's transformative power—the origin for her preaching and prophesying. These embodied spiritual practices require Elaw's access to God's words and also to divine vision. For example, Elaw explains during a visionary encounter with God while recovering from a serious illness that "the room was filled with the glory of God, who had permitted the veil to be removed from my mortal vision, that I might have a glimpse of one of our heavenly attendants—. . . who had a message to deliver to me from God" (77). As in Elaw's previous visions, she can hear the voice of God, who declares prophetically that she will recover from her illness and explains where Elaw must go to fulfill God's call to her. In this moment, Elaw's encounter with God transforms her manner of seeing from human to divine sight. This ability to see divinely enables Elaw to receive the message that God has for her, assuring her of God's continued care and concern even amid her suffering and providing further evidence of God's calling her to a position of spiritual authority and power. However, this access to divine voice and vision is also the source of her preaching and prophesying.

In her narrative, Elaw emphasizes that such displays of transformative sacred power are possible only when she relies and depends completely on God. Just as God's provision for Hagar required her unconditional willingness to follow God's voice and direction, so does Elaw learn that to be filled with divine power, she must rely solely on God. When Elaw disconnects herself from divine voice and vision through disobedience to God's call, she finds herself cut off and shut out from this divine power. For example, after Elaw receives her call to "preach the gospel, and . . . travel far and wide," she begins to doubt that she can find the money to support such a mission (86). Thinking that it might be possible to raise the money to cover her provision first and then follow her call to itinerant ministry, Elaw's spiritual vision begins to suffer. She begins to doubt the validity of the call she receives to preach. Consequently, she acknowledges, "the Spirit of the Lord fled out of my sight, and left me in total darkness. . . . I had lost my spiritual enjoyments; my tongue was also silenced, so that I was unable [to] speak to God: and though my congregation continued to meet every Lord's day, I had no power whatever to preach to them" (87). Elaw's narrative reveals that her lack of belief in God's call and her refusal to rely totally on God for her provision make it impossible for her to embark on her journey. Elaw becomes both spiritually and physically stagnant: as she states, "here Satan bound me down for two years" (86). Her doubt also causes her to lose her spiritual vision and voice, the source of her sacred power—leading her to exclaim, "I had no power whatever" (87).

Eventually, however, Elaw learns from her mistakes and once again puts her full trust in God's provision rather than in worldly materiality. She explains, "I solemnly pledged myself to the Lord, that if He would again bestow on me the aids of His Holy Spirit, I would go forth in His ministry just as I was, not waiting for any further provision or preparation, but trusting alone in His holy words." Elaw's reaffirmation of faith leads to a return of her spiritual power: "I was enabled to preach with more fluency and copiousness than ever before. . . . Heaven again opened to my eyes and ears, because I was at last led to discern the path of obedience, and hearken to the counsel of the Almighty, saying, 'This is the way; walk ye in it'" (87–88). Like Hagar, Elaw must learn that God is willing to meet her in her place of need and, therefore, desires to send her just as she is. As Hagar's narrative illustrates, those called by God need only follow God's command to move and the way will be provided. Once Elaw learns this lesson, her powers of voice and vision return. Her claim that "[h]eaven again opened to my eyes and ears" illustrates her ability to see with divine sight and hear God's voice. Once again, God's words express a call to move—a call to bodily practice: "This is the way, walk ye in it." This call to walk in the way God has chosen refers to the spiritual journey that Elaw has been called to embark on; however, it also reflects a call to itinerancy—to physically "walk this way." Again, we see the intersection of Elaw's spiritual experience and her physical body, as her spiritual mission is enacted and made visible through her bodily practice.

Visionary Practice: Resistance and Redefinition

In her writing about her experience as a preacher and prophet, Elaw makes evident her awareness of and resistance to the "scopic gaze" of her white audience. According to Lindon Barrett, "the scopic is a preeminent cultural matrix of power and order" in the West (216). He explains, vision has been used against Black people in hostile ways to exclude, marginalize, and mark Black bodies as "abject" (215). Because of this hostile manipulation of vision, Barrett contends that Black people have turned to other sensory practices, particularly that of orality, as resources through which to construct an alternative subjectivity. He defines orality and specifically Black oral culture, which includes singing, folktales, preaching, etc. as "revisionary" and as "a form of contestation" that rejects the dominant notion in the West that literacy is the sole marker of meaning, value, and self-expression—a belief that effectively silences Black people by excluding them from Western definitions of civilization and humanity (58, 61).

Elaw demonstrates, through her preaching and prophesying, orality as an oppositional practice for Black people. However, in opposition to Barrett's critical positioning of visionary practice, her text also suggests that the field of vision need not always be hostile. One passage, highlighting Elaw's preaching to white slaveholders in Alexandria, Virginia, makes evident the potentially transformative possibilities of the field of vision by expanding its boundaries beyond the human to include the divine. In this passage, Elaw disrupts the vision of her white southern audience by appealing to an alternative way of seeing enabled only by God. Moreover, Elaw's travels south, her visionary movements, disrupt the social and legal boundaries of race and gender in the South. According to Elaw, the presence of a Black female preacher

> formed a topic of lively interest with many of the slave holders, who thought it surpassingly strange that a person (and a female) belonging to the same family stock with their poor debased, uneducated, coloured slaves, should come into their territories and teach the enlightened proprietors the

knowledge of God; and more strange still was it to some others, when in the spirit and power of Christ, that female drew the portraits of their characters, made manifest the secrets of their hearts, and told them all things that ever they did. This was a paradox to them indeed: for they were not deficient of pastors and reverend divines, who possessed all the advantages of talents, learning, respectability and worldly influence, to aid their religious efforts; and yet the power of truth and of God was never so manifest in any of their agencies, as with the dark coloured female stranger, who had come from afar to minister amongst them. But God hath chosen the weak things of the world to confound the mighty. (92)

Clearly, the white slaveholders that Elaw describes have come to gaze at her—they have come to see a spectacle. In line with Barrett's understanding, the slaveholders manipulate the realm of vision in this scene to render Elaw's body "Other." Elaw is on display in this scene; she is an oddity, a "curiosity," something "surpassingly strange." I read this space that Elaw occupies on display before slaveholders as a metaphorical auction block, which Katherine McKittrick defines as a key site of domination, a space that "serves to spatially position black men and women as objects 'to be seen' and assessed" (72). Although Elaw is a free Black woman and not literally for sale, her body is available "to be seen" and therefore available for consumption by her white audience. Their comparison of Elaw's free Black body to their enslaved property reifies a master narrative of Blackness as "poor debased" and "uneducated" (92). And although Elaw posits herself as "the dark coloured female stranger . . . from afar," giving voice to this master narrative of the Black female body, she positions herself in this role as spectacle only to disrupt the boundaries of race and gender that underlie it and to offer an alternative vision of herself.

Much as Hagar wielded the field of vision to challenge the singular narrative of her body as captive object devoid of agency, so too does Elaw wield her visionary practice as a "counter-power"—renaming herself as a subject who "is certainly seen, but [who] also sees" (Spillers 163). Not only does Elaw reject the supposed knowledge of slaveholders regarding her own body, but her visionary movement enables her to construct an alternative knowledge both of herself and of her audience. Empowered by God's vision of her body as a sacred vessel for divine knowledge, Elaw challenges definitions of the Black (female) body as "altogether knowable, unknowing, and expendable" or as "an intelligible, transparent commodity" (McKittrick xv,

72). Instead, Elaw looks deep into the hearts of these slaveholders, piercing through the veil of seeming "impenetrable whiteness" to reveal secrets unknown.[22] In doing so, she reveals both the limits of their white supremacist patriarchal knowledge and their spiritual blindness.

Using Morrison's analysis of whiteness in *Playing in the Dark,* I link Elaw's encounter with southern slaveholders to the master narrative about whiteness reproduced throughout American literature—a narrative that defines whiteness as "unknowable" and as "blinding" (32–33). The slaveholders' assumptions about Elaw and their positioning of her Black female body as knowable reifies the master narrative about Blackness and reinforces this contrasting narrative of whiteness. Elaw's visionary practice disrupts both of these narratives, as her claim to divine sight that can see even the secrets of their hearts repositions these white southern men as *blinded* rather than *blinding,* as *knowable* by this poor Black woman rather than as *impenetrable.* Unlike the canon of white-authored American literary texts that employ "images of impenetrable whiteness" as an "antidote for" Blackness and Black people, who are most often depicted as "dead, impotent, or under complete control" (Morrison 33), Elaw employs vision, voice, and deep knowing in her text to showcase the Black (female) body as divinely empowered—a body that contests white supremacist patriarchal authority and control.

Through her spiritual practice, Elaw dismisses her white audiences' gaze, proving that this southern space is not simply a site of domination for Black women. Rather, through her visionary movement south, Elaw affirms, as McKittrick claims, that "black women's geographies push up against the seemingly natural spaces and places of subjugation, disclosing, sometimes radically, how geography is socially produced and therefore an available site through which various forms of blackness can be understood and asserted" (xviii–xix). Using McKittrick's theory of space and geography, I argue that Elaw's spiritual practice, her itinerant preaching, prophesying, and positioning of her body before these slaveholders, reveals the constructed boundaries of race and gender to her audience and claims a different way of seeing the Black female body.

Elaw's critical response in the passage above makes a clear distinction between her white audience's perceived knowledge about God and about the Black female body and her own oppositional knowledge of God and of her raced, classed, and gendered body. Beginning first with the perceptions of her audience, Elaw underscores that these slaveholders' racist and sexist knowledge about Black female bodies causes them to identify Elaw as "poor debased, uneducated" and as not free. In short, the slaveholders question Elaw's humanity and therefore her ability to possess any access to spiritual knowledge. They assume that those who do have access to such divine knowledge possess "talent, learning, [and] respectability." In short, whiteness and maleness become prerequisites for divine knowledge and authority. Hence, Elaw's presence in this community, and specifically her claim to spiritual authority and sacred power, create what Elaw refers to as "a paradox," or something "surpassingly strange." Her words make clear that the location and movement of her body within this white racist patriarchal space create a kind of rupture in the social fabric of the community. Even before Elaw speaks, her mere physical presence disrupts the boundaries of race, gender, and even class. According to Elaw's narrative, part of her spiritual performance before this audience includes a display of her prophetic knowledge—the ability to see into the lives of her white spectators and to know "the secrets of their hearts." Elaw's secret knowledge is equally as disruptive if not more so than the rupture caused by her physical presence. In fact, it is her bodily performance of such knowledge—Elaw's gift of foresight and the ability to expose her largely white male audience, naming their weaknesses and sin—which seems to concern them most.

Yet what her spectators see as a paradox, Elaw sees as God's agency, God's willingness to choose a "dark coloured female stranger . . . from afar" to house "the knowledge of God" and to become the arbiter of "the power of truth and of God." Elaw does not attempt to transcend her racially and sexually marked body. Rather, she embraces her Blackness and femaleness—claiming that it is precisely this body (marked as weak, as debased, and as unfree) that God has chosen to "confound the mighty." With her use of the word "confound" Elaw paraphrases from biblical scripture (1 Cor. 1:27–29). This word means also to mystify, bewilder, or baffle, suggesting that Elaw's embodied spiritual performance calls into question the perceived knowledge, wisdom, and power of her white spectators—revealing the limits of their knowledge and their power.

Throughout her narrative, Elaw's spiritual practice continues to disrupt the racial landscape of the South, and the risks she faces in doing so become increasingly apparent. Upon her arrival, Elaw expresses her "fear of being arrested and sold for a slave, which their laws would have warranted, on account of my complexion and features" (91). Here Elaw illustrates the precarious location she occupies in the South as a "free" Black person. In this space, her body is seen by white spectators as an enslaved body. Hence, Elaw's narrative, also communicates a fear of being seen—a fear of the white gaze that not only can envision her body as enslaved but can enact that vision. She explains, "news of a coloured female preaching to the slaves . . . had produced an immense excitement and the people were collecting . . . to gaze at the unexampled prodigy of a coloured female preacher. . . . I observed, with very painful emotions, the crowd outside, pointing with their fingers at me, and saying, 'that's her,' 'that's her'" (91). The gawking and finger pointing mark Elaw's body as spectacle, much as the white slaveholders had in the earlier scene. However, in this moment she articulates the risks involved in a spiritual practice that disrupts social boundaries of race and gender.

Elaw appeals to an alternative spiritual knowledge to assert her freedom within a space that threatens the legibility of her *free* Black body. She asks herself "from whence cometh all this fear?" The question leads her faith to "rall[y]" and her "confidence in the Lord" to "return." Then, "I said, 'get thee behind me Satan, for my Jesus hath made me free.' My fears instantly forsook me, and I . . . came forth before all the people again; and the presence and power of the Lord became greatly manifested in the assembly" (91). Elaw does not allow her audience's gaze to silence her for long. Appealing to her alternative source of knowledge, she constructs an oppositional vision of herself as free in spite of a present threat to render her body as chattel. Elaw acquires confidence from this appeal to divine knowledge and vision—a confidence that enables her to step, once again, before the crowd of spectators and enact a spiritual performance that reveals "the presence and power of the Lord" to all who look upon her. Consequently, Elaw's spiritual vision and knowledge transform her from spectacle to a vessel of sacred power.

After witnessing her presence and power, several white men in attendance from the Methodist Society ask Elaw to preach for them that afternoon. She agrees and the preaching takes place at the courthouse. Elaw recalls, "therein I obtained a very large auditory; and God gave forth proofs that my ministry was from Him, in giving me many seals to it on that day" (91). The proximity of this event of preaching before white patriarchal church leaders to her fear of arrest or enslavement invites a reading of these two events in relationship to one another. I argue that Elaw's physical presence in the courthouse undermines and disrupts this legal space where Black bodies have been marked as criminal and abject. Hartman describes the courtroom of the antebellum South as a place where Blackness was equated with criminality such that "the enslaved could neither give nor refuse consent, nor offer reasonable resistance, yet . . . were criminally responsible and liable." The law recognized "the slave" as "a reasoning subject," possessing a will that was "acknowledged only as it was prohibited or punished. It was generally the slave's crimes that were on trial, not white offense and violation, which were enshrined as legitimate and thereby licensed" (Hartman 82). Given that "neither slaves nor free blacks were allowed to testify against whites" (Hartman 82), Black voices were effectively silenced in the courthouse except as proof of Black criminality. I read Elaw's courthouse performance within this broader social and historical context of the Black body on trial.

Although she has been called before a panel of respected white male leaders to bear witness to her spiritual gifts and talents, Elaw's testimony that "God gave forth proofs that my ministry was from Him" contends that true authentication comes from God, rather than men. She does not believe the white male spectators before her have the power to approve or disprove her ministry. She rejects them as ultimate judge and jury. Rather, Elaw claims it is God who provides a seal of approval to her ministry. Dismissing their right to occupy the role of judge, Elaw transforms the space of the courthouse, proving it to be socially constructed and therefore changeable, from one in which Black people have always been silenced, found guilty and wanting, into a space where the Black female body can, instead, be seen and heard as sacred and holy. This *hearing* that Elaw receives is particularly important given that Black people were denied the ability to testify in court. Therefore, we can read Elaw's courthouse performance as both a spiritual testimony, bearing witness to God's work and presence in her life, and a legal testimony in which she proves the authenticity of her gifts. Through her oppositional bodily performance in the courthouse, one that undermines and disrupts racist and patriarchal constructions of Black women's bodies, Elaw effectively recasts this typically oppressive and dehumanizing space as a place in which the humanity, power, spiritual authority, and agency of Black women can be seen.

Through her courthouse performance, Elaw engages in a practice of "respatialization," to use McKittrick's term (xiv). That is, she resists spaces of domination, which objectify and violently circumscribe Black bodies, by destabilizing the racial-sexual identities produced therein. By enacting a bodily performance in a space where she does not belong, a space where such a bodily practice seems "out of place" (McKittrick xv), Elaw proves such spaces to be socially constructed and, therefore, alterable. Her body reconfigures socially hierarchized spaces, introducing a different kind of knowledge about both non-dominant and dominant bodies—forcing us to rethink what we believe to be true about not only Black femininity but also whiteness.

Elaw's bodily practice disrupts other white patriarchal spaces as well. While traveling throughout the South, Elaw receives multiple invitations to preach in the homes of prominent white families. These become opportunities to use her embodied spiritual practice to critique both the violence and the violation of Black bodies within white domestic space and the marketplace. During her visit to Annapolis, she receives an offer from a wealthy white man there "to give [her] a house and a plot of ground on condition of [her] residing there" (99–100). This offer sounds strangely similar to the one Linda Brent receives from Dr. Flint in Harriet Jacobs's narrative *Incidents in the Life of a Slave Girl* (1861). Dr. Flint offers Brent a home of her own, a marker of security and freedom, in exchange for sex.[23] In both Jacobs and Elaw's texts, the offer of "security" merely extends the arm of white patriarchal control over Black women's bodies. The southerner's offer of a home presumably in exchange for uninhibited access to Elaw's preaching is, like Dr. Flint's, grounded in a desire to control the embodied labor of Black women. Although the proposition Elaw receives from the wealthy man appears to offer her access to white power and privilege via property ownership, in reality it threatens to turn Elaw into a captive body by bounding her down, holding her in place so that this white man might have unlimited access to Elaw's "labors." Thus, by refusing the offer of a home, which I read as a radical refusal to stay in place, Elaw honors the divine call to mobility—to follow the free and open movement of the spirit.

Elaw's intense rejection of the Annapolis man's proposal, which she couches in terms of sinful materiality and a rejection of worldly desires, reflects a tacit rejection of the marketplace that economically determined and controlled the bodily and sexual labor of Black women. She describes her refusal thus: "[I]t was not meet for me to depart from my Master's work, from considerations of worldly interest. I dared not, like Demas, forsake my itinerating ministry, to love this present world: nor was filthy lucre the object I had in view in the service of the gospel . . . ; the love of mammon has no place in the hearts of his true ministers, who love the flock rather than the fleece" (100). Elaw clearly understands that accepting this man's offer would mean choosing to become dependent on human beings, for economic security, rather than relying on God for her provision. Central to her rejection of this offer of economic security within white domestic space is Elaw's fierce criticism of the marketplace and its central values of wealth, greed, and even lust, all of which fueled the physical and sexual exploitation of Black flesh. Although the white people who invite Elaw into their homes believe that as a poor Black woman she might find their wealth and domestic space desirable, Elaw's oppositional spiritual knowledge and values free her from the pull of the market and commodification, as well as the exploitation within that space. In this moment, Elaw proves that she has no price; her bodily practice and spiritual/bodily labor cannot be bought nor contained.

Elaw's *Memoirs* demonstrates Elaw's spiritual practice as resistance to white patriarchal domination, and also showcases her preaching as capable of transforming those who would exploit and denigrate her raced and classed body. For example, while preaching in Mount Tabor (ten miles outside of Annapolis), at the invitation of the local preacher, Elaw explains that "[a] young man was present who behaved very indecorously, and as the people came in he pointed with his finger to me, tittering and laughing. Poor young man; before that meeting was terminated, his laughter was turned to weeping" (100). Here again, Elaw's physical presence disrupts the typical boundaries of race and gender. By occupying the pulpit, a space traditionally defined as white and male, Elaw's bodily practice reveals the constructed nature of such boundaries and definitions—rejecting this white male spectator's narrow vision of the Black female body as spectacle.

Although, as Elaw notes, this man is "a slave-driver, accounted the most profligate drunkard in that vicinity, and habituated to every vice," she facilitates his conversion from a heckler to a believer (100). In addition to providing Elaw with direct, unmediated access to God's voice and direction, her gifts of divine vision and godly knowledge give her the power to transform those who witness her spiritually embodied practice. Members of the congregation tell Elaw that they had never seen the man pay such attention to preaching before and that they were very surprised that he knelt during the concluding prayer. This display of Elaw's embodied spirituality reveals her power over her white spectators. Although this "slave-driver" intended to denigrate her performance as a form of entertainment and spectacle, her bodily practice literally turns this man's laughter to tears—revealing his own weakness and need to experience God's healing power made accessible through her preaching. Consequently, her bodily practice reconstitutes the

Black female body not as a body to be consumed and therefore objectified and dehumanized by the white gaze, but as a body that houses sacred power and divine authority.

Elaw's journey to Hartford, Connecticut similarly displays her transformative sacred power in response to the opposition she faces toward her preaching. She explains that in this city, "some of the most influential ministers of the Presbyterian body greatly opposed me; and one of them, a Mr. House, resolutely declared that he would have my preaching stopped; but he . . . imagined a vain thing; for the work was of God, who made bare his arm for the salvation of men by my ministry" (104). Elaw's words illustrate the confidence with which she engages in her work because she knows that God has authorized her ministry. In the face of active opposition from local ministers, Elaw engages in the practice of healing a man, described as "dangerously ill" through prayer (104). The man's markedly improved health leads his doctor to attend one of her preaching engagements and to testify to Elaw's spiritual power while visiting with Mr. House, who is transformed by the doctor's account exclaiming that "if God has sent her, I bid her Godspeed." As a consequence, Elaw tells us that Mr. House, her "former opponent" relinquished his opposition to her ministry—announcing instead to his congregation God's intention to "do a great work in this city" through Elaw and to "know that it is of God" (105). Mr. House's transformation confirms Elaw's critique of his opposition as vanity and her pronouncement that men would be saved through her ministry. No doubt, Elaw foresees God's saving work to include those new to the Christian faith and those unbelievers, like Mr. House, who initially questioned the authority of her ministry. Elaw's embodied spiritual practice in Hartford—both her preaching and her use of sacred power to heal the sick—thus reveal the transformative nature of her work. Not only does her practice bear witness to God's power from the pulpit, but through divine healing illustrates that her sacred power cannot be confined to the pulpit. Likewise, her performances even lead to the conversion of her strongest opponent.

Claiming her body as a vessel for divine knowledge and power through her preaching, prophesying, and transgressive movements also exposes Elaw to physical threats and dangers. These potential dangers include "savage dogs," which Elaw describes as "very fierce and ferocious creatures" that she must face when preaching in southern states (94), as well as an attempted assault in Maine where Elaw states a "ferocious looking man . . . came close to me, making a demonstration as if he intended to seize or strike me" (128). Though according to Elaw, this man "stood over me as if he would take my life" she claims in this moment, as in every instance where she faces bodily harm, that "God was with me, and I felt no fear" (128). The narrative also demonstrates that divine protection extends beyond just internal peace to include the physical protection of her body. While in Utica, New York, for instance, where Elaw was invited to preach, she testifies that "a number of young men conspired together, and came to hear me, with their hands filled with stones; intending, if I uttered any sentiments which they disapproved of, to pelt me therewith" (132–33). Once again, Elaw attests to God's protection but this time in physical form:

> the presence of the Lord overshadowed the assembly, and the workshop suffered no interruption from the young gentlemen, who came, not to be instructed in the way of the truth, but to sit in judgement on and try my discourse by the standard of their petty opinions. After service, my brother[24] . . . overheard their conversation, discovered their wicked plot and heard them confess that they knew not what ailed them when they entered the chapel; but their arms seemed bound and held down, and were so paralized that they dropped the stones upon the floor. (133)

Here "the presence of the Lord" physically intervenes by paralyzing the arms of would-be attackers. Bearing witness again to the embodied presence of the sacred in her midst, Elaw's visionary experience of God empowers her to preach in the face of such peril, as she claims, without fear.

Not only do these embodied encounters with the sacred authorize and defend her embodied spiritual practices in the pulpit, but I argue the indwelling of divine spirit and voice also emboldens her to critique such assaults on her ministry. Although she refers to her assailants as "young gentlemen," the words that follow offer a scathing critique of their patriarchal and possibly race and class arrogance. Like her criticism of white slaveholders in Virginia, her description of these men as coming "not to be instructed in the way of the truth, but to sit in judgement on and try my discourse by the standard of their petty opinions" undermines their claims to totalizing knowledge. In contrast, Elaw positions her own body, a sacred vessel of divine knowledge, as the source of truth that they have failed to recognize or see. As with her earlier critiques of opponents to her ministry in the United States, Elaw claims such blindness caused by patriarchal, racial, and class arrogance as folly that God would ultimately overcome.

Embodied Travel: Elaw's Transatlantic Crossing

Elaw's international travel to England disrupts normative constructions of race, gender, and class and also challenges the dominant narrative of transatlantic travel and of Black women's mobility, while complicating broader conversations about missionary and colonial travel during the nineteenth century. From the very beginning, Elaw's passage to England reflects her oppositional spiritual practice: a critique of the imperial roots of missionary travel is embedded in her journey. As a free Black woman traveling across the Atlantic, answering God's call to save the British people, her passage literally reverses the slave trade and colonization by affirming the Black female body not as cargo to be exchanged but as sacred.

The disruptive potential of her journey to England becomes visible even before Elaw leaves the United States. During her visit to Virginia some white men she describes as "friendly to the cause of missions" suggest she go to Africa to "labour among the native tribes." She declines, saying that since God has not directed her to do so she does not dare (96–97). This response suggests that humans, including white men, cannot make the call to go and preach. Only God can send her out into the world and only God can direct her path and journey. Elaw's sole source of authority is God to whom her obedience and allegiance lies. This obedience enables her to resist and oppose white patriarchal authority. Elaw's exclamation that only God can send her illustrates the power of divine authority, so much so that these men accept her response and push her no further on the issue. Ultimately, Elaw's decision to travel outside the auspices of any church, denominational body, missionary organization, and without the authority of men grants her the liberty to follow the free and open movement of the spirit.

The men's suggestion that Elaw go to Africa also invokes colonization schemes popular at the time as a means to rid the United States of people of African descent in a kind of reversed Middle Passage.[25] Although colonial missionary travel typically involved white Christian (i.e., "saved") subjects traveling from the West to Africa to redeem "savage" Black bodies, sending Black people who have been brought to the West and "redeemed" reflects a perfecting of the imperial project. During the nineteenth century, the project of exporting the descendants of people kidnapped from Africa to their ancestral home continent was inextricably linked to the notion of spreading Christianity.[26] Organizations like the American Colonization Society (ACS), founded in 1816, were supported by Christian churches, which saw colonization as a means to spread Christianity as well as Western culture (S. Martin 65). Supported by both white pro-slavery advocates and northern white abolitionists, the ACS was also driven, before and after the end of the Civil War, by a belief in white supremacy. Though colonization had the support of some Black leaders, especially those with a strong commitment to Christian missions, many Black people saw such efforts as a threat to Black liberation and citizenship in the United States. Although Elaw positions her journey within a spiritual rather than a political context, her rejection of the suggestion that she travel to Africa to expand her missionary work reflects a disengagement from the violence of "slavery's geographic terrain" to use McKittrick's words (xvii). By choosing an alternative geographic practice (i.e., traveling to England), Elaw engages in an embodied spiritual practice that rejects and critiques an oppressive itinerary in which colonial domination and Christian missions go hand in hand.

Drawing on her own varied experiences in the United States, Elaw displays a powerful argument about the incompatibility of slavery with Christianity. After the untimely death of an enslaved man, described as "a local preacher, a coloured brother and a slave," Elaw reflects "Oh, the abominations of slavery! Though Philemon be the proprietor, and Onesimus the slave, yet every case of slavery, however lenient its inflictions and mitigated its atrocities, indicates an oppressor, the oppressed, and the oppression. Slavery in every case, . . . involves a wrong, the deepest in wickedness" (98). Elaw's description of slavery as "the deepest in wickedness" and her unequivocal rejection of slavery "in every case" challenges Paul's return of an enslaved man to his master and his acceptance of Philemon's authority as master over his property (even as he advocates for Philemon to treat Onesimus as "no longer as a slave but more than a slave, a beloved brother" in v. 16). Paul's diplomatic writing regarding slavery seeks forgiveness for the enslaved man who has run away from his master and clearly aims to avoid alienating the slaveholder by honoring his claim to Onesimus ("I preferred to do nothing without your consent"). In contrast to Paul's diplomacy and to southern Christian slaveholders' selective use of such passages to justify slavery, Elaw defines enslavement simply as an abomination demanding divine judgement rather than negotiation.[27]

Through her rejection of slavery and racism at the heart of the white imperialistic model of Christianity that these southern men espouse, Elaw ultimately challenges their identification of whiteness as righteous and Africanness as heathen. Having witnessed the hypocrisy of white Christians in the North and South, she refuses to see them as *the* source of spiritual authority, believing—as we have seen through her transformative spiritual practice—that she has been called to work for the salvation of all but especially those white Americans and British, whose racism, patriarchy, and elitism prevent them from becoming true Christians.

Through a series of visionary experiences that occur over twelve years, the spirit does move within Elaw, sending her not to Africa but to England in 1840.[28] Elaw wonders what she could possibly have to offer "a country so polished and enlightened, so furnished with Bibles, so blessed with ministers, so studded with temples" (137), which may be why she does not go to England the first time she receives the call. The experience that resolves her to go occurs when she is praying. She hears God's voice respond, quoting the book of Jeremiah, "say not, I cannot speak; for thou shalt go to all to whom I send thee, and what I command thee, thou shalt speak" ([Jer. 1:7] 137). Much as God met Hagar in her place of need, taking her just as she is and providing what she lacks, here God meets Elaw. The reference to the prophet Jeremiah connects Elaw's doubts to Jeremiah's feeling of being unworthy of the divine call to go where God commands and to speak God's word to the people. It also locates her within the broader tradition of biblical prophets, challenging the patriarchal construction of the prophetic voice as a masculine voice. If God has the power, as Elaw quotes from 1 Corinthians 1:27, to use "the weak things of the world to confound the mighty," then surely God can use a poor Black woman to do such work (92).

From her moment of arrival in England, Elaw finds it different from what she had imagined, and readily feels the people of England will benefit from her ministry. Shortly after disembarking from her ship in London, Elaw expresses surprise "to see the shops open" on Sunday, "the people intent on traffic and marketing . . . in the metropolis of the most Christian country in the world" (139). Elaw's initial assessment of England foregrounds what she sees as the hypocrisy of this so-called Christian land, in which monetary gain and material consumption take place on a day that should be set aside for spiritual and physical rest. This assessment echoes Elaw's ongoing opposition to greed as a threat to Christianity. Speaking out against the dangers of "worldly interest," "filthy lucre," and "love of mammon" in her narrative (100), she foregrounds the hypocrisy of British people who "traffic" on the Sabbath and exclaims their deep need for spiritual renewal. Elaw's critique of the British people's "intent on traffic and marketing" places her in conversation with Alexander Crummell, a fellow Black traveler to England. Crummell, whose travel to England began with a speaking tour of Great Britain to raise money for his church, ended up moving to England in 1847. His challenge to the British Anti-Slavery Society drew an inextricable link between British markets and American slavery.[29] Elaw similarly saw the country in a complex light, refusing to idealize it or use it as a foil for condemning the slaveholding United States as Frederick Douglass and William Wells Brown did.[30]

Elaw's visit to the British Anti-Slavery Society, years before Douglass and Crummell, further demonstrates her oppositional practice. Once inside, she feels unwelcomed and scrutinized by the men she encounters:

> Had I attended there on a matter of life and death, I think I could scarcely have been more closely interrogated or more rigidly examined; from the reception I met with, my impression was, that they imagined I wanted some pecuniary or other help from them; for they treated me as the proud do the needy . . . they demanded to be informed, whether I had any new doctrine to advance, that the English Christians are not in possession of? To which I replied, no; but I was sent to preach Christ . . . : they also wished to be informed, how it came about that God should send me? To which I replied, that I could not tell; but I knew that God required me to come hither, and that I came in obedience to His sovereign will. (140)

Here Elaw critiques the anti-slavery leadership's paternalism, their assumption that Elaw is a charity case who has come because she needs something from them rather than to give that which they need. They find it unimaginable that she might have anything to offer theologically to the British Christian community and inconceivable that God would call a poor Black woman to preach to them. Here we see a national, racial and class elitism at play—all of which Elaw critically deconstructs in her narrative.

After her encounter with the men at the anti-slavery society, Elaw steps firmly into her prophetic role, denouncing their antagonism toward her presence and ministry: "Pride and arrogancy are among the master sins of rational beings; an high look, a stately bearing, and a proud heart, are abominations in the sight of God, and insure a woeful reverse in a future life. Infidels will indulge in pomposity and arrogance; but Christians are and must be humble and lowly" (141). Elaw boldly asserts her moral authority and offers a spiritual lesson. As Jeremiah does in the Bible, she demonstrates more clearly her call as "proclaimer" or mediator between the people and

God's word—specifically serving as the vessel through which the voice of divine critique that challenges injustice, hypocrisy, materialism, and greed can be heard (Sawyer 1). Her emphasis on a reversal of what we see here on earth references a theological belief central to African American's historical practice of Christianity, what Yolanda Pierce refers to as a "sense of justice [that] rests on the notion of spiritual retribution" (8). Another key feature of the biblical prophetic tradition, divine retribution was the consequence for failing to heed the prophet's words, always given as a message of warning. Elaw's prophecy that the pride and arrogance of these men will "insure a woeful reverse in a future life" proclaims retribution for their unjust treatment of her on this earth and in this life. And while Elaw does not explicitly reference hell in this passage, her description of their future life as "woeful" suggests an eternal punishment for their earthly sin.

Also central to Elaw's critical response is her characterization of these men, who incidentally have claimed all superior and original knowledge of God, the Bible and Christianity, not as Christians but as "infidels." In contrast to these "infidels," Elaw positions herself "as a servant of Jesus . . . required to bear testimony in his name, who was meek and lowly, against the lofty looks of man, and the assumptions of such lordly authority and self-importance" (141). Again Elaw declares her moral authority and Christ's authority by flipping social hierarchies, questioning the power and influence attached to whiteness, maleness, and wealth. She continues by highlighting that God has chosen a "coloured female preacher" to "preach His Gospel on the shores of Britain . . . to residents in localities plentifully furnished with places of worship and ministers of the gospel,[yet who] had scarcely heard a sermon in their lives" (141). While the members of the anti-slavery society make it clear that the process of conversion and missionary travel occur only when white Christians convert Black people, Elaw rejects this narrative by declaring that the British need conversion, spiritual transformation and renewal—provided by a divinely called, poor Black woman.

Unlike other famous Black travelers to England, Elaw's journey abroad offers a far more nuanced portrait of England and reveals the multiplicity of Black people's journeys. Despite her critiques of slavery in her narrative, Elaw's self-representation as a preacher, prophetess, and missionary (not as an anti-slavery activist) extends critical conversations about the movements of Black people during the nineteenth century beyond forced journeys of captivity/enslavement and voluntary journeys of anti-slavery activism. As a result, Elaw's *Memoirs* provides a more expansive portrait of freedom—one that includes liberation from the formal system of slavery and spiritual liberation from the sin of pride, arrogance, and greed. Beginning with her dedication, the consciousness of this fundamental threat to community both in the United States and in England pervades her narrative. For Elaw, liberation from the sin of race, class, and gender pride and arrogance, as well as the greed of materialism, are foundational for constructing a community fully free from slavery and oppression in all its forms.

Elaw's visionary movement, her prophetic voice, itinerant preaching, and missionary travel to England extends the legacy of Hagar's narrative into the nineteenth century through her resistant movements and visionary encounters with the divine. Through her embodied spiritual practices, Elaw gestures to the existence of a Black female prophetic tradition, demonstrating the centrality of visionary experience in shaping not only Black women's voices but also their movements. Her itinerant movements and international travel as preacher and missionary reveal the disruptive potential of Black women's sacred journeys, which challenge race, gender, and classed definitions of the Black (female) body as captive, poor, and debased, offering a revised vision of her body as a vessel made holy by God and capable of harnessing divine power. Housing the sacred within her body, Elaw's transgressive movements and practices bear witness to the free and open movement of the spirit across socially constructed boundaries of race, class, and gender as well as regional and national borders. In the process, Elaw's journeys push against singular narratives of Black travel in the nineteenth century and challenge geographies of domination including the Middle Passage, colonization, and forms of missionary travel grounded in imperial hegemony. *Memoirs* ultimately grounds Black women's journeys in the sacred and in a divinely authored vision for an alternative community fueled by a deep desire for human liberation.[31] This desire for a home free from oppression persists across the narratives I will explore in subsequent chapters, fueling the journeys and vision of Black women travelers throughout the nineteenth, twentieth, and twenty-first centuries.

· THREE ·

Colonial and Missionary Crossings in Amanda Smith's *An Autobiography*

Amanda Smith's 1893 spiritual narrative *An Autobiography: The Story of the Lord's Dealings with Mrs. Amanda Smith* further demonstrates the intersection of spirituality, mobility, and slavery evident in both Hagar's and Zilpha Elaw's narratives. Unlike Elaw, who was orphaned at a young age, Smith was raised by her parents from whom she inherited a rich legacy of spiritual work and social activism. Born into slavery to Samuel and Mariam (Matthews) Berry in Long Green, Maryland, in 1837, Amanda Berry Smith became free when her father purchased his own freedom and that of his wife and four children.[1] The family moved from Maryland to York County Pennsylvania in 1845 where they were active participants in the Underground Railroad.

As an adult, Smith often found herself in a spiritual wilderness facing struggles and hardships caused by race, gender, and class inequities. She was married twice, widowed by her first and separating from her second husband who, much like Elaw's husband, hindered his wife's spiritual calling. Although Smith gave birth to five children during her lifetime, only one lived into adulthood. Even in the nineteenth century this was a high death toll, and Smith's autobiography indicates the particular vulnerability of Black life as she bears witness to the harsh conditions she faces as a poor Black woman forced to perform underpaid and often arduous labor in white homes with her young babies in tow. These conditions drove her movements from Lancaster to Philadelphia to New York, where she sought out greater wages and increased opportunity for her family.

Despite facing continued economic difficulties and family struggles, Smith's migration to these larger urban centers did expose her to burgeoning religious movements, in particular the Holiness movement. Attracted to and transformed by the doctrine of sanctification, like Elaw, she would become a leading preacher in the Holiness movement (though her roots were in the AME church rather than in the Methodist Episcopal denomination). Through a combination of preaching and singing, Smith's performances grounded in southern Black culture appealed to a wide array of audiences and enabled her to cross race, class, and gender divides even as her preaching exposed her to heightened criticism and attack. Drawing audiences in the hundreds and even at times in the thousands, Smith's preaching, described in newspapers and journals as "eloquent" and "electric," often left attendees crying and shouting.[2]

Although Smith identified herself as "The Colored Evangelist" on the title page of her book and though she is better-known for her preaching, evangelism and her work within the Women's Temperance Movements in the US and in Britain than for her writing, her 500+ page spiritual narrative and travelogue demands closer scholarly attention.[3] Reading across the sacred and secular elements of her work and travel, this chapter extends beyond previous studies by foregrounding how Smith used her mobility as itinerant preacher and missionary to advocate for poor Black children and to speak out about colonization, racism, Black civil rights, and citizenship in the US.[4] In doing so, my analysis makes visible the full impact and significance of Smith's writing about her spiritual journeys and extensive domestic and international travel to broader conversations within the fields of African American Religion and Literature, Black Diaspora Studies, and Travel Writing.

Much like Hagar before her, Smith's writing reveals an embodied spirituality that disrupts boundaries of race, gender, and class. Moreover, like Elaw, Smith foregrounds the positioning of her body as "out of place" through her public performances and through her travel. Beginning with Bishop J. M. Thoburn's preface, *An Autobiography*, presents Smith, much like Elaw, as a "dark female stranger from afar."[5] While Bishop Thoburn acknowledges Smith's "remarkable gifts" and greater "than ordinary power," he writes that when she was in India, "The novelty of a colored woman from America, who had in her childhood been a slave, appearing before an audience in Calcutta, was sufficient to attract attention" (vi). Thus, he suggests she was a spectacle. Although Smith's mission is a holy one, we see a blurred line between Smith's spiritual practice and her body, her singing and preaching, as entertainment and as spirit-filled. Concerned for her safety, her friends advise her not to "perform" in a local theatre in Calcutta, warning her the proprietor "merely wishes to have a good opportunity of seeing you, so that he can take you off in his theatre" (vii). This warning to Smith highlights the looming threat she faced as a traveler and public preacher—the risk of becoming a circulating spectacle, a commodity within the entertainment marketplace. This marketplace, existing both in the US and globally, consisted of "freak" shows, minstrel shows, ethnographic and "tom" shows that featured both Black and blackened bodies. The threat of exploitation by a man who wishes to profit from the display and performance of her body places Smith in close company with other Black women.

In his sociohistorical work *The Showman and the Slave: Race, Death, and Memory in Barnum's America,* Benjamin Reiss presents a woman who was constantly exploited in the way Smith sought to avoid, Joice Heth, an elderly enslaved woman who P. T. Barnum bought in 1835. Marketing Heth as "The Greatest Natural and National Curiosity in the World," Barnum traveled around the country with Heth on display as the 161-year-old "former nurse of the infant George Washington" (1). According to Reiss, crowds came in large numbers to hear Heth tell stories about Washington's birth and about breastfeeding him, as well as "to gaze on—even to touch—her amazingly decrepit body" (2). After Heth's death, Barnum charged fifty cents admission to view her corpse (2-3). Heth's story illustrates quite clearly white audiences' fascination, even obsession, with the Black female body and the ever-present threat of objectification and commodification of women like Smith. Every time Smith performed before a white audience, and in India a largely non-white audience, she faced the threat of consumption by those who come to gaze at her—seeking either pleasure or spiritual renewal from her body.[6] While the risk of commodification was ever-present, Smith's embodied spiritual practice—her visionary encounters with the sacred, her spiritual itinerancy throughout the country, and her travel abroad—disrupts constructions of Black women as commodifiable objects. She uses her own spiritual vision and power to undermine and critique the gaze of her various audiences (Black, white, Indian), and her spirit-led travel challenges the boundaries of race and gender that narrowly define the Black female body as a captive body.

I begin my analysis with a discussion of how Smith's early experiences of slavery, ancestral and communal knowledge about work and spirituality, as well as her experiences as a free Black woman employed in the North shaped her spiritual practice. The work she and her family performed in these contexts is quite distinct from the spiritual work and call by God to spread God's message to people across the globe that motivated her travels. The second half of the chapter will focus on Smith's international journeys and the rhetorical practices she employs in her travel writing. Much like the meaningful and value-filled work her parents and other predecessors performed in the service of individual and collective freedom, it is Smith's spiritual work, her "co-creative" work with God as missionary and preacher that liberates her from the forms of exploitative and violating labor within the marketplace that take up the bulk of her narrative.

Work: A Spiritual Legacy

Work is central to Smith's narrative, and physical and spiritual work central to her embodied spiritual practice. In opposition to the institution of slavery, in which enslaved people are denied access to the value or fruit of their labor, the opening of Smith's narrative describes how her father, Samuel Berry hired himself out throughout the countryside to purchase his own freedom and that of his wife and children. Smith explains, "after working for his mistress all day, he would walk three and four miles, and work in the harvest field till one and two o'clock in the morning, then go home and lie down and sleep for an hour or two, then up and at it again. He had an important and definite object before him and was willing to sacrifice sleep and rest in order to accomplish it. It was not his own liberty alone, but the freedom of his wife and five children. For this he toiled day and night" (18). There is a clear distinction between the labor Smith's father does for his mistress and the work that he does for his family. The labor he performs for his mistress does not belong to him, but after that he does work he can claim as his own, work from which he can profit and benefit. While slavery denies enslaved people control over their labor and redirects the profit their labor yields to their white masters, here Smith chooses to highlight work as meaningful and valuable to enslaved people. Her representation shows Black bodies not as chattel, who exist solely for another's profit, but as human beings who work with meaning and purpose to improve their own lives and that of their family.

Historians such as Jacqueline Jones and Larry Hudson give context for Smith's understanding, attesting to enslaved people's participation in meaningful work. Slaveholders were not the sole arbiters of the nature and meaning of work. Rather, enslaved people exercised agency through performing work for themselves and for the larger community. Hudson notes that enslaved people could win status in slave communities through this type of hard work; Jones attributes to such work "a degree of personal fulfillment" (29). She describes the remembrances of a formerly enslaved woman, Martha Colquitt, in the 1930s, of her grandmother and mother sewing clothing for her and other slave children. Reiterating the personal satisfaction of such work, Colquitt explains, "Dey done it 'cause dey wanted to. Dey wuz workin' for deyselves den" (qtd. in Jones *Labor of Love* 29). Such work has both spiritual and communal value because it sustains self and community. This sustenance is physical as it includes meeting the material needs of the body (i.e., food and clothing), but also spiritual as it enables enslaved peoples to act as agents whose work is chosen rather than coerced.

Likewise womanist scholar Joan Martin argues that the enslaved community developed their own "work ethic" in opposition to the oppressive labor and exploitation of slavery. In *More Than Chains and Toil: A Christian Work Ethic of Enslaved Women,* she defines this work ethic as "a motivating vision of livelihood—that is, the creation and use of intuition, skills, and practices which allow for the sustaining of self and family, and which contribute to the process of liberation from oppression for one's community. . . . [T]he nature and meaning of work itself is found in the quest for concrete freedom and human wholeness in the face of humanly constructed oppression and evil" (80). Martin's definition foregrounds three key elements of the community's alternative work ethic: (1) a commitment to the sustainability of Black life (individual and collective), (2) the pursuit of liberation and the full humanity of Black people, and (3) meaningful work resists oppression and evil.

Notably, an alternative spiritual knowledge shaped the enslaved community's understanding of work. This understanding countered the cosmology of slaveholders, who claimed Blackness was inherently evil and that God had ordained their enslavement and oppressive labor. Grounding their conception of evil within an African cosmology, the enslaved community, in contrast, defined slavery and the "unwarranted, unearned, and undeserved" suffering it caused as a human sin, a human evil—not the command of a supreme God or deity (J. Martin 106). Within this cosmology, they defined labor performed for slaveholders as evil precisely because it was exploitative and caused undeserved suffering. Reconstituting the very nature of work, enslaved people engaged in work for themselves and for their community in spite of and in resistance to the suffering they experienced at the hands of their masters and mistresses. Even if it required as much sacrifice as Samuel Berry's, it gained meaning by sustaining the lives of one another, and by seeking the liberation of self, family, and community. Such work meets the material and spiritual needs of others, whether that be through growing extra food to feed others, sewing clothing to keep others warm or aiding others in attaining freedom—a practice of care Smith's family continues even after achieving their own freedom.

Applying Martin's womanist analysis of work for the enslaved community, I read Smith's father's work as an embodied expression of a meaningful "work ethic"—work as life-sustaining, liberating, and resistant to evil and oppression. Despite Smith's description of her father's slave mistress as "very kind" because she allowed him to purchase his own freedom and that of his family, that kindness did not shield him from the oppressive nature of enslaved labor. Her description of the work he performed as a lime burner, broom maker, and harvester in his mistress's service, as well as the grueling hours he kept to own himself and free his wife and children bears witness to the evil and unjust conditions of slavery that afforded him just 1–2 hours of sleep each night.[7] Yet every hour that her father spends working for the lives and liberation of his family, rather than for his owner, challenges the institution of slavery in which slave labor was a death sentence. Through it he performed work that was not death but was committed to "living and resisting the consequences of evil" (J. Martin 107). Through his own resistant spiritual practice, Smith's father passes on his work ethic as part of a legacy that greatly informs Smith's experiences as a free laborer in the North. I read Samuel Berry's work as both physical and spiritual in nature since it was rooted in a desire for freedom and in opposition to the violence of the slave market, which defines him and his family as commodities.

Smith's mother and grandmother's spiritual practices are no less central to this work ethic. Bearing witness to the spiritual work of her female ancestors, Smith tells us that her mother and grandmother had prayed their mistress's daughter would convert to Christianity, hoping it would lead to the freedom of Mariam and her children, as Samuel had already purchased his freedom (19). They took it as evidence of both God's power and the power of prayer when Miss Celie converted and shortly thereafter asked her mother to promise she would "let Samuel have Mariam and the children" (21).[8] Smith reports that upon hearing Miss Celie's words, Mariam "ran with all her might and told grandmother, and grandmother's faith saw the door open for the freedom of her grandchildren; and she ran out into the bush and told Jesus" (21). Smith's grandmother continues to hold conversations with Jesus in the woods and understands the liberation of her grandchildren as the answer to her persistent prayers. I read this encounter with Jesus in the woods as an extension of Hagar's legacy of wilderness encounters with the divine in Genesis. For Smith's grandmother, as for Hagar and Elaw, the wilderness is both a physical and spiritual place of struggle—a place in which God sees their struggle and meets them in their place of need. Moreover, the grandmother's spiritual experience demonstrates her embodied relationship with the divine—one in which she receives a divine vision (seeing the door of freedom open for her family) and responds to this vision with physical movement—running to the woods. Just as Jesus approaches Elaw while she is outside milking a cow, the grandmother's conversation in the woods with Jesus indicates he enters into her world and lived reality, meeting with the grandmother in her place of need, seeing and hearing her struggle, much as God sees and hears Hagar in the desert and Elaw in the wilderness of the camp meeting. If we read across the narratives, the legacy of Black women's embodied spiritual practices become visible, as does the divine commitment to supporting the physical and spiritual needs of Black women on their path toward liberation.

At the end of the first chapter, Smith bears witness to the real-world impact of her grandmother's sacred power. Describing her grandmother as "a woman of deep piety and great faith," Smith notes, "I have often heard my mother say that it was to the prayers and mighty faith of my grandmother that we owed our freedom. . . . She had often prayed that God would open a way so that her grandchildren might be free. . . . And so . . . , the Lord did provide, and my father was permitted to purchase our freedom" (23). As the passage suggests, Smith and her family's liberation is secured by the spiritual work of her father, mother, and grandmother, reflecting a work ethic that defines this work of liberation as meaningful. Moreover, in line with Martin's description of "co-creative work with a liberating God who acts in human history" that enslaved people performed, Smith's passage makes clear that such liberating work is God-supported (151).

In contrast to her ancestors' divinely supported work of liberation, Smith positions the futility and hypocrisy of Christian slaveholders who seek to thwart the liberatory initiatives of enslaved people. Similar to the slave narratives of Frederick Douglass and Harriet Jacobs, Smith offers a digression about one such slaveholder, Ned Gossage, who died while trying, unsuccessfully, to capture two of his runaway slaves. Smith reflects, "I used to think how strange it was, he being a professed Christian, and a class leader in the Methodist Church, . . . that he should be so blinded by selfishness and greed that he should risk his own life to put into slavery again those who sought only for freedom. How selfishness, when allowed to rule us, will drive us on, and make us act in spirit like the great enemy of our soul, who ever seeks to recapture those who have escaped from the bondage from sin" (18). Smith parallels Ned Gossage's selfishness, greed, and the desire to enslave with the actions of the devil, who threatens to spiritually enslave all humanity. She makes a powerful theological critique of slavery and of the Fugitive Slave Law—establishing slavery and the desire to enslave as sinful and proclaiming death as the spiritual and material consequences of such sin, as in Gossage's case.

Further defining Christianity as offering freedom from bondage, Smith positions slavecatching, the attempt to re-enslave those who God has called to freedom, as antithetical to Christianity. She posits an alternative way of knowing, a spiritual knowledge that challenges dominant constructions of justice, as well as slaveholding theology that defines only white people as made for freedom. Rejecting a disembodied or transcendent freedom that Black people can access only in the afterlife, Smith presents a vision of freedom grounded in the material world. As such, she refuses to equate freedom with death. Rather she highlights the active struggle of enslaved people to attain their freedom now—in this life. This freedom struggle is visible in the tireless work of Samuel Berry to buy his own and his family's freedom, the persistent prayers of Mariam Berry and Smith's grandmother for liberation, and in the flight of enslaved people like the two boys Ned Gossage fails to capture. Thus, not only does Smith equate the desire for freedom with godliness, she further claims the work of liberation as sacred work.

Smith's mother's spiritual work and its role in ensuring justice and liberation persists even after the family has achieved its freedom.[9] Smith underscores the important role her family plays in aiding runaway slaves and helping them to secure their freedom, describing their home as "one of the main stations of the Under Ground Railroad" (31). Biographer Adrienne Israel reports Smith's family began aiding runaways in the 1840s and continued even after 1850, the year the expanded Fugitive Slave Act passed (18). Therefore, it was imperative to keep such practices concealed. Smith describes how white men confronted her parents in the middle of the night, trying to catch them in the act of hiding runaways. Outraged by this invasion of their home, Mariam travels to New Market, where, as Smith notes, the slave catchers live:[10]

as she went she told everybody she met how she had been hounded by these men. Told all their names right out, and all the rich respectable people cried shame, and backed her up. . . . [S]o she stood on the stepping stone . . . right in front of the largest Tavern in the place. There were a lot of these men sitting out reading the news . . . and she opened her mouth and for one hour declared unto them all the words in her heart. Not a word was said against her, but as the spectators and others looked on and listened the cry of "Shame! Shame!" could be heard; and the men skulked away here and there. By the time she got through there was not one to be seen of this tribe. (34)

Smith's narrative about this public and mobile act of resistance illustrates her mother's embodied spiritual practice, much like her grandmother before her. First, this passage reveals Mariam to be a moral authority with the power to speak out against those who have committed crimes by dishonoring or threatening her family. As a result, others in the community listen to her and believe her judgment. Unlike Mariam and Samuel, the slave catchers had committed no legally recognized crime. In opposition to the illegibility of their crimes (the failure of the state to name their actions as criminal), Mariam appeals to a moral law informed by her own spirituality and domestic ideology in her public testimony against the invasion of the Berry home and the threatening of their family. It is this intrusion into domestic space, a sanctuary for the middle class, that Mariam portrays as a crime and violation. Certainly, her appeal to Victorian ideals explains why the "rich respectable people" support her, while incriminating the slave catchers.

The distinction between "rich respectable people" and the "tribe" of slave catchers foreshadows Smith's ethnographic claims of superiority by aligning Black people with Egyptians and creating a spiritual lineage that locates the birthplace of Western Christianity in a Black Egypt. Both Smith and her mother strategically align Black people with Christian principles and moral order, while positioning slave catchers (and by extension practices of captivity) as alien, foreign, and even antithetical to Western Christian values. Mariam's words are also powerful enough to run these men that have threatened her family out of town. While Mariam is not a preacher as Smith later declares herself to be, here she claims the right of Black women to speak publicly.

In claiming a public voice, Mariam disrupts the space of the marketplace, a place where Black bodies are frequently displayed and auctioned off, commodified and objectified, and transforms it into a space where she, a

Black woman, can exercise authority and demand justice. Though Mariam is a free Black woman, this space of the market, and indeed the entire national landscape, has been touched by slavery and its violence. Positioning Black people within this context "as objects 'to be seen,' and assessed," McKittrick claims that "black men, women, and children become part of the slave trade landscape, like other objects for sale" (72). The terrain of slavery, therefore, shapes the very spaces within which Black women move, regardless of their status as free or enslaved. For Mariam, this means that by entering the marketplace, she risks placing her Black female body on display "to be seen," "assessed," and ultimately to be objectified by her white spectators. Yet in this passage the space is transformed.

Masquerading as a static and rigid space in which race and sex differentiation are naturalized, the marketplace is revealed as socially constructed and, therefore, susceptible to transformation by the very bodies it seeks to control and define, such as Mariam's. Her resistant practice shifts the white gaze away from her body to her white assailants, rendering their bodies and their unjust actions public and "transparent."[11] The public display of their bodies and actions is so shameful to these men that, according to Smith, they "skulked away" until they could be seen no longer.

Mariam's disruption arguably goes beyond maintaining her personhood. Her public testimony about the injustices her family suffered at the hands of these white men actually transforms the space of the market into a courthouse—a space in which the larger community can see and judge the men's illegible crimes. Hence, Mariam's public testimony functions much like Elaw's preaching/prophesying as a practice of "respatialization." As discussed in the previous chapter, the courthouse traditionally functioned as a site of domination for Black men and women, regardless of their status as enslaved or as "free." They were often denied the right to testify against white people until after the passage of the Fourteenth Amendment in 1868.[12] While they could be charged in court as criminals, they could not seek justice from the many wrongs committed against them by the larger white community. Yet Mariam turns the marketplace into a figurative courthouse in which a Black woman can be seen as an innocent victim, while the unjust actions of white men can finally be seen and judged as criminal. Mariam's public testimony ultimately vindicates her family and enables them to continue their covert work in helping runaway slaves achieve freedom. This embodied spirituality, which makes evident the possibility of a liberating Black female performance even within a space legally structured for captivity and violence—profoundly shapes Smith's own theology and spiritual practice.

Despite the rich spiritual legacy of work and liberation that Smith inherits from her parents and grandmother forged out of their experiences of slavery, the next section of Smith's autobiography reveals her struggle to live out this legacy within the oppressive contexts of the northern labor market, as a domestic laborer in white homes, and within her own domestic space as a wife and mother. As a free Black woman, Smith initially attempts to find spiritual fulfillment and contentment within domestic space, marrying twice during her life. Smith has five children, two from her first marriage and three from her second marriage. Her first marriage to Calvin Devine receives very little attention in her narrative and ends when her husband dies while fighting in the Civil War.[13] The one child who survived into adulthood, Mazie, is the product of this union. The second marriage, to James Smith, a preacher in the AME Church, receives more attention.

In her autobiography, Smith positions her second marriage to a preacher as a way to answer the call to preach, which she receives in a series of visions. However, like Elaw, Smith's marriage ultimately becomes an obstacle that hinders her ability to heed God's call. She experiences her first spiritual vision and call to preach during an illness in 1855:

> I seemed to go into a kind of trance or vision, and I saw on the foot of my bed a most beautiful angel. It stood on one foot, with wings spread, looking me in the face and motioning me with the hand; it said "Go back," three times. . . . Then, it seemed, I went to a great Camp Meeting and there seemed to be thousands of people, and I was to preach and the platform I had to stand on was up high above the people. . . . O, how I preached, and the people were slain [converted] right and left. I suppose I was in this vision about two hours. When I came out of it I was decidedly better. (42–43)

Smith's vision, much like Elaw's visionary experience, emphasizes the link between spirit and the body. Thus, it bears witness to her embodied spirituality. That this vision occurs during a physical illness is no coincidence. The fragility of Smith's physical body, particularly her feverish state, seems to facilitate this spiritual vision, while her vision of God's desire for her to preach leads to her physical healing.

The references to an angel with hands, feet and wings indicates the centrality of the body within her vision, affirming the divine as both concrete and tangible. Moreover, the command she receives from the angel to "Go back," and preach echoes God's command to Hagar to "Go back" to Abraham and Sarah's household. As in Hagar's narrative, Smith's call to return is in response to her flight away from the place God has called her to be. Just as God spares Hagar's life in the wilderness—offering her a hope and a future, so too has God "spared [Smith] for a purpose" (43). And like Hagar and Elaw before her, she can only realize this purpose by answering the call to move, the call to itinerancy and travel. Later we will see the importance of both this itinerancy as well as preaching to Smith's spiritual legacy. Not only does Smith receive the command, but she also sees the physical manifestation of God's call—a vision of herself successfully preaching in front of thousands of people.

The final articulation of embodiment occurs when Smith awakens from her vision and discovers that her body has been healed. A central characteristic of Black women's theology in nineteenth-century spiritual narratives is this belief that physical illness signifies a deeper spiritual sickness. Bodily illness could often be interpreted as a sign of being out-of-sync with God or, as with Smith at the time, the result of fleeing from God's plan and direction (Moody 66). Given this context, we can read Smith's spiritual obedience—her decision to heed the angel's command to return, to "Go back" and preach—as facilitating her physical healing. Smith's vision demonstrates the intimate connection between spirit and body. Thus, when she finally heeds the call to preach, Smith's faith leads to the liberation of her body, a liberation from sickness, and her spirit.

The inextricable link between Smith's body and her spiritual experience persists in her description of her conversion the following year:

> I sprang to my feet, all around was light, I was new. I looked at my hands, they looked new; I took hold of myself and said, "Why, I am new, I am new all over." I clapped my hands; I ran up out of the cellar, I walked up and down the kitchen floor. Praise the Lord! There seemed to be a halo of light all over me; the change was so real and so thorough that I have often said that if I had been as black as ink or as green as grass or as white as snow, I would not have been frightened. I went into the dining room; we had a large mirror that went from the floor to the ceiling, and I went and looked in it to see if anything had transpired in my color, because there was something wonderful had taken place inside of me, and it really seemed to me it was outside too . . . ! (47)

As with Elaw's conversion, Smith foregrounds the body in her description; however, while Elaw's conversion vision foregrounded Jesus's embodiment (his hands, feet, hair, and robe), Smith's conversion narrative focuses largely on her own body. Typically defined as a spiritual change or transformation, conversion appears here in material terms: clapping hands, running, and walking. Smith's body, then, becomes the conduit of divine power and transformation—a physical vessel whose movements make visible the presence of the sacred in the world.[14] Not only does physical movement become the expression of Smith's spiritual encounter and transformation, but even more important, Smith's vision of her body changes, to the point where her hands "look new." Believing this transformation to be so powerful and complete, she even expects to look physically different in the mirror.

Smith's expectation of a change in her skin color illustrates that racial constructions in nineteenth-century America have profoundly shaped her. Certainly, the sociohistorical construction of whiteness and its legal, social, economic, and even spiritual value informs Smith's language. Yet I argue that while her conversion narrative reveals Smith's operation within these racial constructions, it also demonstrates a tenuous critique of white power and privilege.[15] Central to this critique is Smith's refusal to equate conversion with whiteness. While Smith does imagine herself as "white as snow," a phrase that suggests her internalizing of colonized Christian discourse that equates whiteness with spiritual purity, she also imagines herself as "black as ink or as green as grass." Here Smith strategically removes whiteness from its place as privileged signifier by placing it last in a series of similes that equate Blackness, greenness, and whiteness. Through her own metaphorical images ("black as ink" and "green as grass"), Smith reveals the language "white as snow" to be constructed and undermines the image's supposed universality. Here, Smith desires to express in material terms how powerful a change she has experienced. Perhaps given the particularities of her time and place, there is no physical change more dramatic than that of skin color. This does not, however, mean that Smith desires to change her skin color or wishes to be white. In fact, the rest of her autobiography reveals her attempts to reclaim the spiritual and cultural value of Blackness in opposition to white power and privilege.

Despite the clear command Smith receives from God in an 1855 vision to "go and preach," she evades the call for more than a decade and decides to marry James Smith, her second husband, in 1865 believing that her service as a preacher's wife will satisfy God's command. Smith's initial unwillingness to follow God's call to preach is perhaps unsurprising given that preaching was a position of authority open only to men in the large majority of Christian churches in the nineteenth century. This included Smith's denomination, the AME church, which excluded women from ordination until 1948 (Dodson xxxvii). She tells her reader that she marries James to "have a Christian home and serve God more perfectly. I thought to marry a preacher would be the very thing. . . . I had seen and known the influence of a minister's wife, and how much she could help her husband. . . . Mr. Smith said that was just the kind of wife he wanted" (58). But James Smith fails to keep his promise to join the AME Conference as an itinerant minister, and Smith quickly realizes that the marriage traps her within domestic space—preventing her from becoming an itinerant preacher.

Because Smith's marriage requires she work as a domestic for a white family, it also keeps her locked within a system of exploitative and abusive labor that hinders her attempts to create a home for herself and her children. While it requires her to travel from family to family providing whatever labor they need, it exists in contrast to itinerancy. Smith describes her three months working for Mrs. Colonel McGraw thus:

> O, what I went through during those three months! I had to do all the cooking for the house, and eight farm hands, besides helping with the washing and doing up all the shirts and fine clothes and looking after my children. How I did it I don't know. There were but two other servants in the house . . . so I had no help. . . . My baby seemed to get along nicely for the first three weeks, then she was taken sick with summer complaint, and in six weeks I had to lay her away in the grave. (59–60)

Smith's narrative abounds with experiences like these—attesting to her constant need to travel to find employment, the severity of the conditions and the harsh consequences of such labor to herself and to her family. Although Smith's physical labor never breaks her spirit, as her constant reminders to the reader that "the Lord stood by me" suggest, it becomes clear that her life as a domestic worker offers little fulfillment and comes at a high price—the cost of her own physical health and that of her child, Nell, who dies while she works as a domestic.[16]

Smith's narrative suggests the difference between middle-class white women's experience of being trapped within domestic space and free Black women's experience of continued captivity within white domestic space in the nineteenth century. It aligns with Paula Giddings's examination of Black women's experience of race and sex oppression in the period. She points out that the association between true womanhood and domesticity evidenced by women's "exclusive role . . . as homemaker, mother, housewife" and moral center of the home supported a narrative that Black women, who had to work outside their own homes as domestics and washerwomen for white families to make ends meet, were "unnatural, unfeminine" and even immoral (47–49). This narrow definition of womanhood, therefore, fundamentally excluded Black women, who were often positioned as failed women or as bad mothers even as their cheap labor within white domestic spaces facilitated and reaffirmed white women's seclusion and idealization within the home. While white domestic space served to protect white women and their children, this space posed a continuing threat to the physical and mental health and well-being of Black women and children.

In addition to having her body and labor devalued by white employers, Smith's piety and moral wisdom are also devalued within her own home. Facing a similar opposition from her husband as Elaw experienced, Smith represents him as a threat to her own spiritual growth. Although James Smith is an educated preacher, Smith resists his spiritual authority, particularly his stance on sanctification or holiness. Revealing her husband's attempts to stifle her spiritual growth, Smith states "he had no sympathy with holiness. He had had advantages far above me and was far more intelligent. He would always want to argue on this subject, and I could not keep up on that line and it would throw me back, so I told the Lord one day if He would send James away somewhere till I got the blessing he would never get it away again, but that he hindered me from getting it" (70–71). Smith clearly believes that James has set her back spiritually and refuses to privilege her husband's theological beliefs, despite his educational status. Instead, she does what is necessary to ensure the cultivation of her own spiritual life even if that means distancing herself from her husband.

Smith's theological resistance to her husband places her in firm opposition to the nineteenth-century expectation of "feminine self-sacrifice" that was central to the definition of a "true woman" (Haynes 88). According to Caroline Haynes, within this true womanhood ideal, "woman's primary allegiance is not to God but to her husband. Moreover . . . she is to remain supposedly within her divinely ordained, 'natural' sphere," which ironically requires her to "abdicate her own spiritual development and even her entitlement to salvation to ensure those of her undeserving spouse" (88).

Before actually leaving her husband, Smith attempts to obtain some measure of independence for herself—both economically and spiritually—so that she can continue on her own spiritual path. For example, when James attempts to relocate the family for a new job opportunity as a coachman, Smith resists the move, declaring, "I am afraid to go; you have done me so bad right here where I have just begun to get used to the people, and know how to turn around, and what will it be if I go there out in the country, no church near, and a stranger, and if I give up my washing what will I do? I can help myself a little now" (71). Smith's response testifies to the negative impact of James's job instability and the difficulties she faces from relocation. The move threatens her economic independence—a necessity for Smith in part because of her husband's unreliable employment and wages but also disrupts communal ties and destroys the network of people Smith needs to thrive. In this passage, then, Smith advocates for a physical separation from her husband to maintain the spiritual and economic independence she has achieved in the city, where she has the communal support of friends and the church to sustain her.

Although being a washerwoman and a domestic in white homes was, as historians have noted, frequently demanding, unrewarding, and even dangerous for Black women, for Smith it offers some measure of economic control over her life.[17] Smith's decision to stay in New York City, while James departs for a new job, enables her to maintain her economic independence, community, and facilitates her spiritual growth. The physical distance from her husband provides Smith with the spiritual independence necessary to receive the second blessing (sanctification) that she so fiercely sought.

As with her conversion narrative, Smith's experience of sanctification reveals the embodied nature of her spiritual practice. After receiving the blessing during a church sermon, she tells us, "I don't know just how I looked, but I felt so wonderfully strange, yet I felt glorious. . . . Just as I put my foot on the top step I seemed to feel a hand, the touch of which I cannot describe. It seemed to press me gently on the top of my head, and I felt something part and roll down and cover me like a great cloak! I felt it distinctly . . . and O what a mighty peace and power took possession of me!" (79). Echoing Elaw's embodied experience of sanctification, Smith highlights the intersection of the spirit and the material in this passage. Smith's spiritual reality receives expression only through her body, which functions as a marker of her spiritual transformation. Smith's sensation of "a hand touching her head" reveals God as an unquestionable spiritual and physical presence in her life. So tangible and intimate is this divine connection that God can literally reach out and touch her. Smith's description of "a large cloak covering her body" further demonstrates how this internal change reflects externally onto her physical self. Serving as an outward marker of the internal transformation of sanctification, the cloak represents the Christian's newfound identity in Christ.[18] With this visual reference, Smith once again positions her body as the locus of divine blessing—the vessel through which she encounters the sacred.

This link between the body and Smith's spiritual transformation becomes even more apparent after Smith leaves the church where she receives the gift of sanctification. Smith suggests that her spiritual change gives her a newfound emotional but also physical confidence. As she walks down the street, Smith encounters three prominent Black women from her church, women whose ridicule she fears and who cause her to feel inadequate.[19] Yet Smith acknowledges, "when I got up to them I seemed to have special power in my right arm and I was swinging it around. . . . O I felt mighty, as I came near those sisters. They said. 'Well, Smith, where have you been this morning?' 'The Lord,' I said, 'has sanctified my soul.' And they were speechless! I said no more, but passed on, swinging my arm! I suppose the people thought I was wild, and I was, for God had set me on fire" (79)! Again, Smith's body enables her to express the internal change that she has experienced. In this case, her swinging right arm communicates Smith's newfound empowerment and confidence.

But Smith's encounter with these three women demonstrates an even greater change, as Smith's confidence also manifests through her voice. Smith, who would have been afraid to speak to these women and to share her belief in sanctification with them before her spiritual change, now has a "wildness" about her. Her tongue, much like Hagar's, has become unruly, so much so that she announces, "if there was a platform around the world I would be willing to get on it and walk and tell everybody of this sanctifying power of God!" (79). Illustrating the confidence she has gained from her belief in holiness, Smith's swinging arm and daring tongue mark the continuation of Hagar's legacy of disruptive, embodied movement. Holiness, which "meant absolute trust in God's will," legitimized unruliness and resistance because "its followers not only were given permission to develop and change in response to God's calling but also were licensed to obey God's will over and above the will of all other earthly beings" (Haynes 103). Consequently, after Smith acquires sanctification, she no longer fears what others may think of her and, perhaps most important, she is able to stand in opposition to the various forms of oppression she faces, including patriarchy and racism.

Evidence of Smith's newfound liberation, sanctification enables Smith to overcome her fear of white people. She exclaims, "I was not afraid of them in the sense of doing me harm, or anything of that kind—but a kind of fear because they were white, and were there, and I was black and was here!" (80). Notably, Smith represents the distance between herself and white people as a spatial difference (there vs. here). Yet as she begins her spiritual work, we see her undermining such boundaries, calling them into question and using her body to disrupt raced, classed, and gendered space. This change in how she views race, particularly whiteness, becomes visible when Smith explains "the Holy Ghost had made it clear to me . . . as I looked at white people that I had always seemed to be afraid of, now they looked so small. The great mountain had become a mole-hill" (80). Thus, Smith's spiritual change brings her a new vision—enabling her to see the world differently. Rather than seeing with her own eyes, she appears to see with godly eyes ("the Holy Ghost . . . made it clear") and with this vision Smith sees whiteness as something ordinary rather than fearful. Like Hagar and Elaw before her, this clearing provided by the spirit reveals the Black (female) body "as a site of divine revelation"—a site of alternative ways of knowing (Copeland 24). This alternative knowledge delivered via Smith's sacred vision, suggests that the boundaries of race are permeable. Whatever chasm existed between Blackness and whiteness, between here and there, to use Smith's terms, can now be traversed. Furthermore, as the remainder of this chapter describes, this alternative knowledge about the Black body as sacred vessel informs her travel abroad—empowering her to transgress the raced, classed, and gendered boundaries that held her in place for so long.

If Smith's achievement of this spiritual transformation that brings her power, vision, and the freedom to move occurs only after she creates physical distance between herself and her husband, it is perhaps no surprise that she does not fully begin her spiritual work until this distance from her husband becomes permanent. Smith references James's death rather succinctly and matter-of-factly: "He died in November, 1869, at New Utrecht, NY. Since then I have been a widow, and have traveled half way round the world, and God has ever been faithful" (96). God's faithfulness stands in stark contrast to the unreliability of her husband, who often left Smith alone to meet the material needs of the family and who failed to support her spiritual growth—even belittling her spiritual vision.[20] Clearly, her husband's death was not a loss for Smith but rather a gain, as freedom from her marriage brings with it the freedom to travel and the freedom to fulfill her spiritual calling.

Smith's portrait of her early life experiences both in the southern and northern US demonstrates the persistence of Hagar's legacy for African American people. Through their embodied spiritual practices, even amid conditions of captivity, Black women (and men) reveal themselves as made for freedom. Specifically, Smith's narrative posits the embodied work of liberation as sacred work—a co-creative process between human and divine. The significance of Smith's narrative lies in its grounding of Black women's spiritual practices in the lived material reality of Black women in slavery and in freedom as well as in showcasing their expression of sacred power through embodied acts of resistance. *An Autobiography* further extends Hagar's legacy of unruliness beyond an active resistance to slavery to include Smith's resistance to patriarchal control within marriage, as well as a resistance to white supremacy and racism that continues to shape the realities of Black life in the US. As the remainder of this chapter will lay out, this legacy of unruliness culminates in her travel abroad as the mobility of Smith's body and her rhetoric disrupt dominant legacies of travel (tourist, colonial, and missionary).

"Half Way round the World": Spirituality, Mobility, and the Disruptive Black Female Body

Smith's mobility increases exponentially after the death of her second husband. Traveling across four continents, including North America, Europe, Asia, and Africa, her mobility is extraordinary at a time when the majority of Black women were trapped within systems of domination and oppression throughout the African diaspora. Although Smith has achieved recognition as an internationally renowned preacher and singer, in this section I foreground the lesser studied and oft-overlooked aspects of her spiritual practice, most notably her international travel and how her movements abroad shape and inform her ever-shifting rhetoric. Through this deep dive into Smith as traveler and travel writer, I offer an expanded portrait of her varied theological and literary contributions, as well as a deeper understanding of Black women's legacy of unruliness and itinerancy.

Smith begins her travels around the world in 1878—living abroad until her return in 1890.[21] Although the US slave trade was abolished in 1808, and the Atlantic slave trade effectively ended by the 1860s, the legacy of three centuries of Black bodies circulating as cargo still informed perceptions of Black women travelers in 1878. Unlike white women travelers who largely traveled for leisure as tourists, Black women largely traveled as laborers, migrating to find employment in another location or in the employ of white travelers. Charmaine Nelson describes how even "free" Black bodies were immobilized (i.e., segregated) on ships at the time on the logic that they were a threat to white passengers (32). Yet Smith's travel narrative complicates the dominant construction of the Black body as a body that must be contained. Though Smith's travel is tied to the legacy of forced movement, her mobility also challenges and expands beyond this single story of Black women as captive bodies.

The disruptive nature of Smith's international travel becomes evident in her ship passage across the Atlantic, which she undertakes after receiving a spiritual call from God that sends her first to Europe for a period of rest from preaching and later to India and Africa as a preacher and missionary. She rides first-class because a white woman, Mrs. Kenney, whom Smith refers to as a "dear friend," has paid for her ticket. The anomaly of Smith's presence on the ship unaccompanied and in service to no one is multiplied by her possession of a first-class ticket. From the first moments, it is clear that her presence aboard the ship disrupts social hierarchies, as her mobility calls into question race, gender, and class boundaries. Smith explains that "There were quite a number of aristocratic passengers, and I, being a colored woman and alone, there was quite a little inquiry who I was, what I was going to England for, etc. I must say I did feel somewhat embarrassed" (250). Attributing their reaction to both race and class bias, Smith describes her fellow passengers' perception of her as "a suspicious being of some kind"; they relentlessly question her ability to ride first-class and call her "a fool" for not riding in steerage (250). Like Elaw's experience of being out of place as a lone Black woman traveling abroad, Smith's passage to England stands in stark contrast to the traditional ways in which Black female bodies have circulated across the Atlantic.

Within this context, Smith's mobility abroad and her writing about her travels contests the dominant definition of the Black (female) body—repeating a legacy of unruliness that Smith undoubtedly inherits from her female ancestors but that also reflects the broader spiritual and literary legacy of

Hagar's narrative. Focusing specifically on Smith's tour of Europe, her travels to India, Egypt, and her eight-year-stay in Liberia, I argue that Smith's itinerant spiritual practices as tourist and missionary enable her to shift from spectacle, one who is objectified by the gaze of her white audiences, to spectator, one who sees and who is free to interpret what she sees. Although tourist and missionary travel are firmly entrenched in Western imperial privilege and power, Smith, engaging in an itinerant rhetorical practice, appropriates colonial travel and missionary discourse in order to undermine and critique imperial practices, hierarchies, and values in America and abroad.

The social and historical context informing her geographical and her literary movements can help us understand Smith's tenuous use of colonial discourse in her travel, her shifting at times between fierce critique and a seemingly paradoxical appropriation of typical colonial representations. First, I locate Smith's shifting discourse as part of what Malini Johar Schueller refers to as a "cunning" and "complex" rhetorical strategy to appease her white western evangelical audience (Intro xx). This particular strategy becomes less surprising considering the difficult line Smith, like so many Black writers, had to walk between criticizing the racism and colonial privilege of her readers and financial supporters and meeting their expectations so that they will support her financially.[22] As supporters of the missionary enterprise, Smith's audience would have been supporters of extending Western empire abroad as well. Demonstrating this inextricable link between missions and empire, Schueller maintains that "Missionary activity was seen as related to nation making and empire making, just as the idea of a US empire was always seen in terms of a mission" (39). Within this context, audience expectations necessarily limit Smith's critical vision. Nevertheless, Smith contests such limits, employing an itinerant spiritual practice to creatively surmount these obstacles.

EUROPEAN SOJOURN: FROM SPECTACLE TO SPECTATOR

Although Smith's spiritual itinerancy and international travel are liberating practices, her arrival in Liverpool, England in 1878 illustrates Smith's continued position as spectacle, in which her white audience's objectifying and dehumanizing gaze continues to threaten her.[23] Smith's presence in Liverpool locates her within a tradition of nineteenth-century American travelers for whom Liverpool "was the first port of call" in England, and more specifically within a long lineage of African American travelers, such as Frederick Douglass, William Wells Brown, and William and Ellen Craft who "came to Liverpool to pursue different aims all connected with the pursuit of freedom" (Seed xv). Although Smith travels as a tourist and missionary after the end of US slavery, her brief stop in Liverpool illustrates, like so many African American travelers before her, the comparatively better treatment she receives in England as opposed to the United States. Offering her comparative analysis, Smith shares an experience of the treatment she receives while waiting for a train to take her to a conference in Keswick:

> I was a curiosity. How the people did look at me. I thought I would buy me a newspaper, and then they wouldn't look at me so much, but, lo and behold, that only made it worse. They seemed to wonder what in the world I was going to do with a newspaper. Then I walked up and down, then they walked up and down, as though they wondered what I was walking up and down for. They were very respectful; they did not laugh and make remarks like they would have done in this country, but they seemed to look as though they pitied me. (255)

Smith's status as spectacle continues. The spectators' shock at seeing her walking and reading gives the impression that they are gazing at an unfamiliar animal in a zoo rather than a human being. Much as it was during her ship passage, her subjectivity as a traveler is threatened by what Shirley Ann Tate terms "the white colonial gaze," which "homogenizes Black women's bodies as it dissects and inscribes its own meanings of racialized otherness" (4–5). Smith's reference to these spectators as "respectful" does not lessen the dehumanization of their gaze that marks her body as less than human, and therefore incapable of literacy. When she highlights the difference between the more "respectful" racism she faces in Britain, she offers an explicit critique of American racism, which might be expressed in laughter, demeaning speech or, as Elaw testifies, a threat of physical violence.

The tension in Smith's positioning as subject and object demonstrates a central challenge for Black women travelers who position themselves as mobile subjects over and against the persistent objectification of their bodies. Much as it does in the narratives of Hagar and Elaw, this objectification repeats in a number of ways: the gaze, speech acts such as naming, written words, and through the reproduction of visual images and art that hold the Black (female) body captive. Narrow and singular definitions of embodied Blackness as other, as spectacle, as strange seek to fix them in place. In opposition to this continued threat of objectification, Smith employs an itinerant rhetorical practice that reinforces her "mobile subjectivity," at times drawing from colonial rhetoric while at other times challenging the hierarchies and domination at the heart of colonial and missionary travel. I employ Fish's term "mobile subjectivity" to my analysis of Smith because it recognizes the inextricable link between identity and place.[24] Resisting the fixed identities imposed on Black women, Smith's itinerant rhetorical practice demonstrates a fluid or mobile subjectivity that shifts as she moves across geographical space and national borders. As a result, her embodied and rhetorical movements suggest a far more complex self-representation and tenuous relationship to empire than has been previously noticed.

The comparison of England and the US Smith offers exemplifies her mobile subjectivity—employing a common rhetorical strategy of nineteenth-century African American travel writers. Schueller, for instance, discusses how William Wells Brown and Nancy Prince contrast "the relative humanity afforded black peoples overseas" with the "degrading treatment" they face in the United States (Intro x). Smith engages in a kind of situated knowledge grounded in her unique experience and location as a formerly enslaved African American woman in Europe. As a "situated knower," whose knowledge is fundamentally tied to her social and geographic location, she offers a critical perspective of the US and an alternative vision of Black women.[25] Hence, through her deployment of knowledge about the US and about England, Smith reconstitutes herself as a mobile subject. No longer merely a spectacle for others to gaze at, she moves into the position of spectator—one who actively sees.

Through her travel writing about Europe, Smith reconstitutes an identity for herself as tourist, someone who travels for leisure. Traveling with a group of white "friends," Smith's itinerary included many of the stops found on the American "grand tour" of Europe, which typically consisted of stops in England, Germany, Switzerland, France, and Italy (Nelson 3). Despite her raced, classed, and gendered status in the US, through her tour Smith lays claim to several key privileges of Western travel including (1) "freedom of mobility," (2) "access to sights and cultural spaces," and (3) "the power to comment and interpret" (Schueller, Intro ix). Smith's mobility transgresses social boundaries that delimit the movements of Black women and narrowly define them as objects to be seen. Her appropriation of the rhetoric of Western tourism grants Smith the privilege of interpreting for her readers all that she surveys.[26]

Smith's shifting subjectivity as tourist (spectator) becomes further apparent when she and her friends, the white women with whom she travels, arrive in Paris. Smith's entry in her journal, which up until this point has focused on her missionary work and spiritual experiences, candidly expresses the excitement and pleasure so central to travel and tourism. As Paul Fussell asserts, a traveler is someone who "retain[s] all . . . the excitement of the unpredictable attached to exploration, and fus[es] that with the pleasure of 'knowing where one is' belonging to tourism" (39). Smith voices this excitement and pleasure, speaking excitedly as she discovers her new physical surroundings in Paris: "My! The wonders; not strange, perhaps, to others, but to me; the statuary, and parks, and buildings were lovely to behold" (286). Here Smith mimics the "[m]anners, morals, and class [of] . . . Anglo-American travel writers to Europe" and their "respect for the artifacts of European culture" (Schueller xxii–xxiii). Much like her earlier comparative critique of England and America, this discourse encourages Smith's largely white middle class readers to identify with her vantage point as adorer of Western cultural artifacts. The cunning nature of her identification with such artifacts, important signs of empire, becomes more apparent as Smith's gaze shifts from that of adorer of Western culture to fierce critic of Western imperialism.

Confidently writing from the position of traveler, Smith's text clearly focuses on what Smith sees as opposed to so many earlier entries that focus on Smith being seen. In this new role of spectator and tourist, Smith's usually overexposed and out of place body takes a back seat. Not only does Smith move the reader's lens away from her body and onto the surrounding landscape, but she begins to focus her gaze on the other bodies around her. Employing a more complex representational practice than earlier in the narrative, Smith's strategic negotiation of embodiment through her travels abroad allows her to challenge and revise dominant constructions of Black bodies, while protecting her own body from the objectifying gaze of her audiences.

RE-PRESENTING BLACKNESS IN EGYPT

As Smith travels beyond Europe, we begin to see the bodies of other people of color (African-descended and South Asian people in particular) enter the foreground. During her travel to Egypt, for example, Smith trains her eye on the Black bodies she sees with her own critical gaze shaping how we see them. Though critical conversations about the meaning of Egypt for Black travelers and intellectuals have generally not addressed Smith's work, her unique perspective as a formerly enslaved Black woman among the very few Black travelers to Egypt in the nineteenth century contributes to and expands on representations of Egypt in literature and art.[27]

In the opening of a generous section of her narrative that focuses on her first encounter with Egyptian men in Alexandria, Smith engages in the cultural work of reclaiming Blackness in Egypt. She exclaims,

> And who are these men coming off in the boats? . . . black men—my own race. I had been so long without seeing any of my own people that I felt like giving three cheers! . . . Many of them were fine looking men, black as silk and straight as arrows, well developed, and independent as kings. . . . They didn't know what it was to crouch to any man. I felt proud that I belonged to that race when I saw such nobility in ebony. Then I thought of the passage in the Old Testament history: "Princes shall come out of Egypt." Then I remembered it was the birthplace of Moses, and the hiding place of the infant Jesus from the cruelty of Herod, the king. And out of all the world round it pleased God to bestow this great honor on the black race, which ought to be held in everlasting remembrance. And I prefer being black, if for no other reason than to share this great honor with my race. (295)

In her description of these Egyptian men, Smith takes a strong stance against imperial and colonial representations of Black bodies. First, her characterization of the men as "black men—my own race" is an important political move, identifying Smith not with colonizers and the colonial project, which enables her tourism in the first place, but with the colonized peoples of Egypt, whose plight Smith sees as identical to her own. Through her very calculated and deliberate representation of these Egyptian men, we see Smith fighting for a more just representation of all Black people, their capabilities, and their history. Her attempt to re-value the Black body is most evident through her description of the men as "black as silk and straight as arrows, well developed, and independent as kings" (295). Her reference to nobility provides the ultimate rebuke to racist and imperial representations of Black bodies as inferior, as foreign, as spectacle and as monstrous.

Smith's affirmation of racial pride and her lauding of Blackness as a privilege echoes the strategy David F. Dorr used in the preface to his 1858 travel narrative *A Colored Man round the World*. Dorr was enslaved at the time of his travels. Like Smith, he faced the challenge of claiming credibility for his writing and travel while facing a predominantly white readership, and like Smith he affirmed the civilization of African-descended peoples in Egypt and therefore the value of his own writing. Representing himself as "Colored man around the world" in the preface of his book, Dorr grounds his racial pride in a celebration of the Egyptians as having thick lips, curly hair, and Black skin, while claiming them as ancestors whose "living language," "scientific majesty," and "genius" forms the foundation of his own cultural inheritance (11). Both Dorr and Smith use Egypt to shift the meaning of Blackness in opposition to the narrow racial constructions at work in the US and often reproduced within the tradition of Euro-American travel writing.

Rather than exoticizing the Black body, as we have seen white audiences do to Smith's body, her gaze communicates respect and reverence.[28] Similar to her response at seeing the amazing statues and parks of Paris, Smith stands in awe at the beauty of the Black bodies before her. Using what Schueller refers to as travelers' "power to comment and interpret," Smith co-opts the visual practice of tourism in order to ascribe meaning and value to the Black bodies she sees. Challenging the fixed identities imposed on Black people, Smith's visual practice illustrates that "[t]here is no one gaze, no singular universal way of seeing" (Nelson xiv). Rather than reproduce a colonized gaze by positing these bodies as foreign, Smith sees her own body as inextricably linked to the bodies of these Egyptian men—not only are their bodies linked but so are their histories, their lineages, their struggles, and their destinies. Ultimately, through her visual practice, Smith argues that there are multiple ways of viewing and interpreting Black bodies. Refusing to identify with the white western imperial mission, Smith instead imagines a shared kinship with Black people throughout the diaspora—a kinship based upon the particularities of her experiences of oppression as a formerly enslaved Black woman in America.

Smith's political turn to Egypt also aligns her with Black public intellectuals such as Frederick Douglass, Pauline Hopkins, and Edward Wilmot Blyden who responded to proslavery Egyptologists by placing the origins of civilization in Africa. For instance, Edward Wilmot Blyden, a Black nationalist who traveled to Egypt, describes the pyramids as "the work of my African progenitors" and claims to possess "a peculiar 'heritage in the Great Pyramid'" (Blyden 152). Born in the Virgin Islands, Blyden emigrated to Liberia by way of Venezuela and the United States and wrote the 1873 travel text *From West Africa to Palestine*.[29] Like David Dorr, Blyden's identification with a Black Egypt informs his claims of superiority over Arab people most visible in his reference to "greedy" and "half-naked, shoeless, and sure-footed Arabs" who guide him through the pyramids (150). In contrast, this characteristic of nineteenth-century Black travel writing to Egypt is not present in Smith's narrating. Rather, Smith strategically elides the presence of Arab peoples in Egypt, which problematizes her imperial critique, while enabling her to place the origins of Western Christianity in the hands of Black people. This strategy would have encouraged Smith's white Christian audience to identify Black people as part of their own spiritual lineage, rather than as strange "heathens."

Though Blyden's travel narrative points out the various locations of biblical events in Egypt, he makes no explicit links between the Bible and his African heritage. For example, as Blyden leaves the city of Alexandria, he exclaims that Egypt is the place that "every Sabbath-school boy desires to see, . . . and everything in the scenery through which we passed seemed to call up incidents in Sacred Writ" including "the simple narrative of Joseph and his brethren—of Moses concealed in the ark of bulrushes—of the persecution, hard labour, and exodus of the Jews—of the haughty and tyrannical Pharaoh—and of the flight of Mary and Joseph with the infant savior" (146). Though Blyden expresses the tourist's awe and wonder at seeing the place in which biblical history took place, his observations of the biblical history of Egypt are disconnected from his later discussion of ancient Egypt as African.

By contrast Smith extends the Egyptological discussion by arguing for a spiritual kinship with Egyptians as well as racial kinship, placing Black people at the center of her revisionist history of Christianity and the Bible through her references to Moses and Jesus. Explaining that Moses was born in Egypt includes him within the lineage of all Black people and gives Black people access to the spiritual royalty that Moses represents. Similarly, Smith's highlighting Jesus's protection from King Herod suggests that Black people are responsible for keeping Jesus alive and for enabling the very mission and ministry that he implemented throughout his life. Consequently, Smith makes Black people important contributors to the very existence and spread of Christianity. By these discursive moves, Smith disrupts notions of the Western world as the central contributor to the life and spread of Christianity.

This anti-imperial move on Smith's part becomes even more evident when we consider that her recuperation of Egypt, and therefore Africa, as central to Christianity comes just a page after her tour of Italy, where Smith has nothing but harsh criticism of the people and practice of Christianity, specifically Catholicism, that she observes there. Describing the monks and priests that she sees in the streets as "[o]ld men, with gray hair, who had never done a day's work in their lives," Smith says that "[s]ome of them looked almost like idiots; their brain, and muscle, and thought had never been developed" (288–89). This description stands in stark contrast to her portrayal of Egyptian men as intelligent hard workers and as heirs to the spiritual lineage of Moses and Jesus. Undoubtedly, Smith's representation of these priests and monks expresses an anti-Catholic position. However, given the inextricable link between the Catholic Church and the Roman Empire, so central to the formation of Western civilization, Smith's harsh criticism toward Roman priests seriously undermines Western imperialism and deviates from typical representations of Rome in travel writing as a well-known cultural center and "as a site of memory and replication" for American and European travelers (Nelson 3). Clearly for Smith, Egypt surpasses Rome and even displaces it as the preeminent site of cultural memory and identification.

SMITH'S SHIFTING DISCOURSE IN INDIA

Yet, Smith's rhetoric shifts with her location. Her anti-imperial rhetoric is missing from the section of her travelogue focused on India. In keeping with the broader tradition of women's travel writing, Smith's rhetoric reveals a tenuous relationship to colonial discourse that, as Sara Mills asserts, typically constructs clear binaries between civilized and savage.[30] As Smith shifts between locations abroad, we see her discourse shift as well from a humanizing discourse to an "othering" discourse that expresses her pity for Indian people and her horror and disgust at their cultural practices, which she refers to as "heathen idol worship" (300). Locating herself firmly in the traditional discourse of missionary travel writing, Smith's representation of India as depraved serves to "illustrate the need for Christian conversion" (Schueller 31). At a fair in Allahabad, she laments, "[h]ow sad to see the different idols they worship displayed on their flags and in every possible shape and way. My heart ached, and I prayed to the Lord to send help and light to these poor heathen" (301). While Smith's identification with Egyptians, her ability to see herself in their bodies, enabled her to embrace their full humanity, she has no such identification with Indian people. Smith does not see herself when she looks at them; rather she sees an exoticized "other." Slipping back into the discourse of Western colonial travelers, Smith displaces her own strangeness as a foreigner onto the bodies of Indian people. These bodies are not of African descent and do not fit into Smith's spiritual genealogy that places Africa at the center of Christianity. Here Smith practices a kind of religious, cultural, and even racial imperialism that was quite common in the nineteenth century, including among Black Christians.[31]

Smith's imperial rhetoric becomes increasingly apparent as the narrative of her time in India continues. While sightseeing, Smith encounters what she describes as "the great juggernaut car," referring to a wooden chariot that carried an image of the Hindu deity, Jagannath,[32] "well known in the history of sacrifices in India, whose wheels have crushed so many infants at the hands of their poor mothers" (320). Referring to the oft-reported story by European travelers to India of people throwing themselves under the wagon as a form of self-sacrifice,[33] Smith responds, "How dreadful is heathen blindness. Thank God that the car of the juggernaut for such sacrifice has come to belong to the things of the past; has been superseded by the glorious light of Christian civilization, and judicious Christian legislation" (320). Classic imperial hierarchies are once again at work in Smith's observation, which risks reifying a singular narrative about Indian people as monstrous and barbaric. Positing Indian people as blind and ignorant, this passage celebrates Western imperialism as a humane and lifesaving response to "heathen blindness," while ignoring the realities of oppression and violence stemming from European expansion.

Nevertheless, Smith appears to be aware of the inequities perpetuated by the imperial system. Of her travels through the Indian countryside, she explains: "There are generally two roads; a native road, and an English road; the English roads were better, as a rule; they generally kept in their provinces good roads; we were on the English road, so we had to turn out and go down on the native road, which was very rough, because they never mended them, or made any repairs on them" (301). Noting that the English road was in better shape than the "native road," which had "a great deep gutter about a quarter of a mile in length" (301), Smith's juxtaposition of these two roads draws critical attention to the hierarchized, segregated, and unjust nature of a colonial society. Smith's observation of the impact of the unequal distribution of resources testifies to a system in which all things British are valued at the expense of the country's local inhabitants. This less idealized portrait of colonization stands in stark contrast to Smith's earlier representation of imperialism as a benign, lifesaving force. Yet Smith never attempts to reconcile these two representations—at least not in relation to India.

Although Smith's reimagining of a Black Egypt reveals the subversive potential of her itinerant rhetorical practice that shifts between reproducing colonial discourse and critiquing it, Smith's unequivocal representation of India as a "heathen" and depraved land illustrates the limitations of her critical practice. Unfortunately, Smith's critical appropriation of Egyptology to undermine Western imperial hierarchies rests on the re-inscribing of those hierarchies in India. In short, Smith redeems the humanity of Black people throughout the diaspora at the expense of denigrating India and its people. By creating a discursive distance between herself and Indian people, Smith proves herself an ally of her white audience even as she identifies herself as an heir of a civilized and glorious Egypt—undermining white Western claims to power and privilege.

NEGOTIATING COLONIAL AND MISSIONARY IDEOLOGIES IN LIBERIA

Smith's chronicling of her eight years in West Africa (1882–89) combines rhetorical strategies employed in the Egypt and India sections of her narrative to offer a much more nuanced picture of colonization. In this section of her narrative Smith's discursive and rhetorical shifting continues as she attempts to negotiate the critical mission of her text with the expectations of her audience. Smith's writing about Africa, especially Liberia where she spends the majority of her time, reflects her increased critical awareness of the role of missionary work within colonization, and, much like her presentation of Egypt, her opposition to racist representations of indigenous African people and her critique of the racism underlying white colonial missions. Thus, Smith continues and extends Elaw's critique of racism as a fundamental threat to beloved community.

Smith's oppositional stance is most apparent in her representations of indigenous Africans in Liberia. Mirroring her earlier attempt to free the Black male (Egyptian) body from racist and imperialist definitions, Smith's portrayal of indigenous African women in Liberia posits an alternative vision of the Black female body as beautiful. While living in Monrovia, for instance, Smith depicts the beauty of one of the king's wives who was "not very tall, but very black, beautiful limbs, beautifully built, small feet, as a lady would have, and beautiful hands and arms" (387). Much like her earlier portrait of Egyptian men as strong, agile, and noble, this description of the Black female body as graceful and beautiful opposes typical colonial identifications of Blackness (Nelson 116). Recognizing the power of western science and other knowledge systems to objectify and classify the Black body as monstrous, Smith launches a counter-analysis in which she posits alternative identifications for Black male and female bodies in the diaspora.[34] Her reference to the "small feet" of the African woman she encounters marks her as a "true" lady that Smith's white audience would have easily recognized. Given Black women's exclusion from the category of woman within nineteenth-century Victorian culture, this reflects an important political move for Smith. Though typically a Black woman's body excluded her from achieving the status of "true woman," here Smith describes the African woman's body as grounds for inclusion within the category of woman.[35]

According to Hazel Carby, nineteenth-century Victorian culture defined a "true woman" as possessing four virtues: "piety, purity, submissiveness and domesticity" (23). She goes on to assert that these "internal qualities of character" were discernable through "external physical appearance" (25). Hence, race functioned in the nineteenth century as a prime marker of "true woman" status, meaning that while the white female middle class body was deemed sacred, set apart for a special purpose, the Black female body was seen as strictly a source of labor and "capital accumulation" (Carby 25). Smith's celebration, then, of this African woman's physical features undermines the dichotomizing of white and Black women's bodies and calls for reading the Black female body as human rather than a commodifiable object.

In addition to her reclaiming of the Black (here specifically African) female body, Smith offers a positive and celebratory endorsement of African medicine when she states, "the natives helped in fever cases, and all kinds of sickness, by the use of herbs, which, when skillfully administered, as many know how to do, in my opinion are much better than doctors' medicines" (393). Here Smith privileges African over Western ways of knowing by defending African medicine as far more effective than Western medicine.[36] Her showing that so many African people have access to this knowledge further celebrates their skillfulness and talents.

Smith's adoption of an African child becomes another occasion to demonstrate her deep concern for and her investment in African people.[37] The adoption of indigenous African children was a common practice in

Liberian society in the late nineteenth century, and it was in many ways a continuation of colonialism. Although "adoptions" were often practices of domination that allowed for the economic exploitation of indigenous African children, they could also create extended kinship relationships between Black colonists and indigenous Africans, enabling reciprocal transference of culture (Clegg 94). This is certainly the case of Smith's adoption of two African children, a boy named Bob and a girl named Frances both of whom are given to Smith by their fathers.[38] Although Smith offers little info about Frances and how she comes to adopt her, she offers more details about her adoption of Bob. During her stay in Monrovia, Bob's father pleads with her to take his son, desiring a Western education for him, and Smith obliges, portraying the adoption as an act of economic and spiritual self-sacrifice.[39] Smith believed that by offering Bob a Western, and therefore Christian, education she was improving his quality of life. Nevertheless, she references the particular vulnerability of Black children whose "adoption" often leads to exploitation in both the United States and in Liberia, and seeks to protect him from serving as an apprentice or as a servant. Rather than mirroring an oppressive servant/master hierarchy, her relationship with Bob becomes that of guardian and teacher.[40]

Her initial reluctance toward adoption suggests that Smith sees this relationship not in terms of what she can gain but in terms of what she can give, including her time, energy, and emotional and material resources, in the service of another human being. Smith's level of investment in Bob's well-being becomes quickly apparent, as does her pride in his accomplishments under her teaching. She notes that after just a few months, Bob acquired English and the ability to read the New Testament so quickly that "people were astonished. They could hardly believe that a little while before, he was a little, raw, naked heathen, and could speak but two words of English. . . . Now, when all is considered, I don't believe there is a child in this country, born of Christian parents, that would have shown a capability beyond that child's. It is nonsense to say that a native African is not capable of learning" (399). Smith's use of the term "heathen" in this passage further demonstrates her rhetorical shifting. On the one hand, she seems to support the imperialistic language that her Western audience would have recognized. However, her attributing this perception of Bob as a "raw naked heathen" to Western colonists in Monrovia creates a clear distinction between the dominant Western construction of Africans and her own view of Bob as intelligent and capable. In spite of Smith's colonizing language, her words emphasize the impressive intelligence of Africans and their capacity for learning. However, they also suggest that this capacity can be realized only through the transforming power of Western knowledge. Unlike in her consideration of indigenous medicine, here Smith does privilege Western ways of knowing, specifically the English language and Christian education, over and above African language and culture.

Smith's support of Western culture, particularly religion, becomes increasingly evident in her description of African traditional religious practices. During her visit to Old Calabar (now known as Calabar and located in the southeastern region of Nigeria), Smith observes that "At the house of Ironbar, who is a big chief, the first thing we saw on entering was in one corner of the courtyard a large juju, the head of an elephant, which represents a superstition they all believe in. . . . He dressed like a gentleman, in English clothes . . . went to church nearly every Sunday; and yet he was as full of superstition and heathenism as if he had never heard the Gospel" (379). Here Smith draws a clear distinction between African traditional spirituality, which she posits as "superstition and heathenism," and Christianity. Smith finds most disconcerting what she refers to as Ironbar's "hypocrisy," his ability to embrace both Englishness and Africanness.

This embrace of duality is challenging for Smith, who clearly operates in this passage within a Western imperial worldview that sees and orders the world according to narrow and strict dichotomies: civilized vs. heathen, Western vs. Non-Western, saved vs. damned. Because of this "either/or" ordering principle so central to Western epistemology, Smith defines Ironbar's actions as hypocritical. As a result, she calls into question his conversion, which for Smith requires a literal falling away of all things African. Her definition of conversion in this passage reflects an ideology that was quite popular and central to "mid-nineteenth century missiology," which defined conversion as "induced cultural change," and further contended that "Christianity and 'civilization' were inseparable" (S. Jacobs 6). According to Sandy Martin, religion and culture were completely inseparable within this ideology. Thus, in her depiction of Ironbar, Smith displays a form of colonized Christianity that is particularly dangerous and threatening to indigenous Africans because it requires its converts to violently reject an African self to be transformed into a Western (civilized) Christian self.

To make visible the violence of Smith's colonial gaze, I turn to West African writer, J. E. Casely Hayford, whose book *The Truth about the West Africa Land Question* (1913) underscores the impact of missionaries and their collusion with imperialism. Hayford offers a scathing critique emphasizing the philanthropists' and missionaries' propensity for using violence to further their "good" intentions (4). For Hayford, the life and soul of the nation can be found in its culture. Therefore, he views conversion to Western culture and values with suspicion: "You cannot think great thoughts in Africa by adopting wholesale the . . . way of life of the European. Nature did not intend it. Those who attempt it end in trouble. Nay, worse. It means death" (101). Given this inextricable link between religion and culture that Sylvia Jacobs, Sandy Dwayne Martin, and Hayford describe, conversion, as Smith's depiction of Ironbar implies, required the literal death of African culture.

Ironbar, however, operates not within a Western dichotomous worldview, but rather in a non-Western epistemological framework that embraces duality as wholeness rather than as hypocrisy. Peter Paris confirms the centrality of multiplicity and unity within an African cosmological framework, defining the central elements of this cosmology as including "the realm of the spirit . . . the realm of tribal or ethnic community . . . the realm of family . . . and the individual person who strives to integrate the three realms in his or her soul" (25). The interdependence and integration of these differing realms is key to achieving a sense of wholeness and balance. Paris's explanation of African cosmology, particularly his description of the individual person, makes clear that subjectivity is multiple and shaped by the integration of spirit, community, and family. Because of this "spirit of unity" central to an African worldview, Paris attests to the "eventual formation of a syncretized cosmology comprising an amalgam of Christian and African elements: a cosmology that shaped the African expressions of Christianity both on the continent and in the African diaspora" (26). Paris argues that the result of colonial and imperial expansion throughout Africa and the diaspora was not the destruction of African culture and cosmology but rather the joining of Christian and African traditional spiritual elements. Within this worldview, Ironbar can quite easily embrace a subjectivity that is multiple—part English and part African. This means he can attend church regularly, read his Bible, and pray to the Christian God, and yet still engage in the traditional spiritual practices of his local community that facilitate a connection to ancestors, to nature, and to God, all of which are viewed as sacred practice.[41] And most importantly, he can do these things without contradiction—demonstrating a "both/and" non-Western ordering principle rather than an "either/or"

Western dichotomy. Ultimately, this kind of worldview, one that embraces multiple subjectivity, enables Ironbar to resist the violence of this Western imperial framework that threatens to tear all colonized people in two.

Though Smith defines Ironbar's multiplicity as hypocrisy, his presence in the text draws attention to Smith's own unstable subject position. Although colonial discourse utilizes binaries to construct clear insiders and outsiders, identity is always multiple, shifting, and unstable (Loomba 105). Thus, despite her positioning of Ironbar as outsider (hypocrite), her colonizing gaze makes visible her own unstable, always shifting, mobile subjectivity. Smith does occupy a position of privilege as a Western subject, specifically as a traveler and writer who has the power to ascribe meaning to the people and places she encounters in her travels. Yet, as discussed earlier, Smith is also subject to the colonial gaze of her white Christian audience who expects a particular performance of Blackness—one that reinforces Western colonial values abroad. Consequently, we continue to see Smith, in an attempt to negotiate these two subject positions, engaged in an itinerant practice—most evident in her shifting between her reproduction of colonial discourse and her critique of oppressive colonial practices and values.

The limitations of Smith's dichotomous thinking become evident in her reply to the question, "What is the religion of Africa?" (383). She responds, "they had no real form of religion. They were what we would call devil worshippers" (383). This passage clearly expresses Smith's grounding in traditional nineteenth-century missionary ideology that denied the existence of legitimate religious practices in Africa and commonly considered African traditional religions to be fundamentally evil (S. Jacobs 16). Smith's claims about the absence of religion in Africa locate her firmly within this broader ideology, as does her representation of indigenous Africans as "devil worshippers." Positioning African traditional spirituality as evil, Smith effectively aligns herself with her Christian readers over and against the indigenous Africans she encounters. Nevertheless, by reiterating her mobile and fluid subjectivity, she continues to trouble her identification as Western traveler and Christian missionary.

Despite her grounding within an imperial framework that privileges Christianity as the only religion in Africa, Smith critiques other key elements of missionary ideology, particularly the racist and unjust treatment of indigenous peoples. For example, when responding to the question whether or not white missionaries should go to Africa, Smith explains, "Yes, if they are the right kind. If they are thoroughly converted and fully consecrated and wholly sanctified to God, so that all their prejudices are completely killed out, and their hearts are full of love and sympathy" (423). Reflecting her belief that a true Christian must be "saved deep" (116), here, Smith declares that full conversion necessitates not only a spiritual transformation but also a political shift to an anti-racist stance, which significantly requires the death of white supremacy and racism. Furthermore, this spiritual and political conversion enables missionaries to come to Africa with the central characteristics for success—sacrifice and humility. Those who come out of arrogance and greed, rather than to serve, merely undermine missionary efforts in Africa.

While describing colonization efforts as positive for a time, Smith offers some harsh criticism of its continuation. "God bless the Colonization Society," she writes. "It was raised up at a time of imperative need. . . . It did its work." This is very much at variance with other Black intellectuals of the time, including Richard Allen, Frederick Douglass, Martin Delany, David Walker, and Maria Stewart.[42] However, Smith also calls for the organization's dissolution, disparaging it as consisting of "white people who want the Negro to emigrate to Africa." Claude Clegg explains that supporters of colonization believed in sending Black Christians to Africa for varied reasons including the conversion of African people to Christianity and as a way to reduce the presence of free Black people in the country, who were often viewed as a threat to American unity and as a social problem (33, 4). In contrast to the often-racist motivations of colonizationists, Smith argues for Black people's right to American citizenship, stating unequivocally, "there is a place in the United States for the Negro. They are real American citizens, and at home. They have fought and bled and died, like men, to make this country what it is. And if they have got to suffer and die, and be lynched, and tortured, and burned at the stake, I say they are at home" (452). Here Smith argues that the long-standing sacrifices Black people have made fighting for the nation's liberty and their continued struggles for full freedom in spite of those national sacrifices—facing persistent forms of anti-Black terror and violence in their bid for freedom serves as undeniable proof of Black people's citizenship and birthright. Though it may seem odd that Smith begins her critique of the American Colonization Society by paying homage to it, it may be a way to appease her white readers, who undoubtedly were supporters of the organization, as missions and colonization were often inextricably linked in the nineteenth century.

Ultimately, she agrees with other free Black intellectuals that colonization is a hollow solution for the country's failure to recognize or protect the human and civil rights of formerly enslaved people and their descendants. Responding to claims that Black people do not belong in the United States, that they have failed to and will never make any lasting contributions to society, Smith posits African Americans as "real American citizens." For Smith, the continued violation of Black bodies, as well as their sacrifices for and contributions to the country prove the citizenship rights of Black people, who endured centuries of suffering and continue to endure because they believe that America, however unfair and unjust in its treatment of Black people, is their home.

Smith grounds her unequivocal belief in the US as home, not in an idealized portrait of the country as a land of freedom and Christian civilization but, rather, in the image of Black bodies being lynched, tortured, and burned on American soil. This image contrasts strongly with the representation of Africa by so many people, white and Black, as a heathen land that must be saved.[43] With this image of irrational and barbaric violence on American shores, Smith calls into question notions of a civilized West, refusing to privilege the United States as the source of enlightenment for all those "native Africans living in darkness." One need not leave America to find such terrifying darkness. Smith's writing these words after spending eight years in Africa makes her criticism of American hypocrisy all the more potent.

Although we tend to think of Black women as victims of colonial and imperial oppression because of the coerced movement of Black female bodies, Smith's narrative, like Zilpha Elaw's, necessitates that we move beyond this narrow construction of Black female subjectivity within the nineteenth century. By foregrounding her travel explicitly within the context of colonization, Smith's *An Autobiography* goes further than Elaw's *Memoirs* by underscoring Black women's complex subject positioning as both colonial subjects and colonial others. In spite of her own reproduction of colonial binaries at times, Smith engages in an array of embodied spiritual practices revealing the multidimensionality of Black people, Black subjectivity, and Black bodies. Her travel and writing disrupt dominant constructions of Blackness in general and of the Black female body in particular. As such, her hybrid text (slave narrative, spiritual autobiography, and travelogue) broadens our understanding of Black women's spiritual practices informed by a long legacy of unruliness and mobility, while contributing to larger conversations about the centrality of Black (female) embodiment to Christianity, to Western travel, and to ongoing debates about citizenship, belonging, and the possibilities for Black people at home and abroad. These key concerns raised in Smith's text around Black citizenship, belonging, and home persist and expand in the chapters that follow.

· FOUR ·
Searching for Home in Nancy Prince's *A Narrative*

> What place in the world could sate four hundred years of yearning for a home? Was it foolish to long for a territory in which you could risk imagining a future that didn't replicate the defeats of the present?
> —Saidiya Hartman, *Lose Your Mother*

Nancy Gardner Prince was born a free Black woman in Massachusetts in 1799, just a few years after Zilpha Elaw. Much like Elaw and Amanda Smith, Prince experienced poverty, death, and familial separation in the "free" North. She and her siblings were forced into indentured servitude and her experience of domestic employment in white homes as a child and young adult parallels the legacy of exploitation that punctuates Hagar's, Elaw's, and Smith's narratives. Like Smith's *An Autobiography,* her narrative begins with stories of her ancestor's captivity, enslavement, and struggles for freedom. While both texts reflect the incomplete nature of freedom for Black people in the US, Prince's text offers a more explicit exploration of travel as a pathway to freedom for Black people, especially the obstacles Black women encountered due to unequal access to mobility and the myriad dangers they faced on their journeys. Unlike Elaw and Smith, who received a divine call to preach domestically and internationally, Prince was not a preacher but a businesswoman, missionary, and anti-slavery activist. While Elaw and Smith's itinerancy initially required separation from their husbands, Prince's marriage to Nero Prince facilitated her access to travel, as his job enabled them to move to Russia. Ultimately, Prince's narrative further expands and complicates Black female travel in the nineteenth century by showcasing varying methods for accessing mobility and the varying motivations for travel, which for Prince are social, economic, political, and spiritual in nature. Prince's text not only explores more deeply the material challenges Black women travelers faced in the nineteenth century, but also demonstrates how her spiritual practices both motivate and actively sustain her freedom to travel.

My focus on the spiritual roots and impact of Prince's travel departs from scholarship that positions her 1853 work, *A Narrative of the Life and Travels of Mrs. Nancy Prince,* as a secular travel narrative.[1] Elaw's and Smith's texts more closely adhere to the expectations of the spiritual autobiography; Prince's narrative, on the other hand, does not strictly follow the traditional structure chronicling an individual's journey from sin to redemption. Nevertheless, Prince's spiritual travelogue reveals how the spirit moves in and through her travel, while foregrounding and challenging the systems of oppression and evil she sees at work in the US and during her international journeys to Russia and Jamaica. While other scholars have recognized the hybrid nature of her text, they typically underscore the economic, social, and political aspects of her travel rather than its spiritual nature.[2] In contrast, Carla L. Peterson's 1995 book *"Doers of the Word": African-American Women Speakers and Writers in the North (1830–1880)* and Joycelyn Moody's book *Sentimental Confessions: Spiritual Narratives of Nineteenth-Century African American Women* (2001) address both the sacred and secular elements of Prince's narrative. However, my own study offers an expanded analysis of Prince's travel to Russia, positioning it as central to her spiritual practice and subsequent travels to and from the US and Jamaica. Building on Moody's work, my intersectional approach recovers the sacred elements of Prince's journey by considering how her social and political efforts at home and abroad reflect her ancestors' spiritual legacy and struggles for freedom in the US as well as her spiritual encounters and experiences while traveling abroad. Foregrounding the sacred in my reading of Prince's narrative, my analysis focuses on her employment of a resistant spiritual practice that exposes and critiques race, class, and gender oppression throughout the circum-Atlantic world.

Prince's text illustrates her experience of race, gender, and class injustice in the US and, as Cheryl Fish has argued, launches a powerful critique of the country as a failed home for all African Americans—enslaved and free.[3] Thus, her travel narrative participates in a long legacy of Black travel writing that positions mobility as a way for Black people to escape the injustices of America and explore the possibilities for freedom in various locations abroad. Although the desire to escape injustice and the longing for a livable home where she can thrive initially motivates Prince's travel, I do not read Prince's travel and mobility strictly as an escape from the US and her personal experiences of oppression. Rather, I argue that her travel, specifically her nine years in Russia, leads to a spiritual transformation for Prince that propels her into a life of spiritual activism in the US and in Jamaica.

My reading of Prince's travel to Russia complicates previous scholarship that posits Russia as an idealized space of freedom and possibility for Black people. While Prince's social and economic status improves after she and her husband move to Russia, images of death and violence pervade her writing about the country. Moreover, the realities of violence and threat of death follow Prince wherever she goes including Jamaica where she serves as a missionary, who actively undermines and challenges colonial hierarchies and practices within the country. Through an analysis of Prince's travel abroad, I reveal the foundation of her spiritual practice and activism: her powerful critique of the injustices Black people have faced in the US, her commitment to their ongoing collective struggle for full citizenship, and her linking of injustice at home to the realities of oppressive state power and violence that she witnesses abroad.

To make this link visible between her experiences in Russia, Jamaica, and the US, I turn now to the opening of Prince's narrative. As I will describe, it showcases the US as a space of terror for Black people due to the persistent realities of captivity and enslavement extending beyond the South into the North. It also demonstrates an alternative spiritual legacy of anti-slavery resistance that Prince inherits from her ancestors who pursued freedom through mobility. These key opening themes prepare the reader to understand the whole of her narrative.

Exposing the Terror of Home

For Prince, the experience of terror begins with the repetition of captivity and enslavement that runs through her ancestral lineage. The opening line of her narrative mentions her birth in Newburyport, Massachusetts, but she quickly shifts from the location of her birth to a genealogy of her family in which she notes that her maternal grandfather, Tobias Wornton "was stolen from Africa, when a lad, and was a slave of Captain Winthrop Sargent" (5). Thus, she highlights both genealogy and geography—telling us not only *who* but also *where* she comes from. Like Hagar before her, Prince underscores the intersection of identity and place. She tells us that her "grandmother was an Indian of this country; she became a captive to the English, or their descendants" (5). Prince's narrative therefore marks the historical enslavement of not only African bodies that were forcibly brought to this country but also the captivity of those indigenous peoples already here. Her biological father, who died when she was three months old, she writes, was born in Nantucket, Massachusetts, to parents of "African descent," while her stepfather, Money Vose, "was stolen from Africa" but "succeeded in making his escape from his captors, by swimming ashore" while the slave ship was docked in a Massachusetts port (6). This expanding genealogy and geography illustrates the complex web of slavery that ensnares people from the African continent as well as those indigenous to North America.

Prince also reveals an inextricable link between slavery and the country's bid for independence, noting that "although a slave, [her grandfather] fought for liberty. He was in the Revolutionary army, and at the battle of Bunker Hill. He often used to tell us, when little children, the evils of Slavery, and how he was stolen from his native land" (5). Prince's ancestral memories reveal the hypocrisy of a nation in which slavery and the fight against tyranny coexist, effectively challenging the dominant understandings of slavery and freedom in the US. The term "stolen" defines the practice of enslavement as a criminal and immoral act rather than as a legal and divine right, as pro-slavery apologists argued. Moreover, Prince's grandfather's and stepfather's struggles for liberty complicate the dominant narrative about the source of the nation's spirit of independence by shifting the focus from the Euro-American struggle for liberty and the full rights of citizenship to African-descended people whose fight for individual freedom informed their participation in the nation's larger collective fight for independence.

The opening of Prince's narrative also demonstrates that anti-slavery resistance originates not with white abolitionists but with her African ancestors. Her grandfather and stepfather have the audacity to define themselves as made for freedom in opposition to the dominant positioning of the Black body as what Kimberly Blockett terms "slave-classed."[4] Prince further dramatizes this legacy of anti-slavery resistance through a two-page long retelling of her stepfather's escape from a slave ship while docked off the coast of Massachusetts. Prince's retelling highlights several predominant themes in her text: the anti-slavery resistance of her ancestors, mobility as a tenuous pathway to freedom for Black people, and slavery as a continuing source of terror for Black men, women, and children in the US regardless of their geographical location or legal status as free. Her narration begins:

> My stepfather was stolen from Africa, and while the vessel was at anchor in one of our Eastern ports, he succeeded in making his escape from his captors, by swimming ashore. I have often heard him tell the tale. Having some knowledge of the English language, he found no trouble to pass [as a resident of Massachusetts]. There were two of them [escapees], and they found, from observation, that they were in a free State. I have heard my [step]father describe the beautiful moon-light night when they two launched their bodies into the deep, for liberty.... When day began to break, they laid down under a fence.... [Here Prince begins telling the story in her stepfather's voice] In a few minutes, a man with a broad-brimmed hat on, looked over the fence and cried out, "Halloo boys! you are from that ship at anchor?" Trembling, we answered, yes. He kindly took us by the hand, and told us not to fear, for we were safe.... [W]e were taken to his house and carried to an apartment, where he brought us clothes and food.... No search was made for us; it was supposed we were drowned, as many had jumped over-board on the voyage, thinking they could get home to Africa again. I have often heard my step—father boast how brave they were, and say they stood like men and saw the ship set sail with less than half they stole from Africa. (6–7)

This ancestral story points to the fluid and shifting nature of the slave ship. As Paul Gilroy and Katherine McKittrick argue, ships function as symbols of the Middle Passage (markers of death and enslavement) that also carry the potential for life and liberty.[5] Vose's testimony in Prince's recounting about individual and collective escape foregrounds not only the countless deaths of African captives but also centers "black resistance and struggle" aboard the ship as engendering new possibilities for life and freedom amid a space of violence and captivity (McKittrick x). Despite attempts to dehumanize African captives and to transform them into commodities by stripping away their clothing, culture, and ties to community during the Middle Passage, Money Vose's escape narrative demonstrates African captives' full awareness of their humanity as they engage in "open rebellion" to thwart their captors—even forming new bonds of kinship to help facilitate their escape.[6] Though Prince focuses on her stepfather's escape from the ship by swimming ashore, the story she retells points out that he is not alone in his resistance; another African man escapes with him, and together they share in both the risk and the victory of escape. Vose's story also bears witness to the collective rebellion of many other African captives who jumped overboard—so many, in fact, that no search was made for Money Vose and his companion.

Vose's story and Prince's retelling reference multiple outcomes of this resistance to captivity: drowning, successful escape to the Massachusetts shoreline, as well as swimming home to Africa. Though stories of African resistance to enslavement in the New World were initially transmitted by enslaved people orally, narratives of captives swimming, flying, or walking back to Africa remain part of a central mythology within African American culture and literature. The story of African people escaping captivity is central in Julie Dash's film, *Daughters of the Dust*, which seeks to recover and complicate the story of resistance aboard slave ships. Though I will address Dash's recuperation of this core mythology in chapter 5, here I position Prince's retelling of her stepfather's escape, like Dash's own multi-perspectival storytelling, as a refusal to accept a singular narrative about their captivity or about anti-slavery resistance. In doing so, Prince and, as I will argue later, Dash participate in a long legacy of collective Black struggle born aboard the slave ship.

Prince's narrative, like Dash's film, foregrounds the spiritual resources available to captives and their descendants to resist the soul-killing effects of slavery that sought to turn people made for freedom into objects made for sale. These resources include not only physical escape but also the act of recreating community and kinship ties through what historian Marcus Rediker calls "an oppositional process of culture creation" (265). Through this creative process, African captives "forged new forms of life—new language, new means of expression, new resistance, and a new sense of community" (Rediker 265). Money Vose engages in a similar practice of creative resistance as he forms a new bond with his shipmate who struggles alongside him for freedom and as he "often" retells the story of his enslavement and escape. Money Vose's story of collective struggle bears witness to the new communal bonds formed in opposition to the slave ship's violent practices of separation. I read his commitment to telling this story of collective resistance again and again as an extension of the critical spiritual practice of committing the past to memory through language. Reiterating the centrality of language practices for captives, historian Stephanie Smallwood asserts, "the only means to survive [the Middle Passage] was to divine means to explain it, to define and delimit it. And the only means to achieve that was to speak of it—to probe its contours with words spoken among strangers. Words were the glue that made the crowd . . . into a collective 'us,' whose fate stood in the balance during the journey. Agency aboard the slave ship took refuge above all in the voice, the means by which the 'self' finds realization" (125). Smallwood's words reveal the crucial spiritual work that captives engaged in to survive the assault and terror of the slave ship. This assault was not only physical but spiritual as the ship's oppressive practices aimed to transform people into things and tore African captives from their sources of meaning, identity and power: community, tribe, ancestors, and kin.[7] Just as captives aboard the slave ship employed language in creative ways to sustain their humanity and to reconstitute community across the breach caused by the Middle Passage, Prince's retelling of her stepfather's escape similarly testifies to the creation of an "us" through her use of first person plural ("*we* answered, yes," "*we* were safe," "no search was made for *us*"). Moreover, Vose's assertion that he and his shipmate "stood like men and saw the ship set sail with less than half they stole from Africa" demonstrates the use of language to explain, define, and delimit his experience of captivity. Rejecting the violent process of the slave ship that sought to transform him into a commodity, Money Vose's language reconstitutes his subjectivity as a man, as human, and therefore as worthy of freedom (Prince 7).

Drawing on M. Jacqui Alexander's definition of spiritual work as a kind of *body praxis* "central to our mapping of subjectivity" (316) as well as "an antidote of oppression, healing work" (312), I position the creative practices of captives, like Prince's grandfather and stepfather, their use of language to reconstitute the self as a means of survival aboard the slave ship, as spiritual work. Employing language through creative practices such as singing, storytelling, and dramatization, enslaved people, as Prince's narrative reveals, used their bodies and voices to commit their experiences of captivity to memory and in the process constructed meaning and a collective subjectivity from those experiences. This commitment to memory reflected "an effort to retain historical identity" amid a brutal process that attempted to strip away history in order to transform human beings into things (Rediker 284). The ability to remember, then, to construct oneself as a historical being, is a fundamentally human and humanizing practice. If as Alexander claims, "healing work is a call to remember and memory is embodied" (316), then memory becomes an embodied spiritual practice—one that facilitates the healing work of reconstructing (redefining) the self as fully human, as sacred and therefore as made for freedom. This critical theorization of memory as oppositional spiritual practice and as healing (human) work informs my reading of Prince's narrative and her rhetorical foregrounding of her stepfather's escape story. Through this ancestral memory, Vose resists the violent stripping of the slave ship and an institution of slavery grounded in a will to forget.[8] Both Money Vose through the repeated oral telling of his story and Prince through her written reproduction of his story insist on their right to active remembrance and, in passing down that story to future generations, engage in a spiritual practice that challenges the legacy of dispossession and enslavement inherited by African captives and their descendants.

Reflecting this critical practice as part of her ancestral spiritual legacy, Prince participates in this spiritual practice of remembering by retelling their stories (albeit in written rather than oral form). This legacy of remembering constructs an alternative communal narrative about slavery and freedom in the US that, as we have already seen, complicates singular narratives about American slavery (which impacted both African and Native American people) and about the Revolutionary War by placing the collective freedom struggles of African-descended peoples alongside and in tension with America's national struggle for independence. Prince's text also challenges the geographic or "spatial histories" of slavery and freedom in the United States, drawing on the marginalized knowledge and experience of her ancestors to craft an alternative story about this new world.[9] The geographical memory constructed in the opening through Prince's focus on her ancestor's experiences of captivity in Massachusetts and the image of Vose's escape from a slave ship docked off the Massachusetts coast redefines slavery as a national institution though our dominant national mythology tends to cast it as a southern one. The presence of anti-slavery allies in the state, one of whom aids Money Vose's escape from captivity, does not erase the reality of slavery in the North and its foundation to the entire nation's history and economy.

The continuation of Prince's narrative in which she reveals the aftermath of Money Vose's escape further complicates the construction of the US as a space of freedom and refuge. Immediately following her retelling of her stepfather's escape, Prince undercuts the previous moment of victory and further complicates the relationship between mobility and freedom for Black people. First, she reiterates her stepfather's kidnapping from his home in Africa, stating that he was "was selling his bamboo baskets, when he was seized by white men, and put in a boat, and taken on board the ship that lay off; many such ships there were" (7). Second, she shifts abruptly to Vose's employ as a sailor for twelve years on a ship that was stolen by the British during the Revolutionary War. Referencing the violence and oppression that sailing exposed Black men to, Prince explains that "[Vose] was pressed into their [the British's] service. He was sick with the dropsy a long while, and died oppressed, in the English dominions" (7). Thus, the terror that Money Vose experiences aboard the slave ship and during his risky escape repeats as he is kidnapped a second time and pressed into service by the British. Prince's grandfather, stepfather, and brother were all sailors, and sailing provided many Black men opportunity and freedom during the nineteenth century, including access to physical and economic mobility—a way to earn a living for their families.[10] Hence, Vose's story was not unusual. Enslaved men and women often escaped slavery via ship passage, including Frederick Douglass who escaped slavery dressed as a sailor and Robert Smalls who commandeered a Confederate ship into Union Army territory in 1862 leading himself and many other enslaved families to freedom.

Prince's condensed writing locates the second seizure of Vose aboard a merchant vessel just two sentences after his kidnapping by white men in West Africa, underscoring the close link between the ships and the repetitions of violence that Prince and her ancestors face. These repetitions reveal the tenuous nature of the ship as a space of captivity and freedom and further complicate the equation of mobility and itinerancy with freedom by illustrating Black people's continued exposure to the threat of violence and captivity even after achieving legal freedom. Money Vose's second seizure aboard a merchant ship reveals the failures of the United States to protect the rights of Black people who participated in and contributed to the economy while facing the continual threat of being kidnapped and held captive. America's legacy of freedom and independence, in other words, does not accrue to African-descended people. Rather, Prince's emphasis on illness, oppression, and death at the end of Money Vose's story suggests that America's only inheritance for Black people is one of dispossession and death.

The remainder of Prince's opening turns away from the focus on her male ancestors to demonstrate the impact of such terror and violence on Black families, women, and children in particular. The death of Prince's biological father as well as her stepfather's captivity and eventual death has terrible consequences for Prince's mother and her eight children. Describing her mother as "like a lunatic" (9) after losing Vose, Prince explains that "[h]er grief, poverty, and responsibilities, were too much for her; she never again was the mother that she had been before" (7–8). Illuminating how oppression and suffering destroys her mother's health, Prince's descriptions link her mother's mental, spiritual, and emotional instability to the dire social and economic circumstances that make it impossible for her to care well for herself and her children.

Further illustrating the tremendous strain the northern labor market places on Black families and homes, Prince explains that despite the family exhausting all resources in order to stay together, she (at the young age of eight) and her sisters were hired out as domestic servants in white families while her brothers were apprenticed or became sailors. Prince writes of her family, "[S]o we were scattered all about" (9). This forced separation demonstrates how America's rootedness in violence and economic exploitation leads to both individual and communal brokenness. Despite the legacy of freedom fighting Prince inherits from her ancestors, her representation of her own experiences and those of her family members as "free" laborers illustrate that the exploitation of Black labor and the separation of families extended beyond the institution of slavery in the South to wage slavery in the North. Thus, Prince and her family's ongoing struggle to construct a home in the US reveals the incomplete nature of freedom for African Americans. By foregrounding her own and her family's exclusion from the full benefits of US citizenship, Prince represents the nation as a failed home, challenging constructions of the North as a haven and safe space for freedom seekers.

Prince's critique of the oppressive violence she experiences while employed in white domestic spaces further demonstrates that slavery haunts the entire national landscape, undermining Black people's efforts to construct spaces of freedom and belonging in the US. Like Amanda Smith, Prince experiences labor in white homes as emotionally draining and physically destructive. No matter how hard Prince works, she cannot seem to ever command enough money for her labor to provide for her family. One of her strongest critiques is of a Christian family that employed her when she was fourteen. She first agrees to leave her prior situation to work for the family after claiming a "determin[ation] to get more for my labor" (10). However, the only thing she gets for her labor is abusive treatment and ill health. Much like Smith, she must work long hours, including all hours of the night. The family of seven requires her to work on the Sabbath and to get up at 2:00 a.m. on weekdays to begin multiple tasks, including washing clothes, answering the door, and waiting on all seven family members. Describing her labor as "very severe," Prince also endures harsh complaints about being too slow and the poor quality of her work (11). She must perform multiple tasks at the same time, while being ill-treated and underappreciated and ultimately leaves the job because of deteriorating health.

Through her narrative, Prince bears witness to the impact of such exploitative conditions. She explains, "Hard labor and unkindness was too much for me; in three months, my health and strength were gone. I often looked at my employers, and thought to myself, is this your religion? I did not wonder that the girl who had lived there previous to myself, [*sic*] went home to die. They had family prayers, morning and evening. Oh! yes, they were sanctimonious! I was a poor stranger, but fourteen years of age, imposed upon by these good people" (11–12). Prince's raw portrait of this white middle class Christian home stands in stark contrast to nineteenth-century domestic ideology, which idealized white domestic space as guided by Christian morality and the virtues of gentility and kindness that would provide a safe haven from the exploitative greed and materialism of the market.[11] Prince's scathing critique of her employers reveals the hypocrisy of their religious practice that allows them to abuse rather than care for the "stranger" in their midst. Their persistent prayers reflect a mere outward display of faith with no impact on their heart or their actions. Rather than a safe haven, their home becomes a space in which Black female bodies are continually violated and broken; Prince makes this anti-Black violence evident in her description of her own broken-down body after just three months of labor and that of the Black girl employed before her who "went home to die." This phrase reveals the expendability of Black labor within white domestic space and the realities of wage slavery in the North, where Black women could be worked to the point of death because a cheap replacement was always available and waiting. Prince's critique of Christian hypocrisy echoes that of other Black writers, such as Frederick Douglass, Harriet Jacobs, and Harriet Wilson, who demonstrate that masters and mistresses who professed to be Christians were often the harshest and most abusive.

While Douglass's and Jacobs's slave narratives reveal Christian hypocrisy as foundational to the institution of slavery, Wilson's 1859 autobiographical novel, *Our Nig; or Sketches from the Life of a Free Black, In A Two-Story White House, North. Showing that Slavery's Shadows Fall Even There*, underscores the similar violence (physical and psychic) a young Black girl named Frado sustains while working in a middle-class white Christian home as an indentured servant in New England. Both Prince and Frado are abused in their respective "homes" and are worked to the point of sickness and physical deterioration of their bodies.[12] These stories make a powerful critique of white domestic space. Though this space is typically represented within domestic ideology as the heart of Christian goodness and morality, both Prince and Wilson reveal them as violent and destructive toward Black women, underscoring the complicity of white domestic space with slavery and racial injustice. The enslaving, whether literal or figurative, of Black women as laborers within this domestic space attests to their inability to achieve a certain kind of freedom through mobility that Prince has shown, through her stepfather's narrative, as a viable possibility for Black men. Through such juxtaposing of southern slavery with violence and racial oppression in the North, both Prince and Wilson illustrate how Black people have been alienated from the US nation and from full and equal participation in the rights and protections of citizenship.

Though Prince has the freedom to leave her place of employment after three months, her description of her older sister Silvia's imprisonment within a house of prostitution further demonstrates how "slavery's shadows" extend beyond geographical borders—haunting northern domestic spaces in which Black women are exploited and held captive. According to Prince, Silvia is "deluded away" while traveling to Boston in search of better employment, suggesting that this movement was coerced rather than voluntary. Likely, the poor working conditions and devaluing of Black labor to which Prince attests propel Silvia on the road in search of sustainable rather than destructive and dehumanizing labor. Prince follows her sister to Boston in order to save her. But as single Black women, both confront the realities of sexual terror while traveling. Upon her arrival in Boston Prince looks for a house to stay overnight and passes up several, despite the "kind invitations" she receives from female "greeters" at the door, describing them as "suspicious" (13). Though Prince does not elaborate, it seems reasonable to assume they are houses of prostitution. Shortly thereafter, we discover Silvia's captivity within such a house. Clearly, she was tricked into believing she was entering a "good" house, unlike Prince who portrays herself as a savvy traveler able to escape the many dangers of Black female mobility. On an earlier journey to find work, for instance, Prince says she only stayed with friends or places with a referral.

Prince determines to rescue Silvia, bringing along a male acquaintance named Mr. Brown for protection. Upon entering the house where her sister is confined, Prince finds her sister "seated with a number of others round a fire, the mother of harlots at the head" (14). After Prince embraces her sister, the old woman ("the mother of harlots") "opened a door that led down into a cellar kitchen" and commands Prince to come down. When Prince, instead, entreats her sister to leave this house with her, the "old woman seize[s] [Silvia] to drag her down into the kitchen," exclaiming that "she owes me, she cannot go" (14). Prince and her sister manage to escape because Mr. Brown threatens the woman with his cane. Later, Prince describes the "house [as] the way to hell going down to the chambers of death" (15).

Prince's critical representations of the house underscore how domestic space can be corrupted by evil—more precisely by those patriarchal capitalistic values that commodify and exploit women's bodies for sexual labor. Her representation of domestic space as unfree and unsafe challenges the dominant construction of domestic space and the violation and terror Black women face in such spaces. The image of Prince's sister sitting around a fire suggests initially the image of the ideal hearth so central to the true womanhood ideal.[13] And yet that idealized image quickly becomes distorted as Prince describes the "mother of harlots at the head." This passage, with its suggestive references to domestic ideology, places the mother figure at the head of domestic space, as she is imbued with spiritual and moral power within the home. According to Lisa Logan, "the ideal or 'true woman' opposed the moral degeneracy of the market with Christian values and gentle, self-sacrificing, and virtuous maternal influence" (48). Yet in Prince's narrative, the image of motherhood is desecrated as the home fails to function as a space of morality and protection from the pull of the market and the oppressive patriarchal values of greed and materialism. Her representation of the instability of her mother's mental health and the dissipation of her childhood home due to poverty and abuse reveals the incongruity of domestic ideology with the harsh realities poor Black women faced.[14] Here the mother at the head is a harlot instead of angel, morally corrupt, her kitchen a prison. Moreover, her house serves not as a space that sustains spiritual growth and nurtures life but as a space of terror and enslavement that conceals hell and death. In spite of its geography within supposedly free territory in Boston, just as in the southern US this space marks the Black (female) body as "worthy of captivity, [sexual] violence, . . . and objectification" (McKittrick 40).

Through rescuing her sister, Prince challenges this dominant construction of Black female embodiment. In demanding Silvia's freedom Prince declares Black women as worthy of freedom rather than captivity. Moreover, while the house functions as a space of domination that contains and conceals violence, Prince's description of the house as "the way to hell going down to the chambers of death" reflects a spiritual and spatial practice of resistance that reveals the terror and violence the house seeks to conceal through its external display of domesticity: a hearth, a fire, and a mother at the center. That physical force and a patriarchal weapon, Mr. Brown's cane, are necessary to free Silvia further undermines ideas of the house as a space of safety and protection. If, as McKittrick has argued, "it is in the material landscape, at work, in the home, and within the community, where the [Black] body is . . . retranslated as inferior, captive, and accessible to violences" (82), then Prince's critical portrait of such spaces in the northern US reveals a geography of terror and enslavement in which Black (female) bodies are unprotected and alienated within the nation-space.

Despite Prince's resistance to the varying assaults against Black embodiment and despite her continual search for sustainable work and a habitable place of belonging in the US, seven years after rescuing Silvia, she still finds herself trapped within a cycle of exploitative domestic labor and inescapable poverty. In the face of endless struggle, Prince claims spirituality and mobility as her pathways to freedom. First, she turns to Christianity and faith for spiritual strength and sustenance, perhaps in an attempt to avoid the mental and spiritual break that her mother suffered. Deteriorating in health and emotionally anguished, Prince bears witness to the significance of spiritual strength for her survival: "Care after care oppressed me . . . all hope but in God was lost" (17). Unlike Elaw and Smith, Prince does not give a long, detailed account of her spiritual conversion. She simply states, "I resolved . . . to seek an interest in my Savior, and put my trust in Him; and never shall I forget the place or time when God spake to my troubled conscience. Justified by faith I found peace with God. . . . After living sixteen years without hope, and without a guide, May 6th, 1819, the Rev. Thomas Paul, baptized myself" (17). Although Prince marks this moment as her official conversion, her account feels disconnected from the rest of her narrative and is more formula than testimony. As I will discuss in the next section, she experiences a much fuller and more compelling spiritual transformation in Russia.

A Stranger Abroad

Prince decides to leave the US, "after seven years of anxiety and toil" following her sister's rescue for a new potential home in Russia (20). Thus, Prince finally actualizes the same desire for mobility that her ancestors expressed by turning to the ship as a pathway to freedom. Yet she escapes, not as a sailor, as her stepfather and brother did, but as the wife of a sailor. She writes, on "September 1st, 1823, Mr. Prince arrived from Russia. February 15th, 1824, we were married. April 14th, we embarked on board the Romulus . . . bound for Russia" (20–21). Prince's marriage to a former sailor turned court attendant to the Russian tsar suggests that she has not forgotten her ancestral legacy of achieving freedom through mobility. No doubt her memory of how her stepfather, grandfather, and brother "achieved a tenuous freedom in the Americas through the male occupations of soldiering and maritime life" informs her resolve to leave the country (Gunning 43).

Recognizing through her own experiences and Silvia's the limited access Black women have to acquire such subjectivity, Prince finds an alternate access to mobility through marriage. Reflecting on Prince's decision to leave the US, Sandra Gunning notes that it "suggests . . . the particular site of the United States could not sustain a viable black female existence" (43). Therefore, despite the meager outcomes for Prince's Black male ancestors, for whom mobility brings increased economic opportunities but also exposes them to capture and premature death, for Prince the opportunity to board a ship offers a far more viable future than those open to the women in her family. Such future possibilities include violence and exploitation as domestic laborers in white homes, prostitution, and, for Prince's mother, the mental and physical deterioration that occur from the responsibilities of caregiving with no economic or emotional support. If the body Prince inhabits denies her access to the mobile subjectivity of her male ancestors, the joining of her body with that of a Black man, through marriage, provides her with access to the ship's mobility that she so deeply desires.

Adopting her husband's name and the title of wife in exchange for increased mobility, Prince engages in a gendered performance that affirms the conventions of marriage even while seeking to break out of domestic constraints. She adopts what Gay Gibson Cima terms a *host body*, which Cima defines "as a life-like body shield" that "may be donned in print through a set of rhetorical moves, or in person" (4). The host body provides women who claim a public space for their life and work "with a certain safety . . . by aligning with and simultaneously resisting acceptable 'American practices'" (Cima 4). As such, we can read Prince's decision to marry as an alignment with gendered conventions, and her new identity as wife as a performance that grants her respectability and credibility as a traveler, speaker, and writer. She offers little information about her husband, their relationship or domestic life. She narrates his death only through a note that "death took him away" (40).

Without offering the critical portrait of marriage as an obstacle to a divine calling that appears in Elaw's work and Smith's, Prince refuses to construct marriage as a desired ideal by shifting the focus of her narrative to her travel and work. Her elusive portrait of her union reflects a radical departure from the cult of true womanhood and domestic ideology that position marriage as the central value and as integral to women's sphere of power and influence. For Prince, marriage is a means to achieve mobility and freedom; however, she constructs her subjectivity not primarily as a wife but as a traveler (tourist, missionary, ethnographer), a businesswoman, who, as Carmen Birkle notes, "professionalizes the domestic sphere and sells her labor force" as a successful seamstress in Russia, as well as an activist fighting against slavery and all of its vestiges at home and abroad.[15] Hence, in line with Cima's theorization of [Black] women's embodied resistance to social norms, Prince both aligns herself with the traditional gendered practice of marriage even as she resists the practices of true womanhood through her mobility, public spiritual activism, and economic ambition. Through this tenuous and ever-shifting gendered performance, Prince effectively shields herself behind the host body of wife even while rejecting the traditionally defined practices of true womanhood that seek to contain female bodies within domestic space. Ultimately, this enables Prince to cross gender boundaries while maintaining her respectability.

Beyond reducing her marriage to the margins, Prince offers little explanation for why she leaves the US for Russia. From what little information we do have, Prince suggests in this passage, "Care after care oppressed me . . . all hope but in God was lost," that her frustration as a poor, underpaid domestic laborer fuels her decision to leave the country. Travel for Prince clearly offers a possible way out of a less than subsistence existence and begins a search abroad for a more livable place, in other words, a home.

Given her narrative's documentation of Black people's ongoing struggle to survive in the US, Prince's decision to leave the country for Russia must be read in light of the Colonization Movement and increased interest in Black emigration in the nineteenth century as a response to America's failure to extend full citizenship rights to people of African descent.[16] While Amanda Smith's autobiography introduced the struggle over citizenship and entered into conversation about Black emigration, her travel like Elaw's was motivated by a spiritual call rather than a desire for a new home. Unlike

Smith, who despite her critiques of racism, claimed the United Sates as the unequivocal home of Black people, Prince's representation of the United States as a failed home places her in a long line of Black travelers and emigres who left the States in search of what Saidiya Hartman calls "free territory," a legacy I will address further in chapter 6. Prince's narrative contributes to this larger conversation about Black citizenship and emigration from the United States, while also expanding beyond Smith by engaging in her own search for home abroad and extending the geographic boundaries of that search beyond the continent of Africa.

Given this context of nineteenth-century Black emigration and Prince's ongoing desire for a livable place (a home), the question is raised: Might Russia be the remedy for Prince's longing? She spent nine years of her life in Russia and a significant portion of her narrative recounting her life there, though, as Kristin Fitzpatrick has argued, much of the scholarship on her narrative privileges her experiences in the US and Jamaica (268). This chapter builds on and expands beyond the work of scholars, such as Sandra Gunning and Kristin Fitzpatrick, who position Russia as central to Prince's political and cultural work evident in her narrative. Scholarship that does provide a deeper analysis of her travel to Russia focuses on the secular impact of her journey, specifically Prince's improved social and economic status while in Russia as compared to the US. My analysis expands beyond previous readings by foregrounding the spiritual significance of Prince's time in Russia—demonstrating how the spiritual transformation that she undergoes there informs the sacred roots of her travel. Furthermore, I offer a more nuanced reading of Prince's portrait of Russia, one that further complicates the positioning of the country as an idealized space of freedom and tolerance in stark contrast from what she experiences in the US.[17] Despite Russia's lack of participation in the Atlantic slave trade and the government's often "outspoken progressive position," Black people were often exoticized and objectified in Russian society.[18]

While I agree with Gunning and Fitzpatrick's claims that Prince uses her travels to Russia to expose the racial injustice in the US and Jamaica, her representation of Russia invites alternative readings. Shifting the narrative focus away from her own body and onto Russian social and political practices, Prince appropriates the voice of a Western tourist in this section of her text. In the process, Prince offers a much more tenuous portrait of Russian society and politics than scholars have typically noted, one that demonstrates Russia's problematic racial ideologies, while exposing the realities of political suppression, violence, and the ever-present threat of death.[19]

Prince's portrayal of Russia offers a stark contrast to her description of her life of deprivation, hardship, and economic instability in the United States. Of her initial arrival to Russia, Prince explains, "I spent six weeks very pleasantly, visiting and receiving friends, in the manner of the country. While there I attended two of their parties; there were various amusements in which I did not partake, which caused them much disappointment. I told them my religion did not allow of dancing or dice playing. . . . As they were very strict in their religion, they indulged me in the same privilege" (21–22). Here Prince highlights her immediate acceptance within Russian society, in spite of racial and religious difference. Her narrative, then, testifies to an abrupt shift in class location for Prince, who is no longer worked to death for less than subsistence wages for employers who exploit her and are perpetually dissatisfied by her labor. She now has the leisure time for a social life. Thus, Prince's gracious welcome into Russian society stands in stark contrast to her alienation within the US.

This shift in status, enabled by her newly attained mobility, becomes more apparent in Prince's description of her first meeting with the Emperor and Empress of Russia. She explains that both of them welcomed her "with great politeness and condescension" (23). Further emphasizing their generosity, Prince notes "[t]hey presented me with a watch. . . . It was customary in those days, when any one married, belonging to the court, to present them with gifts . . . ; there was no prejudice against color; there were there all casts, and the people of all nations, each in their place" (23). Attesting to the existence of a class hierarchy rather than a racial hierarchy in Russian society, Prince illustrates how her relocation to Russia enables a shift in her social and class status. Specifically, Prince's physical mobility allows her to move in a social stratum that certainly would have been closed to her in the US, where she is denied the dignity and respect afforded her in Russia. This newfound class and social status also leads to a shift in subjectivity for Prince.

As Prince appropriates the voice of Western tourist, her narrative indicates a similar shift in subjectivity from spectacle to spectator evident in Smith's *An Autobiography*. This change allows for Prince's previously raced, gendered, and classed body, a body that was denied mobility and economic security in the US, to masquerade as an apparently objective (bodiless) observer. This shift from autobiographer to tourist is most evident through Prince's objective narrative voice in which the personal "I" disappears from her text. Shifting the gaze away from her body, Prince offers detailed descriptions of Russian fashion, religion, and the streets of St. Petersburg: "The Russian ladies follow the fashions of the French and English. Their religion is after the Greek Church. . . . The principal church is on the Main street. . . . There is another spacious building called the Market, half a mile square, where all kinds of articles many be bought. Between the Market and the church there is a block of buildings where silver articles of all kinds are to be purchased. Besides these buildings, Main Street is lined with buildings with projecting windows, to the extent of twelve miles" (35–37). Prince's description, which continues for several pages, effectively illustrates her new role as distant observer, apparently absent from the scene she describes. This shift in subjectivity is possible because of the performative nature of tourism and travel, which James Buzzard defines as offering "an imaginative freedom" that "encourages the fashioning of special identities . . . which are congruent with that freedom" (81–82). Prince's lengthy descriptions of Russian society and culture reflect this imaginative freedom of the traveler that enables her to move the reader's gaze away from her own body and onto Russia.

Wielding the tourist's power to shift the gaze through observation, Prince initially appears to construct Russia as a space of freedom in opposition to the racial oppression of the US. However, a closer reading of the text reveals a preoccupation with instability, violence, and death in Russian society that belies the pleasantness, amusement, and open acceptance in her initial experience of it. Taking this tenuous representation of Russia into account, I argue Prince, like Smith, employs in her narrative not only the tourist's power to observe but also to comment and interpret. Looking at a fuller picture of the country Prince constructs, one can hardly call her portrait ideal.

Prince's description of the Black servants employed in the tsar's court further complicates her portrait of Russia. She explains, "The number of colored men that filled this station was twenty; when one dies, the number is immediately made up. Mr. Prince filled the place of one that had died" (23). This unusual statement that job vacancies occur only as a result of death could reflect job stability and satisfaction. Employment conditions in Russia do appear more favorable for people of color than those Prince and her siblings faced in the US. But Prince's description of the court's hiring practices suggests unsettling racial ideologies at play. Her words, "when one dies, the number is immediately made up," indicate, a mere substitution of bodies at work in the tsar's court—one that calls to mind the substitution of bodies on a slave ship, where there is an equal concern with ideal numbers and achieving a "full complement."[20] Just as investors in the slave trade denied the full personhood or individuality of enslaved people, so too does Prince's explanation of service in the Russian court suggest that Black people were reduced from individual persons to bodies only, valued primarily for their labor. As historians have noted, just as many white abolitionists hostile to slavery in the United States were also firmly entrenched in white supremacist ideologies and practices, Russian opposition to slavery coexisted with a general acceptance of dominant Western constructions of Blackness (Blakely 34). Hence, Prince and her husband likely faced racist ideologies that called their full humanity into question in Russia even if they had much improved their social position.[21]

Prince's account of the Decembrist Revolt in 1825 and the violence and inhumane punishments that the tsar deployed to end it further complicates any notion of Russia as a space of freedom. She explains that after the attempted overthrow of the tsar, "There was a general seizing of all classes, who were taken into custody. The scene cannot be described; the bodies of the killed and mangled were cast into the river, and the snow and ice were stained with blood of human victims . . . the bones of those wounded, who might have been cured, were crushed" (31). Likewise, for those still alive after the revolt was suppressed, Prince explains, "A stage was erected and faggots were placed underneath, each prisoner was secured by iron chains, presenting a most appalling sight to an eye-witness . . . then fire was set to the faggots, and those brave men were consumed. Others received the knout [whip], and even the princesses and ladies of rank were imprisoned and flogged in their own habitations. Those that survived their punishment were banished to Siberia. The mode of banishment is very imposing and very heart-rending, severing them from all dear relatives and friends, for they are never permitted to take their children" (32–33). These terrifying and "heart-rending" scenes of burning flesh, women being flogged and ripped away from their children—families being torn apart indefinitely, seem eerily similar to the oppressive violence of slavery in the southern United States, as well as the anti-Black violence used to terrorize "free" Blacks throughout the US and in Jamaica. Certainly, Prince was well aware of the institutionalized violence used to suppress and subjugate Black people in America. Her shock and amazement, as well as her inability to find the words to describe what she witnesses hint at the precariousness of

Prince's position as a Black woman who flees the US to escape its violence and degradation only to be confronted with violence and oppression that appear shockingly the same.

Here we see the true power and value of Prince's critical practice—it enables her to see and question oppression and injustice beyond the borders of the nation. Moreover, Prince's narrative, which chronicles her own failed escape, makes clear that merely fleeing from such oppression is not a viable solution. My reading of Prince's account, therefore, differs from that of Cheryl Fish, who claims that Prince identifies with the emperor (Nicholas) as a "heroic survivor" (*Black and White* 47). Her descriptions of state-sponsored violence in Russia diminishes such identification. The revolution and its violent aftermath forces Prince to see the intersection of oppression at home and abroad. But I believe her own more personal experiences with death in Russia lead to a spiritual transformation that propels her into a life of activism both at home and during her travels.

While her narrative chronicles many intimate experiences with death, including a cholera outbreak in 1831 and the death of her husband in 1833, her most transformative brush with death is the St. Petersburg flood of 1824 in which "many of the inhabitants drowned" (26). Recalling the terror of her experience, Prince remembers that on the day of the flood, "I was left alone. At four o'clock in the afternoon, there was darkness that might be felt, such as I had never experienced before. My situation was the more painful, being alone, and not being able to speak [the language]" (27). Here Prince's voice shifts from that of the distant observer of the terror and violence, a tourist with the power to comment and interpret, to an active participant in such terror. With her own embodied experience at the center of the text once more, Prince's narration reveals an interior struggle with homelessness and alienation. Although Prince is in her home in St. Petersburg, she emphasizes her utter aloneness, her physical disconnection from community, and her social isolation as well since she has not yet learned to speak Russian.

If read through the lens of the sacred, Prince's experiences of the flood demonstrate an inextricable link between the physical and spiritual alienation that she experiences. This link becomes clearer when describing her own near-death experience after falling into a sinkhole caused by the flood. Prince explains, "I made my way through a long yard, over the bodies of men and beasts, and when opposite their gate I sunk; I made one grasp, and the earth gave away; I grasped again, and fortunately got hold of the leg of a horse, that had been drowned. I drew myself up, covered with mire, and made my way a little further" (27). This part of Prince's account employs greater materiality than her narrative typically does; you can almost feel the weight of Prince's body as she is nearly sucked under the earth, and indeed the weight of all life (people, animals, and plants) that is drowned in the deluge.

Prince's representation of her experiences disrupts the possibility of Russia as a potential home for Black émigrés disillusioned by racial injustice in the United States. The immanent realities of death, insecurity, and lack of stability are human conditions that follow the traveler everywhere. Prince may be able to escape racial injustice in Russia, but as the very earth beneath her gives way, Russia becomes a place of violence, terror, and near death. This confrontation with terror has a profound spiritual impact on her. Revisiting the pit where she nearly died, Prince exclaims

> It was large enough to hold a dozen like myself, where the earth had caved in. Had not the horse been there, I should never again have seen the light of day, and no one would have known my fate. Thus through the providence of God, I escaped from the flood and the pit.
>
> My helper, God, I bless thy name;
> The same thy power, thy grace the same;
> I 'midst ten thousand dangers stand,
> Supported by thy guardian hand. (28)

If we strictly read Prince's travel to Russia in terms of her national critique of slavery, colonization, and racial injustice, we miss the spiritual work Prince engages in here. Much like Hagar in the desert, Prince's experience of the flood represents the wilderness as a place of material and spiritual struggle but also a space of divine encounter. Prince's narrative, like Hagar's, attests to God's willingness to enter into her place of material and spiritual need by facilitating her physical survival during the flood and enabling her spiritual shift from a place of alienation and despair to one of belonging. Utterly transformed by her near-death experience, Prince bears witness to the reality of this new life that God has offered her by saving her from both a literal and spiritual pit. This newfound reality that God is with her, sustaining her through all of the obstacles and inherent terrors of the world transforms her understanding of home and leads to a spiritual transformation that propels Prince to embark on travel not as an escape from such dangers but to actively engage in the struggle against violence, terror, and oppression in the world.

Though Russia serves as a space of spiritual renewal and transformation for Prince, her ruminations on the persistent realities of terror and death through political violence, outbreaks of disease, and natural disasters raises serious questions about the viability of Russia as a habitable place for Black people and for all those who love freedom and desire to live. Reiterating Russia as an unlivable place, Prince announces the death of her husband and the deterioration of her own health. She returns to the US because, as she claims, "life seemed desirable" (40). Thus, she positions her return to the US as a lifesaving decision in contrast, suggesting that staying in Russia would have killed her too. Paradoxically, returning to the US gives her the potential for renewed life.

Despite what must have been a conflicted "homecoming" given the loss of her husband and the reality of facing once again a place that made her survival and thriving as a full human being nearly impossible, Prince's return to the US in 1833 reflects her renewed commitment to social and political activism through her lecturing and writing. Notably, she joins the anti-slavery society, becoming a supporter of and fighter for Black liberation as well as women's rights.[22] Prince's engagement in the social concerns of her day further illustrates the transformative experience that I believe she undergoes in Russia—a spiritual transformation that leads to a more formal and lifelong commitment to a spiritual practice rooted in active resistance to and prophetic critique of the failures of not only American slavery but also the failures of Western imperialism and colonization more generally.

Though Prince's description of her seven years stay in the United States spans just two pages, her narrative foregrounds an embodied spiritual activism and a growing critical voice that challenges the injustices she witnesses at home. She highlights, for example, her involvement in the Boston Female Anti-Slavery Society[23] until as she notes "contention broke out among themselves" (42) due to women's leadership in the abolitionist movement. Apparently, some members, Black and white, believed that "sexual integration and the full participation of women as speakers would distract abolitionists from their original goal" (Fish, *Black and White* 50). Despite her personal commitment to anti-slavery efforts, Prince expresses disillusionment with the organization and criticizes the systemic inequities that threaten the abolitionist movement. Prince writes

I may not see so clearly as some, for the weight of prejudice has again oppressed me, and were it not for the promises of God, one's heart would fail, for *He* made man in his own image, in the image of God, created he him, male and female, that they should have dominion over the fish of the sea, the fowl of the air, and the beast of the field, &c. This power did God give man, that thus far should he go and no farther; but man has disobeyed his Maker, and become vain in his imagination, and their foolish hearts are darkened. We gather from this, that God has in all ages of the world punished every nation and people for their sins. The sins of my beloved country are not hid from his notice; his all seeing eye sees and knows the secrets of all hearts. (42–43)

Here Prince's voice shifts further away from an observer who merely testifies to the injustices she witnesses, as in Russia, to a prophetic critique of such oppression. Like Zilpha Elaw before her, Prince transcends the limitations of her own human (flawed) vision by relying on God's perfect vision. Empowered by God's "all seeing eye" that "sees and knows the secrets of all hearts," Prince's prophetic critique challenges gender inequities and the marginalization of women's contributions as "man-made" rather than God-authored.

Given that Prince, like Elaw and Smith, faced readers who would question the truth and authenticity of her voice and vision, her reliance on divine authority offers a protective shield for her bold criticism of the US as a space that has and continues to limit her attempts to claim herself as fully free simply because of the body she inhabits.[24] However, Prince's words are rooted in her love for the very country that has forsaken and oppressed her, which she claims in the phrase "my beloved country." This critical love not only fuels her prophetic warning to a nation whose destruction she foresees if it does not turn from its sinful ways, but also informs her departure from the United States to Jamaica on November 16, 1840, as a missionary following the abolition of slavery on the island in 1838.[25]

Prince's prophetic voice and critical vision are primary expressions of her embodied spiritual practice—practices that deepen and expand with her travel to and from Jamaica. I posit that Prince's anti-slavery efforts in the US and her desire to help newly freed Black people in Jamaica demonstrate the inextricable link between political and spiritual work in her narrative. For instance, Prince claims as her purpose for becoming a missionary to Jamaica, "to aid, in some small degree, to raise up and encourage the emancipated inhabitants, and teach the young children to read and work, to fear God, and put their trust in the Saviour" (45). Thus, her travel has sacred and secular roots, as she aims to respond to both the spiritual and material needs facing Black Jamaicans after emancipation. However, her narrative also reveals a fundamental connection between Prince's investment in Jamaica and her commitment to freedom struggles in the US.

Demonstrating her concern for both the US and Jamaica, Prince offers a complex representation of Black Jamaicans that challenges American stereotypes: "it may be hoped they are not the stupid set of beings they have been called; here *surely we see industry;* they are enterprising and quick in their perceptions, determined to possess themselves, and to possess property besides, and quite able to take care of themselves. They wished to know why I was so inquisitive about them. I told them we had heard in America that you are lazy, and that emancipation has been of no benefit to you; I wish to inform myself of the truth respecting you, and give a true account on my return" (50). Prince's words reveal her concern with not only the spiritual welfare of newly freed Jamaicans but also an investment in the economic and social reality of the inhabitants. Thus, her spiritual work is connected to her larger political mission of fighting for justice for Black people in the West Indies and in the US. Like Elaw and Smith, Prince holds a critical vision toward slavery and racial and economic injustice that extends beyond US borders. However, her mission statement above also suggests that her ethnographic witness to the ingenuity and independence of newly freed Jamaicans will further the cause of freedom in the US by showcasing the economic benefits of emancipation.

Paralleling the challenges Amanda Smith faced in writing about the people and places she encountered in her travel to West Africa, Prince's narrative reveals the difficulty in constructing complex portraits of Black people abroad while negotiating her own social and cultural privilege. Consequently, scholars have read Prince's representation of Black Jamaicans and particularly her inclusion of their voices in conflicting ways. Carla Peterson, for example, asserts that "Prince's narrative progressively enacts a shift in power relations as she increasingly positions the Jamaicans as subalterns whose consciousness she must retrieve and for whom she must speak, and as her cultural enterprise transforms them into native Others in need of racial uplift" (92). Joycelyn Moody, on the other hand, offers a more tenuous positioning of Prince, arguing that through her depiction of Jamaicans "shows herself as both the colonizer and the colonized" (98). Cheryl Fish similarly maintains that Prince, through her inclusion of Jamaican voices, "is simultaneously making a narrative space for a transgressive ex-slave voice as she co-opts this voice from an ethnographic perspective" (*Black and White* 59). Thus, in her attempt to speak *of* Black Jamaicans in a way that reveals their full humanity, Prince risks speaking *for* them—appropriating their voices and experiences for her own ends. This scholarship confirms that there is no way for Prince to completely escape the Western imperial worldview that shaped American travelers in the nineteenth century. I argue, nonetheless, that Prince's making room for the voices of Black Jamaicans, allowing them to speak for themselves showcases their agency and resistance as forceful critics of colonial and missionary rule in Jamaica rather than as passive consumers of colonial ideologies.[26]

While Prince's status as a Western traveler with privilege in Jamaica certainly informs and at times limits her writing about Jamaica and the people she encounters, her precarious relationship to Western culture as a Black woman "at once inside and outside the society she wished to condemn" (Carby 42) also broadens her critical vision. Thus, Prince's status as both an insider and an outsider, her tenuous experience as a traveler shaped by Western culture and excluded from its full benefits because of race and gender, makes her an effective witness to and intense critic of its racist and colonial practices. If Prince's location, however much it shifts, does shape her critical vision, then her continued critique of racial injustice and colonialism becomes a central part of her embodied spiritual practice. After all, Prince's critique is not divorced from her lived experiences in the US or abroad; nor is her critical vision separate from her material reality as a raced, gendered, and classed being. Because Prince's criticism is grounded in her material reality (embodied), it is not completely free of the class and cultural biases that Peterson, Moody, and Fish see as reflected in her narrative. Nevertheless, despite the privileged position Prince occupies as traveler and ethnographer, her narrative voices a powerful critique of slavery and colonialism, which she sees as inextricably linked—a critique even more commanding than what we find in Zilpha Elaw's narrative or even Amanda Smith's because of her commitment to foreground Black voices, perspectives, and experiences beyond those of African Americans.

Although Prince attempts to maintain the role of ethnographer by claiming simply to observe Black Jamaicans' experience of freedom, her embodied spiritual practice disrupts her ethnographic voice to reveal her explicit critique of the continued racial and economic injustice of colonialism in a supposedly free Jamaica. Offering a "truer" account of the lives of newly emancipated Jamaicans, Prince couches her description of the people she encounters within their material context, especially the larger social and economic challenges they face. In addition to being "worn out and degraded" by slavery, Prince notes that

> Those who are able to work, have yet many obstacles to contend with, and very little to encourage them; every advantage is taken of their ignorance; the same spirit of cruelty is opposed to them that held them for centuries in bondage; even religious teaching is bartered for their hard earnings, while they are allowed but thirty-three cents a day, and are told if they will not work for that they shall not work at all; an extraordinary price is asked of them for every thing they may wish to purchase, even the Bibles are sold to them at a large advance on the first purchase. Where are their apologists, if they are found wanting in the strict morals that Christians ought to practice? Who kindly says, forgive them when they err. "Forgive them, this is the bitter fruit of slavery." Who has integrity sufficient to hold the balance when these poor people are to be weighed? Yet their present state is blissful, compared with slavery. (53)

Although emancipation became a reality in Jamaica before the US, Prince's narrative makes it clear that emancipation does not automatically lead to freedom. Her statement that "the same spirit of cruelty is opposed to them that held them for centuries in bondage" illustrates the continued link between slavery and colonization, which continues similar systems of hierarchy and power in which Black people are treated as inferior. As such, her critical portrait calls out colonial oppression such as the continued economic exploitation of Black Jamaicans by withholding fair and livable wages and the commodification of their spiritual practices.

As well as white employers, Prince criticizes Christian leaders and missionaries as they cheat Black people out of their meager wages by charging them for Bibles and by making them pay for religious instruction at weekly, monthly, and annual intervals.[27] Given the immoral and unjust treatment of newly freed Blacks, Prince argues that we cannot and should not judge them by strict moral standards. By attributing whatever moral degradation may exist among Black Jamaicans to the "bitter fruit of slavery," she holds the institution of slavery and those in power responsible for their material and spiritual suffering. She quotes a local inhabitant saying "the Macroon hunters take all" (54), to reiterate this critique of white missionaries. Prince explains that "Macroon hunters" "is a nickname [Black Jamaicans] give the missionaries and the class-leaders—a cutting sarcasm this!" (54). This identification of missionaries with the macroon, a form of Jamaican currency, makes visible the greed of local missionaries and their participation in colonial systems of exploitation.[28]

Colonial systems of power and control persist not only through the economic exploitation of Black people but also through violence against them. Prince explains: "A few young people met to celebrate their freedom on an open plain, where they hold their market; their former masters and mistresses, envious of their happiness, conspired against them, and thought to put them down by violence. This only served to increase their numbers; but the oppressors were powerful, and succeeded in accomplishing their revenge, although many of them were relations. . . . What little the poor colored people had gathered during their four years of freedom, was destroyed by violence; their fences were broken down, and their horses and hogs taken from them" (57–58). Prince's account unequivocally testifies to this shift from the violence of slavery to colonial violence and rule, in which white planters still hold the power to control the local economy and continue to control the lives of Black people through terrorization. As in her representation of the violence of Russian society, here too Prince's focus on the violence and terror that undergirds Jamaica, serves as a deterrent or, as Cheryl Fish claims, a warning to potential Black emigrants.[29] Like Russia, Jamaica is not a potential home for African Americans. Unsurprisingly, then, Prince departs Jamaica as well.[30]

Prince's sea voyage from Jamaica to the United States is one of the most revealing parts of her narrative as it showcases her growing spiritual activism and resistance. While her spiritual practice in Jamaica was focused externally on the social and political conditions she observed on the island, during her ship passage Prince displays a spiritual activism that is both personally and collectively focused. She links her individual struggle for freedom with that of her fellow Black passengers on board the ship, as well as with those Black people she witnesses on shore. I argue that the architecture of the ship makes it impossible for Prince to conceal herself behind the shield of tourist or ethnographer as in Russia and Jamaica. Rather, her positioning while on the ship becomes more precarious as she is subject to another gaze besides that of the audience, one that is far more difficult to evade—the white gaze of the captain aboard her ship and of slaveholders ashore as her ship docks in various southern ports.

The Journey Home: Prince's Spiritual Practice aboard the Ship

In 1842, Nancy Prince returns from Jamaica to the United States on a ship that should be headed to New York. Instead the Captain stops in Key West, New Orleans, and along the Texas coast. Along the way, she discovers that he has tricked her and has made a plan with slaveholders on shore to sell her and the other Black passengers aboard the ship into slavery. Prince discovers that the captain has deviated from the planned itinerary through her skills of navigation (reading the stars), which suggest the ship is headed in the wrong direction. Once she discovers the plot, Prince confronts the captain and warns the other Black passengers aboard the ship (74–75). This moment demonstrates her savvy as a traveler and her tireless commitment to advocating for the safety of all Black people. Yet Prince finds herself captive aboard this ship; she cannot leave or she will be enslaved, as she informs the reader, a "law had just been passed [in Key West] that every free colored person coming there, should be put in custody on their going ashore" (Prince 79). Although Prince embarks on the ship passage in order to escape violence and terror in Jamaica, the liminal status of the ship as a paradoxical marker of mobility and captivity demonstrates once again the inextricable link between travel and terror for Black people. The fluid and ever-changing space of the ship, which Kristin Fitzpatrick defines as "a contested space" (275), reveals Prince's complex and tenuous subjectivity; her status as free is equally liminal and unstable because of the location of the ship in a southern port. Her narrative reveals once again that geography matters, and reiterates, as Hagar's narrative made clear, that identity is tied to place.

Positioned on the ship's deck as a "spectacle" before the white southerners on shore at each of the unexpected stops, Prince notes that "people were very busy about me; one man asked me who I belonged to, and many other rude questions. . . . There were a great many people that came to see the vessel; . . . they watched me very closely" (77). Much like Elaw and Smith, Prince finds herself under the objectifying white gaze that places her body as captive and suspicious. Nevertheless, Prince does not give into fear, nor does she despair. Exclaiming that "[God] is with her," she instead stands boldly on the ship's deck and employs an array of embodied spiritual practices in her struggle for individual and collective freedom. To ward off the threat of enslavement, Prince engages in a spiritual activism that takes three forms: (1) bearing witness to injustice, (2) questioning racial hierarchies, and (3) using biblical prophecy to challenge slaveholding power and authority.

Prince's spiritual practice begins with bearing witness to the injustice around her, shifting from the oppressive gaze of white onlookers to her own critical vision. From her vantage point on the ship's deck, she observes that men and women of color, young and old, are chained "in pairs at the wrist"—imprisoned because of "impudence" or boldness and "theft" (77). The charge of "theft" was made against those enslaved people (i.e., fugitives) who attempted to escape slavery because they had literally run away with their bodies—bodies that did not belong to them under the law. Once again, the unrecognizability of Black humanity under the law within nineteenth-century America comes into play.[31] Prince also notes that "Every ship that comes in the colored men are dragged to prison" (78). These "free" Black travelers, whose citizenship is denied, find themselves marked instead as criminal and as a threat to the social order. Thus, Prince's narrative demonstrates that within the context of the United States, freedom and citizenship are narrowly defined as white (and male), while Blackness is criminalized. Within this context every Black body becomes a captive body (either enslaved or incarcerated—Prince's text suggests no distinction between the two).

Though here Prince's gaze faces outward onto the Black bodies around her, her observations reveal the precarity of the Black female body, particularly one traveling alone on the deck of a ship docked in a southern port. Despite the threats of commodification, incarceration, and enslavement that she faces, through her verbal sparring with the slaveholders on shore, Prince critically questions the oppression of Black men and women she sees—asking them, "who made you Lord over God's inheritance?" (77). Prince's question challenges slaveholding theology and its accompanying hierarchies of authority, which positioned slaveholders as godlike with absolute and total control over the lives and bodies of enslaved people.[32] Paralleling her earlier critique of patriarchy in the Anti-Slavery Society, her question reveals the presumed authority of slaveholders as human constructed rather than God-ordained. Prince's theological critique extends beyond the status of slaveholders to their definition of Black people as criminal, as dangerous, and as property to be bought and sold. In opposition to dominant definitions of Blackness, Prince claims Black people's true identities as God's inheritance, meaning sons and daughters of God.

Of course, Prince's bold spiritual practice comes with consequences. Revealing both the danger and the necessity of her anti-slavery activism, Prince explains, "[The slaveholders] told me I was very foolish and should worry about my own safety. . . . I found it necessary to be stern with them; they were very rude; if I had not been so, I know not what would have the consequences" (77, 79). The slaveholders' response to Prince's verbal questioning highlights her own vulnerability and though Prince offers only a paraphrase of their words, I read the men's command that Prince worry about her own safety as a latent threat. Hence, Prince's embodied spiritual practice (her public spiritual activism) reiterates the dangers that Elaw and Smith faced as Black women itinerants speaking, preaching, and prophesying in the public arena.

Third, in response to the threats of the men and the clear danger she faces of being dragged off to prison and enslaved, Prince uses the Bible as prophetic word to challenge their definitions of Blackness, citizenship, and freedom. Although she is not a preacher like Elaw and Smith, Prince's final words to the slaveholders effectively transform the ship's deck into a pulpit: "I am sure the Lord will take care of me; you cannot harm me. . . . I pointed them to the 18th chapter of Revelation" (79), which reads as follows:

> they will stand far off, in fear of her torment, and say, "Alas, alas, the great city, Babylon, the mighty city! For in one hour your judgment has come." And the merchants of the earth weep and mourn for her, since no one buys their cargo anymore, cargo of gold, silver, jewels and pearls . . . cattle and sheep, horses and chariots, slaves—and human lives. "The fruit for which your soul longed has gone from you, and all your . . . splendor are lost to you, never to be found again!" The merchants of these wares, who gained wealth from her, will stand far off, in fear of her torment, weeping and mourning aloud. (Rev. 18:10–15)[33]

Prince's employment of biblical text locates her in a legacy of Black women prophetic leaders, like Maria Stewart, an anti-slavery activist/lecturer in Boston from 1831–33 who used the Bible to affirm the divine origins of her prophetic critique. Like Prince, Stewart deployed the text of Revelation in her jeremiads, comparing the United States to Babylon with its selling of human flesh and announcing the destruction that awaits the nation because of its failure to follow God's commandments.[34] In both its biblical form, as seen in the book of Jeremiah, as well as in African American jeremiads, the role of the prophet is to deliver God's message to the people—especially God's critique of the nation's injustice, hypocrisy, materialism and greed and to remind the people of God's impending judgement and destruction if the nation does not change its ways. Though the jeremiad portends destruction, the prophet's critique, grounded in a radical hope, seeks transformation and change for the people.[35] Yet the prophet's message of warning and hope has often been met with open hostility. John F. A. Sawyer notes the original Jeremiah, "was almost lynched by the people" after delivering his message (101) and Maria Stewart was forced to leave Boston after a brief period of lecturing on account of her radical message. In this moment aboard the ship's deck, we see Prince facing a similar hostility as her message reveals the urgency of spiritual and social change. Offering a prophetic judgment of the city of Babylon, this passage in Revelation that Prince cites warns that because of Babylon's great sin, it is condemned to destruction and all those who profited from its sinfulness will suffer God's judgment. Powerfully prophetic in its judgment, this passage highlights the sin of national pride and is focused on destroying the nation's source of wealth—most notably the slave trade. Drawing an unquestionable parallel between America and Babylon in the Revelation passage, Prince effectively links the nation's trafficking in human flesh to the greed and pride that destroyed Babylon and, as she posits, will ultimately destroy the US as well.

Although these southerners see her as a commodifiable Black body, one they can surely enslave for profit, Prince's response confirms that God protects her body. Proclaiming her moral vision and authority, Prince opposes the men's vision of themselves as godly and justified in their actions— positioning them instead as hypocritical, unjust, and sinful. While their practices may be considered legal under state law, Prince assures them that God's law will not allow such injustice to go unpunished. It's no surprise, then, that these men find Prince threatening—so much so that they are not willing to touch her, though they continue to watch her closely. Though they have the power of the law on their side, as Fitzpatrick notes, "Prince is dangerous. Her freedom of speech and movement defy their equation of blackness with slavery and could incite other Blacks to demand the same liberties she possesses. Her very existence testifies to the possibility of black literacy, self-determination, and potential racial and gender equality" (275). Indeed, Prince's radical spiritual practice repositions her body as an explicit threat rather than of value to the slavocracy. Her words are so dangerous that southerners ask the ship's captain to leave.

Ultimately, at the end of this scene we see Prince, like her stepfather in the beginning of her narrative, risking bodily harm on the ship's deck in order to affirm her own claim to freedom. However, Prince's deployment of jeremiadic discourse reveals the expansive strategies Black women spiritualists used to protect their own individual bodies, to sustain their mobility, and to advocate for the collective freedom of all Black people. Making it to New York in October of 1842, Prince wins this particular battle and protects her right to travel once again aboard the ship as a free, mobile subject rather than be taken ashore as a captive body.

Although Prince's travels end rather triumphantly with her radical resistance aboard the slave ship that secures her right to return home, she ends her narrative not with this very public victory and performance but with a poem titled "The Hiding Place." Offering a far different image of freedom than that offered on the ship's deck, the poem's narrator states,

> I'm in a wilderness below,
> Lord, guide me all my journey through,
> Plainly let me thy footsteps trace,
> Which lead to heaven, my hiding place.
>
> Should dangers thick impede my course,
> O let my soul sustain no loss;
> Help me to run the Christian race,
> And enter safe my hiding place. (89)

Prince's concluding her narrative with this image of hiding contrasts strongly with her triumphant self-exposure and subsequent fight for freedom on the deck of a ship. At first, the title of the poem and repetition of the words *hiding place* call into question the exultant nature of her return home. Prince finds herself, upon her return to the US, faced not with a welcoming portrait of home, but rather "in a wilderness," where she faces "dangers thick." For Prince, these struggles include having her personal belongings stolen, her business broken up multiple times, and having to move repeatedly because of an inability to provide economically for her needs (85). Consequently, the wilderness for Prince, as for Hagar, is a place of spiritual and material struggle but also a place in which God meets Black women in their place of need.

The imagery of the wilderness places Prince's narrative firmly within the Puritan spiritual narrative tradition, especially John Bunyan's *Pilgrim's Progress*, which represents the Christian as a wanderer who must journey through a wilderness, life here on Earth, before arriving at the intended destination—heaven. Yet for Prince, as for Hagar, Elaw, and Smith, the dangers of such a journey are not simply metaphorical but are reality as well.[36] As Fitzpatrick claims, "The freedom she experiences as an American citizen abroad melts away upon reentry. . . . Freedom at home is at best a conditional, uncertain state. . . . Rather than a returning citizen, she is a fugitive in her own land, where the journey out is less perilous than the journey home" (277). Extending Fitzpatrick's claim that Prince loses her freedom upon returning home, I have argued throughout this chapter that Prince's travels illustrate again and again the untenable nature of freedom, stability, and protection anywhere in the world—not just in the US. The ending of Prince's narrative both calls into question the United States as a potential home *and* contests the very notion of home as a physical place to be discovered.

The freedom and stability Prince experiences abroad is always conditional. As we witness from her accounts of Russia, Jamaica, and her ship passage to the US, Prince still faces serious dangers, violence, and the realities of political and social oppression. Her journey, therefore, leads to a far more complex and nuanced critique of oppression and injustice that extends beyond national borders—one that recognizes that such systems of oppression are global in nature, inextricably linked to each other. Moreover, her ability to redefine home as a spiritual condition, rather than a physical location, as the poem suggests, enables her to engage in a powerful spiritual practice aimed not at escaping the terrifying realities of suffering and oppression but rather becoming actively engaged in transforming and destroying such violent and hierarchical institutions.

Although some scholars, those few who attend to the poem at all, might read this positioning of home as an otherworldly dream, I would like to claim otherwise.[37] Read within the context of a narrative that clearly delineates a spiritual practice grounded in lived experience, I assert that Prince's poem attempts to explain how to be at home in the wilderness, here on earth rather than in the next life. In other words, this poem is not strictly about the journey toward a heavenly home, though this reading is most certainly present. Rather, these verses, which radically redefine home as a state of being, maintain that Prince can be at home in any place—even while held captive on a ship docked in a slave state, surrounded by terrifying slaveholders who wish nothing more than to devour her. What Prince and indeed Zilpha Elaw and Amanda Smith recognize is that all of humanity lives in a state of alienation. We are all strangers in a strange land. The spiritual lives of these women offer hope, which, for Prince, is not simply a future vision that we must wait for but rather a call to action.

For Prince, then, the image of home offered in "The Hiding Place," a safe place, where one feels protected and secure from the troubles of the world, reflects not an otherworldly ideal but a vision for constructing spaces of freedom here on earth. Though her narrative bears witness to an evolving and increasingly radical spiritual activism, the most powerful example of Prince's commitment to prophetic critique and to transforming the nation-space into a space of freedom for Black people does not appear in her text. In 1847, Prince led several members of the Black community in Boston in expelling a known slaveholder from a local home. According to an eyewitness account reprinted in a local newspaper, Prince "with the assistance of the colored women that had accompanied her . . . dragged [the slaveholder] to the door and thrust him out of the house. By this time quite a number, mostly women and children had gathered near by, whom Mrs. Prince commanded to come to the rescue, telling them to 'pelt him with stones and any thing you can get a hold of,' which order they proceeded to obey with alacrity. The slaveholder started to retreat, and with his assailants close upon him ran out of the court" (Sterling 222). Though Prince excludes this event from her narrative, this key moment further reveals her resistant practice in opposition to the oppressive forces of slavery that extended into the North. Moreover, this aggressive act of physically expelling a slaveholder from a home in the Black community illustrates, in spite of the ever-present risks and dangers, Prince's commitment to creating and sustaining community in which Black people can live fully and freely in the world. This account in which women and children bond together to remove the threat of violence, exploitation and captivity from the community reveals Prince's investment in a communal practice of freedom—one that reflects a commitment to protecting *all* members of the community (enslaved and free). I locate this struggle for justice that crosses gender, class, and age boundaries as part of the legacy of collective Black resistance that the opening of Prince's narrative recounts. Moreover, Prince's willingness to risk her life for the freedom of others and her identification with the struggles of fugitive slaves harkens back to the freedom struggles of her ancestors and other unknown Middle Passage survivors who claimed the strangers around them as kin and built new communities that actively resisted slavery in all of its forms.

This profound collective act of resistance demonstrates the preservation and protection of home—the assertion of the Black community and the homes within it as safe havens from racial and economic injustice and violence. Through this construction of a space where slavery is outlawed and where supporters of the institution are trespassers, Prince and those who aid her engage in an oppositional practice, what McKittrick terms a practice of "respatialization," that reconstitutes for men, women, and children of color the notion of home as a refuge. Reflecting slavery's reproduction and transmission across varying social spaces, Prince's narrative showcases how slavery haunts our landscape including "ships . . . homes, communities, nations" (McKittrick xvii). In order to end the transmission of captivity and violence through space, Prince builds on and extends beyond the "place-based critiques" she employed throughout her various journeys by using physical force to maintain a space of freedom for Black people.[38] Moreover, Prince's willingness to use her own body to protect the lives of other Black people reflects a critical spatial practice that, as McKittrick asserts, Black women use to "negotiate their surroundings" and "employ . . . alternative geographic formulations" that interrogate and remap spaces of domination—ultimately remaking them into places that are livable and habitable by Black people (xix). Hence, despite attempts to destroy Black homes and to deny Black freedom in the nation-space (private and public), here we see Prince, with the aid of her fellow communal activists, constructing a home space in which slavery is outlawed in opposition to the larger nation that has outlawed freedom for Black people.

The public nature of this resistance to slavery, led by a community of Black women and children, is particularly significant in light of domestic ideology's positioning of the (private) home as the proper sphere for women's anti-slavery efforts. Moving beyond private domestic space and individual homes, these women and children engage in a public spiritual practice that reconstitutes kinship and community and actively resists the practices of separation on which slavery depends. Despite Prince's geographical location in a space fully corrupted by slavery, Prince uses her bodily practice to transgress spatial boundaries of gender, race, and class. Resisting the Fugitive Slave Law's attempt to transform the entire nation into an auction block, Prince contests the capture and sale of Black bodies in Boston, Massachusetts, just as she did from the ship's deck while docked in southern territory. Ultimately, Prince's oppositional practice rejects the notion that space "just is" (McKittrick xi). Creating a home space that is not inherently free or innately safe but rather a place in which freedom and safety are defined as fundamental human values that must be practiced, Prince and her fellow community members produce free space, in opposition to a larger context of anti-Black violence, by engaging in an ongoing, active struggle to ensure all Black men, women, and children can live as fully human.

Though this moment of radical spiritual activism is excluded from her text, this does not undermine the power of Prince's narrative, which demonstrates the constraints placed on Black women's subjectivity and autobiographical practice in the nineteenth century. Certainly, her decision to exclude this event from her autobiographical travelogue reflects a key moment of concealment in which Prince perhaps recognizes the potentially negative repercussions of the radical representation of Black womanhood exemplified through her embodied resistance to the institution and laws of slavery. No doubt, this act of physical and collective rebellion in which Prince actively breaks the law would have undermined attempts to represent herself as respectable and trustworthy before white middle class readers in particular. Moreover, as literary scholars have long argued, withholding the details of such events was for nineteenth-century Black women writers such as Prince a form of self-protection and a way to negotiate the financial pressure on and economic necessity of their writing. Anthony G. Barthelemy highlights the particular challenges Black women writers faced when he exclaims, "Each [Black woman writer] lived under the shadow of capture and sale" (xxxiii), as they faced the continued threat of a "literary return to the auction block" (xxxiv), meaning a return to the threat of commodification and consumption before the white gaze—a threat that, as we have already seen, both Elaw and Smith were subject to as itinerant preachers. Although Prince was born free in the North, the publication of her expanded *Narrative* in 1853, just three short years after the expansion of the Fugitive Slave Act, suggests that this threat of returning to the auction block was not just a literary fear but quite probably a literal fear as well, since the new law threatened the safety and security of free Blacks throughout the US. This historical context also explains not only the narrative's preoccupation with slavery and Prince's tenuous attempts to represent herself as a free subject throughout her text, but also the omission of her 1847 attack on a slaveholder.

Given how visibly this historical event bears witness to a radical spiritual practice rooted in a communal legacy of resistance, it becomes imperative to offer a critical reading of it. Moreover, in our critical engagement with this alternative text beyond the published narrative, we can speak into the historical silencing of African American women writers. Not only does such an approach enable us to better navigate the formal complexities of such works (the tension between concealment and exposure, and between distant observer and embodied critic/activist), but it also ensures that we do not participate in a narrow and singular conception of Black female subjectivity that Hagar, Elaw, Smith, and Prince's narratives bear witness to and struggle against. Considering this alternative textual representation of Prince and her local Boston community, therefore, complicates her subjectivity and her spirituality while also offering a fuller portrait of Black female and Black collective resistance.

While Prince's narrative, with its vacillation between individual and collective Black struggle, marks a subtle departure away from Elaw and Smith's focus on their individual lives and journeys, Dash's 1991 film *Daughters of the Dust* breaks entirely from these earlier texts by shifting the lens away from the single individual life to foreground instead the Black community and its multiplicity of experiences, journeys, and spiritual perspectives. Nevertheless, Dash's film expands on and deepens our discussion of the central themes Prince's narrative introduces: the continued vulnerability of Black people in the US, their complex and intersecting journeys across the diaspora, and their ongoing struggles to build a home in the face of unfreedom. With this film, then, the legacy of Black women's embodied spirituality from Hagar's biblical narrative visible in Elaw, Smith and Prince's nineteenth-century texts expands into the twentieth century.

· FIVE ·

Mapping Sacred Movement in Julie Dash's *Daughters of the Dust*

> Not only humans made the Crossing. . . .
> The Sacred energies that accompanied the millions who had been captured and sold for more than four centuries had indeed inhabited a vast geography. . . .
> —M. Jacqui Alexander, *Pedagogies of Crossing*

As I have argued throughout *Spirit Deep,* the sacred moves. It informs and shapes the journeys of Black women. These words from M. Jacqui Alexander serve as an invocation of this truth as it relates to the bodies of those transported across the Atlantic during the Middle Passage. "[T]he geographies of crossing and dislocation," as Alexander writes, which have long characterized the movements of African-descended peoples also transform the sacred, which is always fluid and ever-changing (290). Julie Dash's groundbreaking 1991 film *Daughters of the Dust,* much like the other texts I have examined here, moves Black women and the particularities of their spiritual experiences from the periphery to the center. It actively foregrounds Black women's voices and their embodied and sacred knowledge. In doing so it makes visible the varied geographies of the spirit Alexander references by expanding our conversation about the sacred beyond Christianity. Through an analysis of *Daughters,* this chapter will highlight how the varying geographies of Black diasporic peoples lead to varied expressions of the sacred and transform their understanding of and relationship to the divine. Dash has identified her film as a work of "speculative fiction," but, like Judith Weisenfeld, I see *Daughters* also as a spiritual "text" that, following in the legacy of Hagar's narrative and nineteenth-century Black women spiritualists, takes seriously the movement of the sacred in the lives of Black women.[1]

With the shift in this chapter to new spiritual geographies, as well as to a new medium and new time period, this chapter extends my commitment to move beyond what Houston Baker has described as the limits of singular models and selective frameworks. Rather than offer a "single model" (Baker 9) of embodied spiritual practices at work in Black women's lives, through this chapter and the next I will expand beyond the selective experience of nineteenth-century Black women spiritualists by foregrounding the varying spiritual legacies of Black women in the twentieth and twenty-first centuries. *Daughters* expands the spiritual lineage of Black people in two ways: by presenting a communal, rather than an individual spiritual narrative, and by embracing Islam and African cosmology as alternative spiritual geographies that have informed Black people's experiences in the New World.[2] In analyzing this text, I respond to literary and theological scholars' demand for "more expansive approaches" (Hucks 90) to the study of African American women's literature and religion, taking up Barbara Christian, Judylyn Ryan, and Tracey Hucks's challenge that we "expand the mapping of the African American religious continuum" (Ryan 267). *Daughters* documents alternative knowledge that dominant narratives about Black women in US history and film have left out. Including it ensures that *Spirit Deep* expands literary and theological conversations about Black women's spiritual journeys beyond a singular spiritual framework, while also demonstrating the intersections between Black women's journeys in the nineteenth and twentieth centuries.

While the previous chapter analysis of Nancy Prince's life and legacy ended with a vision of Black female-led collective struggle against the forces of slavery, *Daughters* extends this exploration of the central role of Black women in constructing and sustaining community—spaces of freedom and belonging for Black people into the twentieth century. Dash's film takes place in 1902 on Ibo Landing, one of the Sea Islands off the coast of Georgia and South Carolina. It tells the story of an extended African American family, the Peazants, on the eve of migrating north. The film showcases various members of the family as they gather for a reunion before a large portion of them leave the island in search of increased opportunities for education, social mobility, and economic progress in the "promised land" of the North. Though the film takes place at the turn of the twentieth century, its positing of separation as the central theme and spiritual conflict of the story emphasizes that slavery's traumatic legacies of dislocation and dispossession continue to shape people's lives. Yet much like Hagar's narrative, *Daughters* offers an alternative legacy to that of slavery's alienation and dispossession expressed through the diasporic spiritual practices of the Black characters in the film—often led and facilitated by women.

These spiritual leaders and facilitators include most notably Nana Peazant, the family elder born in slavery and whose mother survived the crossing from Africa to the United States; Eula, the wife of Nana Peazant's great-grandson Eli; and the Unborn Child, a girl growing in Eula's womb. As the primary source of ancestral wisdom, Nana Peazant employs her African-derived spiritual practices to ensure the family's continued connection to the past. Eula also grounds her spiritual practice in African cosmology, ensuring the continuation of Nana Peazant's and the ancestors' spiritual legacy. The Unborn Child crosses the spiritual realm of the ancestors into the material world of those already born, a journey both Nana Peazant and the ancestors or "old souls" facilitate to help hold the family together. A representative of the Peazant family's future, the Unborn Child embodies the possibility of wholeness through sustained communal and ancestral connection in the face of the varying conflicts and impending separation that threaten to tear the family apart. These divisions are most visible in the character of Yellow Mary, a cousin whose return to Ibo Landing in search of a place of belonging makes visible conflicts and spiritual disconnection within the family. However, her transformation by the end of the film, most evident in her decision to stay in Ibo Landing, reveals the possibilities for restoration and wholeness. Thus, *Daughters* positions the work of reconstituting self and community, facilitated in and through Black women, as healing and therefore as deeply spiritual work that enables Black people to resist and thrive in the face of the continuing threat of dislocation and dispossession.

Cinematic Practice

Daughters is the first feature film directed by an African American woman to achieve widespread commercial distribution. Beyond this, its approach to filmmaking was groundbreaking. Dash learned her craft at UCLA as part of the Los Angeles School or LA Rebellion, a group of young Black filmmakers informed by the radical freedom fights and anti-colonial struggles of the 1960s in the US and globally. Challenging the racism at the foundation of Western cinema, Dash's filmmaking expands beyond the narrow representations of Black people, Black women in particular, that the US film industry continually reproduces.[3] It reflects what N. Frank Ukadike calls "a movement toward thoroughgoing cinematic decolonization" (102–3).

Like Nancy Prince, Dash engages in a spiritual practice of storytelling that bears witness to and challenges slavery's legacy of dispossession that has informed representations of Black people historically and in the present. In order to expand the range of stories about Black experience and thereby challenge dominant constructions of Blackness, Dash embraces multiplicity, blending multiple voices, bridging varying spiritual geographies of Black characters in the film, and recovering and layering multiple histories. The film employs multi-perspectival film techniques, including tableaux and co-narration. This rejection of the single-voiced narrative in her cinematic practice reflects what Joel Brouwer refers to as its "kaleidoscopic perspective" (5). As Brouwer claims, Dash's deployment of the kaleidoscope functions as a metaphor for the unique visual, and I argue spiritual, practice of the film, which demonstrates that for the characters in *Daughters* there is no one way of seeing.

The kaleidoscope appears in one of the early scenes of *Daughters* in the hand of Mr. Snead, a northern Black photographer who Viola, a member of the Peazant family, has hired to photograph the reunion. Dash has described Snead as having "a secret mission." She explains that beyond his contract to take photographs for the family, "He has another agenda. He's going to take pictures of these very, very primitive people and go back and have a showing of what he's photographed" (38). Not only does Snead's "secret" ethnographic mission align his photographic practice with the colonizing roots of Western science, but his identification with the kaleidoscope, invented by a Scottish physicist, similarly reiterates his privileging of Western scientific knowledge and achievement.[4] Bringing the kaleidoscope as a novel gift for the Peazant children, he explains its mechanics: "If an object is placed between two mirrors, inclined at right angles, an image is formed in each mirror. Then, these mirror images are in turn reflected in the other mirrors, forming the appearance of four symmetrically shaped objects" (Dash 82–83).[5] Building on Brouwer's claim that Dash uses the kaleidoscope as a metaphor, I argue Snead's statements about the toy directly illuminate the perspective of the film and Dash's cinematic practice.

First, Mr. Snead's statement that the kaleidoscope uses mirrors to produce the appearance of multiple objects reflects the power and significance of the device that enables multiple ways of seeing. Likewise his delight in the kaleidoscope—"[i]t's beauty, simplicity and science, all rolled into one small tube. I think the children will enjoy it" (83)—underscores his privileging of Western science and his joy in possessing and displaying a totalizing and fixed knowledge about the kaleidoscope and how it works. The shift from Mr. Snead's delight in the kaleidoscope as scientific device to the children's joyful experience of it as a new toy, however, gestures toward another possible way of seeing. Since children would clearly lack access to the science behind the kaleidoscope, their enjoyment must come from its "beauty" and "simplicity." Quite distinct from Mr. Snead's method of viewing, which privileges totalizing knowledge of the object being viewed, the children imagined here do not require an understanding of the science to enjoy the beauty of the kaleidoscope. These imagined children, with their ability to simply appreciate the beauty of the kaleidoscope and find joy in the varied and ever-changing images it produces without a full understanding of what they are seeing, in many ways exemplify the idealized manner of viewing this film.

Through her deployment of the kaleidoscope in the film opening, Dash addresses the challenges of viewership and the film's intended impact on the audience's way of seeing. Dash recognizes the existence of multiple viewing practices and expectations from her audience as she notes that those who are "not used to spending two hours as a black person, as a black woman," may not recognize the cultural practices and images she portrays on the screen (40). Nevertheless, one of the goals of her film, through its "kaleidoscopic perspective," is to challenge viewers to move beyond the unknown (the unfamiliar)—to see and embrace multiple itineraries and representations of, as well as varied possibilities for, Black subjectivity and history. Thus, like the kaleidoscope, *Daughters'* mission is to bear witness to the myriad images of Blackness and to reveal the fluid, shifting, and ever-changing nature of Black (female) subjectivity. As such, the film disrupts dominant attempts to construct a fixed or singular definition of Blackness. By disrupting their preconceived knowledge of the world, Dash shifts viewers out of their position of privilege and invites them to adopt a spirit of curiosity, openness, and possibility as represented by the kaleidoscope.

In contrast to Snead's colonial and ethnographic deployment of the camera as a tool to capture the Peazant family for later display, a process of transforming them into objects held in place by the camera's technology, Dash employs what Judith Weisenfeld has called her "empowered eye" as director to reconstitute the subjectivity of Black people, especially Black women who she positions as both her primary audience for the film and as the film's primary storytellers.[6] This reconstitution takes place through documenting their embodied practices, which includes performing the role of griot, a traditional role of transmitting the "sacred histories" of the community common in West African societies.[7] Nana Peazant declares, "the ancestor and the womb are one." As such, she and other Peazant women become bearers of an ancestral spiritual knowledge housed in and conveyed through their bodies. Continuing the legacy of Hagar and nineteenth-century Black women spiritualists, *Daughters* testifies to the sacredness of Black women's bodies.

Dash's decolonized cinematic spiritual vision manifests in the opening montage of the film, a series of fragmented tableaux or "living pictures" that introduce audiences to the context of the film's story and to Dash's focus on community.[8] That each focuses on a different character demonstrates Dash's commitment to illustrating the multiple trajectories and spiritual practices of Black people. Nana Peazant appears as a young woman holding Sea Island soil in her hands and in the film's present bathing in the river like her African ancestors before her. Bilal Muhammed, a historical figure who lived on the island, chants a prayer in Arabic, holding an open text handwritten in Arabic, presumably a copy of the Qur'an.[9] Eli stands by as Eula engages in the African-derived spiritual practice of calling on the ancestors for aid, placing a handwritten letter for her deceased mother underneath a glass of water. Viola, Nana Peazant's granddaughter, who hired Snead, returns to the island by boat along with her cousin Yellow Mary, who holds a St. Christopher charm.

As I have discussed, scholars of West African religions highlight the centrality of the community to African cosmology. The individual has no identity apart from the community, which consists of all life—including animals, plants, living people, the ancestors who have passed on and those yet to be born. Dash's film reflects a similar notion of community through Eula's attempt to communicate with the dead and through the voiceover that follows the opening montage, as the Unborn Child tells us that "Nana prayed and the old souls guided me into the New World." It describes how those members alive in the present (the living), those from the future (the unborn), and those from the past (the ancestors or "old souls") work together to ensure the survival of the Peazant family (Dash 80). Therefore, the film affirms the movements of the sacred in the past, present, and future lives of Black people.

The montage presents a range of spirituality. Nana Peazant and Eula demonstrate West African spiritual beliefs. Bilal Muhammed is a Muslim Sudanese captive who survived the Middle Passage to the West Indies and Sea Islands. Viola is a Christian missionary who has returned to the island from the North. Yellow Mary's St. Christopher charm represents the syncretic spiritual practice of Santeria from Cuba, where she migrated for work. Viola's travel by boat, Nana Peazant's bathing in the river, Bilal's prayer by the ocean, and Yellow Mary's charm displaying the patron saint of travelers invoke crossings in journeys of captivity, migration, missionary, or return. They link each character's identity to geography and place and introduce key spiritual practices that have shaped their journeys and been transformed by their movements (Petty 90). They also reference how the various spaces of the diaspora (US North and South, Africa, and Caribbean) are connected.

The film's opening also introduces audiences to a second key element of Dash's decolonizing cinematic practice: her multivocal narration. The inclusion of two female voices off screen in the opening minutes of the film, that of a woman and a child, gestures toward the co-narration technique Dash employs to tell her story. It reflects the impossibility of any single, dominant perspective as representative of Black women's experience. Although Nana Peazant and the Unborn Child are the primary narrators, the film also foregrounds the experiences and perspectives of additional characters, Viola, Eula, and Yellow Mary in particular. These characters reflect the diversity of Black women's spiritual experience, embodied knowledge, and make visible the community's healing and transformation. Mirroring Dash's centering of Black female voices, the following sections highlight several Black women while also considering how their spiritual experiences intersect with that of Black men significant to the life of the community.

Viola

Dash's commitment to decolonization becomes particularly evident in her representation of the character Viola, whom she uses to de-center Western Christianity and critique it as a colonizing force. The screenplay introduces Viola as a Christian missionary, much like Zilpha Elaw, Amanda Smith, and Nancy Prince, who predate her. Like them, Viola espouses Western notions of progress and civilization, which she equates with both Christianity and technology. Her return to the Sea Islands with a Bible and a photographer reflects Christianity and the promising technology of the camera as important markers of civilization and progress.[10] As Viola explains to Yellow Mary and Trula, her traveling companion and lover, Mr. Snead's function is to "document our family's crossing to the mainland." This pronouncement, along with her reference to Mr. Snead as "my photographer," reiterates the value Viola places on her family's journey to the mainland as a marker of their progress and photography as an expression of her own civilizing practice.

The film further aligns Viola with Western notions of progress as she quotes Shakespeare, exclaiming "What's past is prologue." She tells the approving Mr. Snead and the amused Yellow Mary and Trula, "I see this day as their [her family's] first steps toward progress, an engraved invitation, you might say, to the culture, education and wealth of the mainland" (Dash 79). The quote comes from Shakespeare's *The Tempest* (1611). In the play, Antonio has usurped the title of Duke of Milan from his brother Prospero and sent him and his baby daughter, Miranda adrift at sea. In the second act of the play he presses Sebastian, the brother of the king, to murder the king, saying, "We all were sea-swallow'd, though some cast again / (And by that destiny) to perform an act / Whereof what's past is prologue; what to come, / in yours and my discharge" (2.1.247–50). Thus, he states that they are in control of their destiny and must write their own futures and perform their own drama in which they become heroes and aspire to greatness. The past as prologue merely provides the setting for this drama. What really matters is what they choose to do from here on.

Viola's reference to this passage suggests she seeks to marginalize the past. Rather than focus on the legacies of African-descended people in the West (defined largely by the Middle Passage and slavery), over which she has no control, Viola wishes to write a new narrative for herself and her family, one in which Black people can achieve greatness rather than be consigned to lives of powerlessness as victims of sexual and economic oppression and violence. Her statement to Mr. Snead of the advantage her family will gain by stepping "toward progress" reveal she privileges Western culture and epistemology (ways of knowing). The reference to Shakespeare can be read as evidence of her internalization of and entrenchment within this culture and epistemology. Viola effectually minimizes the importance of the past, as prologue—relegating it to the role of a few introductory lines before the "real" or "main" action begins.

Many scholars have been intensely critical of Viola, viewing her as a fully acculturated victim of Western colonization. In an interview with Dash about the film, bell hooks stated that if Viola "had her way, she would strip the past of all memory and would replace it only with markers of what she takes to be the new civilization. In this way Christianity becomes a hidden force of colonialism" (hooks and Dash 37). Following this argument, we might read Viola's Western devaluing of the past as juxtaposed against African cosmology, which greatly values the past as inextricably linked to the present and future represented by Nana Peazant, Eula, and the Unborn Child.

Catherine Cucinella and Renee Curry's essay "Exiled at Home: *Daughters of the Dust* and the many post-colonial conditions" offers a similar reading of Viola. "[H]er post-colonial condition is one of utter assimilation," they write. "She wants a Christian patriarchal future.... [S]he is not interested in the past. To her mind, the past ... represents exile from Jesus Christ, her God" (212). While I agree that the film urges us to be critical of Viola's valuing of Western culture and singular narrative of progress, I question the claim that Viola is fully assimilated.[11] In the film we see her engaged in a critical practice that questions the authority of Western epistemology—a resistance that complicates scholarly readings of her as "utterly assimilated."

In fact, *The Tempest* offers a critical look at Western imperialism and the process of colonization. The play offers a critical reflection on the land theft, enslavement and colonizing of indigenous peoples—practices of domination that have been central to Western colonization. Prospero is typically read as the figure of Western imperial power, who, upon being shipwrecked on a strange island, immediately subjugates the indigenous population, using manipulation and force to claim the land as his rightful property. Caliban embodies the voice of colonized and indigenous people, who after permitting the colonizers to enter, find themselves stripped of their land and power and enslaved. Caliban resists Prospero's perceived authority and power, and Viola's reference to the play invokes his story.

Given the centrality of memory in *Daughters*, I foreground Caliban's memory in this analysis. For example, Caliban, resisting Prospero's claim to the island, declares:

> This island's mine by Sycorax my mother,
> Which thou tak'st from me ...
> For I am all the subjects that you have,
> Which first was mine own king; and here you sty me
> In this hard rock, whiles you do keep from me
> The rest o' th' island. (1.2.331–43)

Here Caliban claims the island as his by birthright and blood lineage, a natural inheritance which juxtaposes strongly with Prospero's illegitimate claim by theft, manipulation, and violence. His counter-memory undermines Prospero's power and authority by appealing to alternative ways of knowing—knowledge that Prospero does not control. Prospero dismisses him:

> Thou most lying slave,
> Whom stripes [wounds from severe beating] may move, not kindness.
>   I have used thee
> (Filth as thou art) with humane care, and lodged thee
> In mine own cell till thou didst seek to violate
> The honor of my child. (1.2.344–48)

Prospero's disavowal of Caliban's testimony as the words of a lying, savage, rapist, as Francis Barker and Peter Hulme claim, reproduces the colonial violence of historical and discursive erasure through which "European colonial regimes articulated their authority over land to which they could have no conceivable legitimate claim" (206).

Daughters echoes these practices of resistance and disavowal in an exchange between Viola and Mr. Snead on the boat ride before they arrive at Ibo Landing. According to the screenplay, from the boat, Viola notices "a small deserted island [with] the remains of a small crumbling shanty" (Dash 83). She explains to Snead that her Uncle Spikenard used to live there, recalling, "He was from Africa, and just after the [Civil] war, he moved from the plantation to that little house on the waterfront." Addressing Yellow Mary, she asks "Remember how when Uncle Spikenard used to get angry, he'd talk funny so the children couldn't understand him? He'd speak in African words and sounds. You know, Uncle Spikenard told me, just before the war they'd keep boatloads of fresh Africans off on some secret islands around here" (Dash 84).

Viola's testifying to the existence of an illegal slave trade long after its official ban in 1808 positions memory as the site of a counter knowledge that has been passed down from generation to generation as a kind of ancestral inheritance. Attempting to correct her, Mr. Snead asserts: "Viola, our government banned the transporting of Africans for slavery fifty years before the Civil War" (Dash 84). Much as Prospero disavows Caliban's testimony, Mr. Snead uses his Western patriarchal knowledge to dismiss Viola's memory.

But Viola persists. She tells him, "Not back off on these islands. Noooo! Just before the war, they were still running and hiding salt water Africans, pure bred, from the Yankees" (Dash 84). Although Mr. Snead remains unconvinced, Viola privileges the ancestral and communal knowledge that she has inherited from her uncle over Western authority and power. Thus, Viola's memory functions as a site of spiritual resistance, holding fast to the experiential and embodied knowledge of southern Black communities.

Through this interchange between Viola and Mr. Snead, the decolonizing cinematic spiritual vision of this film becomes evident in Dash's refusal to privilege a single history or a single genealogy. Rather, the film's kaleidoscopic perspective demands that we consider alternative ways of knowing to counter the dominant narrative about Black people's experiences in the West. Dash's decision to place this alternative knowledge and wisdom into Viola's mouth renders her body as a site of ancestral spiritual memory that challenges Mr. Snead's espousal of the official US historical record. This official record, as Joseph Roach has argued, "tends to discredit memory in the name of history" by privileging the static written word over living (embodied) oral memory (*Culture and Performance* 125). Therefore, in making visible that which has been erased from the official record, Viola demonstrates the incomplete and even fraudulent nature of the Western historical archive of slavery.

Nonetheless, the dominant narrative of Western Christianity influences Viola's perspective. Sharing her testimony with the children of the Peazant family, she tells them, "When I left these islands, I was a sinner and I didn't even know it. But I left these islands, touched that mainland, and fell into the arms of the Lord." When her niece, Myown asks her, "What's out there, Auntie Viola?" Viola says, "Life, child, the beginning of a new life." When Myown asks, "Who's out there?" Viola responds, "Jesus Christ, baby, the Son of God" (Dash 115–16). Viola's testimony that she had to leave the Sea Islands to find God resembles Amanda Smith's representation of India as a place devoid of God's presence. It reveals her internalization of traditional Western hierarchies that often informed nineteenth-century missionary ideology. However, unlike Smith who offers a critical portrait of Western missionaries to Africa and of the United States' hypocrisy, Viola posits Africa as heathen and godless and the West as the unequivocal source of salvation and progress. She does not question Western Christianity as a colonizing force.

Linking the Georgia Sea Islands with Africa, her comments define Black diasporic space in similarly narrow ways that erase the diverse spiritual geographies of Black people. The "new life" Viola describes is not only spiritual but also social, as the mainland offers wealth, education, and progress as she described to Mr. Snead, Yellow Mary, and Trula at the opening of the film, linking Western civilization with Christianity.[12] If the mainland is the source of life, then the Sea Islands are a place of death, spiritual and social if not physical. Her ability to critique and resist the totalizing gestures of Western epistemology does not let her see how her own expression of Christianity espouses Western colonial ideals.

From the outset, however, Dash's film challenges Viola's colonizing gestures. For instance, Yellow Mary and Trula laugh candidly at her claims about the culture, education, wealth, and progress offered by the mainland. Without this laughter, Viola's authority established by her knowledge of her family and of Uncle Spikenard's stories would give similar credence to her claims about the island's relationship to the mainland. But the laughter dislodges the weight and power of Viola's words, and Viola becomes visibly uncomfortable.[13] She averts her gaze and shifts uneasily in her seat. In the face of such laughter, the viewing audience cannot uncritically accept Viola's words. In this scene and throughout the film, Dash positions Black female characters as critical viewers and, through their critical spectatorship, encourages the audience to adopt an oppositional rather than a passive gaze. Bell hooks defines the term "oppositional gaze" as "a site of resistance . . . a critical gaze . . . the power of the dominated to assert agency by claiming and cultivating 'awareness'" (*Black Looks* 116). Through this critical spectatorship, viewers "actively resist the imposition of dominant ways of knowing and looking" (hooks *Black Looks* 128). The moment of exchange between Viola, Yellow Mary, and Trula demonstrates what Janell Hobson describes as Dash's "authority behind the camera to reshape the [viewer's] gaze" ("Viewing" 54). Thus, we can see Viola's colonizing rhetoric as evidence of a system of value to be interrogated and contested.[14]

Although Dash's film intensely criticizes all colonizing gestures, including Viola's expression of Christianity, it does not dismiss her faith tradition. Dash employs the "Hand" ceremony (a ritual of remembering to tie the family together across geographic distance) as a syncretic blend of the various faith traditions represented in the Peazant family: African spirituality, Catholicism, Islam, and Protestant Christianity. Haagar leaves the ceremony in anger, shouting "Hoodoo . . . Hoodoo! Hoodoo mess! Ain't no roots and herbs going to change nothing" (Dash 161). In contrast, Viola overcomes her initial reluctance to stay and participates in it, bending down to kiss both her Bible and the "Hand" that Nana Peazant has created to protect them and bind the family together after the coming migration. This small but momentous gesture marks a considerable shift in Viola's understanding of and relationship to the past. It suggests a growing awareness that progress requires a living connection to the past and to the Sea Islands, facilitated through ancestral memory, rather than a separation from it. As such, Viola's participation suggests that she does have the capacity to resist and alter the colonizing ideologies and practices she has internalized as part of Western Christianity.

Bilal Muhammed

Dash further de-centers Western Christianity as the sole spiritual geography possible for Black people by placing Viola's spiritual journey alongside that of Bilal Muhammed. Viola describes him as "that ol' heathen," but the film's opening tableaux reveals him as a devout man of faith. It challenges other representations from members of the community who describe Bilal and his religious practice as spectacle, including one woman, described as "the hair-braider" in the screenplay, who refers to him as "that old crazy Bilal" (Dash 130). The inclusion of Bilal Muhammed reflects the film's spiritual work, offering multiple images of Black spiritual expression, as well as Dash's cinematic spiritual vision.

Dash based Bilal Muhammed on a historical man by the same name, who lived and practiced Islam in the Sea Islands before the time of *Daughters*. As Dash told hooks in an interview, after being taken from the Sudan at the age of 12, Bilal Muhammed "worked as a slave in the West Indies before being brought to the Sea Islands" (hooks and Dash 36). He retained his spiritual connection to his home in the Sudan through embodied memory, which included transcribing Muslim sacred texts from memory and praying five times a day. As Dash notes, the historical Bilal "never stopped practicing his faith" and passed that spiritual legacy onto his five daughters, who "by the turn of the century [when *Daughters* is set], . . . were still carrying on the tradition of Islam" (36). Her inclusion of Bilal points to the complex spiritual geographies and lineages of Black people and showcases her deployment of what Sheila Smith McKoy terms *diaspora time* as a fundamental expression of her cinematic spiritual vision.[15] Explaining her inclusion of this historical figure from an earlier century, Dash states

"I knew *actually* that he was living and practicing his faith in the 1800s. I wanted him to be a part of this day too" (37).

Her decision to include a historical figure from the century before her film takes place further illustrates the roots of Dash's spiritual practice in a cosmology that views time differently than in Western cultures. As McKoy notes, "time ... in African Diaspora cultures is startlingly different from the ways in which Western cultures construct time" (208). Within West African cultures, from which many African diaspora cultures derive, time is cyclical, rather than linear as conceived in the West, meaning that the past, present, and future are not distinct periods but are connected and fluid. Highlighting this cyclical and fluid nature of what she terms *diaspora time* or *limbo time,* McKoy explains, "the roots of limbo time are located in West African belief in the cycle of time. . . . In essence, tradition binds Diaspora cultures to their African roots across space and time in that the ancestor—the mythical and spiritual embodiment of another time—maintains a constant relationship with the living" (209). Dash's deployment of *diaspora time* becomes evident, then, through the figure of Bilal, who I argue functions as an ancestor—"the mythical and spiritual embodiment of another time." By including a historical figure from a century before the time period of the story, Dash grounds her film even further in the past. Bilal recounts his forced journey to the Sea Islands on a slave ship called *The Wanderer,* providing an ancestral tie to the past for the characters in the film (including Mr. Snead, who interviews him, and Eli, who hears Bilal's story) and for the viewing audience who similarly witnesses Bilal's story.

As a film dedicated to transmitting a more expansive communal history of Black people's experiences of slavery and colonization in the New World (particularly in the US), Dash's inclusion of Bilal Muhammed in her film extends our knowledge about slavery in several key ways. First, his inclusion reflects the diverse physical geographies of Black people who had multiple points of origins and who survived multiple passages throughout the diaspora. Bilal Muhammed's narrative reveals, as Joseph Roach asserts, that the Middle Passage was not necessarily always a transatlantic journey but often times a circum-Atlantic passage uniting multiple locations throughout the diaspora. Not only does Bilal Muhammed's presence in the film demonstrate Dash's desire to showcase the interconnection of Black people across diasporic space, but his presence also makes visible their tangible connection across time.

Like *Daughters of the Dust* itself, Bilal's narrative is a communal spiritual narrative. It reflects the varied spiritual geographies that have shaped and informed Black people's experiences of slavery and colonization. As such, Dash's claim that Bilal Muhammed "never stopped practicing his faith" and her portrayal of him in the film as a devout Muslim man unswayed by others' attempts to convert him to Christianity affirms that Christianity was not the only spiritual force shaping the lives of enslaved Africans brought to the New World. Moreover, Christian conversion reflects just one of many viable spiritual practices open to Black people—many of whom opted for a syncretic blend of Christianity and African-derived spiritual practices as a method of transforming and thereby resisting Christianity as a colonizing force.

Nana Peazant

Nana Peazant's role as the family elder whose mission is to practice, cultivate and pass on alternative ways of knowing highlights the role of African cosmologies as shaping forces in the Gullah community of the Sea Islands. These ways stand in stark contrast to the epistemological, social, and physical violence of the (white) West. Like Bilal Muhammed's, Nana Peazant's presence in the film helps illustrate the spiritual continuities that undermine attempts to strip Black peoples of their spiritual and cultural roots. Through Nana Peazant, the film asserts Black diasporic spiritual practice grounded in African cultures as a defense against slavery, colonization, and their legacies, including physical violence (lynching and rape) and spiritual violence (disconnection and alienation).

The four interconnected dimensions of African cosmologies—the spirit, the community, the family, and the individual—come into play here. As Peter Paris explains, the individual "strives to integrate the [other] three realms in his or her soul" (25). Community, here, includes everything currently in the world (animate and inanimate), extending to unborn children still in the womb, all of which are connected to each other, to God, spirits, and the ancestors (Mbiti 20). Because the realms are interdependent, rather than hierarchical, the individual is not privileged above the community. The individual finds meaning and purpose only in relationship to the larger community of the spirit, tribe, and family.[16] Dash's film invokes this interconnectedness at the heart of this cosmology through countless images, including the colored glass bottles tied to a tree that serve as a reminder of the ancestors, the frizzled hair chicken and newspaper clippings on the wall that are used to ward off evil spirits, Eula's glass of water under her bed that enables her to communicate with her deceased mother, and of course the Unborn Child who is as much a part of this Sea Island community as the living and those who reside in the ancestral realm.

While the principal goal of this African cosmological framework is the achieving of balance and harmony between the various realms and dimensions of life, *Daughters* reveals a spiritual imbalance underpinning the central conflict of the film. This disharmony divides Yellow Mary from her community, as most of the women in it reject her. It comes between Eula and Eli because Eli fears the Unborn Child is the product of rape. It divides Eli and Haagar from Nana Peazant. Eli articulates his disavowal of his great-grandmother's spiritual wisdom and power by destroying the bottle tree, and Haagar calls her embodied spiritual practice "hoodoo mess." Hence, the film portrays disconnection between living members of the family, and disavowal of the elders, ancestors who have passed on, and those yet to be born.

Nonetheless, Nana Peazant determines to restore harmony by binding the family and community together before many of them make the journey north. To do so she calls on the ancestral spirits, the "old souls," to access their spiritual power and help. For example, she brings Eli to visit the grave of her dead husband, Shad Peazant, telling him, "It's up to the living to keep in touch with the dead. . . . Man's power doesn't end with death. We just move on to a new place, a place where we watch over our living family." (Dash 93). In line with this she assures Eli, "you won't ever have a baby that wasn't sent to you. The ancestors and the womb, . . . they're one, they're the same. Those in this grave, like those who're across the sea, they're with us. They're all the same" (Dash 94). Nana Peazant's words reiterate the interdependence, and therefore inseparability, of all life, including those alive, those who have "passed on" and those who have yet to be born, as well as those who survived the Crossing and those who remained behind "across the sea." Thus, she offers Eli a way to access the spiritual power and protection of the ancestors.

But Eli's response challenges Nana Peazant's spiritual vision and the alternative perspective she offers: "How can you understand me and the way I feel? This happened to my wife. My wife! I don't feel like she's mine anymore. When I look at her, I feel I don't want her anymore. . . . Why didn't you protect us, Nana? . . . were the old souls too deep in their graves to give a damn about my wife while some stranger was riding her?" (Dash 95). In his moment of spiritual struggle, Eli falls back into Western patriarchal values. As bell hooks explains, here we see "a connection between . . . [Eli's] patriarchal sense of ownership, and the mentality of the unknown rapist" (hooks and Dash 50). Employing the language of ownership, Eli positions himself as master over Eula's body. As a result, Eli's words foreground the violation of his own patriarchal claim to his wife's body rather than Eula's traumatic experience of violence.

Nana Peazant counters Eli's espousal of Western patriarchal values with her critical reminder that "You can't give back what you never owned. Eula never belonged to you, she married you." Appealing to African spirituality as an alternative source of strength and knowledge, she urges Eli to instead, "Call on those old Africans, Eli. . . . Let those old souls come into your heart, Eli. Let them touch you with the hands of time. Let them feed your head with wisdom that ain't from this day and time. Because when you leave this island . . . you ain't going to no land of milk and honey" (Dash 97). Drawing from her own embodied spiritual practice, Nana Peazant rejects the notion of marriage as ownership of another human being, linking such patriarchal claims of ownership to slavery and the ownership of Black bodies as chattel. Instead, she encourages Eli to draw strength and sustenance from a spiritual tradition and epistemology that promotes embodied healing evident in the incarnational language she uses: "come into your heart," "touch you," "feed your head." As hooks says, "he has another tradition that he can relate to and which can give him a sense of masculinity that is not disrupted by the actions of the oppressor" (hooks and Dash 50). This healing enables a continuity of relationships across time and space in opposition to the white supremacist patriarchal value system that underpins slavery and colonization, as well as the continuing legacies of violence (lynching and rape) that inform the film's broader context and the intracommunal consequences of these legacies of domination.

Nana Peazant's creation of the "Hand" and holding a "Hand" ceremony before the family's departure north broadens her field of spiritual work from the individual (Eli) to collective healing. As she narrates, "I've been working on a plan" (Dash 87). Nana Peazant intends to bind the family together through this ceremony even though they will be separated by time and geographical distance. In her screenplay, Dash describes the "Hand" as "a small leather pouch" sewn together, "a 'charm bag'" (Dash 150). As she sews, Nana Peazant steps into the role of griot, transmitter of communal history and keeper of family memory. Beginning with her own childhood memories, she explains to those around her, "my mother cut this from her hair before she was sold away from us. Now I'm adding my own hair. There must be a bond . . . a connection, between those that go up North, and those who across the sea. A connection!" Nana Peazant includes other "bits and pieces of the 'scraps of memories' from her tin can" in the pouch (Dash 152). Through this oral transmission of her memories and sewing of material artifacts together, Nana Peazant engages in a circum-Atlantic performance. It challenges traditional Western historiography and speaks into the erasures of the archive. Circum-Atlantic performances are grounded in embodied memory and in collective human experience rather than in textual knowledge.[17]

As the earlier disagreement between Mr. Snead and Viola about the end of the slave trade makes visible, Western historiography privileges the written text as fact and singular truth. However, just as Viola's reference to oral ancestral knowledge in the form of Uncle Spikenard's memory challenges the official history of slavery, Nana Peazant's childhood memories reveal the limitations of the dominant historical archive of slavery, which may document the sale of enslaved bodies for profit but fails to record the traumatic impact of family separation resulting from the sale of human beings. Nana Peazant's ceremonial performance via oral transmission of memory and joining of her mother's hair with her own stand in contrast to this erasure. She bears witness to the legacy of slavery's violent separation of families and Black people's resistance to it through the deployment of spiritual practices to remember what has been lost and to rebuild that which has been broken.[18]

Dash's screenplay and subsequent interviews have described *Daughters* as an untold story about slavery and its consequences. This includes the emotional and spiritual impact of slavery's lesser considered violence: separation, dislocation, and alienation. Dash's inclusion of the "Hand" as a literal and figurative collection of memories, showcases the sacred practices Black diasporic peoples employed to counter this legacy of dispossession and loss. While it demonstrates the centrality of the ancestors and the past in holding the family together, Nana Peazant's spiritual practice also reveals the potential power of this sacred object to transform the family and community by healing the divisions among the various members. In the film, after finishing the sewing, Nana Peazant "holds up the 'Hand' she has made, [and] the St. Christopher's charm [that Yellow Mary wears] is wrapped around it. She takes Viola's Bible and lays the 'Hand' on top of it. Then, with a firm grip,

Nana takes a hold of Bilal's shoulder." She then exclaims, "This 'Hand,' it's from me, from us, from them (the Ibo). . . . Just like all of you. . . . Come, children, kiss this hand full of me." (Dash 159).

Nana's "Hand" ceremony reconstitutes community across time, space, and lines of difference. Affirming the interconnection of the family and community across time and geographical distance, the "Hand" unites those who remain across the sea and those ancestors lost, but not forgotten, from the Middle Passage and slavery with the family members who will go north and those who will remain in the South, as well as those yet to be born. As a result, through this sacred ceremony, Nana Peazant as spiritual priestess ensures that the past, present, and future generations remain connected. Her tying together of symbols from Christianity and Santeria with her own spiritually empowered objects and the inclusion of Bilal Muhammed in the ceremony suggests that *Daughters* embraces a kind of religious syncretism that inextricably links the diasporic spaces of Africa and the Americas, including the US, the Caribbean, and Brazil.[19] Much as Nancy Prince did, Nana Peazant reimagines community beyond blood kinship ties through the participation of Bilal and Mr. Snead as well as Eula, who, as some of the older women in the family remind her, is a Peazant by marriage, not by blood. The "Hand" ceremony erases such distinctions, as well as those separating the Muslim Bilal and the northerner, Mr. Snead. It points to the diasporic spiritual legacy of rebuilding community and reconstituting kin in the face of slavery's ongoing legacies of separation, division, and dislocation. In short, the "Hand" ceremony bears witness to the possibilities of restoration and wholeness.[20]

Eula

Although I have positioned Nana Peazant's sacred work as central to the success of the "Hand" ceremony, in truth, Eula Peazant's own embodied spiritual practice makes its communal transformation possible as well. This includes her intervention when Haagar interrupts this ritual to verbally attack Yellow Mary for wanting to remain in Ibo Landing as part of the family and community. During this disruption, Eula calls on the power of the word (Nommo) to help facilitate the healing of the community. According to Janheinz Jahn, Nommo is "the life force, which produces all life, which influences 'things' in the shape of the *word* . . . a unity of spiritual-physical fluidity, giving life to everything, penetrating everything, causing everything. . . . All change, all production and generation are effected through the word" (124–45). Dash's film, like many African cultures, privileges this power of the spoken word (i.e., Nommo) to create and transform.[21] This critical power and knowledge ensures Black people's survival and wholeness in the face of the legacies of colonization and the Middle Passage that threaten to tear them apart. Nana Peazant, for instance, uses this power to call the "old souls" to the aid of Eli and Eula, and to initiate the Unborn Child's entrance into the present.

Eula employs Nommo in similarly empowering and transformative ways. Revealing the embodied nature of her spiritual practice, Eula's body is in visible physical distress when she exclaims to the Peazant women, "If you're so ashamed of Yellow Mary 'cause she got ruined . . . Well, what do you say about me? Am I ruined, too?" (Dash 155). She goes on,

> As far as this place is concerned, we never enjoyed our womanhood. . . . Deep inside, we believed that they ruined our mothers, and their mothers before them. . . . Deep inside we believe that even God can't heal the wounds of our past. . . . Even though you're going up North, you all think about being ruined, too. You think you can cross over to the mainland and run away from it? You're going to be sorry, sorry if you don't change your way of thinking before you leave this place. If you love yourselves, then love Yellow Mary, because she's a part of you. Just like we're a part of our mothers. . . . We're the daughters of those old dusty things Nana carries in her tin can. . . . We carry too many scars from the past. Our past owns us. . . . Let's live our lives without living in the fold of old wounds. (Dash 156–57)

Eula clearly shares Nana Peazant's traditional West African values of community, the ancestors as a key source of spiritual strength and sustenance, the interrelatedness of all beings, and the centrality of the past in shaping the present and the future. Much like the public speech acts Elaw, Smith, and Prince used to teach and reprove others, Eula's monologue places her firmly in the roles of preacher and prophetess—both central expressions of an embodied spiritual practice. Through her prophetic vision, Eula seeks to reshape her listeners' fantasies about the mainland and the North as a "promised land" free from the legacies of anti-Black violence, as well as their misconceptions about themselves, their bodies, and their worth. By naming individual traumas, both her own and Yellow Mary's experiences of rape,

Eula emphasizes the communal nature of such trauma. Her belief, like Nana Peazant's, that we are all connected informs her claim that her trauma and Yellow Mary's is shared and that other women cannot avoid this reality by calling them "ruint."

In her rebuke, Eula highlights how Black women have been denied access to the category of woman because of the dominant construction of the Black female body as inferior and impure. She challenges the dominant claim that "There is nothing sacred about Black women's bodies" (Guy-Sheftall 18). Regardless of whether or not she has been raped, every Peazant woman must realize that to be a Black woman in this place is to be "ruint." All Black women share this history of rape and sexual violence, she argues, referencing "our mothers, and their mothers before them" (Dash 156). Thus, Eula's deployment of the word as sacred practice (Nommo) reunites Black women though this shared history, resisting the disconnection and division resulting from colonial ideologies and legacies of enslavement.

Eula's monologue also emphasizes Black women's participation in such practices of domination through charges of ruination and the use of denigrating words such as "heifer" for Yellow Mary, proving their failure to see the sacredness of all Black female bodies. Eula tells them that they are connected and sacred: "If you love yourselves, then love Yellow Mary, because she's a part of you. Just like we're a part of our mothers." She models an alternative way of being in the world—one grounded in self and communal love rather than in hierarchy and domination. By engaging in a spiritual practice that testifies to her experience of rape and simultaneously claims her body as sacred, Eula disrupts the pure/impure binary used to mark the boundaries of womanhood and demonstrates a paradoxical truth about Black women: as Judith Weisenfeld argues, "potentially devastating experiences" such as sexual violation do not "diminis[h]" "black women's religious power" (55). Like Nana Peazant, Eula understands that the members of the family planning to go north require a spiritual transformation and interior healing so they are prepared to withstand and resist the ideological, linguistic, and physical violence that they will inevitably face.

Eula's speech articulates a healthy relationship to the past as central to individual and collective healing. Like Nana Peazant, she understands that the past shapes who we are and our reality. For Eula, both the past and those who have "passed on" are important sources of strength and sustenance whenever needed. Early in the film, Eula says to Yellow Mary, "My Ma came to me last night, you know. She took me by the hand. . . . I needed to see my

Ma. I needed to talk to her. So I wrote her a letter, put it beneath the bed with a glass of water, and I waited. I waited, and my Ma came to me. She came to me right away" (Dash 119). Eula's claim that her mother comes to her "right away" and takes her by the hand suggests the immediacy with which one can access the ancestral world. She implies that there is no discernable separation between the spiritual and material realms and demonstrates the ancestors' power to easily mediate between a spiritual and material reality. Eula has not imagined this encounter. Rather her mother appears before Eula as real and tangible as if she were still alive. As Nana Peazant explains in the graveyard with Eli, death is not the end for us: "We just move on to a new place, a place where we watch over our living family" (Dash 93).

Yellow Mary teases her for still needing her mother, and implicitly for her spiritual practice as well. But it is clear she has won spiritual strength, comfort, and guidance from ancestral wisdom. The film does not reveal exactly what Eula's mother tells her or what Eula communicates to her mother in her letter, but the viewer assumes she seeks help with the emotional and spiritual distance between her and Eli, her experience of sexual violation, and the impending birth of her first child. Eula's spiritual practice, her ability to find strength, wisdom, and healing from the ancestors, as Nana Peazant urges Eli to do in the graveyard, keeps her grounded and enables her to resist the urge to run away from the past and from trauma. Moreover, unlike others in the family, her spiritual practice keeps Eula from internalizing the dominant cultural and social definition of Black women as not sacred. Rather, Eula reveals the possibilities for healing and points to alternative ways of being in the world. She affirms Nana Peazant's decolonizing vision of community grounded in love as a practice of liberation rather than in hierarchical division and domination. As a result, Eula can assert with confidence to the other Peazant women that despite their shared history of sexual violence and violation, "we're all good women" (Dash 157).

The Unborn Child

The final key element of Dash's cinematic spiritual vision is evident in the continual presence of the Unborn Child throughout *Daughters*. Her spiritual work, along with that of Nana Peazant and Eula, is essential to achieving the communal transformation and healing that the film calls for. Even before she physically appears on screen or before she enters the material world of

Ibo Landing, the Unborn Child's significance to the film becomes evident through her co-narration of the story with Nana Peazant. Through the presence of the Unborn Child as co-narrator, Dash posits a cinematic spiritual vision, an alternative method of viewing and seeing that resists any kind of totalizing knowledge about the community, rejects a linear notion of time, and refuses the privileging of a single telling.

Similar to her deployment of Bilal Muhammed, Dash's inclusion of the Unborn Child challenges a Western linear notion of time. Eli's oldest uncle, Daddy Mac, refers to the Unborn Child as "our child of the future" (Dash 142). Her appearance reveals the collaborative work of the living, the ancestors, and the unborn across time and space. Her first words in the film are "My story begins on the eve of my family's migration North. My story begins before I was born. My great-great-grandmother, Nana Peazant, saw her family coming apart. Her flower to bloom in a distant frontier" (Dash 80). The Unborn Child's presence as an agent in the drama of the story before her physical birth along with Nana Peazant's vision of the future separation of her family and subsequent calling forth of this child from the future to aid her family in the present, reveal *diaspora time* at work in the film. The Unborn Child's co-narration illustrates tangibly the connection and inextricability between the ancestral world and the world of the living, the link between the past, present, and future, as well as the importance of using a multi-perspectival approach when telling a communal spiritual narrative of Black people in the US.

Unlike the single-voiced model of the spiritual narrative exemplified in Zilpha Elaw, Amanda Smith, and to some extent in Nancy Prince's narrative, Dash's film rejects such individualism by adopting a "theoretical stance" that claims there is never just one way of seeing.[22] Adopting a communal and multi-perspectival approach, *Daughters* reminds us, in Brouwer's words, "that we never know everything, and our perceptions are bound by our point of view at any particular moment. . . . There are always other stories to tell, stories which the storyteller ignores while privileging the stories she tells" (11). Rather than privilege a single totalizing viewpoint, which as we have seen in previous chapters is a central characteristic of cultural imperialism, Dash "open[s] up the possibility of varying interpretations," thereby asserting that "many truths exist, and when seen differently by different people in different contexts, they are no less true" (Brouwer 12). As Toni Cade Bambara claims, "The dual narration [that] pulls together the past, present, and future [is] a fitting device for a film paying homage to African retention, to cultural continuum. The duet [between Nana Peazant and the Unborn Child] also prepares us for the film's multiple perspectives. Communalism is the major mode of production. . . . [*Daughters*] asks that the spectator honor multiple perspectives rather than depend on the 'official' story" (124, 133). Thus, *Daughters* resists totalizing truth, much as it did in the opening conflict between Mr. Snead and Viola's contrasting narratives about the slave trade.

Dash's cinematic practice, her embrace of multiple ways of seeing, also becomes evident through the varying ways in which characters in the film interact with the Unborn child. Moreover, their interactions with and relationship to the Unborn Child reveals the characters' differing levels of spiritual awareness and possibilities for growth. Only the children of Ibo Landing can physically see the Unborn Child with the naked eye as they play with her on the beach. Much like their simple appreciation of the kaleidoscope, the children's ability to see and play with the Unborn Child suggests an all-embracing faith in the face of mystery and paradox. Their interactions with the Unborn Child contrast sharply from that of Mr. Snead and Haagar. Though Mr. Snead briefly sees her through his camera lens, he dismisses her as an apparition when she disappears. Haagar does not recognize the Unborn Child's presence, even when the child tugs on her dress. Both have a limited vision that rejects alternative ways of knowing. The camera's capture of the Unborn Child's image points to the possibilities of the camera as a technology that, when in the right hands, has the capacity to expand our vision and transcend our human limitations.[23]

By contrast Nana Peazant and Eula are clearly aware of the Unborn Child's presence through their interactions with her. Moreover, she is significantly linked to both Nana Peazant and Eula's spiritual practices. It is Nana Peazant's calling on the ancestors for help that brings her into the material place of Ibo Landing before her birth, and the Unborn Child tells us that Eula can feel her presence in the world. She states, "Years later, my ma told me she knew I had been sent forward by the old souls" (Dash 133). Hence, even though she is a child still growing in the womb, the Unborn Child engages in an embodied spiritual practice that intersects with Nana Peazant, Eula, and the ancestors.

Describing herself to be on a "spiritual mission," a traveler "on the journey home," the Unborn Child acts as a mediator between the spiritual and material worlds, as well as between the past, present, and future. For example, while the children look at a Sears Christmas catalog entitled the Wish Book, the Unborn Child points at something she wants with an indigo-stained finger. The indigo stain links her to Nana Peazant, whose hands are also stained from working with the indigo dye during slavery. Dash employs the stain imaginatively in her film as a visible embodied marker of slavery, even though historically the dye did not remain on the hands (hooks and Dash 31). As with her inclusion of Bilal Muhammed, here Dash displays her employment of *diaspora time* in the making of her film—revealing the cyclical and fluid nature of the past, present, and future. Thus, the Unborn Child's indigo-stained finger links her in a physical way to slavery even as she represents future generations to come, a sign for all Black diasporic people, the descendants of those who survived enslavement and colonial dominance. In spite of relentless legacies of violence, as the Unborn Child reminds us at the film's end, "we remained" (164). We are still here.

Perhaps the Unborn Child's most important spiritual practice is the healing and reconciliation of her parent's marriage. She leads Eli to the family graveyard where Eula awaits them. Under the power and direction of the spirit, he becomes transformed and able to walk on water while Eula tells the Unborn Child the myth of Ibo Landing. In this myth, the enslaved Ibo walk on the water back to Africa and away from bondage. The screenplay notes explain that Eli has "witnessed and performed things that he could not have done" without the guidance and vision of the ancestral spirit, which includes seeing "that the fury growing inside of Eula's womb is, in fact, his Unborn Child" (Dash 142). This transformative spiritual vision enables the displacement of Eli's patriarchal vision, which defined Eula as "ruint" property, with a non-Western spiritual vision that enables Eli to unconditionally embrace his wife and Unborn Child not as objects to be owned but as sacred beings. In Eula's deployment of Nommo through the retelling of the myth, the past, present, and future intersect, enabling Eli to recognize that the ancestors have sent the Unborn Child to him (Dash 142). In this moment, the womb and the tomb unite, as Eli's encounter with those who have passed on (beyond the grave) and his recognition of the child in Eula's womb enables a kind of spiritual rebirth for Eli and ensures the possibility of new life—not only for Eli but for the next generation.

This scene of Eula's oral storytelling and Eli's rebirth further demonstrates the film's kaleidoscopic vision, as it reflects one of multiple retellings of the Ibo Landing myth, which themselves are a retelling of a passage in

Paule Marshall's novel *Praisesong for the Widow*. By describing the enslaved Africans brought to the Sea Islands the myth gives voice to their experience of captivity and their resistance to it.[24] Eula's recitation to her Unborn Child positions the story as undeniable truth narrating,

> It was here they brought them. They took the Ibo off the boats, right here where we stand. . . . The minute those Ibo were brought ashore, they just stopped, and took a look around. . . . When those Ibo got through sizing up the place real good and seeing what was to come, my grandmother said they turned, all of them, and walked back in the water. . . . They just kept walking, like the water was solid ground. And when they got to where the ship was, they didn't so much as give it a look. They just walked right past it, because they were going home. (Dash 142)

Eula's narration highlights the multiple histories and genealogies of Black people throughout the diaspora. The statement that it was "right here" links the present with the past in a concrete way. As she recollects the "old souls" through her retelling, Eula engages in a spiritual practice of remembering and transferring that memory to her child. She connects them to her present, elaborating that not only were the Ibo able to see "everything that was to happen," but "They even saw you and I standing here." Eula's ability to call forth the ancestors through her retelling of the past and the ability of the Ibo captives to see into the future reveals the permeable boundaries between the past, present, and future.

Bilal Muhammed, however, offers Mr. Snead another telling with a different kind of truth, exclaiming, "I came with the Ibo. Some say the Ibo flew back home to Africa. Some say they all joined hands and walked on top of the water. But, Mister, I was there. Those Ibo, men, women, and children, a hundred or more, shackled in iron . . . when they went down in that water, they never came up. Ain't nobody can walk on water" (Dash 151–52). He acknowledges Eula's version of walking on water as well as an alternative version that the Ibo flew home, while privileging his own telling as absolute truth. But the film refuses to do so. Focusing the camera on Eli while Bilal Muhammed speaks the words "Ain't nobody can walk on water," reminds the viewer that Eli disproved that statement just a few scenes earlier when he walked on water. As the screenplay states: "[Eli] has come from the graveyard and he is walking on the water. Eli is walking toward the floating, rotting, Figurehead broken off years ago from the prow of a slave ship" (Dash 141). The film, therefore, reiterates the possibility that the Ibo did indeed walk home.

Yet the myth's real truth and power lies in its construction and retelling by a community determined to fashion an alternative legacy for themselves and their descendants—a legacy defined by liberation and agency rather than captivity and domination. Through Eula's version, the film gives voice to the community's sacred work of storytelling that Abena Busia defines as possessing the power to restore diasporic subjects to wholeness.[25] Storytelling, then, is both a sacred and decolonizing practice that Dash employs to weave disparate and fragmented histories, identities, and people together.

To do this sacred work, the film rejects the notion of any totalizing truth. In this moment of tension between Eli and Bilal, Dash encourages us as the audience to become active, critical spectators, to decide for ourselves what is possible. Thanks to the critical spiritual work of the film, we must claim our own truth fully aware of the dangers inherent in privileging a particular truth, including the erasure of alternative perspectives, experiences, and ways of knowing.

No character in *Daughters* better demonstrates the inherent dangers of privileging a singular truth than Haagar, who is often portrayed as antagonistic in the film. Scholars have often found her problematic. Linking Dash's Haagar with the biblical figure Hagar, scholar Foluke Ogunleye, asserts, for instance, that "Haagar bears a resemblance to a negative character in the Holy Scriptures. The biblical Hagar is a supplanter who was eventually driven away from Abraham's house, losing the opportunity of being part of the Abrahamic covenant. Dash casts Haagar in the role of outcast as she storms away from the communion scene [Nana Peazant's "Hand" ceremony] without kissing Nana's charms" (163). I have acknowledged that Hagar is a disruptive figure, reading this unruliness as a central characteristic of Black women's embodied spiritual practice. Dash's Haagar is also a disruptive figure.[26] When Viola and the hairbraider try to censor her, she exclaims, "I'm a fully grown woman, and I don't have to mind what I say." Like Hagar's, her unruliness is essential for her survival. Thus, while Hagar's disobedience to Abraham and Sarah serves as a form of resistance to and protection for both herself and her child from abusive treatment, Haagar's tenacious verbal resistance to authority in order to create a better life for her children reveals a capacity to survive even in the face of tremendous obstacles and hostile conditions. As she explains, "I done born five children into the world and put two in the grave alongside their Daddy. I worked all my life and ain't got nothing to show for it" (Dash 129–30).

The similarities between Haagar and Hagar largely end with this tenacity to survive in oppressive conditions. Hagar, for instance, is in a state of involuntary exile within Abraham's household because she has been taken from her own land and enslaved. Hence, when Sarah casts her out, she escapes her enslavement. Haagar's exile, however, is self-imposed. For instance, after yelling "Hoodoo. Hoodoo! Hoodoo mess! Ain't no roots and herbs going to change nothing. Don't go and spoil everything! Old Used-To-Do-It-This-Way don't help none today," according to the script, "Haagar walks away, [then] looks back in anger, ignoring Nana Peazant's open arms and the pleas from her own daughters. Haagar turns inward, perhaps to remain unenlightened and disenfranchised forever" (Dash 161). While Hagar's narrative in Genesis suggests that she will return home to Egypt (Africa) to find a wife for her son, Haagar is clearly fleeing from her physical home and from family connection. Her turning away, therefore, reflects both an external geographical rejection as well as an internal relational rejection of community.

Thus, it is not Haagar's unruliness that makes her a problematic character, as the film showcases Nana Peazant, Eula, Viola, and Yellow Mary engaging in a variety of disruptive practices. Rather the film positions her relationship to the community and to family as a problem. Although Haagar is a Peazant by marriage, Nana Peazant claims her as one of her daughters when she pleads with Haagar, "Come, come child . . . I love you 'cause you're mine" (Dash 161). Not only does Haagar reject her mother-in-law's love and her ancestral inheritance by refusing to participate in the "Hand" ceremony, but she also walks away from her own daughters, who wish to participate. The seriousness and weight of this rejection becomes apparent as Myown cries out desperately to her mother as she leaves, "Mama, please!" Here Nana Peazant and Myown's pleas signify both their sadness that they have lost a loved one but also their fear of the consequences of Haagar's rejection of community. Their grief indicates Dash's clearest assertion in this film that, as Toni Morrison declares "When you kill the ancestor, you kill yourself" ("Rootedness" 64).

Within an African cosmological framework, to reject the lifeline of community and all the spiritual resources that come with it is to threaten one's very survival. This does not necessarily mean those who migrate north have rejected or will reject the lifeline of the community, as the film suggests this turn away from community must be internal as well. Dash's analysis of Haagar's actions in this scene as "self-righteous" point to a clear turn inward for Haagar that accompanies her turning away from community. Furthermore, Dash posits an embrace of individualism at the expense of community as self-destructive. Refusing to equate such individualism with the achievement of enlightenment (i.e., knowledge) and freedom, Dash affirms one can find these spiritual fruits or gifts only in community.

Yellow Mary and Hagar's Return

Although Haagar invokes the biblical figure Hagar with her unruliness and strategies for surviving in the difficult places of life (i.e., the wilderness), I conclude this chapter by positioning Yellow Mary as another possible Hagaric figure. In the beginning, the film portrays Yellow Mary as a wanderer, an itinerant figure with a propensity for movement. She explains to Eula, "The only way for things to happen or for people to change is to keep moving. People sitting still, men sitting still, don't get it with me, y'know" (Dash 121). Similar to Hagar's, Yellow Mary's journeys are informed by exploited labor, captivity, flight, and return. Though she initially leaves the Sea Islands of her own accord, she ends up traveling to Cuba for economic reasons—in service as a wet nurse and nanny to a white family in Cuba. Though she expresses her desire to leave the family after the husband rapes her, as Yellow Mary retells it, "I wanted to go home [to Ibo Landing] and they keep me . . . they keep me" (126). Following in a long legacy of Black women travelers before her, Yellow Mary's travel initially begins as a migratory journey to improve her economic status. However, her mobility is compromised as she becomes, like Hagar, a captive body exploited for domestic and sexual labor. As such, Yellow Mary bears witness to slavery's afterlife; its recurring legacies of violence and captivity continue to threaten the mobility of Black women across time periods and geographical boundaries. Despite the persistent dangers Black women face, Yellow Mary's disparate journeys and spiritual practice point to the alternative inheritance Hagar offers her daughters: a legacy of Black female mobility as well as resistance to the practices of captivity and violence that seek to hold them in place. For instance, Dash explains in her screenplay that Yellow Mary escaped her captivity and sexual exploitation in Cuba by using "a folk remedy to dry up her breast milk" (126). Thus, like Hagar's disobedience to Sarah and flight into the wilderness, Yellow Mary employs creative practices of resistance to regain her freedom and mobility.

Like the biblical Hagar and unlike the film's Haagar, Yellow Mary returns home. While Haagar turns away from community and rejects her ancestral spiritual inheritance, Yellow Mary returns to the community in search of home—a place of belonging and a deep desire for reconnection. Initially she plans only to visit Ibo Landing, as she and Trula have plans to go to Nova Scotia. However, by the end of the film she changes her mind. Nana Peazant's "Hand" ceremony creates for Yellow Mary a thorough spiritual transformation. She announces to Nana Peazant and for all to hear, "I'm not like the other women here. But I need to know that I can come home, . . . to hold on to what I came from. I need to know that the people here know my name. I'm Yellow Mary Peazant! And I'm a proud woman, not a hard woman. I want to stay. I want to stay and visit with you here" (Dash 154). Yellow Mary's own words testify to her status as a disruptive figure—a woman whose sexuality, her experience of rape, prostitution, and her same-sex relationship, mark her as strange and seemingly out of place in Ibo Landing. Her return to the Sea Islands proves disruptive for the Peazant family even as her journey home facilitates a powerful spiritual transformation for herself and for the larger community.

The film heightens Yellow Mary's disruptive potential by visually contrasting Yellow Mary and Viola, who share a boat ride to Ibo Landing in the opening, as well as through the characters' descriptions of her. While Viola returns wearing a conservative plain-style dress with a Bible and a photographer, Yellow Mary returns wearing an ornate dress with a can of store-bought biscuits and her lover beside her. As Sheila Petty has noted, these visual cues contrast Viola's bodily and spiritual purity with Yellow Mary's worldly life and her transgressive potential (92–93). Further inscribing her status as out of place through language, several of the women in the Peazant family call her "heifer," while Viola laments "all that yellow wasted," suggesting that Yellow Mary has squandered her greatest asset: light skin.

Paule Marshall's *Praisesong for the Widow*'s description of the conflicted positioning of light skin within the Black community sheds light on Yellow Mary's status. Light skin, Marshall writes, is "[a] color both sacred—for wasn't it a witness?—and profane: 'he forced my mother my mother / late /

One night / What do they call me?'" (19). Marshall's words point to both the prizing of light skin, but also to its shameful origins in interracial rape. Thus, Viola's and the other women's words reveal a collective desire for and valuing of Yellow Mary's skin tone even as that skin tone serves as a visual reminder that the Black female body is, as Jeannine King asserts, "violable, not sacred" (480).

Even some of the Peazant children join in the verbal ostracizing of Yellow Mary, as one of them exclaims, "Yellow Mary's no family woman, she's a scary kind of woman" (Dash 123). The characters' demeaning and dehumanizing language reinscribes dominant ideologies of race, gender, and sexuality—marking Yellow Mary's body as devalued, beyond the category of woman, and therefore as less than fully human. Much like the biblical figure Hagar, Yellow Mary's disruptive potential lies not only in her sexually transgressive body but also in her disordering of the domestic space, which she rejects in the film by exclaiming, "You know I don't like messing around in no kitchen" (Dash 112). She, therefore, rejects the dominant ideology of true womanhood that continued to shape the expectations for women at the turn of the twentieth century when *Daughters* takes place.

Although Eula and Yellow Mary are both victims of rape, the Peazant family defines Yellow Mary as particularly "ruint" because of her disruptive embodied practice—one that makes her sexuality visible and that gives voice to the realities of sexual violence that many of the Peazant women would rather keep silent. Eula rejects that silence, but only after Yellow Mary connects them in the only instance of a character in the film using the term rape. In the scene that follows one in which Myown describes her as "a new kind of woman," Yellow Mary tells Eula of the rape she has suffered in response to Eula's own disclosure: "[T]he raping of colored women is as common as the fish in the sea," she says (Dash 123). It is the only moment in the film that defines sexual violation as an act of violence and terror against Black women rather than as a condition (i.e., "ruint") that shames and devalues them. Notably, Yellow Mary also links this violence against Black women with lynching—violence used to punish and keep Black men and women silent. She counsels Eula not to tell Eli who raped her because, "There's enough uncertainty in life without having to sit at home wondering which tree your husband's hanging from" (Dash 124). However, this is a selective silence, and throughout this scene Yellow Mary reveals her commitment to truth-telling within the Black community, as she is honest about who she is, where she has been, and the struggles she has faced. Through her willingness to tell the truth, Yellow Mary disrupts the silence and shame around sexual violence and bears witness to lynching and rape (including her captivity in Cuba) as practices of terror employed by white Americans to extend slavery's hold into the twentieth century.[27]

It is Eula who commanded the Peazant women to "love Yellow Mary," and invites them, "Let's live our lives without living in the fold of old wounds," after which Nana Peazant, Yellow Mary, and Eula share an embrace. In this moment, the film affirms that such an embrace is central to individual healing and to the restoration and spiritual growth of the entire community. Yellow Mary's reclamation as a pathway to healing and wholeness similarly points to the necessity of reclaiming Hagar. In a sense, Yellow Mary's return marks a kind of figurative homecoming for the biblical Hagar, whose own exilic journey I have argued must finally come to an end. Throughout this study, I have sought to embrace Hagar and her many daughters—returning her to rightful place in a lineage of spirit-filled Black women. By reclaiming Hagar and her spiritual daughters, we reject slavery's legacy of dispossession and alienation. *Daughters of the Dust* reveals that our alternative spiritual inheritance is grounded in collective liberation, interdependence, as well as a connection to the past and those who have come before.

The central project of *Daughters* is in many ways similar to my own—to reconsider the often-silenced and usurped voices of Black women, who like Hagar, Zilpha Elaw, Amanda Smith, Nancy Prince, Viola, Nana Peazant, Eula, and Yellow Mary have had their stories rendered invisible, marginalized, and misrepresented. Just as my project seeks to expand our understanding of and approach to Black women's spirituality and mobility, Dash, through her *cinematic decolonization,* rejects dominant ways of viewing and seeing Blackness, and especially Black femaleness in film. Rather than reproduce this legacy of marginalization and misrepresentation, *Daughters* offers us a new vision, a new story—one that calls for a critical awareness of the diverse spiritual geographies of Black people throughout the diaspora and, therefore, a more expansive portrait of Blackness. Stepping into the role of "modern-day griot" as Jennifer Marchiorlatti describes her, Dash wields cinematic storytelling to do the sacred and transformative work of reconstituting Black humanity and Black community in critical response to the many divisions and hierarchies caused by slavery, colonization, and their legacies. Thus, her film reminds us that stories matter. The stories we tell about Black people have real-world consequences. They not only tell us who we have been and how we came to be in the present, but they can also show us who we might become in the future. With chapter 6, the final chapter of *Spirit Deep,* I turn to Saidiya Hartman's *Lose Your Mother,* a travel narrative that extends this spiritual work of recovery and storytelling into the twenty-first century—considering the challenges and possibilities of such a critical practice in a more contemporary context.

· SIX ·

Secular Journeys, Sacred Recovery in Saidiya Hartman's *Lose Your Mother*

> I am a reminder that twelve million crossed the Atlantic Ocean and the past is not yet over. I am the progeny of the captives. I am the vestige of the dead. And history is how the secular world attends to the dead.
> —Saidiya Hartman, *Lose Your Mother*

This final chapter focuses on Saidiya Hartman's 2007 work of travel writing, *Lose Your Mother: A Journey along the Atlantic Slave Route,* and expands my discussion of the significance of Black female mobility in two key ways. First, Hartman's text extends the legacy of Black travel into the late twentieth and early twenty-first centuries. Second, Hartman demonstrates the inextricable link between Black people's journeys in the past and in the present while inviting us to locate their varied movements within the broader context of Western travel. Her text interweaves several strands: It chronicles her personal travel to and throughout Ghana as a Fulbright Scholar. It also recounts the perspectives of the Ghanaian people she encounters along her journey and the experiences of African Americans who emigrated to Ghana in the 1950s and 60s in search of "a free territory," a livable place free from racial injustice and terror. Finally, it includes Hartman's imaginative and critical retellings of historical events from the Middle Passage. *Lose Your Mother* is more than an autobiography and more than a personal travel account—it is a work of cultural history aimed at retrieving and reimagining those voices lost or silenced by the official historical record. Thus, Hartman continues the important cultural, political, and spiritual work of recovery and of constructing new stories about slavery and about Black people's ongoing freedom struggles that have echoed across the previous chapters in this study.

In the prologue, Hartman explains that she first visited Ghana as a tourist in the summer of 1996. She then returned in 1997 for a year-long stay as a Fulbright Scholar to research slavery. As Hartman describes it, her project worked toward the retrieval of the voices and lives of the captives who have been lost, forgotten, or silenced. Its objective was to bridge the profound divide between the past of slavery and what she terms its afterlife—the "skewed life chances, limited access to health and education, premature death, incarceration, and impoverishment" Black people in the US continue to face (6). She writes, "Slavery had established a measure of man and a ranking of life and worth that has yet to be undone. If slavery persists as an issue in the political life of black America, it is . . . because black lives are still imperiled and devalued by a racial calculus and a political arithmetic that were entrenched centuries ago. This is the afterlife of slavery" (6). Like Julie Dash's 1991 film *Daughters of the Dust,* Hartman's travel narrative makes visible the inextricable link between then and now, between past and present. Hartman claims that "[s]lavery is a dimension of the present that we're still living" (Hartman et al. 111). Her journey moves beyond the singular narratives about slavery in an attempt to overcome erasures and silences in the historical archive as well as active practices of forgetting. These narratives conflate Black people's experience of slavery in the past and its consequences in the present ignoring the realities of class, geographical, and national difference. Hartman identifies these silences and erasures as fueling the continued experience of alienation that delimits Black life in the US. Hence, historical recovery becomes one critical method Hartman employs to challenge the singular narrative of slavery with all of its accompanying silences and erasures.

Hartman chooses Ghana to engage in this work because of its central role in the slave trade and "because it possessed more dungeons, prisons, and slave pens than any other country in West Africa" (7). She also names the long legacy of Western travel to the country as a factor. The journeys of African American tourists and émigrés seeking to bridge the divide between their African and American selves as well as the colonial journeys of European travelers shape and inform her contemporary journey. In retracing their steps from the West to Ghana, Hartman challenges the blindness of Western travelers and the subsequent historical and literary erasures reproduced in their writing about Africa. In so doing she develops and employs a critically self-aware and expansive gaze in her encounters with Ghanaian people that enables her to tell and reclaim stories of Africa and of African people long silenced.

Hartman's text extends her critical gaze to her own historical project by foregrounding the limits of recovery practices and the challenges she faces in her attempt to recuperate the voices and lives of enslaved people. In spite of this emphasis on the failures of her work, I align Hartman's practices with those of Julie Dash because of the centrality of storytelling to their critical and spiritual work. Both Hartman and Dash push beyond the limits of the historical archive and the singular narrative constructed about slavery and about enslaved people and their descendants by offering alternative narratives of the past that reimagine Black people's lives. Through her attempts to offer a "fuller portrait" of their lives, Hartman, like Dash, engages in decolonizing work that challenges the archive's violent fragmentation and disfiguration of Black lives by constructing a counternarrative that makes visible the humanity of enslaved people. Although Hartman defines her project as secular, I position her commitment to wholeness, to a fuller portrait of Black life, and to freedom, as sacred work because her work reaffirms the sanctity of Black life and demonstrates a deep-rooted belief in the possibility for a liberated future. In this sense, Hartman continues the legacy of Black women travelers foregrounded in previous chapters.

Slavery is the thematic and historical throughline that persists across all of the texts in my study, from Hagar's narrative through the spiritual autobiographies of Zilpha Elaw, Amanda Berry Smith, and Nancy Prince, as well as the multiple journeys of Black people foregrounded in *Daughters of the Dust* and *Lose Your Mother*. Although Hartman possesses Western and class privilege, her experience as "a descendent of the enslaved" (Hartman 6) in the US informs her journey and the shape of her narrative, much as it did for Elaw, Smith, and Prince. Hartman's text reminds us, therefore, that it is impossible to talk about Black people's legacy of travel without talking about slavery. Moreover, like *Daughters,* Hartman's book reveals the intersection of the Atlantic slave trade with other diasporic journeys that resulted from slavery: the journeys of her ancestors who migrated from the Caribbean to the US, the journeys of Black people who returned to West Africa, especially Ghana, as émigrés seeking to escape the confines of Jim Crow, de facto segregation, and anti-Black violence in the US, the journeys of African American tourists in search of their roots, and even the journeys of flight that fugitives in Ghana embarked on in order to escape the reach of the slave trade as it devastated the country.

The complexity of these disparate, yet intersecting journeys, including those of European colonizers to Africa, demonstrates Hartman's own critical practice—moving beyond singular narratives by embracing multiperspectival storytelling. Like Julie Dash's diasporic spiritual practice in *Daughters*, Hartman's critical practice foregrounds alternative ways of knowing that challenge colonizing practices and hierarchies. Hartman's literary decolonization, visible through the structure of her travel narrative, mirrors Dash's cinematic decolonization. Moreover, her text demonstrates that decolonization informs her bodily practice, meaning how she moves through and engages with the world around her. Through her rhetorical and physical movements (literary and bodily practice), Hartman challenges the colonial roots of European and African American travel to Africa and contests the narrow representation of Blackness reproduced by the historical record. Like *Daughters of the Dust*, Hartman's *Lose Your Mother* showcases the complexity of Black being, mobility, and spirituality.

The fluid and multiple journeys Hartman foregrounds in *Lose Your Mother* require that we move beyond frameworks focused solely on a single type of journey. While current scholarship on *Lose Your Mother*, offers a cogent analysis of memory and loss in Hartman's text, it does not consider the text as a work of travel writing.[1] As such, this scholarship does not consider the text in light of the continuities across varied kinds of journeys—coerced and voluntary—and the intersections between them. Hartman's interweaving of such journeys throughout her narrative demands a scholarly approach that addresses the fluidity and multiplicity of her text. As Alasdair Pettinger and Angela Shaw-Thornburg note, if we are to move Black travel writing to the foreground of academic study, we must employ new and alternative approaches that can expand beyond incomplete readings of African American literary texts.[2] This chapter enacts their vision by offering a more expansive reading of *Lose Your Mother* that foregrounds Hartman's critical engagement with a long legacy of Western and Black travel to Africa.

Although Hartman traveled as an academic scholar and with no explicit spiritual purpose, *Lose Your Mother* fits into this book's explorations of the spiritual journeys of Black women by revealing the thematic and historical continuities across the centuries. By ending my study of African American women's spirituality and travel with Hartman's travel narrative, I aim to make these continuities and intersections across their differing texts and journeys more apparent. My intersectional approach creates opportunities for new dialogues that illustrate the ongoing and continuing significance of earlier Black women's journeys and narratives for our understanding of and approach to Black women's diasporic movements in the twentieth and twenty-first centuries.

In addition to extending the legacy of Black women's travel, *Lose Your Mother* also expands the legacy of Black women's spiritual work that the previous chapters bear witness to. Though Hartman characterizes her work in Ghana as academic and therefore as secular, spirituality and movement intersect within her narrative. My analysis of Hartman's text makes legible the sacred within her journey and especially within her recovery efforts. As such, my analysis disrupts the binaries between sacred and secular, especially the binary between academic and spiritual work Hartman constructs in her text.

Hartman's embodied spiritual practice includes her travel to Ghana, her movements within various spaces along the slave route, and her employment of vision and imagination as tools of decolonization. M. Jacqui Alexander's conception of decolonizing work is instructive for positioning Hartman's commitment to decolonization as spiritual work. She begins by defining *colonization* as a "process of fragmentation" that is "linked in minute ways to dualistic and hierarchical thinking: divisions among mind, body, spirit; between sacred and secular" and as instrumental "in creating singular thinking" (281). Given this definition of colonization grounded in division and separation, the political work of *decolonization* becomes fundamentally about satisfying "the deep yearning for wholeness" by engaging in practices of interconnection and interdependence—practices that reflect the intersection of mind, body, and spirit—of sacred and secular. Because, as Alexander explains, "enforced separations wreak havoc on our Souls," we must build bridges across that which would divide us to return to a state of wholeness and reconnection (281). Extending Alexander's definition of colonization and of decolonizing practices as spiritual work to Hartman's own project, I link her own bridge building work to a similar *yearning for wholeness* and to a similar rejection of *singular thinking* that threatens to fragment and divide. Hartman's decolonizing practice and commitment to wholeness becomes evident through her relentless critique of colonization and its hierarchies, her attempts to redress the violence of the archive by creating a counter-history that humanizes rather than objectifying the captives, and through her commitment to cross-cultural dialogue with the Ghanaian people she encounters even when their differing perspectives challenge her own.

Beyond a Single Story: Hartman's Critical Vision

Hartman's travel to West Africa and her journey through Ghana locates her within a much broader tradition of African American travel to Africa, which spans over two centuries. In this *Lose Your Mother* reflects the intersection of Africa and Black people's deep yearning to belong. As James Campbell asserts, "Africa has served historically as one of the chief terrains on which African Americans have negotiated their relationship to American society" (xxii). As he notes, African American travelers to Africa such as Langston Hughes, Richard Wright, Gwendolyn Brooks, and Maya Angelou embarked on their journeys with an imagined view of the continent as "an idyllic homeland" (Campbell xxi). Hartman distinguishes herself from this view, writing that unlike so many African American travelers before her "neither blood nor belonging accounted for my presence in Ghana" (7). Like Amanda Berry Smith, she rejects the idea of the continent as home. Yet she shares other African American travelers' desire for belonging.

Hartman opens her travel text by illustrating her positioning in Ghana as *obruni*, meaning stranger, a word Ghanaian children use to address her. Describing such an interaction as her "welcome" to the country, Hartman explains, "Obruni forced me to acknowledge that I didn't belong anyplace. . . . I was born in another country, where I also felt like an alien and which in part determined why I had come to Ghana. I had grown weary of being stateless. Secretly I wanted to belong somewhere or, at least, I wanted a convenient explanation of why I felt like a stranger" (4). Although she may have harbored an image of an idyllic homeland at one time, as the narrative unfolds Hartman's self-positioning as a stranger in Ghana enables her to navigate and resist the long legacy of Africanist discourse. This beginning allows her to move beyond limited representations of Africa as either dream or nightmare—representations that erase the complexities of the continent and its varied peoples.[3] John Gruesser's article "Afro-American Travel Literature and Africanist Discourse" reveals that African American travel writers have often participated in such erasure. Defining Africanist discourse as "texts written about Africa by Western authors" (5), he writes that their deployment of Africanist discourse "has frequently stymied the attempts of Afro-Americans to produce more accurate depictions of the continent than those of their white counterparts" (5). Hartman, however, as this chapter will demonstrate, rejects this dichotomy in her refusal to position Africa as "an idyllic homeland" or as "a grave" (233).

In contrast to the persistent erasures and silences expressed in travel writing about Africa, Hartman's narrative offers an expansive vision of Ghana and of the African people she encounters even as she remains critically aware of the limitations of her own perspective as a privileged Western traveler. This tension between shortsightedness and vision, between blindness and sight, echoes throughout Hartman's narrative as John and Mary Ellen Ray, Black émigrés she meets in Ghana, continually remind her to "open your eyes" and to "get out and see" (173, 176). At Hartman's first stop for lodging in Ghana, the Marcus Garvey House, Stella the housekeeper tells her, "No matter how big a stranger's eyes, they cannot see" (21). Hartman herself echoes the sentiment a page later noting, "I doubted whether my way of seeing things had any footing in reality" (21–22). This foregrounding of blindness highlights Hartman's limited perspective and failure as a witness. Accordingly, it destabilizes the traditional status of travelers as authoritative and objective witnesses. From this place of failure Hartman works to develop a practice of vision rooted in liberation, rather than domination. She pushes beyond what Mary Louise Pratt identifies in *Imperial Eyes: Travel Writing and Transculturation* as the common self-positioning of European travelers to Africa as innocent and passive. Pratt links colonial practices of seeing and observation that Hartman rejects with violence and domination. Hartman acknowledges her culpability for such practices even as she tries to resist an active participation in the violence of erasure that her limited vision and shortsightedness enacts.

Hartman's critical preoccupation with blindness and travel persists in chapter 9 "The Dark Days," which foregrounds tropes of blindness and sight in order to challenge traditional Western conceptions of vision, as well as conceptions of light and dark. For a time she ignores John and Mary Ellen's advice to explore her surroundings, to see that "the zone of privilege doesn't extend very far." Hartman finally does "get out and see" after a power outage in Osu plunges her into darkness (176). This power outage erases, if only temporarily, access to electricity, which is a major class division in Osu. Hartman describes herself as "unprepared" for the outage even though she knew "at least 60 percent of Ghanaians regularly lived without electricity" (173). The darkness becomes an opportunity for reflection on the physical darkness around her—an opportunity to expand beyond typical literary representations of darkness.[4] She observes a "kind of velvety black that was rare ever to see in cities, because artificial light robbed the sky of this jetty density" (174). Navigating Osu at night with a flashlight, Hartman contrasts fears she would have had of being assaulted in New York or Oakland with her sense of safety in Osu. Hartman's descriptors, *velvety* and *jetty density*, represent the darkness as soft and smooth, a protective cover that envelops her. Her absence of fear as she walks through Osu suggests that darkness is not inherently fearful or terrifying. Location matters. This walk opens up possibilities and discoveries for Hartman. As she notes, "over the course of weeks, I began to experience a kind of relief when the lights went out, as if the world were meeting me on my own terms or pardoning me from my flawed perception. The darkness provided a welcome retreat from my failure [to understand Ghana] and, to my surprise, the threshold to a world I had failed to notice" (175).

Nonetheless darkness also makes Hartman aware of her own blindness before the power outage. Hartman explains, "the people hidden from view and the things I had failed to notice now bumped into me in the night. . . . In the deep hole of night lived all the people whom I passed by during the day but failed to see. . . . The beggars, the poor, . . . the toilers who tidied and swept the world for those who owned it . . . all resided in this nocturnal world" (175–76).

Beyond her own personal failures, Hartman seeks to locate her journey as a Western traveler to Ghana within the broader legacy of colonial travel to Africa. For Hartman, the tension between blindness/sight and between darkness/light reflects a key intersection between her own travel and colonial journeys. "I was self-conscious about my flashlight," she writes, saying she "feared it was the equivalent of the pith helmet worn by colonial administrators. Illuminating the world seemed like an act of violence" (174). Here Hartman reveals how metaphors of darkness and light inform colonial journeys to Africa, within which colonizers positioned themselves as bearers of light over and against the darkness of Africa and of African people.[5] Hartman locates her mobile practices within this broader legacy, as she connects her own flashlight with a history of colonial violence. This critical shift introduces a new perspective, a new way of seeing her own journey and the Ghanaian people she encounters—a perspective that is crucial to her practice of bridge building across the disparate journeys of African Americans and Africans.

Hartman's practice of vision demonstrates, as Charmaine Nelson claims that the "process of vision, of viewing, is classed, raced, and sexed, and the way one sees and what one sees are both products of that person's identification and location and a part of what confirms and reinstates both.

Viewers do not merely see what *is*. Rather, vision must be addressed not as a process of objective reading but as a process through which identifications are imagined and assigned" (xiv). Nelson's theorizing of vision illuminates Hartman's own critical viewing practices which similarly reject the notion of vision as singular or objective. Throughout her narrative, Hartman engages in a decolonizing viewing practice that embraces a multiplicity of gazes and multiple ways of seeing the spaces she moves through, the people she encounters in the present, as well as various ways of seeing the past. Given M. Jacqui Alexander's definition of colonization as a "process of fragmentation" (281), I position Hartman's own viewing practice as decolonized because her bridge-building work reflects a process of interconnection and interdependence—a practice that embraces multiplicity, complexity, and even contradiction over the ease of simplistic binaries.

Juxtaposing her own decolonized viewing practice against a colonized vision, Hartman explains,

> I lived in darkness, not the darkness of African inscrutability or the gloomy cast of a benighted landscape but rather in a blind alley of my own making, in the deep hole of my ignorance. . . . In Western philosophy . . . [n]ot being able to see clearly is tantamount to ignorance, and since early modernity the ignorance of the West had been projected onto Africa—the heart of darkness, the dark continent, the blighted territory. But I knew better. My flashlight was a defense not against dark, dark Africa but against my own compromised sight, my own thickheadedness. I had been in Ghana nearly half a year and I barely understood the world around me. (174–75)

Here Hartman links her inability to see, her failure as witness, to a long legacy of Western blindness in Africa. Yet she also asserts a critical difference, saying, "I knew better." That is, unlike colonizing predecessors, she knows how not to project her own blindness onto Africa or onto the African people she encounters. Instead, she claims ownership of her blindness and employs a critical practice that enables her to explore its roots and consequences. Reversing her gaze, Hartman turns inward to expose her own interior failings, flaws, and limitations rather than projecting the fear of such failure and limitation onto the bodies of "others" deemed strange and alien. Ultimately, Hartman's self-positioning as stranger and as foreign enables her to resist the violence of colonial vision that seeks instead to project that strangeness and foreignness onto African people.

Hartman's resistance to colonial journeys to Africa persists as she situates her own travel, tenuously, within a legacy of African American émigrés. According to Hartman, "[t]he revolutionaries had come to Ghana believing they could be made anew, reborn as the African men and women they would have been had their ancestors not been stolen four hundred years ago. . . . They left the [United] States hoping to leave slavery behind too. America had made them, but Ghana would remake them. They had faith that the breach of the Middle Passage could be mended and orphaned children returned to their rightful homes" (39).[6] Although Hartman questions their faith, slavery also propelled her across the Atlantic. Like the revolutionaries, she too had a yearning to belong, for a country "in which your skin wasn't a prison." Hartman conveys this shared longing with the question, "What orphan had not yearned for a mother country or a free territory?" (39).

Yet Hartman asserts her unequivocal difference from the revolutionaries: "The dreams that defined their horizon no longer defined mine. The narrative of liberation had ceased to be a blueprint for the future. The decisive break the revolutionaries had hoped to institute between the past and the present failed" (39). She shares their longing but has a starkly different vision of the past and of the future. For instance, Hartman claims, "While the Afros [revolutionaries] were far too intelligent to believe the past could be forgotten, they definitely wanted their distance from slavery and colonialism. They valued history to the extent that it aided the task of liberation. So it was more common for them to disparage the slave mentality than to claim the slave" (40). They construct, she writes, "a grand narrative" of a glorious African past in order to "reverse the course of history, eradicate the degradation of slavery and colonialism, and vindicate the race" (40). By contrast Hartman claims enslaved ancestors and the reality of slavery as part of her inheritance. She criticizes their practices as creating separation and division. As Hartman's passage illustrates, the revolutionaries' desire for distance from the past, from slavery, and from colonialism, as well as their refusal to claim "the slave," reinforces the break the Middle Passage caused and reinforces colonial divisions.

Moreover, though their vision for the future expressed through Pan-Africanism reflects a desire for belonging and connection, Hartman's critique reveals the limitations of this political vision that constructs a singular view of Africa. While Pan-Africanism is an ideology and social and political movement based on the assertion of a unified Africa, its definition is complex and varied—often manifesting differently on the Continent than throughout the diaspora, which explains one source of conflict between African Americans and Ghanaian people that Hartman attests to in her book.[7] Thus the revolutionaries' vision of a glorious return and redemption that can wash away the shame and pain of the past rests on multiple erasures. As Hartman notes, "Utopias always have entailed disappointments and failures. They cast a harsh light on the limits of our imagination, underscore our shortsightedness, and replicate the disasters of the world we seek to escape." Revealing the nightmare beneath the dream, Hartman reiterates that utopia "never turns out to be the perfect society. Look hard enough and you'll . . . see the African elites . . . fashioning themselves after Europe's kings and the captives trailing behind them in tow. You'll discern the disease of royalty beneath the visage of eternal glory. You'll witness the dream of freedom crash and burn" (46). This passage clearly challenges the revolutionaries' utopic vision of Ghana as Hartman's description links "the visage of eternal glory" to disease and posits "the dream of freedom" as a destructive vision. Moreover, utopia blinds us precisely because it rests on an erasure of the past and on a narrow vision for the future.

Disconnected from history and from the lived experience of African people in the present, the revolutionaries' romanticized vision of Africa and of Ghana ignores the deep divisions between Africans and African Americans, including the complicity of African people in slavery, differing experiences of racism, and class hierarchies. Hartman finds, as Kevin Gaines did, that Ghanaian people "did not share African Americans' sensitivity to white racism" and "many Ghanaians considered African Americans much better off for their enslaved ancestors' travails and misfortune" (Gaines 157, 283). Hence, the dream of freedom in Ghana depends on the silencing and erasure of the ongoing impact of slavery, colonization, and class hierarchies in Ghana. Like Hartman's initial blindness in "The Dark Days," the blindness of the émigrés, she argues, only exacerbated their sense of alienation and further divided them from the very people with whom they wished to belong.

Seeking to expand beyond the shortsightedness of the revolutionaries, Hartman works hard to distance her own journey to Ghana from theirs, as well as that of some African Americans who followed them, "scores of black tourists who, motivated by Alex Haley's *Roots*, had traveled to Ghana and other parts of West Africa to reclaim their African patrimony" (41). She notes Maya Angelou's curious avoidance of the slave forts in her 1962 journey to Ghana and Sylvia Boone's description of the country as "a dream come true" in her 1974 travel guide, disputing the positioning of Ghana as a glorious return to African Americans' homeland.[8] She claims this distance for herself and her contemporaries, emphasizing, "My generation was the first that came here with the dungeon as our prime destination. . . . For me, the rupture was the story. Whatever bridges I might build were as much the reminder of my separation as my connection" (41–42). The intersection and divergence of Hartman's journey from preceding travelers becomes apparent in the tension between connection and separation. Through her recovery efforts, Hartman seeks a connection between the past and the present and a way across the breach in her identity as African American—the break caused by the Middle Passage. In opposition to the desire for kinship and return, stemming from "the sickness of nostalgia" (Hartman 106), she embraces bridge building as a critically engaged practice that requires wrestling with the complex and varied histories and geographies of African-descended people in the past, as well as confronting the multiplicity of their experiences in the present. Moreover, her words illustrate that the bridge she seeks to build is tenuous and shaped as much by separation and loss as it is by connection.

This tension ultimately saves her reclamation and her imagining of the past from nostalgia. Locating nostalgia at the heart of her critique of Pan-Africanism in her article "The Time of Slavery," Hartman claims "the desire for . . . a return to ancestral land, an abiding nostalgia, and unmet and perhaps unrealizable longings for solidarity throughout the black world" as the animating force of Pan-Africanism (759). Nostalgia, with its desire for an idyllic return, inevitably erases the separation and rupture between Africa and the diaspora. Thus, Hartman's tethering her project of bridge building to this separation and loss enables her own vision of the present (and future) to push beyond the limitations of a utopian vision that foregrounds the experiences of African Americans over that of Africans from the continent. For Hartman, nostalgia also reflects an active rejection of history. As Svetlana Boym explains, nostalgia is "a longing for a home that no longer exists or has never existed. Nostalgia is a sentiment of loss and displacement, but it is also a romance with one's own fantasy. Nostalgic love can only survive in a long-distance relationship" (151). The romance and fantasy at the heart of nostalgia conflicts with Hartman's own practice of freedom, her attempt to construct a more expansive vision of the past and the present. Conversely, nostalgia "desires to obliterate history and turn it into private or collective mythology"—a fantasy "determined by the needs of the present" (Boym 152). This erasure of history leads to the narrow utopian vision that she resists throughout her narrative. In the case of the émigrés or revolutionaries, their desire for a glorious past that can redeem their inheritance of enslavement inevitably requires the obliteration of "the slave"—an act of violence that Hartman bears witness to again and again in her narrative.

Even in the slave forts, where Hartman initially begins her research in Ghana, she finds this obliteration of history and the erasure of the lives of enslaved people. Though these structures were built to hold captives before transporting them to the Americas for sale, the Ghanaian government has transformed many of them into museums as a way to facilitate tourism. Hartman criticizes this industry known as roots, or heritage tourism, which seeks to profit from the desire for return, belonging, and home through the creation of goods and experiences.[9] Through her own visit, Hartman reveals how the narratives of redemption, progress, and nostalgic return constructed for tourists in the slave forts disrupt the work of remembering.

Upon reaching the slave fort, Hartman notes "The sign posted on the hurricane fence warned: 'No one is allowed inside this area except tourists'" (84). The slave fort, then, is a closed space, exclusive, and designed only for those willing and able to pay for a sense of belonging and connection, to repair the break caused by the Middle Passage. Outside of the fort known as Elmina Castle, Hartman receives handwritten letters from two young Ghanaian boys written to Black tourists. One of them begins, "Beloved Sister, please write me. We are one Africa . . . the same people and I know it's because of the slave trade that's why you left here to U.S.A. and I want you to know that you are my sister and I am your brother according to the history of our ancestors and Africa is both of us motherland so you are welcome back home" (84–85). This letter clearly reproduces the vision of Pan-Africanism that propelled Black émigrés to Ghana—the utopian vision of a united Africa, Africa as the motherland and home to Black people throughout the diaspora. Here in this letter is the welcome and homecoming that so many Black travelers before Hartman sought. However, Hartman's own experience of strangeness and alienation in Ghana disrupts this singular vision. She has already learned she is *obruni* (stranger), not a sister. This enables Hartman to develop a new way of seeing—a critical gaze and perspective leading to a more expansive vision that resists the blindness of previous travelers to Ghana.

Hartman asks, "[h]ow could these scruffy adolescents love me or anyone else like me? You could never love the foreigner whose wealth required you to inveigle a handful of coins. It was not the kind of relationship that cultivated tender feeling." Hartman sees and names the class and national privilege informing the interaction. Instead of focusing on this response, however, Hartman foregrounds the boys' perspective, imagining they yearn

> to break out of this dusty four-cornered town and never see the castle again or the sign barring their entrance. . . . In their eyes, I must have appeared a foolish woman who acted as if slaves existed only in the past . . . as if dispossession were her inheritance alone. Looking at me, the boys imagined the wealth and riches they would possess if they lived in the States. After all, who else but a rich American could afford to travel so far to cry about her past? Looking at me, the boys wished their ancestors had been slaves. If so, they would be big men. (89)

Hartman's attempt to enter into the boys' perspective reveals the difficult work of bridge building. This work of connection requires not an erasure of difference but a confrontation with that difference—their varied ways of seeing the world. The division Hartman recognizes between herself and the Ghanaian boys marks the slave forts, as Elizabeth MacGonagle describes them, as "contested spaces" (250). As Sandra Richards notes, they are sites "produced for outsiders" and yet require Ghanaian support to authenticate the performance (626). The end result of this construction of "one collective memory," which MacGonagle defines as "a fiction" (252, 257), and the concomitant failure to integrate varied and often-tenuous histories and perspectives within the slave forts is the reproduction of *forgetting* in spite of the central mission and invocation of heritage tourism to *remember*. Such practices of forgetting, which Hartman locates at the heart of heritage tourism and of the revolutionaries' idyllic vision of return, undermine the decolonizing work necessary for building free territory.

Though Hartman challenges heritage tourism practices, she does come with her own yearnings that often disrupt and oppose the needs and desires of the Ghanaian people she encounters. In line with her understanding that the boys seek funds to survive, she explains that even if their letters might have "seduced" other African American tourists and given them a sense of "solidarity with their newfound kin," "most Ghanaians weren't fooled by the mirage, even when their survival necessitated that they indulge the delusion. The story of slavery fabricated for African Americans had nothing to do with the present struggles of most Ghanaians. What each community made of slavery and how they understood it provided little ground for solidarity"

(165). Hartman's critical gaze reveals the cavern of difference (economic and social disparity) undermining the facade of solidarity. The boys' letters are motivated by their own dreams, their own utopian vision, which differ from that of African Americans who visit the slave forts.

Hartman notes that while "African Americans wanted to regain their African patrimony and to escape racism in the United States," alternatively, "Ghanaians wanted an escape from the impoverishment of the present, and the road to freedom which they most often imagined was migration to the United States." More succinctly: "African Americans entertained fantasies of return and Ghanaians of departure." As a consequence, "From where we each were standing, we did not see the same past, nor did we share a common vision of the Promised Land" (165). Once again, Hartman demonstrates that vision and sight are not singular or fixed but rather multiple and fluid—dependent on our location in the world. Ghanaians and African Americans see things differently. At the slave forts, Hartman illustrates blindness and shortsightedness as persistent threats to the work of bridge building between these two visions. Notably, in the passage above Hartman posits this blindness to differing perspectives as the consequence of a singular story of slavery, which privileges the needs of African Americans over that of Ghanaian people. She refers to this story as a *mirage*, a *delusion*, and as a *fabrication* because it silences the lived experiences of Ghanaians in the past and present. This disconnection at the heart of the Pan-Africanist vision espoused in the boys' letters—the erasure of their own experiences as Ghanaians—inevitably destroys, rather than creates, possibilities for solidarity and connection. Hence, Hartman's text reveals that only in rejecting the singular story of slavery can we adopt a more expansive vision of the present and of the future.

Beyond a Single Story: Sacred Recovery

Although this singular narrative privileges African Americans' perspective, Hartman extends her critique of the limitations and dangers of such a narrative for her own recovery efforts as she enters and moves throughout Elmina Castle, where she continues to encounter the narrative of return and welcome: "'Return' was the word that reverberated throughout Elmina Castle, as though the only life possible was the one that existed in the past. . . . *Return to the motherland. Welcome back. It's good to be home*" (89). Here we see the same story that Hartman encounters in the boys' letters as she links the envy-tinged welcome she receives from the boys at the entrance to the slave fort with the persistent narrative of return and welcome that accompanies her movements through the holding cell and dungeon. Noting the absurdity of this narrative, Hartman asks, "How could a slave fort be a welcome house?" (90).

Challenging the narrative of welcome and return with its promise of finding what one has lost (one's mother or motherland), Hartman foregrounds the emptiness she finds in the dungeon. Voicing the failure of her attempt to access the past through the dungeon, Hartman states, "No revenants lurked in the dungeon. The hold was stark. No hand embraced mine. No voices rang in my ears. Not one living creature dwelled here. . . . I moved back and forth with the slumped shoulders of defeat. I traced the perimeter of the cell disappointed. . . . My hands glided over the walls . . . but the brush of my hands against stone offered no hint or clue. What I wanted was to feel something other than bricks and lime. What I wanted was to reach through time and touch the prisoners" (118–19). Here the physicality of the dungeon becomes palpable as Hartman's body meets brick and mortar and stone but that does not lead her to reconnection, recovery, or return. Not even after making the trip multiple times. After blaming her friend Phyllis, who accompanied her on her first visit, for ruining the atmosphere with discussions of Terry McMillan and *Titanic* she concludes, "I blamed Phyllis for what didn't happen. Only later did I realize there was nothing to see. I hadn't missed a thing" (118). Though Hartman represents her failure to discover or witness anything in the dungeon as personal, referring to herself repeatedly as a "failed witness," I would like to suggest an alternative reading—one that considers this disconnect between Hartman and the past as a larger consequence of how the slave fort has been rhetorically constructed for tourists. In other words, the very narrative of welcome and return that tourists encounter outside of and within Elmina Castle makes it impossible for Hartman to engage with the past, just as it hindered connection and solidarity between African Americans and Ghanaians.

This experience of rupture follows Hartman from the dungeon to the museum inside the slave fort, where she encounters another singular narrative about slavery and its impact. It lies in a collection of "items for which the slaves had been exchanged" and accompanying facts about the "benefits of the trade—new agricultural crops and animals, literacy, and Christianity—as well as the drawbacks of the slave trade—the suffering of millions of enslaved people. You learned that despite the terrible ordeal, the descendants of the slaves triumphed in the end" (116). "[H]ow do you weigh literacy and Jesus and luxury goods against four centuries of rout [defeat] and the millions [of people] gone?" asks Hartman. Like the narrative of welcome and return, here again she locates a practice of erasure evident in the museum's incomplete portrait of slavery and its consequences. She notes, "Even in the museum, the slaves were missing. None of their belongings were arranged nicely in well-lit glass cases. . . . None of their sayings were quoted on placards. . . . Nor was their family life and social organization described. . . . The museum was as bereft as the underground" (116). This description recalls her earlier claim that "there was nothing to see" in the slave fort, in the dungeon, or apparently in the museum. To better illustrate this *nothing*, Hartman juxtaposes what's missing—expressed in the word *bereft* which ties this lack to wanting, to desire, to longing and expectation—with what we do see in the museum. Through this juxtaposition, Hartman makes visible the circumscribed narrative of the slave trade and its consequences through a superficial presentation of pros and cons followed by a presumably happy ending. She notes, "You learned that despite the terrible ordeal, the descendants of the slaves triumphed in the end. Large portraits of Bob Marley, Muhammad Ali, Martin Luther King Jr., James Baldwin, and Angela Davis concluded the story on an upbeat note" (116). The problem for Hartman is twofold: The story of slavery has neither concluded, nor has it been redeemed as the museum suggests.

From her vantage point, Hartman sees not triumph or victory over slavery but rather the afterlife of slavery signaling the incomplete and unfinished nature of freedom. For Hartman, the singular story of progress and redemption is similarly incomplete precisely because of its "dismissal or refutation of slavery's enduring legacy" and because "the language of progress . . . establishes the remoteness and irrelevance of the past" ("Time" 771). Given the continued assault on Black life in America, Hartman claims that any attempt at memorializing slavery becomes a practice of silence and erasure—a failure to see the ways in which slavery persists into the present. Hence, she states, "The reverberations of slavery . . . are so immediate and unceasing that you can't even begin to think about memorialization, because people are still living the dire effects of the disaster" (Hartman et al. 111).

The themes of silence and erasure persist throughout the chapter, "So Many Dungeons," as Hartman chronicles the missing voices, experiences, and artifacts of enslaved people in the dungeon and museum. After all, this is what we would expect to find in a museum—artifacts connecting us to another time and place. But in the slave fort, Hartman finds only a singular narrative that has erased her (and her ancestors') experience of alienation and of dispossession. The "crush of empty space" that she discovers in the slave fort leaves her feeling even more like a stranger, more alienated and without a home. Hartman ties this failure of the dungeon and museum to bear witness to the voices and experiences of enslaved people, this failure to bridge the past and the present inextricably to the lack of stories. She notes, "Like most people willing to cross the threshold of a slave dungeon, I wanted to give the dead their due. But I was unsure how to accomplish this. . . . In the dungeon, there were remains but no stories that could resurrect the dead except the stories I invented" (116).

Here we catch a glimpse into Hartman's critical practice—her response to the emptiness and the silence that she finds is storytelling. Naming this practice "critical fabulation," Hartman asserts that narrative enables her to construct a "counter-history" of enslaved people capable of revealing their humanity ("Venus" 3). In her essay published a year after *Lose Your Mother*, "Venus in Two Acts," Hartman highlights three key elements of her critical practice: (1) "re-presenting [historical] events in divergent stories and from contested points of view," (2) "displac[ing] the . . . authorized account" (i.e., the master narrative) by unveiling the "fictions of history," and (3) "imagin[ing] what might have happened or might have been said or might have been done" (11). Hartman's overview of her critical practice reflects a similar commitment to multi-perspectival storytelling that we witnessed in Dash's film particularly through her multiple retellings of the Ibo Landing myth. I define this work of making visible the humanity of the enslaved by retrieving what has been lost through the bridge-building work of storytelling as decolonizing work and, therefore, as sacred. In response to the loss, dispossession, and alienation of slavery and the Middle Passage she confronts in the dungeon and in the official historical record, Hartman's decolonizing (sacred) work, grounded in connection and recuperation, attempts to remedy the open wound caused by slavery and the violence of the record she finds at the fort. This wound, she makes clear, remains open, continuing to shape Black people's struggles to live as fully human in the world and in particular African Americans' attempts to establish a home in the US "in the aftermath of catastrophe and devastation" (3).

Hartman's confrontation with history in the dungeon, the museum, and in the archive intersects in key ways with Toni Morrison's engagement with the historical record in her own writing. Moreover, Hartman engages in a critical practice that I see as closely aligned with Morrison's process of "literary archaeology"—a term Morrison coined to describe her own writing practice as a critical response to and engagement with the historical record. In her essay "The Site of Memory," Morrison explains the process of "literary archaeology" that she employs in order to "gain access to [the] interior life" of enslaved people (71). She explains, "you journey to a site to see what remains were left behind and to reconstruct the world that these remains imply. What makes it fiction is the nature of the imaginative act: my reliance on the image—on the remains" (71). These remains become her "route to a reconstruction of a world, to an exploration of an interior life that was not written and to the revelation of a kind of truth" (74).

Although Hartman identifies herself as a literary scholar and Morrison as a writer of fiction, I have chosen to foreground the intersection between their projects for two reasons. First, both highlight the failures of the historical record and its inability to tell the full story of Black people, describing their encounters with the archive as an encounter with "nothing" or with the "incomplete."[10] Moreover, they commit themselves to the work of retrieving the voices, experiences, and interior lives of Black people that the historical archive of slavery has lost or silenced. While both bring to the archive their critical lens and skepticism of its silence, Hartman positions such erasures as a painful loss, a wound, while Morrison claims these gaps as significant for herself as a writer of fiction—opportunities for her creativity, as these "interstices of recorded history" become the locus for her novels ("On *Beloved*," 280).

Recognizing the value of the interior lives of enslaved people, Morrison claims that her purpose as a Black woman writer is to unveil what had been silenced, censored, and forgotten.[11] Taking up this work to remedy the historical erasures and marginalization of Black lives, especially those of enslaved people, Hartman engages in a similar process of resisting and challenging the singular narrative of slavery produced by the archive, which as Hartman notes, "dictates what can be said about the past and the kinds of stories that can be told" (17). Since the gaps and silences in the archive make it impossible to tell the entire story of slavery *and* its afterlife, Morrison and Hartman use their writing to "tell an impossible story" and to narrate the "unspeakable" or the "unwritten."[12] Telling impossible, unspeakable stories demands a critical practice grounded in both imagination and speculation—a consideration of not only the actual, as Morrison notes, but also the possible. Hartman's exploration of "what might have happened, or might have been said or might have been done" demonstrates her similar concern with *the possible* ("Venus" 11). Thus, despite their differing self-identifications, Hartman as cultural historian and literary scholar, like Morrison as literary artist, employs imaginative storytelling to challenge the archive.

As a result, Hartman's critical imaginative work gives her far more access to the lives of enslaved people than the museum or official tours ever could. With this access, she constructs a more expansive and humanizing narrative of the enslaved people she seeks to reclaim. In contrast to the numbers and figures provided in the slave fort to quantify the loss and impact of the slave trade, Hartman's practice of storytelling (much like Nancy Prince's retelling of her ancestors' struggles for freedom) enables her to avoid "the violence of abstraction." In opposition to this violence that Hartman encounters within the slave fort and the museum, a violence that participates in a continuing erasure of the lives of enslaved people, Hartman engages in the far more difficult work of constructing "a human history" through her critical practice of storytelling.[13] *Lose Your Mother* provides multiple examples of this practice. However, to best illustrate this important critical and, as I will argue, sacred work that Hartman deploys, I turn to her chapter titled "The Dead Book," as it offers the fullest expression of this imaginative practice and its intersection with literary archaeology.

The opening of "The Dead Book" differs in significant ways from the previous chapter, "So Many Dungeons." While Hartman struggles to find any stories in the slave fort, which has been narrowly defined by a singular narrative of slavery, in this next chapter, Hartman shifts from the confining and limiting space of the slave fort to the ocean. The opening lines of this chapter illustrate the profound impact of space, geography, and location on Hartman's recovery work. She begins: "It is said that if you look at the sea long enough, scenes from the past come back to life. It is said that 'the sea is history.' And 'the sea has nothing to give but a well excavated grave.' Looking at the Atlantic, I thought of the girl. There were countless others buried at the bottom of the ocean, but she was the one I had my eyes set on. If I concentrated hard enough I could see it all happening again" (136). Just as in "The Dark Days," where we see Hartman shifting from blindness to sight, here in "The Dead Book," Hartman shifts from being a "failed witness" in the dungeon to seeing clearly once again. Facing the sea and free from the touristic practices, structures and narrative within the slave fort, in this

Figure 1. "Abolition of the Slave Trade, or The Inhumanity of Dealers in human flesh exemplified in Capt. Kimber's treatment of a Young Negro Girl of 15 for her Virgin Modesty," Isaac Cruikshank (London: S. W. Fores, April 10, 1792). (Library of Congress, Prints & Photographs Division, British Cartoon Prints Collection, LC-USZC4-6204)

chapter the sea (a fluid and open space of possibility) facilitates her access to the image and to memory. Thus, the chapter opening aligns with Morrison's own process of literary archaeology, her "reliance on the image—on the remains in addition to recollection, to yield up a kind of a truth" (71).

Like Morrison, Hartman begins with what she can see—the image of a girl, which is her point of entry into the past and the beginning of her recovery work in this chapter. The image of the girl that Hartman sees begins with an eighteenth-century anti-slavery print created to dramatize William Wilberforce's court case against Captain Kimber, a slave ship captain accused of murdering a fifteen-year-old African girl for disobedience, more specifically, for refusing to provide sexual entertainment for the crew. The sketch depicts an enslaved girl hanging precariously by one leg, her body nearly fully exposed for all to see—the crew, the captain, the captives, as well as the larger viewing public.

This visual reproduction of an act of violence on board a slave ship, ironically named the *Recovery*, becomes the impetus for Hartman's critical reflection on the violence of the historical archive of slavery. For Hartman, this print reflects a repetition of violence as it reproduces the initial violence against the girl and illustrates the multiple appropriations of the girl within the archive—each imagining producing another violation. Hartman states,

> If I concentrated hard enough I could see it all happening again. The billow of the ship's sail shuddered in the rush of air. . . . The *Recovery* was a world all its own. Three sailors, the captain, and the girl were the only ones visible on the ship. What happened next, no one could agree on, except, of course, that the girl ended up dead. Everything else depends upon how you look at things or where you were standing when her body was suspended from the slaver's mast. No one saw the same girl; she was outfitted in a different guise for each who dared look. She appeared as a tortured virgin, a pregnant woman, a syphilitic tart, and a budding saint. And the explanation of how she came to hang in the air, flailing like a tattered banner, was no less fanciful: The girl declined to dance naked with the captain on the deck. The girl snubbed the captain and refused his bed. The girl had the pox and the captain flogged her as a cure for the venereal disease. The captain, the surgeon, and the abolitionist all disagreed about what happened on the deck of the *Recovery*, yet they all insisted they were trying to save the girl's life. (136–37)

Here Hartman reminds us once again that vision is not singular or fixed but fluid and inextricably linked to place. Who we are and where we stand determines what and how we see. Hence, the varying imaginings of the girl in the minds of these white men (the captain, surgeon, and William Wilberforce) reflect their own desires and motivations projected onto the violated body of this captive girl.

Hartman's critique of the archive, however, extends beyond images to consider the violence of language. As she explains, "I am as guilty as the rest. I too am trying to save the girl" from the archive's circumscription of her life to "a handful of words: *the supposed murder of a Negro girl.*" Linking this archival erasure to the girl's death, Hartman asserts, "[h]ers is a life impossible to reconstruct, not even her name survived. . . . With a name she might have been more difficult to forget." Quoting Michel Foucault, she explains, "A name would have afforded the illusion of knowing her and made less painful the fact that the girl 'never will have any existence outside the precarious domicile of words' that allowed her to be murdered" (137). For Hartman the violence against the girl is multiple and extends beyond whippings and sexual assault to include the violence of representation especially through language.[14] Nor is the captain's whip the only marker of violence in the archive. The continued appropriation of the girl to meet the needs of white men (physical, moral, political) reflects a monstrous repetition of violence. Her missing name is further evidence of the violent stripping away of her humanity by the historical record (and the slave ship). Even the slave ship has a name. But more violent than the lack of words, the void and silence where her voice should have been, these various stories or "fictions," as Hartman terms them, circumscribe her life—reducing the girl to summary phrases about what could have or did in fact happen to her body ("Venus" 10). In short, the archive and the various ways in which she is imagined within it position the girl as object rather than as human. Most importantly, for Hartman, the physical violence that leads to her murder is the inevitable consequence of such linguistic violence that erases her personhood and humanity—consigning her to *oblivion*. In other words, the linguistic erasure precedes and incites the physical erasure of her body.

Yet Hartman's goal in "The Dead Book," as she claims in her essay "Venus in Two Acts," reflecting on the challenges and limitations of her project, is "to do more than recount the violence" of the archive (2). Rather, in this chapter, she aims to "tell a story . . . capable of retrieving what remains dormant . . . without committing further violence in my own act of narration" (2). In "The Dead Book" Hartman wishes to retrieve the humanity of the fifteen-year-old girl, using her own creative and critical practice of storytelling to challenge the violence of the archive and the incomplete history it offers.

What follows, then, is Hartman's attempt to access what Morrison terms "a kind of a truth" by making room for another possibility, making room for the only story that has not been told in the archive—that of the girl. In opposition to the physical and spiritual violence enacted upon Black people, I argue that Hartman's response to the violence—her attempts to make known the interior life of this fifteen-year-old girl—reflects a key intervention that challenges the violent erasures of the archive. Hartman begins her reconstruction of the court case with the perspectives of the captain, the third mate, the surgeon, abolitionist William Wilberforce, as well as the words of John Weskett, an expert in English insurance law, to showcase the legal theories used in court to argue that "natural death was not in itself sufficient to distinguish slaves from other commodities that withered and decayed. Death was just a variant of spoilage. A dead girl was not really all that different from rotten fruit" (Hartman 148). These voices reproduce the violence of eighteenth-century law and of the archive—all of which render the girl illegible. Missing from these stories and from these testimonies about the girl is her life, her humanity. Faced once again with oblivion (the erasure of the captives) that she finds in the dungeon and slave fort museum, Hartman seeks to recover the life of this specific enslaved girl in an effort to tell a more human history.

Moving from the image of the girl that she sees to the violating imaginings of her from the archive, Hartman ends the chapter with another perspective, one that the archive has failed to document. Engaging in the work of literary archaeology, Hartman's narrative makes visible the interior life of this girl held captive aboard the slave ship *Recovery*, which offered up not restoration, as the name suggests, but destruction:

> There was nothing inside her mouth, since she had decided against eating. . . . When she landed on the ship, the wish, which had taken root in the holding pen in Calabar, blossomed. No matter what new torment the captain inflicted, nothing would pass her lips. Not even the hands attacking her each night could break her resolve. The hands swarmed her body and pinched her thighs and stabbed her insides and nipped her breasts and strangled her throat and stuffed their claws in her mouth so that she could hardly breathe. . . . For twenty-eight days, she had climbed through the hatchway and poured onto the deck with the others and not eaten. Once they had lost sight of the coast, her hunger had disappeared too. (151)

Hartman's imagining of the girl's experience from her own perspective (from where she stood on the slave ship) does important critical work, as this alternative testimony challenges the ship's claim to restoration or as the testimonies of the captain and crew suggest—salvation. Rather, Hartman's imagining foregrounds the violence of the ship, representing it instead, as historians indicate, as an uninhabitable space, a floating tomb whose "cavernous form signaled . . . a powerful and dangerous capacity to consume" (Smallwood 124). Yet Hartman pushes beyond a mere recounting of this violence by also making visible the girl's agency and desire. This unnamed "wish" and her refusal to eat make visible the girl's resistance to the violating practices of the slave ship that seek to transform her from person to commodity.

According to Hartman, doctors aboard slave ships often identified African captives' refusal to eat as a symptom of mental illness, specifically "melancholy," which was marked by "lowness of spirits and despondency" (252, note 144). Though the archival record positions the girl's refusal to eat as a consequence of insanity, reflected in the claim "Some said she had lost her mind," Hartman's imagining of her interior life offers an alternative possibility (152). She counters this master narrative reproduced within the archive by attributing the girl's stubborn refusal to eat or to dance as resistance to captivity and to the violence of the slave ship. In short, she rewrites the girl's practice of resistance as human agency rather than as illness. In her counternarrative, Hartman writes of the girl:

> She had discovered a way off the ship. It worried her that the ancestors might shun her, or the gods might be angry and punish her by bringing her back as a goat or a dog, or she would roam the earth directionless and never find her way beyond the sea, but she risked it anyway, it was the only path open. When the two boys plummeted into the sea, they had made leaving look so easy. She curled into a ball in the corner of the deck. Her body hurt and she trembled. . . . [H]ad it been possible for a corpse to speak, she would have said, "You are wrong. I am going to meet my friends." All they could see was a girl slumped in a dirty puddle and not the one soaring and on her way home. (152)

Hartman's reclamation of the girl's interior life reflects an agency born out of a cosmology that enables her to challenge the violent stripping and work of the slave ship. In particular, the girl's spiritual practice illustrates that there are some things worse than dying (i.e., slavery) and that death is not the end. Hence, through Hartman's imagining, she gives voice to the discredited knowledge that enslaved people and their descendants cultivated. Through narrative, Hartman speaks against the silence of the archive and challenges the master narrative (i.e., the dominant account produced by European and Anglo-Americans) that defined African captives as blank slates, as incapable of reasoning, knowledge production, devoid of history or culture and therefore, as not human.[15]

On the other hand, the imaginative work Hartman employs in order to recuperate the humanity of the unnamed girl risks aligning her with the white patriarchal voices in the archive who appropriate the fifteen-year-old-girl for their own purposes and desires. Although Hartman's intentions are far different from those of the men who witnessed and participated in her death, her desire to retrieve the girl, to "save her from oblivion" makes her "as guilty as the rest" (Hartman 137). Revealing the complicated nature of historical recovery, Kenneth Greenberg, explains, "retelling a story involves a kind of violation" in part because "the act of retelling . . . often involves transforming the people or events of the past into objects we can use in the present. It does not matter whether we praise or vilify the dead—the full complexity of their lives usually gets lost as we remember them for purposes and in contexts that they cannot share" (23).

Similarly aware of the potential violence of such work, Hartman foregrounds the limits of storytelling as a practice in "Venus in Two Acts." Describing recovery as "an impossible goal," in the essay, Hartman asks several key questions revealing her critical awareness of her historical and literary project: "how does one recuperate lives entangled with and impossible to differentiate from the terrible utterances that condemned them to death, . . . that identified them as units of value, . . . that stripped them of human features? . . . How can narrative embody life in words and at the same time respect what we cannot know?" (3). And perhaps most important for Hartman, "How does one revisit the scene of subjection without replicating the grammar of violence?" (4). The danger of reproducing the archive's violence is ever-present for Hartman, informing the care with which she handles the remains found in the archive. Thus, while William Wilberforce and the artist of the abolitionist print transform the girl into a *usable* anti-slavery symbol, Hartman intends to understand what has been lost: the girl's life. Moreover, she seeks to protect her by fashioning a counternarrative of resistance and agency capable of challenging the archive's objectifying record that, as Hartman notes, "yields no exhaustive account of the girl's life, but catalogues the statements that licensed her death" ("Venus" 10).

This latter point reflects a key difference between Hartman's counternarrative and how the official historical record presents the girl: Hartman makes no claim to absolute truth or absolute understanding. Much as she does in "The Dark Days," Hartman extends her critical lens to herself, acknowledging her own limitations of knowledge, of understanding, and of sight. She says she is "as guilty as the rest of them," echoing her own critical reflections on the very recovery work she employs in this chapter. Thus, at the end of her imaginative retelling of the girl's life and death aboard the slave ship, Hartman states: "If the story ended there, I could feel a small measure of comfort. I could hold on to this instant of possibility. I could find a salutary lesson in the girl's suffering and pretend a story was enough to save her from oblivion" (153). Much as Morrison claims her own process of literary archaeology as one that enables her to "explore two worlds—the actual and the possible" (75), here Hartman defines her imaginative act as an "instant of possibility." This willingness to explore both the actual and the possible enables both Hartman and Morrison to expand beyond the limited singular narrative of the archive.

Through my comparison of Morrison and Hartman, I do not wish to argue that their projects are exactly the same. One key point of difference is the extent of their employment of imagination. While Hartman, a trained academic scholar, foregrounds her commitment to "Narrative restraint, the refusal to fill in the gaps and provide closure" as necessary for her critical practice and project ("Venus" 12), Morrison positions herself as a fiction writer who, in contrast to the literary critic, can give her imagination free rein to invent ("Site of Memory" 71–72). Despite these differences, both Hartman and Morrison's writing reflect a commitment to "paint as full a picture of the lives of the captives as possible" (Hartman, "Venus" 11). As part of this commitment, both writers recognize the limits of the archive, its silence and erasure, and both employ imagination and speculation (what would have or might have happened) as a way to challenge the archive and to destabilize the dominant historical record. Their work, like that of Julie Dash, gives voice to those who have been marginalized and silenced—exploring the alternative possibilities for Black life and Black humanity by reimagining and expanding the kinds of stories that can be told about Black people. Their stories, unlike those of the archive and official historical record, begin with a core belief in the sanctity of Black life. As such, Dash, Morrison, and Hartman's projects fundamentally reveal the intersection of the sacred and secular at work in such recovery efforts.

The concern for Black life and the desire to protect the humanity of Black people reflects the core attributes of the word *sacred,* which means set apart, worthy or deserving of respect, protected from violation. Hartman's narrative bears witness to the archive's brutal misnaming of the fifteen-year-old girl ("sulky bitch" and "syphilitic tart") in order to contest the definitions reproduced in the official historical record that render the girl as object and abject. In contrast to "names that deface and disfigure" ("Venus" 10), Hartman's narrative or counter-history makes visible that which the archive has effaced: the girl's dignity and humanity. Although she cannot save the girl from physical violation and destruction, and even as she marks the limitations of her project, Hartman's narrative also reveals the power of imagination and language to construct a fuller life—one that recognizes the girl's body (interior and external) as sacred and, therefore, as made for freedom. As a result, Hartman's travel text continues the long legacy of sacred work that the varying narratives in this study bear witness to again and again. Despite differences in genre, geography, and time period, all claim the Black (female) body as sacred and free.

I position Hartman's deep concern for the fifteen-year-old girl she unearths from the archive, her careful attention to the girl's life, her death, and how she is remembered and defined through language as representative of an *ethics of care*. I borrow this term from Christina Sharpe's seminal work, *In the Wake: On Blackness and Being*, in which she asserts, "Living . . . in the wake of slavery, in spaces where we were never meant to survive, or have been punished for surviving and for daring to claim or make spaces of something like freedom, we yet reimagine and transform spaces for and practices of an ethics of care (as in repair, maintenance, attention)" (130–31). For Sharpe, an ethics of care can "counter . . . the violence of abstraction" and even more than that, this ethic, which she describes as a way of seeing, of being, of remembering, "contains mercy" and points to the existence of "Black being that continually exceeds all of the violence directed at Black life; Black being that exceeds that force" (134). Though Hartman does not use the word care to describe her critical practice, care informs her desire to redress the violence of the archive and underlies her deepest fear—that she might "subject the dead to new dangers and to a second order of violence" ("Venus" 5). Unlike the violence of the archive that renders the girl's life unseeable and unknowable (abstract), Hartman's narrative constructs an "account of care" for the girl that imagines a possibility of being, of existence beyond the violation and destruction of her body.[16] In so doing, Hartman's account demonstrates that the force of slavery, though brutal and unrelenting, is not total. Through this commitment to care and this belief in the possibility of *Black being* that can exceed the force of slavery and its violent repetitions, we see the intersection of the sacred and secular in Hartman's work.

Yet Hartman resists aligning herself with the sacred throughout her narrative. Though she maintains the separation of the sacred and the secular in her own characterization of her work, *Lose Your Mother* demonstrates more of a tenuous or conflicted relationship with the sacred than a decisive break from it. Her resistance to the sacred is grounded in her critique of Christianity in Ghana, particularly because of its deployment as an instrument of colonization and its use as a fair trade for slavery. Hartman also positions herself in opposition to "the faithful," who desired "to enter the world anew, to be born again cleansed of the past," noting that they "were steadfast in their belief, whereas I wavered and doubted" (54). In *Lose Your Mother*, "the faithful" include not only the Christians Hartman encounters in Elmina while visiting the slave forts but also the African American revolutionaries who envision their own rebirth through migration to Ghana. Hartman links Ghanaian Christians and Afros because of what she sees as their shared desire for rebirth and to leave the past behind. In contrast, she defines herself as "the skeptic among the faithful" (39). Nonetheless, Hartman's text demonstrates the significance of faith and hope in the lives of Black people and showcases her similar commitment to struggle against the despair that threatens to imprison her and the people she encounters.

Hartman's resistance to despair becomes visible as she distinguishes herself in key ways from John and Mary Ellen. After decades in Ghana, they have become disillusioned. John asks Hartman, "Do you know what it feels like to be living in a place for nearly twenty years, scraping to get by and still being treated like a foreigner?" (44). Mary Ellen tells her, "We're losing my husband" (43), depicting a kind of spiritual death in his despair. Hartman reflects, that "like many exiles he no longer hoped for anything." She contrasts John's state of having "no question [he] hoped to answer in the dungeon" with herself: "It was the opposite for me, I was willing to enter the dungeon again and again and encounter the disaster anew . . . because at this late date, I was still hoping for a different outcome. I was convinced that even now lives hung in the balance. My own as much as anyone else's" (44).

Here Hartman positions herself in contrast to John's despair, which she claims as a consequence of "the pain and isolation of . . . exile." She explains, "The unrealized dreams of two continents had embittered John. Resentment and loneliness were the proof of his statelessness" (43). Despite Hartman's doubt about the possibilities for freedom, the possibility of a future that "did not end in defeat," she sustains hope through her willingness to enter the dungeon and re-engage the past. Her hope, however, is not superficial but radical, in line with what Junot Díaz describes in his essay, "Radical Hope." He explains, hope "is not blind optimism," but rather a "practice" that is "our best weapon against despair, even when despair seems justifiable" (13). In opposition to a "blind optimism," Hartman grounds her hope in engaged action and in struggle—reflected, as we have already seen, in her repeated return to the slave forts, in her ongoing dialogue with Ghanaians despite the steep divide between their experiences of the past and their present perspectives, in her persistent and relentless questioning of the singular stories she encounters in the slave fort museum and in the archive, as well as in her willingness to question her own project: "what, if anything, could I remember after hundreds of years of forgetting?" (157). Such questions disrupt any claims to authority, to totalizing knowledge, to certainty. Yet, they ensure that her work, like Morrison's, remains anchored in two worlds: the actual and the possible.

All of these critical practices (struggle, returning to the dungeon again and again, cross-cultural dialogue, and unceasing questioning) illustrate Hartman's belief in what's possible despite her full awareness of the actual. Radical hope, then, works toward a future possibility that is both tethered to and is born from a willingness to see and transform the harsh realities of the present world.[17] John's exilic perspective illustrates the other side of Hartman's questions—giving voice to despair and hopelessness as an inevitable consequence if Hartman relinquishes her yearning and struggle for free territory. He reminds her of what's at stake—her life hangs in the balance as she faces the very real possibility of enduring a spiritual death similar to John's.

Revealing this spiritual struggle as a shared one, Hartman shifts from John's despair to a remembrance of her great-grandfather and the spiritual inheritance she receives from him. She explains,

> Like John, I was stateless too. I had never been at home in the world. It was a sensibility I had inherited sitting on my great-grandfather's knee in Morning Pilgrim Baptist Church as he implored in his scratchy baritone voice along with the other congregants, "Lord, I'm going home, / No more toils, no more care, / No more grief to bear." Even as a child I perceived the gravity of these words and I knew they contained an appeal as well as a complaint. Abandoned by all but God, song after song declared. It was a feeling that seemed too ancient for my thirty-six years, but I came by it honestly. I was trying to get to the bottom of it, and for me it began in a holding cell. (44)

While this memory illustrates Hartman's experience of alienation and homelessness as part of the legacy of enslaved people and their descendants, it also reflects an ancestral spiritual practice that served as a bulwark against despair and hopelessness in the face of evil. Though Hartman, a self-identified atheist, does not identify with or claim a spiritual practice as her own, she bears witness to a legacy of spirituality that wards off despair. This legacy reflects bell hooks's definition of spirituality "as an oppositional mode of being that enables [Black people] to combat some of the hopelessness confronting us" (hooks and West 54). Just as Hagar, and nineteenth-century Black women itinerants Zilpha Elaw, Nancy Prince, and Amanda Smith testify that God has not abandoned Black people but rather offers them an inheritance and legacy other than slavery (a hope and a future), Hartman's memory of her great-grandfather's church points to a core principle of the sacred for Black Christians—in opposition to America's practices of alienation and dispossession grounded in slavery, God remains faithful to Black people.

Alongside this sacred practice that testifies to an alternative legacy—the possibility of a hope and a future for Black people, I position Hartman's recovery work as challenging the emptiness of the dungeon and its suggestion that slavery's devastation was a totalizing defeat. As such, she positions herself, as a descendant of the enslaved, as living and breathing evidence that the destruction of the dungeon was not total. Hence, although Hartman identifies her work as secular, her text reflects her commitment to "an oppositional mode of being," transmitted through her grandfather's spiritual legacy and further cultivated through critical practices that ward off hopelessness and the spiritual death that John epitomizes and that threatens her own health and well-being.

I read Hartman's willingness to keep showing up, to keep asking questions and to keep imagining what might have been in the past and what might be possible in the future, in spite of her persistent doubts, as a kind of spiritual practice, albeit one that exceeds the bounds of any specific (singular) tradition, institution, or framework. Central to this spiritual practice is her radical hope. Although she defines her recovery efforts as "an impossible goal," in "Venus in Two Acts," Hartman also clarifies that such work "rather than leading to pessimism or despair must be embraced as the impossibility that conditions our knowledge of the past and animates our desire for a liberated future" (13). Here Hartman explains that while the impossibility of recovery may cause us to doubt, we must use it to fuel our continued work and struggle toward liberation, rather than as proof of our inevitable defeat. As such, Hartman asserts that central to this work of liberation is honoring our human connection to the enslaved, whose lives necessitate that we "imagine a future in which the afterlife of slavery has ended" ("Venus" 13).

Hartman's belief in the possible even when faced with impossibility reflects what theologian Kelly Brown Douglas refers to as "an inherent absurdity in black faith" (170). This absurdity, she writes, "speaks of freedom in the midst of bondage. It speaks of life in the midst of death" (170). I locate Hartman's belief in the possibility of creating a liberated future in spite of the ways in which "the ghost of slavery haunts our present" (Hartman 133), as akin to enslaved people's belief in freedom even, as Douglas claims, "when nothing around them said freedom" (170). Thus, while Hartman renounces the religious tradition of her ancestors, her critical work remains grounded in core principles and practices that have informed a long legacy of Black faith and, as we have seen throughout *Spirit Deep,* that have enabled Black people to survive and protect their humanity in unlivable and hostile places.

In the slave forts as well as throughout her travel across Ghana, Hartman engages in a critical (spiritual) practice that makes room not only for a fuller portrait of the lives of the captives but of all Black people—a practice grounded in hope and imagination, which requires a fundamental belief in what's possible. Moreover, despite her self-positioning as a doubter in opposition to "the faithful," Hartman's continued critical engagement, questioning, imagining, and yearning reveal not only a commitment to struggle with the differing perspectives of the Ghanaian people she encounters on her journey but also a profound faith reflected in her willingness to ask questions she does not know the answer to and in her willingness to "risk imagining a future that didn't replicate the defeats of the present" (33).

Building Free Territory

Hartman's resistance to despair and her persistent belief in the possible continues in the final chapter of her book, "Fugitive Dreams," even as her experience of alienation intensifies during her journey along the interior slave route in Ghana. Initially, she feels overwhelmed by the chasm between her own perspective and that of her fellow travelers to Gwolu—the last stop on her journey along the slave route: "The deeper into the heartland of slavery we entered, the greater the isolation I experienced. Most of my colleagues didn't experience slavery as a wound" (215). While her experience of alienation intensifies on this leg of her journey, we see Hartman reversing her critical gaze away from her African colleagues and their limited perspectives on the past and the present to foreground, as well the limitations of her own journey, her search for free territory, and her desire for restoration. Though Hartman admits to wanting "to build a bridge across our differences," she concedes that "Whatever remained of Pan-Africanism, which had espoused solidarity among all African people . . . , and encouraged each and every one of us in the diaspora to dream of the continent as our home, no longer included the likes of me. . . . I couldn't surmount the barricade that separated me from the others. . . . And I was reluctant to admit that I was as much at fault as the others" (217–18). Here Hartman tethers her critique of the utopian vision of Pan-Africanism to a self-reflexive admission of her own fault—her own singular perspective as African American.

Although she asserts she cannot "surmount the barricade that separated" her from her fellow travelers on the journey, her arrival in Gwolu marks another key shift in her perception—an opening and possible way across the divide. In Gwolu, Hartman discovers new stories. As a community of "fugitives" who had evaded captivity, the people in Gwolu were able to construct "a narrative of liberation in which the glory of the past was the entry to a redeemed future. My narrative was a history of defeat, which at best was the precondition for a victory, long-awaited, but that hadn't yet arrived. This was the story I had been trying to find. And in listening for my story I had almost missed theirs" (232–33). In this passage, Hartman attests to the limitations of her search for the lost stories of the enslaved. In her attempt to discover the silenced and forgotten stories of those who had been captured, Hartman nearly misses another key experience of slavery, one central to Ghanaian people—the story of fugitives—those who escaped and stood down slavery. This story of the fugitives reveals a stark contrast between "the history of slavery" in Gwolu—a history of resistance and overcoming, a history of fugitives and warriors, a history of triumph and pride vs. her own story, which is one of death and sorrow, of masters and slaves—"an irredeemable past" that makes it "hard to envision a future in which this past had ended" (233).

While Hartman does not find what she is initially looking for in Gwolu, her time there enables her to see beyond her singular perspective as a descendant of enslaved people to embrace a more expansive vision of slavery that includes the descendants of fugitives. Ultimately, her narrative provides not only a more complex portrait of slavery but also a new way of seeing identity, community, and belonging that enables Hartman to resist despair. In her description of the fugitive community, Hartman notes, the ever-growing reach of the slave trade in Ghana turned everyone into "a captive on reprieve" (222). Men, women, and children fled in search of a place of freedom, seeking to escape both captivity and participation in the trade, either as a slave raider or trader. Though initially free territory for those in flight was the "unknown territory to which they were heading, as if freedom were a city waiting for them in the distance" (223), eventually that free space becomes, in Hartman's reimagining, a place that the fugitives build together. Hartman explains, "they embraced becoming something other than who they had been and naming themselves again." As a result, in this new community, "[n]ewcomers were welcome." Abandoning all concern for ancestral or linguistic difference, "they put down their roots in foreign soil and adopted strangers as their kin . . . and blended their histories." They created "collectivity . . . from the ground up, not one they had inherited, not one that others had imposed" (225).

Hartman's vision, her imagining of what she calls "the fugitive's dream" rejects the stability and safety of inherited and imposed identities as well as the vision of free territory tied to a singular place. Rather, Hartman foregrounds the difficult work of *building* and *becoming* over imposed identities and inherited visions. In contrast to the initial vision of freedom as "a city waiting for them in the distance," here we see freedom as a practice that requires the fugitives and refugees to leave all that they knew behind to begin anew, to reject inherited and imposed identities in favor of building a community and a collective with strangers. In this new place, everyone is a stranger in a strange land; the condition of stranger is shared rather than projected onto a single group. The fugitive's dream challenges the divisive and hierarchical nature of colonizing discourse, which projects the condition of stranger onto the other or the *not-me*, in favor of a decolonized vision of free territory that calls us to embrace the condition of stranger as a shared human reality. This recognition of the stranger as *me* rather than *not-me* enables us to construct spaces that invite rather than exclude.[18] Hence, the work of building community requires adopting strangers as kin, blending histories and building a new collectivity "from the ground up."

Here, at the end of her travels, Hartman delineates a practice of freedom that would be required in order to create the free territory she yearns for. As Nancy Prince concludes in her own nineteenth-century travel text, home, belonging and free territory could not be found abroad—not in Russia nor in Jamaica. And as Hartman's own narrative demonstrates, Ghana is not the locus of freedom either. There is no place free of oppression that African Americans can simply travel to. Instead, Hartman's narrative, like Prince's, claims that we must do the difficult work of creating such spaces wherever we find ourselves. The final chapter of her book offers another possibility—revealing Hartman's own hopeful vision for freedom and suggesting what the work of building free territory requires.

In order to engage in this work of building and becoming, M. Jacqui Alexander explains, "we would need to become fluent in each others' histories, to resist and unlearn an impulse to claim first oppression, most-devastating oppression, one-of-a-kind oppression, defying-comparison oppression. We would have to unlearn an impulse that allows mythologies about each other to replace knowing about one another" (269). Here, Alexander concretizes the practice of freedom that Hartman employs throughout her travel narrative. Fully committed to this creative work of becoming, Hartman attempts to become fluent in multiple histories (her own and others) even though this means confronting the paradoxes between them. Her journey also reveals a commitment to resisting the desire to position her own experience of suffering, oppression, and injustice above those of the Ghanaian people she encounters. And finally, she is thoroughly committed to moving beyond the singular identities and narratives of African Americans and of African people that divide us.

The ending of Hartman's text further illustrates her ability to "make peace with contradiction and paradox," her willingness to embrace a "dialectics of struggle" that is absolutely necessary for building a collective informed by multiple perspectives, as well as often conflicting and tenuous journeys, histories, and geographies (Alexander 266). Offering the clearest vision of her approach for bridging the divide between America and Africa, in the final pages of her book Hartman states, "The bridge between the people of Gwolu and me wasn't what we had suffered or what we had endured but the aspirations that fueled flight and the yearning for freedom. . . . If an African identity was to be meaningful at all, at least to me, then what it meant or was to mean could be elaborated only in the fight against slavery" (234). Challenging the Pan-Africanist claim that African Americans and Africans are linked by a single common history, Hartman's narrative foregrounds both groups' complex and multiple histories. These divergences and tenuous differences threaten to disrupt any singular historical narrative. Yet Hartman asserts that a bridge is still possible.

In full awareness of the challenges in building that bridge, Hartman's ending suggests a possible way forward—a bridge based on shared longings and desires for freedom expressed through struggle. This shared longing, however, is not enough. Work must be done to construct a shared vision of free territory. Hartman concludes,

> If after a year in Ghana I could still call myself African American, it was because my Africa had its source in the commons created by fugitives and rebels. . . . The legacy that I chose to claim was articulated in the ongoing struggle to escape, stand down, and defeat slavery in all of its myriad forms. It was the fugitive's legacy. . . . It wasn't the dream of a White House . . . but of a free territory. It was a dream of autonomy rather than nationhood. It was the dream of an elsewhere, with all its promises and dangers, where the stateless might, at last, thrive. (234)

Significantly, Hartman extricates the dream of free territory from race and from nationhood. Rather, for Hartman, we build free territory by continuing the legacy of fugitives and rebels—a legacy that includes all those who struggle against slavery "in all of its myriad forms."

Unlike her African colleagues in Ghana who limit their Pan-Africanist vision to the borders of the continent, Hartman adopts a more expansive definition of belonging, a "dream that exceeded the borders of the continent . . . a dream of the world house" (233). Hartman's vision echoes Alexander's assertion that the "yearning to belong is not to be confined only to membership or citizenship in community, political movement, nation, group, or belonging to a family." For Alexander, our full humanity is realized only in and through our interdependence rather than our separation. Thus, Alexander argues "As human beings, we have a sacred connection to one another, and this is why enforced separations wreak havoc on our Souls. There is great danger, then, in living lives of segregation. Racial segregation. Segregation in politics. Segregated frameworks. Segregated and compartmentalized selves" (281–82). Expanding beyond inherited and imposed racialized and nationalist identities that segregate, separate, and compartmentalize human beings, Hartman argues that free territory is not about nationhood or returning to "the great courts and to the regalia of kings and queens" as many of the émigrés believed (234). For Hartman, nationalist and racialized visions of "a White House" or a glorious return to Africa reinforce separation and division rather than engaging in the difficult work of bridge building that Hartman commits to throughout her journey. Moreover, her text challenges us as readers and scholars to ensure that our own lived experiences, our movements through the world, and our critical reading practices reflect a commitment not to singular narratives and journeys but to the ongoing sacred work of decolonization and the unfinished project of freedom.

Throughout this chapter, I have positioned the political and cultural work of Hartman's travel narrative as deeply spiritual because it is grounded not in despair but in radical hope—a hope tethered to the harsh realities of the past with its legacies of violence, dispossession, and domination, and to an unseen but imagined future, what Hartman refers to as "the not yet" or "the as-yet-incomplete project of freedom" ("Venus" 14). Just as the speculative (what might have happened) grounds Hartman's critical reading of the archive, her work toward the creation of a liberated future is equally grounded in the speculative (what might be possible). I define Hartman's relentless commitment to mine, to imagine, to struggle toward "instant[s] of possibility" as we look back to the past and forward to the future as sacred work precisely because such practices make "a place for the living" and enable us to "envision an alternative future" (14). Thus, if we desire to transform ourselves and our world, if we desire to live fully and freely, then the critical and spiritual work of Hartman's text, just like that of the women before her, offers a way forward.

Coda

[H]ow easily Black women's lives are carelessly unearthed, the evidence of our work scattered and thrown away.
—P. Gabrielle Foreman, *Activist Sentiments*

But this is not the end of the story, for all the young women—our mothers and grandmothers, ourselves—have not perished in the wilderness.
—Alice Walker, *In Search of Our Mothers' Gardens*

I have ended this study with *Lose Your Mother* because it calls attention to the stakes of recovering Black women's stories and journeys from the past even while showcasing the limitations of such recovery efforts. Hartman's text reveals that our critical and mobile practices can challenge the erasure and marginalization of Black women's bodies and lives *or* they can reinforce these practices of domination. In opening this study with Hagar and closing it with Hartman, I have sought to demonstrate the long legacy of dispossession and disinheritance that Black women have faced *and* to make visible the necessity, which Foreman notes, of caring for Black women and ensuring that their lives and legacies are not simply "scattered and thrown away." In my own attempts to recover the sacred running through the journeys of Black women from Hagar to Hartman I have aimed to do precisely this, recognizing that offering a fuller portrait of the lives of Black women demands that we tend to their whole lives (the external and the interior, body and spirit) and the complexity of their journeys.

A full portrait also means that we must take seriously the stories Black women have told about their lives. In doing so, we unearth what Black women know and how they know it. Looking closely at their spiritual journeys reveals a persistent vulnerability running through the stories of Black women. We see it in Hagar's captivity—her experience of economic and sexual exploitation, an exploitation that continued to threaten the lives of Elaw, Smith, and Prince as they encountered and testified to various forms of captivity in the United States, including southern slavery, wage slavery in the North, and uninhabitable conditions that threatened their own and their family members' physical and mental health and well-being. Their texts showcase the increased vulnerability Black women have faced as travelers: the near stoning Elaw faced as an itinerant preacher throughout the United States, the threat and fear of kidnapping that Prince experienced in northern cities and on ships, as well as the persistent danger of capture, imprisonment, and enslavement they confronted in their travels throughout a country in which Black bodies were defined as not free and not sacred—a country in which the mobility of Black people was viewed as a threat. Their texts remind us that leaving the country does not remove vulnerabilities—in international waters and lands they continued to face verbal hostility, the threat of kidnapping, political and social terror, and anti-Black violence. Dash's twentieth-century film and Hartman's twenty-first-century travel text remind us that though these legacies of violence and exploitation have their roots in historical systems of oppression and hierarchy (slavery and colonization), they persist into our present, continuing to inform the movements of Black people throughout the world.

In bringing together a variety of sacred and secular texts crossing multiple time periods in this study, I have sought to make visible the singular story constructed about Black women historically—the single story of Black women as captive bodies, not as sacred but as strange and alien. This story troubles each narrator from the biblical Hagar through Elaw, Smith, and Prince in the nineteenth century. It continues to haunt Black women in the centuries that follow, as Dash's film and Hartman's travel narrative reveal. Euro-American theology, visual art, film, and literature have fashioned a legacy of dispossession and disinheritance for Black women. Yet all the texts in this study point to an enduring alternative spiritual legacy that they have claimed for themselves. Through the retelling and reproduction of their own stories that showcase the multiplicity and complexity of their journeys, the women in *Spirit Deep* challenge singular narratives about the Black (female) body, about their spirituality and movements through the world.

Though the narratives in *Spirit Deep* showcase mobility as a refusal to accept the limitations of one's conditions: flight from captivity, from systems of domination, from physical and mental violence and as movement toward a potentially more livable place, they also demonstrate Black women's experience of mobility as complicated and fraught. The route from mobility to freedom is never straight. Despite the inherent tension between mobility and freedom and the ongoing threats Black women have faced, their journeys reveal possible pathways to restoration, to liberation not only for themselves but also for their communities. Despite the many differences between them, all of the texts in this study bear witness to a critical (spiritual) practice rooted in a commitment to struggle, to wholeness, and to interdependence.

Thus, not only do the vulnerabilities Black women face persist into the twentieth and twenty-first centuries but their spiritual legacies persist and expand as well in response to these continued threats. These legacies inform the vision of and the possibilities for liberation these texts offer: freedom grounded in a collective "We" rather than an independent and disconnected "I." Freedom as a practice—something we do and continually struggle toward rather than something we are given. Freedom as the livable, habitable spaces we create in the world rather than some idealized place "out there" to which we might travel. They demonstrate that the individual yearning for freedom, for belonging, the search for home or "free territory" is not merely an individual or even a national yearning but a global and therefore a human one.

Bringing disparate texts together, I have sought not only to make visible the intersections between the journeys, longings, and visions of the travelers. Reading these works through a womanist lens, as I have invited us to do from the outset, enables us to place the sacred and secular elements of these texts in conversation with each other. It enables us to search for and locate Black women's deep spiritual knowing, which requires moving beyond sacred text, beyond the limits of strictly spiritual texts. Our understanding of the sacred may begin with such texts but it need not and must not end there.

Moving beyond this sacred/secular divide makes visible the significance of Hagar's legacy of unruliness and that of her daughters. This core expression of Black women's spiritual practice and knowing has often been dismissed, silenced, or misrepresented. In reclaiming Hagar's narrative of unruliness and locating embodied practices and movements at the core of Black women's spirituality, *Spirit Deep* makes visible an alternative legacy for Black women who resist and challenge systems of domination that narrowly circumscribe their lives, bodies, and communities. Thus, Hagar's legacy of talking back and challenging social hierarchies, flight from captivity, truth-telling, and deep knowing that she is made for freedom persists not only through Elaw, Smith, Prince, Dash, and Hartman's texts but well beyond. Moreover, the narratives in this study reveal the continued relevance of nineteenth-century Black travel writing in the twenty-first century. As we have seen, the spiritual journeys of Black women are a call to meaningful and necessary individual and collective struggle, not only in previous eras, but also in our contemporary moment. In the latest season of oppression in which I write, we have witnessed continued political struggles over citizenship and national identity, the continued circumscribing and policing of the mobility of Black and brown people, as well as unceasing threats to Black life by state-sponsored and white supremacist violence and terror. Even now, I write these closing words in the wake of mounting losses—most recently Breonna Taylor, Ahmaud Arbery, and George Floyd.[1] They remind us of what's at stake in reclaiming Black life, Black bodies, and journeys, that as Hartman claims, lives still hang in the balance.[2]

Yet this study is filled with faith-filled Black women who refuse to accept death as the end and dispossession as our sole legacy. This legacy of Black women's unruliness and radical hope persists into our present age where we continue to see Black women activists, preachers, educators, and public servants committed "to stand down, oppose and defeat slavery in all of its myriad forms" (Hartman 234)—and, I would add, wherever we find it. To name just a few examples, this legacy lives on through organizers, writers, public speakers and educators Brittany Packnett Cunningham, Alicia Garza (co-founder of Black Lives Matters), and Rachel Cargle.[3] It also includes local activists like Takiya Thompson, who tore down a Confederate statue in Durham, North Carolina, in 2017. As she explained, inspired by a long legacy of Black activism, she had decided "I am tired of living in fear. I am tired of white supremacy keeping its foot on my neck and the neck of people who look like me" (Katz). Bree Newsome, who traveled to Columbia, South Carolina, in 2015 to remove the Confederate flag from the state capitol building, lived the legacy. After climbing to the top of the flagpole, she announced with the flag in her hand: "You come against me with hatred, oppression, and violence . . . I come against you in the name of God. This flag comes down today" (Phillip). Then she quoted from Psalm 27:1, "The Lord is my light and my salvation, whom shall I fear?" She was arrested when she reached the ground. But her response echoed Nancy Prince's assertion to white slaveholders that "I am sure the Lord will take care of me; you cannot harm me." Similarly, Rev. Michelle Higgins, Director of Faith for Justice, a

St. Louis based coalition of faith-based activists, lives out and continues a long legacy of biblical activism. Clarifying her mission on a 2015 podcast, Higgins described herself as "honored to be a servant in a season of oppression in St. Louis" where she had been called to "set the working poor free" from both spiritual and "literal chains" ("Stories").

These women are unapologetic in their truth-telling and thoroughly committed to Black liberation. They adopt an intersectional vision for justice that moves the marginalized voices of Black women to the fore. Given Packnett Cunningham, Garza, and Cargle's national visibility, I have chosen to foreground the words of lesser-known Thompson, Newsome, and Higgins in order to highlight the breadth and depth of embodied practices of Black women whose everyday public resistance testifies, like that of the women in this study, that the Black (female) body is sacred and therefore made for freedom. They remind us that our critical engagement with the past cannot and must not end with the text, just as our understanding of the past must always bridge the present. As Deborah McDowell has claimed, "These times call for resistance that stretches beyond discursive realms" (316). Our projects of recovery and critical work as scholars must serve to mobilize our resistance to systems of domination in the present and urge us to a deeper engagement in practices of healing and wholeness for the living bodies in our midst and the restoration of our present world.

Notes

Introduction

1. Pettinger, *Always Elsewhere,* xii; Schriber, *Telling Travels.*

2. The web series *Black Folk Don't* reflects the pervasiveness of this myth that associates travel, especially international travel, with whiteness even as its episode "Travel" challenges the myth that Black people don't travel: www.pbs.org/video/2250428204/.

3. These works include Paul Gilroy's *The Black Atlantic* (1993), the special issue of *BMa:* "Black Travel Writing" (2003), Farah Griffin and Cheryl Fish's *A Stranger in the Village* (1999), Cheryl Fish's *Black and White Women's Travel Narratives* (2004), Jennifer Bernhardt Steadman's *Traveling Economies* (2007), and Gary Totten's *African American Travel Narratives from Abroad* (2015).

4. This legacy of literary scholarship begins with Joanne Braxton's *Black Women Writing Autobiography* (1989), Francis Smith Foster's *Written by Herself* (1993), and Carla Peterson's, *"Doers of the Word"* (1995). See also Moody's *Sentimental Confessions* (2001), Douglass-Chin's *Preacher Woman Sings the Blues* (2001), and Haynes's *Radical Spiritual Motherhood* (2011).

5. Bendixen and Hamera's introduction to *The Cambridge Companion to African American Travel Writing (2009);* Farah J. Griffin and Cheryl J. Fish's introduction to *A Stranger in the Village;* Tim Youngs's "Pushing against the Black/White Limits of Maps." Angela Shaw-Thornburg also notes the "hybridity" of African American travel writing as one explanation for its marginalization (47).

6. Gafney *Womanist Midrash* (2017); Katie Cannon, *Katie's Canon* (1995); bell hooks, *Talking Back* (1989).

7. See M. Shawn Copeland's book *Enfleshing Freedom* (2010) and Carla L. Peterson's "Foreword: Eccentric Bodies" in *Recovering the Black Female Body* (2001), in which she argues that the assault on Black people was both external and internal.

8. The misnaming of Black women originates with European travel to Africa. See Barbara Omolade's essay "Heart of Darkness" for an exploration of the master narrative constructed about the bodies of African and African-descended women, as well as Jennifer L. Morgan's essay, "'Some Could Suckle over Their Shoulder'" for a

deeper analysis of the role of European travel in the construction of the Black (female) body as monstrous.

9. Copeland, *Enfleshing Freedom;* Hortense Spillers, "Mama's Baby, Papa's Maybe."

10. Here I borrow language from William L. Andrews's book, *To Tell a Free Story (1986).* Although *Spirit Deep* addresses work produced more recently than the eighteenth and nineteenth century, I invoke his words in order to suggest that "free telling" is an ongoing struggle and desire for the Black women whose texts I read here.

11. In my critique of singularity as a methodological approach and framework, I draw from M. Jacqui Alexander, who defines "singular thinking" or thinking that focuses on "only one" as divisive, hierarchical and as a practice of negation that undermines the work of decolonization, which seeks wholeness and freedom (281).

12. See Kimberly Wallace-Sanders's introduction to the edited collection, *Skin Deep, Spirit Strong* (2002) and Beverly Guy-Sheftall's essay, "The Body Politic," for evidence of the devaluation of Black women's bodies.

13. See Black feminist scholar M. Jacqui Alexander's book *Pedagogies of Crossing,* 298.

14. McKittrick, *Demonic Grounds (2006).*

15. M. Jacqui Alexander's work informs my thinking about the sacred/secular divide and about the link between knowledge and embodiment. Alexander's commitment to knowledge grounded in a reintegration of spirit and body mirrors the recovery work that *Spirit Deep* undertakes. This work is absolutely necessary because, as Alexander notes, this "way of knowing" is often discredited and marginalized "in spite of the work of feminist theologians and ethicists" (15).

1. Spirituality and Mobility in Hagar's Narrative

1. All quoted biblical passages and translations come from *The HarperCollins Study Bible* (NRSV), unless otherwise stated.

2. I have borrowed this phrase from biblical scholar Savina J. Teubal and use it throughout the chapter when referring to Hagar's divine promise and inheritance.

3. Womanist scholars who foreground the significance of Hagar in their work include Delores Williams, Renita Weems, Wilda Gafney. Though she does not identify as a womanist scholar, see also Nyasha Junior's book *Reimagining Hagar* (2019).

4. Sarai and Abram are pre-covenant names. Later in the text (Gen. 17:4–5, 15), as a mark of God's new covenant with them, God changes Sarai and Abram's names to Sarah and Abraham. Throughout this chapter, I refer to them by their new names.

5. I draw from Sadler's article "Genesis," in which he asserts that Hagar "is objectified, presented only as a solution to a problem for which she is not responsible. Sarai, thus, tells her husband, Abram, in verse 2 to bo '-na' ('go into') Hagar. That sexual language is used for this nonconsensual contact should remind us of enslaved Africana foremothers and forefathers raped by masters and enslavers who used their bodies for sexual gratification and their offspring as slaves" (75).

6. I employ the term "mistress" to connote ownership and authority over enslaved people that is "comparable" or "equivalent" to that of the master (Jones-Rogers xv).

7. Slave narratives that testify to the violence and abuse of white slaveholding women include Frederick Douglass's *Narrative of the Life of Frederick Douglass* (1845), Solomon Northup's *Twelve Years a Slave* (1853), and Harriet Jacobs's *Incidents in the Life of Slave Girl* (1861). For additional historical evidence about the central role of white women as supporters of and active participants in the institution of slavery see Paula Giddings's *When and Where I Enter* (1984) and Stephanie Jones-Rogers's *They Were Her Property* (2019).

8. See Hugh R. Page Jr.'s *The Africana Bible (2010)* and Bernadette J. Brooten's *Beyond Slavery (2010)*.

9. See Marcus Rediker's Introduction to *The Slave Ship* (2007) and Stephanie Smallwood's *Saltwater Slavery* (2007).

10. Biblical slavery is varied, complex and fluid, differing by region, time period, and community. Nevertheless, the common feature of biblical slavery across such differences was a common grounding in a principle of othering. Those most likely to be enslaved were foreigners, while the risk of being enslaved by one's own people was far greater for the most vulnerable members of the community and those with the least power—women and children. See David P. Wright's essay, "'She Shall Not Go Free as Male Slaves Do'" (2010) and Gafney's *Womanist Midrash,* pp. 72–84, for deeper readings of Israel's debt slavery laws and the particular vulnerability of women who were foreigners. For a deeper analysis of slavery within early Christianity, see Jennifer A. Glancy's essay, "Early Christianity, Slavery, and Women's Bodies" (2010).

11. Drawing on Julia S. Jordan-Zachery's *Shadow Bodies* (2017), I define (mis)naming as a discursive practice used to inscribe or fix a variety of meanings to the Black female body, Hagar in particular. For a broader conversation of Black feminist critics about the misnaming and misrepresentation of Black women through the circulation of stereotypes and tropes, see Kimberly Wallace-Sanders's *Skin Deep, Spirit Strong* (2002), Patricia Hill Collins's 2nd ed. of *Black Feminist Thought* (2009), Shirley Anne Tate's *Black Women's Bodies and The Nation* (2015), and Janell Hobson's *Venus in the Dark* (2018).

12. Hagar's narrative is not the only biblical text that can serve as an alternative to the Exodus narrative. The book of Esther, in which a young woman becomes the savior of the marginalized Jewish people, is another story that has been appropriated by both Black women and men. Though Esther's narrative, like Hagar's, focuses on a woman's spiritual experience and power, it lacks the significance that the Exodus narrative holds in Black theology.

13. See Albert Raboteau's assertion that "[b]y appropriating the story of Exodus as their own story, Black Christians articulated their own sense of peoplehood. Exodus symbolized their common history and common destiny" (*A Fire in the Bones*, 33).

14. Adam Clark similarly calls for a more expansive conversation about Hagar across spiritual itineraries in his article "Hagar the Egyptian." Clark claims that Hagar's encounter with the Judeo-Christian God is fundamentally shaped by her African-derived womanist spirituality stemming from her Egyptian origins.

15. See Galatians 4:21–5:1 for Paul's full allegory of Hagar and Sarah, especially verse 30 in which he paraphrases Sarah's command to disinherit Hagar found in the Genesis text. Teubal further clarifies the impact of Paul's allegory, noting that "Paul (albeit in a different context) has clearly defined the slave (Hagar) as 'of the flesh,' and therefore inferior to the free woman (Sarah) who, though not 'of the Spirit' herself, is of superior stature for having received 'the promise'" (xxiii).

16. One exception is Edmonia Lewis, a nineteenth-century sculptor with African American and Native American ancestry, whose sculpture, "Hagar in the Wilderness," depicts Hagar using the neoclassical form. According to art scholars Kirsten Buick, David Driskell and Elsa Honig Fine, Lewis's representation of Hagar identifies with Black people and their experiences of oppression. We can reposition Lewis's Hagar, then, as a critical response to traditional representations of Hagar that exclude Black people from the American cultural and social landscape.

17. See Janet Gabler-Hover's *Dreaming Black/Writing White* (2000). Examples of Hagar novels written by white southern women include: E.D.E.N. Southworth's *The Deserted Wife* (1849) and *Virginia and Magdalene; or the Foster Sisters* (1857), Harriet Marion Stephens's *Hagar the Martyr; or, Passion and Reality: A Tale of the North and South* (1855), as well as Charlotte Moon Clark's *The Modern Hagar: A Drama* (1882).

18. See Saidiya Hartman's article, "Seduction and the Ruses of Power," for a more extensive analysis of rape within the institution of slavery. Hartman argues that rape of Black women was a legal impossibility because under the law, the Black (female) body existed solely for the full enjoyment of the master.

19. Scholarship exploring the cultural anxiety around the Black female body and Black women's critical responses to it include: Michael Bennett and Vanessa D. Dickerson's *Recovering the Black Female Body* (2001); Kimberly Wallace Sanders's *Skin Deep, Spirit Strong* (2002); Carolyn A. Brown's *The Black Female Body in American Literature and Art* (2012); and Shirley Anne Tate's *Black Women's Bodies and the Nation* (2015).

20. See Hazel Carby's seminal book *Reconstructing Womanhood* (1987) for a cogent analysis of the oppositional definitions of white and Black women constructed within the institution of slavery.

21. See Greene, 14–16 and 84, for a deeper analysis of southern Christians' biblical justifications for slavery and Gabler-Hover, 7.

22. Williams's *Sisters in the Wilderness*, 23–26 and 153; Clark, "Hagar the Egyptian," 53.

23. For more on Hagar's cultural and spiritual significance within Black communities, see Delores Williams's *Sisters in the Wilderness*, 2 and Wilda Gafney's *Womanist Midrash* in which she testifies to the importance of Hagar as a spiritual ancestor within Black churches, 40.

24. Although Hall is solely concerned with Anglo-Americans during the First Great Awakening (1730–60), his definition of itinerancy as the transgression of social boundaries is useful for my own thinking about Black women's itinerant practices in the nineteenth century.

25. See McKittrick, *Demonic Grounds*, xv.

26. Like Williams and Gafney, I read Hagar's encounter with "the angel of God" as an encounter with God. See Williams's *Sisters in the Wilderness*, 20 and Gafney's *Womanist Midrash*, 43.

27. McKittrick, xvi.

28. As domestic workers, Elaw, Smith, and Prince would have been continually exposed to the threat of sexual violence. Although Elaw, Smith, and Prince never explicitly name this threat, I will argue in subsequent chapters that this may have been something they silenced in their narratives.

29. Isaac's age is uncertain. However, Sarah's concern over her son's inheritance comes after he is weaned from breastfeeding and after she sees Isaac and Ishmael playing together (Gen. 20:8–9). This suggests that Isaac is a few years old at this point in the narrative but still a young child.

30. Teubal, 168 and 176; Williams, *Sisters in the Wilderness*, 32–33.

31. See Gafney's *Womanist Midrash* in which she claims that "Hagar receives the first divine annunciation to a woman in the canon of a promised child and promise of a dynasty. Hagar will become the Mother of Many Peoples" (42).

32. This positioning of Sarah as obedient wife who submits to the authority of her husband offers an incomplete narrative about her life. It ignores the power she deploys in her household especially in relationship to Hagar whose body she offers up for exploitation and whose exile she demands. In both of these instances, Abraham follows Sarah's commands regarding Hagar—demonstrating her total power and authority over her "slave-girl." For a deeper and more complex reading of Sarah, see Teubal, *Ancient Sisterhood* (1997).

33. See McKittrick's claim that the placing of Black women's bodies "hardens spatial binaries"—marking the boundaries for belonging (xv).

34. See Genesis 16:13–14 for the full description of Hagar's naming.

35. I borrow language from the ESV translation of Genesis 16:13: "So she called the name of the Lord who spoke to her, 'You are a God of seeing,' for she said, 'Truly here I have seen him who looks after me.'"

36. I draw from Gafney who links Hagar's seeing of God to the Exodus 33:20 passage in which God states to Moses that no one can see God and live (42).

37. I borrow the phrase, "subject constituting practices" from Shirley Anne Tate, who claims that attempts to control the Black female body through discourse are incomplete (not totalizing). In other words, Black women also possess the ability to engage in practices of "autonomy," "critique" and alternative "knowledge production" that reconstitute Black women as subjects rather than as objects (6).

38. Andrews, *To Tell a Free Story*, Preface and 19–31.

39. For more on the Egyptian and African roots of Hagar's spirituality, including her naming practices, see Williams, *Sisters in the Wilderness*, 153 and Clark, 53.

40. For additional readings of Sarah's abuse, see Renita Weems, 6; Gafney, 35; and Brooten, 13. See also Exodus 1:11–22 and 2:11–12 for examples of the brutality of Hebrew enslavement that mirrors Sarah's oppression of Hagar.

41. Although Sarah's initial authority over Hagar was absolute, her command to Abraham to expel Hagar and Ishmael suggests that Ishmael's birth has limited her

power in some way, perhaps because he is Abraham's son. See, for example, Genesis 21:11, which states, "And the thing [Sarah's command] was very displeasing to Abraham on account of his son." Sarah's directive to "cast out" Hagar and Ishmael into the desert foreshadows the Pharaoh's edict to throw all male children born to Hebrew women into the Nile (Exod. 1:22). In both instances, such ruthlessness, whether exercised at an individual or national level, stems from a deep desire to withhold power from "foreigners." Reading the Genesis and Exodus narratives in tandem makes visible the repetitions of violence at micro and macro levels and demonstrates oppression as a fundamentally human problem—a systemic evil that persists across cultural, historical, and geographic locations.

42. See Alexander, 300–311.

43. Here I echo Virginia Whatley Smith's claims about the inextricable link between slavery and travel in her essay, "African American travel literature."

2. Visionary Movement in Zilpha Elaw's *Memoirs*

1. Elaw does not mention her exact date of birth. William L. Andrews places Elaw's birth "around 1790" in *Sisters of the Spirit* (7), while Kimberly Blockett places her birth closer to 1793.

2. See Blockett's Harvard Divinity School lecture, "#sayhername" (2018), for more on Elaw's childhood and biography: https://hds.harvard.edu/news/2018/04/25/video-sayhername-recovering-zilpha-elaw%E2%80%99s-rebellious-evangelicalism#

3. These itinerant women include Jarena Lee, Rebecca Cox Jackson, Julia Foote, and Sojourner Truth to name a few.

4. Although Elaw's immediate audience was British given the publication of her text in London, I believe she wrote for a transatlantic audience because of her commitment to ministry on both sides of the Atlantic, her intent to return to the United States (though it's unclear whether she did), as well as her conclusion, which clearly expands her audience beyond her British community of friends and supporters to include "all Christians" (159).

5. Blockett claims that Elaw was "reduced to obscurity by the time of her death [in 1873]." For more on her recovery of the latter part of Elaw's life after the publication of her 1846 narrative, see Blockett's Harvard Divinity school lecture.

6. Gabrielle Foreman addresses the vulnerability of Black girls in northern white domestic spaces in her book *Activist Sentiments* (2009). See also Hazel Carby's *Reconstructing Womanhood* (1987), which links southern slavery and northern systems of economic exploitation in Black women's writing.

7. See bell hooks's essay, "Representing Whiteness in the Black Imagination," 174.

8. See Joanne Braxton, Francis Smith Foster, Joycelyn Moody, and Richard Douglass-Chin.

9. See Braxton, *Black Women Writing Autobiography*, 50; Moody, *Sentimental Confessions*, 24.

10. According to Elaw, her husband Joseph Elaw died after a long illness on January 27, 1823 (85).

11. Such writers include Frederick Douglass, Frances Harper, and Harriet Jacobs.

12. See Andrews's *To Tell a Free Story,* especially 1–5.

13. Williams, "Visions, Inner Voices, Apparitions, and Defiance in Nineteenth-Century Black Women's Narratives" (1993), 81.

14. See McKittrick, xv and Blockett, "Moving Subjectivities in the Evangelical Narrative of Zilpha Elaw," 105.

15. Though Elaw preached before white and Black audiences, her narrative foregrounds hostile receptions she received by white men and women (American and British) to her preaching. Elaw for instance is mocked by slaveholding men who come to hear her preach, patronized by British (male) members of the anti-slavery society, reports having the door slammed in her face by a white woman in Maine after announcing her arrival as an itinerant preacher, and is chastised by a British woman who argues that women preachers are unbiblical.

16. Scholarship on the Black prophetic tradition includes: Wilson Jeremiah Moses's *Black Messiahs and Uncle Toms* (1983), David Howard-Pitney's *The African American Jeremiad* (2005), and Willie J. Harrell Jr.'s *Origins of the African American Jeremiad, 1760–1861* (2011). These texts construct a predominantly male prophetic lineage. However, Harrell's text includes a chapter on Black women prophetic voices including Stewart, Truth, and Harper. Though the majority of the chapter foregrounds Stewart's writing, the text does gesture toward a lineage of Black female prophetic voices.

17. See Stewart's and Truth's primary publications: *Productions of Mrs. Maria W. Stewart* (1835) and *Narrative of Sojourner Truth* (1850).

18. Copeland, 2.

19. See the introduction to Acts in *The HarperCollins Study Bible* (NRSV), as well as note 8.26–40 for additional context on the book of Acts and on the Ethiopian eunuch.

20. As stated in Deuteronomy 23:1, "No one whose testicles are crushed or whose penis is cut off shall be admitted to the assembly of the Lord."

21. Sanctification was so controversial that even Methodists disagreed on whether or not it was a valid theological tenet. See Bettye Collier-Thomas's book, *Daughters of Thunder* (1998), for more on this schism within the Methodist Church over holiness doctrines.

22. The phrase "impenetrable whiteness" comes from Toni Morrison's theoretical text, *Playing in the Dark* (1992).

23. See chapter 15, "Continued Persecutions," in Jacobs's narrative.

24. Elaw references "her only surviving brother," who she travels to Utica to see for the first time since she was 6 years of age (132).

25. See Blockett, "Moving Subjectivities in the Evangelical Narrative of Zilpha Elaw," 103.

26. See Sylvia Jacobs's edited collection, *Black Americans and the Missionary Movement in Africa* (1982), as well as Esme Cleall's *Missionary Discourses of Difference* (2012).

27. I use the term *selectively* because Paul's writings also include passages that suggest a much more complicated relationship between slavery and Christianity, including this passage from Galatians: "There is no longer Jew or Greek, there is no longer slave or free, there is no longer male and female; for all of you are one in Christ Jesus" (3:28).

28. In April 1828, Elaw has a visionary encounter in which "the Spirit" assures her that she will travel to England (90); however, she writes that she does not leave the country until July 1840—twelve years later (138).

29. See Harrell's analysis of Crummell, 171–72.

30. See Douglass's "Reception Speech" at Finsbury Chapel, Moorfields, England, May 22, 1846 in his Appendix to *My Bondage and My Freedom* (1855), as well as William Wells Brown's *The American Fugitive in Europe* (1855).

31. Andrews's claim that Elaw's text offers a "serious reflection on liberating communal alternatives" and expresses the desire for "an inchoate community of the Spirit that transcends normal social distinctions in the name of a radical egalitarianism" (*Sisters* 20) shapes my thinking about community. I draw also from Walter Brueggemann, who defines prophetic ministry as "a way of evoking, forming, and reforming an alternative community" that is radically opposed to systems of domination and is grounded in a "vision of *God's freedom*" (4, 7).

3. Colonial and Missionary Crossings in Amanda Smith's *An Autobiography*

1. The 1840 US Census listed the Berry family as free. See Adrienne M. Israel's biography *Amanda Berry Smith* (1998) for an extended discussion of Smith's family and their experiences of enslavement and freedom (9–19). Although Israel spells Smith's mother's name as Miriam, I have opted to use the same spelling Smith employs in her autobiography.

2. For more on Smith's preaching style and impact, see Israel's biography, which chronicles her preaching from 1889 to 1899, including her representation in various periodicals.

3. Smith joined the Women's Christian Temperance Union in 1875, becoming a popular speaker and national evangelist for the organization. She embarked on a speaking tour across England for the British Women's Temperance Association (BWTA) in 1893. For more on Smith's social activism in the temperance movement, including her role in the Black Club Woman Movement, see Israel's biography especially p59–65, 98–105, and 126–32.

4. See the following studies of women preachers: Richard J. Douglass-Chin's *Preacher Woman Sings the Blues* (2001), Elizabeth Elkin Grammar's *Some Wild Visions* (2003), Susie C. Stanley's *Holy Boldness* (2002).

5. J. M. Thoburn was a white Methodist minister who served as a missionary in Calcutta. On May 25, 1888, he was elected to serve as Missionary Bishop to India and Malaysia by the Methodist General Conference ("One More Bishop"). An

internationally renowned figure and a man of prominence within the world of missions, Thoburn's preface was a strong recommendation to readers.

6. Smith's narrative does not explicitly describe the audience. However, it most likely included local Indian inhabitants of Calcutta, white missionaries and spiritual itinerants like Thoburn, and perhaps white tourists as well.

7. Sleep deprivation was a common but often overlooked expression of slavery's violence and dehumanization. John Jea testifies to this in his slave narrative, *The Life, History, and Unparalleled Sufferings of John Jea* (1811), 4.

8. Although Miss Celie's use of the word *have* implies that she wishes to bestow freedom with no monetary remuneration, the narrative suggests that the word *have* is conditional—meaning that if Samuel saves enough money, he should be allowed to buy his wife and children.

9. Smith does not name her grandmother in her narrative, nor does she address her disappearance from the text explicitly, but the beginning of chapter 2 suggests that her grandmother remains in slavery, while the rest of the family moves north, as she explains her mother "hated to leave her mother, my dear grandmother" (24).

10. Smith describes New Market as located "on the Baltimore and York Turnpike" and lists a number of white men (slave catchers and slaveholders) who reside there (32). Given that New Market was just under a mile from their house, Smith notes she and her family were familiar with the slave catchers who "used to watch our house closely, trying every way to catch my father" (32).

11. Katherine McKittrick, 72.

12. See Claude A. Clegg for an example of how courthouses were utilized as sites of slave auction, 54–57. See also Kenneth S. Greenberg's introduction to *The Confessions of Nat Turner (2017)* for further examples of the kinds of restrictions placed on the freedom of "free" Blacks.

13. Smith does not state when her first husband, Calvin Devine, died, and she offers few details about this loss except that he "enlisted and went South with the army" during the Civil War and "never returned" (57).

14. See womanist scholar M. Shawn Copeland's *Enfleshing Freedom* and M. Jacqui Alexander's *Pedagogies of Crossing*; both shape my understanding of the body as not separate from the spirit but rather as the medium for the spirit's movement in the world.

15. See Elizabeth Elkin Grammer's 2003 study, *Some Wild Visions,* for further discussion of the racial context in which Smith lived and wrote, 15–17 and 94–97. See also Israel's discussion of the impact of racial constructions on Smith's 1893 autobiography as well as her letters and correspondence.

16. Smith loses four children in her lifetime. Though Smith provides little details about these losses, Adrienne Israel attributes them to the poor working and poor living conditions that Smith and her children endured, 24 and 36–41.

17. See Giddings, *When and Where I enter* (1984) and Jacqueline Jones, *Labor of love, labor of sorrow* (1985), as well as *American Work* (1988).

18. See Isaiah 61:10: "I will greatly rejoice in the Lord, my whole being shall exult in my God; for he has clothed me with the garments of salvation, he has covered me with the robes of righteousness."

19. Given Smith's membership in the A.M.E. church, these fellow church members are presumably Black women.

20. Caroline Haynes's analysis of Evangelical Christian representations of God, particularly in the person of Jesus, as a "loving partner" (104), has shaped my thinking. According to Haynes, this image was "enticing for the Christian feminists because it offered them an alternative . . . to their demanding and dominating spouses. Thus, these women could bypass oppressive forms of male authority without shirking their Christian true woman image" (104).

21. Smith notes that she arrives in New York from Liverpool on Friday, September 5, 1890 (502).

22. The sale of *An Autobiography* and itinerant preaching tours would have been important sources of income for Smith after her return to the US, especially to help fund the orphanage and school she opened just outside of Chicago to serve Black children who were excluded from local orphanages and schools.

23. For a more detailed analysis of Liverpool in the nineteenth century, see David Seed's *American Travellers in Liverpool* (2008) and Jacqueline Nassy Brown's *Dropping Anchor, Setting Sail* (2005).

24. See Fish's Introduction to *Black and White Women's Travel Narratives* (2004).

25. See Patricia Hill Collins's *Black Feminist Thought* (2009). I employ her positioning of Black women as "situated knowers" (22) in order to argue that Smith's unique location as a Black woman impacts her perspective and gives her access to alternative ways of knowing.

26. See Mary Louise Pratt's *Imperial Eyes*, 67.

27. Scott Trafton's *Egypt Land* (2004) offers an analysis of nineteenth-century Black travelers to Egypt including David Dorr, Frederick Douglass, and Edward Blyden. Although Trafton does address sculptor Edmonia Lewis's and writer Pauline Hopkins's representations of Egypt in their visual and literary art, the study foregrounds male intellectuals and travelers.

28. We might alternatively read Smith's language as expressing an (always illicit) desire for the Black body. If one of the purposes of exoticism is to make the unfamiliar familiar (see Ashcroft 98), then Smith's use of colonial travel discourse becomes a way of appropriating the familiar to engage her audience in a critique of imperial practices.

29. Blyden's engagement in Egyptology in the nineteenth century reminds us that this ongoing critical conversation was not contained solely within the US but crossed the circum-Atlantic as well. For more on Blyden's intellectual career, see Hollis R. Lynch's edited work *Black Spokesman* (1971).

30. In her 1991 study, *Discourses of Difference*, Sara Mills positions the civilized/savage binary as central to imperial discourse (87). She asserts that women travel writers occupy a tenuous relationship to such discourse because of their status as women, which further complicates their ability to adopt the traditional voice of Western colonial traveler (2–4).

31. See Jacobs, *Black Americans and the Missionary Movement in Africa* (1982).

32. See Jones, Constance A., and James D. Ryan. "Jagannath Temple in Puri." *Encyclopedia of World Religions: Encyclopedia of Hinduism,* Constance A. Jones, Facts on File, 2nd edition, 2016.

33. For an example, see "AFFAIRS IN INDIA.; The Great Juggernaut Saturnalia. The Sacrifice of Human Victims." *The New York Times.* August 31, 1864. https://www.nytimes.com/1864/08/31/archives/affairs-in-india-the-great-juggernaut-saturnalia-the-sacrifice-of.html. For more on the long tradition of Western female travelers to India and their construction of a discourse of difference in their writing about Indian people, see Indira Ghose's *Women Travellers in Colonial India* (1998).

34. For further analysis of how Western science, literature, photography, and art were deployed to provide evidence of the inferiority of Blackness and to construct a definition of the Black female body as monstrous, see Kimberly Wallace-Sanders's edited collection, *Skin Deep, Spirit Strong* (2002) and Henry Louis Gates's edited collection, *"Race," Writing, and Difference* (1986).

35. Smith's inclusion of Black women within the ideal of true womanhood places her in close company with writer, speaker, and educator Anna Julia Cooper, who published her seminal work *A Voice from the South* in 1892—just one year before *An Autobiography* was published. Like Smith, Cooper attempts to revalue the Black female body by positing the Black woman as a "moral force," one whose "unique position" as both Black and female makes her an invaluable resource on all national issues. Cooper includes Amanda Smith along with Frances Watkins Harper, Sojourner Truth, and Charlotte Forten Grimké on a list of noteworthy Black women whose "work and influence" helped further the advancement of Black people in America (44, 45).

36. Smith's negative opinion of Western medicine reflected the unjust and racist treatment of African Americans by doctors in the US. Western doctors demonstrated a continuing disrespect for the Black body through repeated violation, including experimenting on Black bodies and performing medical procedures without the consent of Black patients, as well as the posthumous theft of Black bodies for medical research. Such violations continued as part of standard medical practice in the US well into and beyond the twentieth-century. See Harriet Washington's book *Medical Apartheid* (2006) and Rebecca Skloot's biography *The Immortal Life of Henrietta Lacks* (2010).

37. See Israel's biography for additional information about Smith's adoption of African children.

38. I have borrowed this term "transference" from Mary Louise Pratt's text *Imperial Eyes,* in which she argues that although colonizers emphasized the acculturation of indigenous peoples into Western cultural practices, this sharing of culture went both ways (Intro 6). One obvious expression of colonial culture is the Western names of Smith's adopted children. Her autobiography does not explain how they received these names but undoubtedly the presence of missionaries informed these naming practices. It's unclear, for instance, whether Bob's father, referred to as Jack in the text, chose to rename his son because of his desire for Western acculturation or because missionaries conferred these names on them.

39. I read Smith's adoption of Bob (and Frances) as a reflection of her broader commitment to children's welfare, which becomes more apparent after she returns to the United States in 1890. Nine years after her return, Smith opened the Amanda Smith Industrial Orphan Home in Harvey, Ill in 1899. In addition to teaching and religious instruction, she also took on the daunting work of fundraising to keep the orphanage open, which she continued until her retirement in 1912.

40. Smith's adoption is grounded in a deep desire to protect Black children from exploitation. This desire to protect Black children is most visible in her orphanage and in her own work in arranging and overseeing adoptions of children from the Amanda Smith Industrial Orphan Home. Israel explains that "vulnerable orphans often lived with families who forced them to work under slavelike conditions. Smith tried to shield the children she placed from such abuse by personally visiting the families that adopted children from her home" (128).

41. See John S. Mbiti's seminal work, *African Religions and Philosophy* (1969), for a deeper analysis of African traditional religions, especially the role of nature in spiritual practices like those Smith references. Rejecting the Western sacred/secular divide, Mbiti notes that within African cosmologies, "Nature in the broadest sense of the word is not an empty impersonal object or phenomenon: it is filled with religious significance.... God is seen in and behind these objects and phenomena.... This is one of the most fundamental religious heritages of African peoples. It is unfortunate that foreign writers, through great ignorance, have failed to understand this deep religious insight of our peoples; and have often either ridiculed it, or naively presented it as 'nature worship' or 'animism'" (56–57).

42. Although Maria Stewart is often the sole Black woman included in conversations about colonization, Smith's narrative can broaden our understanding of Black writers' engagement with this issue during the nineteenth century and expand Black women's contribution beyond a singular voice. For additional information on Black travelers and African colonization see Farah J. Griffin and Cheryl J. Fish's edited collection, *A Stranger in the Village* (1998).

43. See Sylvia Jacobs's edited work *Black Americans and the Missionary Movement in Africa* (1982).

4. Searching for Home in Nancy Prince's *A Narrative*

1. Nancy Prince published the first edition of her narrative in 1850 and a second revised edition in 1853 with a reprint in 1856. All quotations in this chapter come from the 1853 edition of *Life and Travels of Mrs. Nancy Prince*.

2. Scholarship foregrounding the secular elements of Prince's journeys include Cheryl J. Fish's "Journeys and Warnings" (2001), Kristen Fitzpatrick's "American National Identity Abroad" (2004), Sarah Brusky's "Nancy Prince and her Gothic Odyssey" (2004), Carmen Birkle's essay, "Traveling and the Discourse of Economy in Nancy Prince's Travel Narrative" (2009), as well as Amber Foster's article, "Nancy Prince's Utopias" (2013).

3. See Fish's article "Journeys and Warnings: Nancy Prince's Travels as Cautionary Tales for African American Readers" (2001) and her book, *Black and White Women's Travel Narratives* (2004).

4. The term "slave-classed" connotes how the consequences and legacies of slavery accrue to the Black body regardless of legal status. See Blockett's "Moving Subjectivities in the Evangelical Narrative of Zilpha Elaw" (2003).

5. Gilroy, *The Black Atlantic,* 4 and 17; McKittrick, *Demonic Grounds,* xii.

6. Marcus Rediker, *The Slave Ship,* 265; Stephanie Smallwood, *Saltwater Slavery,* 60. I borrow the phrase "open rebellion" from Frederick Douglass's 1855 *My Bondage and My Freedom,* 285. Douglass's narrative, like Prince's, locates his individual struggle for freedom within a broader collective resistance to enslavement.

7. Smallwood, like Orlando Patterson, defines the terror of the slave ship as the process of "social annihilation" (60) or "social death" (30) that marked the new status of enslaved people—commodities excluded from human community. I, however, have chosen to define this terror as a spiritual assault in order to underscore the interior violence of practices of cultural stripping, forced forgetting, and the metaphysical separation of captives from kin. Hartman illustrates the spiritual violence of such practices in her book *Lose Your Mother:* "It expunged all memories of a natal land, and it robbed the slave of spiritual protection. Ignorant of her lineage, to whom could the slave appeal?" (157).

8. Rediker, 278–85; Smallwood, 61; and Hartman, *Lose Your Mother,* 157.

9. I borrow the phrase "spatial histories" from McKittrick, who posits an inextricable link between geography and history. For McKittrick, space is produced (shaped and defined) in and through human histories; therefore, shifting attention to the knowledge and experiences of marginalized subjects enables us to "imagine new geographic stories" (ix–xi).

10. See Gunning, "Nancy Prince and the Politics of Mobility, Home and Diasporic (mis)Identification" (2001), 43 and Gilroy, *The Black Atlantic,* 12–13 and 226, note 25. Both note the tenuous nature of liberty achieved via ships/sailing as the passage of legislation in the nineteenth century, such as the Negro Seaman's Acts in the 1850s, aimed to curtail the freedom of Black sailors in the wake of Denmark Vesey's rebellion.

11. See Lisa Logan, "*Uncle Tom's Cabin* and Conventional Nineteenth-Century Domestic Ideology," 46–47, as well as Jane Tompkins's *Sensational Designs* (1986).

12. See also Carla Peterson, *Doers of the Word,* 94.

13. This moment around the hearth stands in stark contrast to the ending lines of the 1861 slave narrative, *Incidents in the Life of a Slave Girl,* when Linda Brent exclaims, "The dream of my life is not yet realized. I do not sit with my children in a home of my own. I still long for a hearthstone of my own" (Jacobs 201).

14. Though Prince omits the details of the abuse she experienced at home, she does note that her "step-father was not very kind" to her or to her sister, Silvia (12). See also Joycelyn Moody's reading of Nancy and Silvia's experience of abuse within the domestic space in *Sentimental Confessions.*

15. Carmen Birkle, "Traveling and the Discourse of Economy in Nancy Prince's Travel Narrative," 28–29.

16. See the previous chapter on Amanda Smith for a deeper discussion of the American Colonization Society and motivations for Black emigration.

17. See Fitzpatrick, 268 and Gunning, 45.

18. See Allison Blakely, *Russia and the Negro* (1986), 28–29.

19. Cheryl Fish's *Black and White Women's Travel Narratives* (2004) and Fitzpatrick's "American National Identity Abroad" (2004) position Russia as an idealized space of racial acceptance in Prince's narrative. Alternatively, Amber Foster's article, "Nancy Prince's Utopias" (2013) and Sarah Brusky's "Nancy Prince and Her Gothic Odyssey" (2004) argue for more complicated readings of Russia as an unstable space of terror.

20. See Smallwood, *Saltwater Slavery:* "the operative unit of the slave ship was not the individual captive person, but rather the aggregate that formed the 'complete' human cargo. The slave ship, then, could not proceed on its way toward American retail markets until its decks were crowded with the requisite number of captives" (68).

21. A telling example of such racist ideologies in Russian society is Nicholas Dobroliubov's claim in an 1868 article that "[w]e do not think it necessary to deal with the differences between the skulls of Negroes and of other lower races of man and the skulls of people among civilized nations. Who is not aware of the strange development of the upper part of the skull among these [lower] races . . . ?" (qtd. in Blakely 34). See also Gunning's claim that Prince never feels fully at home in Russia because Black people maintained a "peripheral status as exotic curiosities" in the country (66, note 34).

22. Prince's activism includes lecturing (1839), organizing an attack on a slave-catcher (1847), multiple publications of *A Narrative (*1850/53/56), and speaking at the National Women's Rights Convention (1856). See Moira Ferguson's *Nine Black Women* (1998) for a full chronology.

23. Though Prince refers to the organization vaguely as "the Anti-Slavery Society," Cheryl Fish specifies her membership in "the biracial Boston Female Anti-Slavery Society during the 1830s" (*Black and White* 49).

24. For more on nineteenth-century Black women writers and the challenges of audience, see Frances Smith Foster's *Written by Herself,* 78–83 and Moody, 25.

25. Although the British Emancipation Act was signed in 1833, it created a system of de facto slavery in which formerly enslaved people served as apprentices to former slaveholders. A second bill was passed in 1838 granting full and immediate emancipation of all apprentices. Prince's text, however, bears witness to the continued economic exploitation of newly freed Black Jamaicans and the use of anti-Black violence to terrorize and control the free Black population. See also Thomas C. Holt's *The Problem of Freedom* (1992).

26. While here Prince foregrounds the agency of Black Jamaicans, at other moments in her text her Western privilege blinds her to such resistance. One example is

Prince's refusal to follow the authority of the Black Jamaican class leader that she is assigned to help (46). Ostensibly, Prince disagrees with the class leader's theology in some way; however, Black Jamaicans practiced a syncretic blend of African traditional spirituality and Christianity, which as Gunning notes, enabled them to challenge the authority of white missionaries and to resist colonial systems of power (54–55). Prince's conflict with the class leader demonstrates her own religious imperialism and her refusal to trust the spiritual knowledge and experience of Black Jamaicans—a key source of their agency and resistance.

27. Prince's critical portrait of white missionaries in Jamaica also extends to her own mistreatment, as she narrates an attempt of the white American Congregationalist missionaries she works with to take possession of her money and material resources (61). See Sandra Gunning's article, "Nancy Prince and the Politics of Mobility, Home and Diasporic (Mis)Identification."

28. See Gunning, 53.

29. See Fish, "Journeys and Warnings."

30. Prince makes two trips to Jamaica in 1840 and 1842. The first time she leaves the island (1841) in order to raise money. Though she returns with additional resources in May 1842, the deteriorating conditions and increased anti-Black violence lead to her second abrupt return a few months thereafter.

31. See Hartman's *Scenes of Subjection* (1997).

32. See SallyAnn H. Ferguson's article "Christian Violence and the Slave Narrative" (1996) for a deeper analysis of slaveholding theology.

33. All quoted biblical text taken from *The HarperCollins Study Bible*, New Revised Standard Version (1993).

34. See, for example, *Productions of Mrs. Maria W. Stewart* (1835), 56–72.

35. See Jeremiah 1:10 in which God declares Jeremiah's mission as prophet as critical and constructive: "See, today I appoint you over nations and over kingdoms to pluck up and to pull down, to destroy and to overthrow, to build and to plant" (NRSV).

36. See Mary G. Mason's article, "Travel as Metaphor and Reality in Afro-American Women's Autobiography, 1850–1972," 355.

37. See, for example, Fish, *Black and White*, 63.

38. I employ McKittrick's phrase "place-based critiques" to foreground how Prince's location in the world shapes and informs her critical practice.

5. Mapping Sacred Movement in Julie Dash's *Daughters of the Dust*

1. See Dash's interview with bell hooks in *Daughters of the Dust: The Making of an African American Woman's Film* (1992) and Judith Weisenfeld's essay "'My Story Begins before I Was Born'" (2003).

2. Of course, Islam is also a colonizing force. The film's inclusion of the historical figure Bilal Muhammed—an African captive who was stolen from the Sudan as a

boy and brought first to the West Indies and later to the Sea Islands illustrates the significant role of Islam in the colonization of Africa.

3. In contrast to popular 1990s Black male-directed films, such as *Boyz N the Hood* (John Singleton, 1991) and *New Jack City* (Mario Van Peebles, 1991), *Daughters of the Dust* was turned down by every major Hollywood studio because executives believed the film had no viable audience. In interviews and in her own writing about the film, Dash attributes this rejection and exclusion to "a concerted effort" to marginalize Black women filmmakers (M. Martin 15) and to tell a single story of African American people (Dash, *Making* 8, 16, 25).

4. Scottish physicist David Brewster invented the kaleidoscope in 1816, though the device did not make its way to the United States until the 1870s when Charles Bush began producing his own version of the toy. Given the geographic and social isolation of Ibo Landing, Mr. Snead's kaleidoscope would most likely be the children's (and many adults') first physical encounter with the toy. See Gillian Holmes, "Kaleidoscope." How Products Are Made. MadeHow.com. 18 May 2020 http://www.madehow.com/Volume-6/Kaleidoscope.html. See also "kaleidoscope." *The Columbia Encyclopedia,* Paul Lagasse, and Columbia University, Columbia University Press, 8th edition, 2018.

5. All film quotes taken from Dash's screenplay in *Daughters of the Dust: The Making of an African American Women's Film* (1992).

6. Weisenfeld's essay "'My Story Begins before I Was Born'" (2003) introduced the term "empowered eye," inspired by Toni Cade Bambara's article title, "Reading the Signs, Empowering the Eye" (1993).

7. See Jennifer A. Marchiorlatti's article, "Revisiting Julie Dash's *Daughters of the Dust*" (2005) for additional context about the role of the griot in African society and in Dash's film.

8. Tableaux refers to a series of static images in a painting or fixed poses in live theatre typically used to encourage deeper contemplation of the art and its meaning. See King's, "Memory and the Phantom South in African American Migration Film" (2010) for an extended analysis of Dash's use of tableaux to visually communicate the fragmentation and rupture caused by migration.

9. Although Dash refers to Bilal's transcribed text in her screenplay notes as a "homemade Koran" (77), Lena Brøndum explains in her essay, "The Persistence of Tradition" (1999) that the historical Bilal Muhammed transcribed another sacred Muslim text, the *Risala,* from memory (155). For additional historical context on Bilal Muhammed's life see also Allan D. Austin's book *African Muslims in Antebellum America* (1997).

10. I locate Viola within a larger cultural understanding of the camera and of photography as "the very foundation of progress" (Wallace and Smith 7). This linking of photography and progress is best expressed through Frederick Douglass's many writings on pictures during the 1860s, especially his lecture "Pictures and Progress" (1864–65).

11. See also Sheila Petty's more nuanced reading of Viola in *Contact Zones* (2008).

12. Of course, Yellow Mary's reverse route in which she travels from the Mainland to the Sea Islands calls Viola's spiritual journey into question as her presence in this life-giving place illustrates the possibilities for wholeness, healing and spiritual transformation that are possible in the Sea Islands.

13. Yellow Mary and Trula also laugh at Mr. Snead's description of the kaleidoscope as an invention that displays the dominance and genius of Western science. However, Mr. Snead appears oblivious to the critical nature of their response.

14. See Jacqueline Bobo's *Black Women as Cultural Readers* (1995) for further analysis of Black women's spectatorship.

15. Although Sheila Smith McKoy capitalizes diaspora, I have chosen to follow standard usage and lowercase it throughout.

16. For an expanded understanding of African cosmologies, see Sheila Smith McKoy's article, "The Limbo Context: Diaspora Temporality and Its Reflection in *Praisesong for the Widow* and *Daughters of the Dust*" (1999). Janheinz Jahn's book, *Muntu* (1958) also explores the central philosophical concepts of African cosmologies, including *Nommo*.

17. See Roach, "Culture and Performance," 125.

18. See Marchiorlatti 112 and Everett 865 for more on *Daughters* as a film that challenges traditional historiography as well as Western practices of forgetting.

19. For more on religious syncretism, see Albert Raboteau, *Slave Religion,* 16–42 and Gayraud Wilmore, 50.

20. See Weisenfeld 50–51 for further analysis of the possibilities for healing and transformation in the film.

21. The philosophical concept of Nommo has played a key role in African and African American literature and culture. For a deeper discussion of Nommo in African and African American poetry, see Jahnheinz Jahn's *Muntu* (1958). See Angela Davis's essay "Black Women and Music" (1990) for more on the role of Nommo in the spirituals and the blues. Finally, Debra Walker King's book, *Deep Talk* (1998) discusses the central role of Nommo in the naming practices evident throughout the African American literary tradition.

22. See Joel Brouwer 10–11.

23. See also Jeannine King 479 for a close reading of Mr. Snead's encounter with the Unborn Child through his camera lens.

24. Explaining the importance of this myth to the Sea Island Community in her interview with bell hooks, Dash notes that "almost every Sea Island has a little inlet, or a little area" that people claim as Ibo Landing. Dash explains, "that message is so strong, so powerful, so sustaining to the tradition of resistance, by any means possible, that every Gullah community embraces this myth" (30).

25. See Abena P. Busia's essay, "What Is Your Nation?" (1989), 196–97 and 210. See also Brøndum, 155–57.

26. See Petty 98 for a more nuanced reading of Haagar's disruptive and resistance practices.

27. See Anna Everett 858 and 863–64.

6. Secular Journeys, Sacred Recovery in Saidiya Hartman's *Lose Your Mother*

1. See Harvey Neptune's "Loving through Loss" (2008), Meg Samuelson's "Lose Your Mother, Kill Your Child" (2008), and Pramod Nayar's "Mobility, Migrant Mnemonics and Memory Citizenship" (2013). One exception is Christine Levecq's essay, "What Is Africa to Me Now?" (2015). The article offers a brief one-page discussion that locates Hartman's text within a broader tradition of twentieth and twenty-first-century Black travelers to the continent.

2. See Shaw-Thornburg 53 and Pettinger ix who argue for a more expansive definition of travel and alternative reading practices.

3. For more on the dream/nightmare dichotomy in Africanist discourse, see John Gruesser's, *Black on Black* (2000).

4. See for example Toni Morrison's literary critical study of race and American literature, *Playing in the Dark* (1992), in which she asserts that within American literature, darkness is "terror's most significant, overweening ingredient" (37).

5. In Hartman's representation of darkness, she challenges the myth of the Dark Continent that identified Africa as a land of darkness, savagery, and "social and moral regression" in Western literature about Africa (Brantlinger 215). According to Patrick Brantlinger, the myth, which developed in response to the British slave trade and empire building during the nineteenth century, reflects the "projection and displacement of guilt for the slave trade, guilt for empire, guilt for one's own savage and shadowy impulses" onto the African continent and its people (215).

6. These Black expatriates to Ghana, including W. E. B. Du Bois, Julian Mayfield, Sylvia Boone, and Maya Angelou, were called Afros (short for Afro-American) by the Ghanaian people (Hartman 36–37).

7. See also Gaines 157 for a deeper analysis of the complexity and multiplicity of Pan-Africanist visions in Ghana.

8. Hartman 37 and 41. See Angelou's *All God's Children Need Traveling Shoes (1991)* and *Boone's West African Travels,* 236.

9. See also Jemima Pierre's "Beyond Heritage Tourism" (2009), Sandra L. Richards's "What Is to Be Remembered?" (2005) and Jennifer Hasty's "Rites of Passage, Routes of Redemption" (2002). See Hartman, "Time of Slavery," 759.

10. See Hartman, "Venus in Two Acts," 4, and Morrison's essay "On *Beloved,*" 280.

11. See "The Site of Memory," 70.

12. Hartman references *impossible stories* and the *unspeakable* on p. 10 and p. 1 of "Venus in Two Acts," respectively. Morrison references the *unwritten* parts of history on pp. 70–71 of "The Site of Memory."

13. Here I borrow language from Marcus Rediker's work *The Slave Ship,* 12.

14. See also "Venus in Two Acts" (2008), where Hartman positions the "numbers, ciphers, and fragments of discourse" in the archive as foreclosing the humanity of enslaved people and therefore as an expression of the archive's violence (3).

15. See Morrison, *Playing in the Dark,* 50; Gates, *"Race," Writing, and Difference* (1986); and Cedric J. Robinson's *Black Marxism* (2000) for an explanation of the

dominant narrative about Africans and African-descended people as possessing "no civilization, no cultures, no religions, no history, no place, and finally no humanity that might command consideration" (Robinson 81).

16. I borrow this phrase from Sharpe's *In the Wake* (2016), 131.

17. My thinking about hope has also been shaped by Martin Luther King Jr., especially his collection of sermons, *Strength to Love,* 9 and 38–39. For King, hope is a synthesis of the actual and the possible, a willingness to see the reality of the world we live in (rather than act from a place of moral, intellectual, and spiritual blindness) while practicing a steadfast belief in a future possibility in which the struggles, tragedy, and suffering of today will come to an end. This belief in a future possibility is what enables us to sustain our difficult work in the present in order to, as Junot Díaz notes, "create a better, more loving future" (13).

18. Here I borrow the term "not-me" from Toni Morrison's book *Playing in the Dark,* 38.

Coda

1. Louisville Metro Police shot and killed Breonna Taylor while she slept in her home in Kentucky on March 13, 2020. Two white men shot and killed Ahmaud Arbery while he was jogging in Glynn County, Georgia on February 23, 2020; it took months for local police to arrest his murderers. A Minneapolis police officer asphyxiated George Floyd while he was restrained in handcuffs on May 25, 2020.

2. Hartman, *Lose Your Mother,* 6.

3. See the following websites for additional info on Brittany Packnett Cunningham: https://brittanypacknett.com/bio, Alicia Garza: https://aliciagarza.com/, and Rachel Cargle: https://www.rachelcargle.com/. #BlackLivesMatter was developed in 2013 through the work of three Black women organizers: Alicia Garza, Patrisse Cullors, and Opal (Ayo)Tometi. See https://blacklivesmatter.com/herstory for more.

Bibliography

Alexander, Jacqui. *Pedagogies of Crossing: Meditations on Feminism, Sexual Politics, Memory, and the Sacred.* Durham: Duke University Press, 2005.

Andrews, William L., ed. *Sisters of the Spirit: Three Black Women's Autobiographies of the Nineteenth Century.* Bloomington: Indiana University Press, 1986.

———. *To Tell a Free Story: The First Century of Afro-American Autobiography, 1760–1865.* Urbana: University of Illinois Press, 1986.

Angelou, Maya. *All God's Children Need Traveling Shoes.* New York: Vintage, 1991.

Arana, R. Victoria, editor. "Introduction: Black Travel Writing, a Kaleidoscopic Genre." *BMA: The Sonia Sanchez Literary Review* 9, no. 1 (Fall 2003): 1–11.

Ashcroft, Bill, Gareth Griffiths, and Helen Tiffin. *Postcolonial Studies: The Key Concepts.* New York: Routledge, 1996.

Austin, Allan D. *African Muslims in Antebellum America: Transatlantic Stories and Spiritual Struggles.* New York: Routledge, 1997.

Baker, Houston A., Jr. *Blues, Ideology, and Afro-American Literature: A Vernacular Theory.* Chicago: University of Chicago Press, 1984.

Bambara, Toni Cade. "Reading the Signs, Empowering the Eye: *Daughters of the Dust* and the Black Independent Cinema Movement," In *Black American Cinema,* edited by Manthia Diawara, 118–44. New York: Routledge, 1993.

Barker, Francis, and Peter Hulme, "The Tempest and Oppression," In *Shakespeare the Tempest: A Casebook,* edited by David Palmer, 200–210.

Barrett, Lindon. *Blackness and Value: Seeing Double.* Cambridge: Cambridge University Press, 1999.

Barthelemy, Anthony G. Introduction. *Collected Black Women's Narratives,* edited by Henry Louis Gates Jr., xxix–xlviii. New York: Oxford University Press, 1998.

Bassard, Katherine Clay. *Spiritual Interrogations: Culture, Gender, and Community in Early African American Women's Writing.* Princeton: Princeton University Press, 1999.

Bendixen, Alfred, and Judith Hamera. Introduction. *The Cambridge Companion to American Travel Writing,* edited by Alfred Bendixen and Judith Hamera, 1–9. Cambridge: Cambridge University Press, 2009.

Bennett, Michael, and Vanessa D. Dickerson, eds. *Recovering the Black Female Body: Self-Representations by African American Women*. New Brunswick: Rutgers University Press, 2001.

Birkle, Carmen. "Traveling and the Discourse of Economy in Nancy Prince's Travel Narrative." In *In-Between Two Worlds: Narratives by Female Explorers and Travellers, 1850–1945*, edited by Béatrice Bijon and Gérard Gâcon, 17–33. New York: Peter Lang, 2009.

Blakely, Allison. *Russia and the Negro: Blacks in Russian History and Thought*. Washington: Howard University Press, 1986.

Blockett, Kimberly. "Disrupting Print: Emigration, the Press, and Narrative Subjectivity in the British Preaching and Writing of Zilpha Elaw, 1840–1860s." *MELUS* 40, no. 3 (Fall 2015): 94–109.

———. "Moving Subjectivities in the Evangelical Narrative of Zilpha Elaw." *BMA: The Sonia Sanchez Literary Review*, special issue on Black travel writing, Spring 2004.

———. "#sayhername: Recovering Zilpha Elaw's Rebellious Evangelicalism." Women's Studies in Religion Program Lecture, Harvard Divinity School, April 25, 2008, https://hds.harvard.edu/news/2018/04/25/video-sayhername-recovering-zilpha-elaw%E2%80%99s-rebellious-evangelicalism#.

Blyden, Edward Wilmot. "From West Africa to Palestine." 1873. In *Black Spokesman: Selected Published Writings of Edward Wilmot Blyden*, edited by Hollis R. Lynch, 145–57. London: Frank Cass & Co., 1971.

Bobo, Jacqueline. *Black Feminist Cultural Criticism*. Malden, MA: Blackwell, 2001.

———. *Black Women as Cultural Readers*. New York: Columbia University Press, 1995.

Boone, Sylvia. *West African Travels*. New York: Random House, 1974.

Boym, Svetlana. "Off-Modern Homecoming in Art and Theory." In *Rites of Return: Diaspora Poetics and the Politics of Memory*, edited by Marianne Hirsch and Nancy K. Miller, 151–65. New York: Columbia University Press, 2011.

Brantlinger, Patrick. "Victorians and Africans: The Genealogy of the Myth of the Dark Continent." In *"Race," Writing, and Difference*, edited by Henry Louis Gates Jr., 185–222. Chicago: University of Chicago Press, 1986.

Braxton, Joanne M. *Black Women Writing Autobiography: A Tradition within a Tradition*. Philadelphia: Temple University Press, 1989.

Brekus, Catherine A. *Strangers and Pilgrims: Female Preaching in America, 1740–1845*. Chapel Hill: University of North Carolina Press, 1998.

Brøndum, Lene. "'The Persistence of Tradition': The Retelling of Sea Islands Culture in Works by Julie Dash, Gloria Naylor, and Paule Marshall." In *Black Imagination and the Middle Passage*, edited by Henry Louis Gates Jr. and Carl Pedersen, 153–63. New York: Oxford University Press, 1999.

Brooks, Daphne. *Bodies in Dissent: Spectacular Performances of Race and Freedom, 1850–1910*. Durham: Duke University Press, 2006.

Brooten, Bernadette J. Introduction. *Beyond Slavery: Overcoming Its Religious and Sexual Legacies*, edited by Bernadette Brooten, 1–29. London: Palgrave Macmillan, 2010.

Brouwer, Joel R. "Repositioning: center and margin in Julie Dash's 'Daughters of the Dust.'" *African American Review* 29, no. 1 (Spring 1995): 5–17.

Brown, Carolyn A. *The Black Female Body in American Literature and Art*. Routledge, 2012.

Brown, Jacqueline Nassy. *Dropping Anchor, Setting Sail: Geographies of Race in Black Liverpool*. Princeton: Princeton University Press, 2005.

Brown, William Wells. *The American Fugitive in Europe. Sketches of Places and People Abroad*. 1855. Boston: John P. Jewett and Co. Documenting the American South, https://docsouth.unc.edu/neh/brown55/menu.html.

Bruce, Dickson D. *And They All Sang Hallelujah; Plain-folk Camp-meeting Religion, 1800–1845*. Knoxville: University of Tennessee Press, 1974.

Brueggemann, Walter. *The Prophetic Imagination*. 40th anniversary ed., Minneapolis: Fortress Press, 2018.

Brusky, Sarah. "Nancy Prince and Her Gothic Odyssey: A Veiled Lady." In *Gender, Genre and Identity in Women's Travel Writing*, edited by Kristi Siegel, 167–80.

Buick, Kirsten, "The Ideal Works of Edmonia Lewis: Invoking and Inventing Autobiography." *American Art* 9 (Summer 1995): 5–19.

Bunyan, John. *The Pilgrim's Progress*. 1678. Edited by W. R. Owens. New York: Oxford University Press, 2003.

Busia, Abena. "What Is Your Nation? Reconnecting Africa and Her Diaspora through Paule Marshall's *Praisesong for the Widow*." In *Changing Our Own Words: Essays on Criticism, Theory and Writing by Black Women*, edited by Cheryl A. Wall, 196–211. New Brunswick: Rutgers University Press, 1991.

Buzzard, James. *The Beaten Track: European Tourism, Literature, and the Ways of Culture, 1800–1918*. Oxford: Clarendon Press, 1993.

Caldwell, Patricia. *The Puritan Conversion Narrative: The Beginnings of American Expression*. Cambridge: Cambridge University Press, 1983.

Campbell, James T. *Middle Passages: African American Journeys to Africa, 1787–2005*. New York: Penguin, 2006.

Cannon, Katie G. *Katie's Canon: Womanism and the Soul of the Black Community*. 1995. New York: Continuum Press, 2008.

Carby, Hazel V. *Reconstructing Womanhood: The Emergence of the Afro-American Woman Novelist*. New York: Oxford University Press, 1987.

Christian, Barbara. "Fixing Methodologies: *Beloved*." In *Female Subjects in Black and White:Race, Psychoanalysis, Feminism*, edited by Elizabeth Abel, Barbara Christian, and Helene Moglen, 363–70. Berkeley: University of California Press, 1997.

Cima, Gay Gibson. *Early American Women Critics: Performance, Religion, Race*. Cambridge: Cambridge University Press, 2006.

Clark, Adam. "Hagar the Egyptian: A Womanist Dialogue." *The Western Journal of Black Studies* 36, no. 1 (2012): 48–56.

Cleall, Esme. *Missionary Discourses of Difference: Negotiating Otherness in the British Empire, 1840–1900*. London: Palgrave Macmillan, 2012.

Clegg, Claude A., III. *The Price of Liberty: African Americans and the Making of Liberia*. Chapel Hill: University of North Carolina Press, 2004.

Coan, Josephus R. "Redemption of Africa: The Vital Impulse of Black American Overseas Missionaries." *Journal of the Interdenominational Theological Center* 1 (Spring 1974): 27–37.

Collier-Thomas, Bettye. *Daughters of Thunder: Black Women Preachers and Their Sermons, 1850–1979.* 1st ed., San Francisco: Jossey-Bass, 1998.

Collins, Patricia Hill. *Black Feminist Thought: Knowledge, Consciousness, and the Politics of Empowerment.* 2nd ed., New York: Routledge Classics, 2009.

Connor, Kimberly Rae. *Conversions and Visions in the Writings of African-American Women.* 1st ed., Knoxville: University of Tennessee Press, 1994.

Cooper, Anna Julia. *A Voice from the South.* New York: Oxford University Press, 1988.

Copeland, M. Shawn. *Enfleshing Freedom: Body, Race, and Being.* Minneapolis: Fortress Press, 2010.

Cucinella, Catherine, and Renee R. Curry. "Exiled at Home: *Daughters of the Dust* and the many post-colonial conditions." *MELUS* 26, no. 4 (Winter 2001): 197–223.

Dash, Julie. *Daughters of the Dust: The Making of an African American Woman's Film.* New York: New Press, 1992.

———, director. *Daughters of the Dust.* Geechee Girls Productions, 1991. Kino Video: Kino International, 1999. DVD.

Davis, Angela, "Black Women and Music: A Historical Legacy of Struggle." *African Intellectual Heritage: A Book of Sources,* edited by Molefi Kete Asante and Abu S. Abarry, 765–77. Philadelphia: Temple University Press, 1996.

Díaz, Junot. "Radical Hope." In *Radical Hope: Letters of Love and Dissent in Dangerous Times,* edited by Carolina De Robertis, 11–13. New York: Vintage, 2017.

Dodson, Jualynne E. Introduction. *An Autobiography: The Story of the Lord's Dealings with Mrs. Amanda Smith, the Colored Evangelist,* edited by Henry Louis Gates Jr., xxvii–xlii. New York: Oxford University Press, 1988.

Dorr, David F. *A Colored Man round the World.* Edited by Malini Johar Schueller. Ann Arbor: University of Michigan Press, 1999.

Douglas, Kelly Brown. *Stand Your Ground: Black Bodies and the Justice of God.* Maryknoll, NY: Orbis Books, 2015.

Douglass, Frederick. "*My Bondage and My Freedom.*" In *Frederick Douglass Autobiographies,* edited by Henry Louis Gates Jr., 103–452. New York: Literary Classics of the United States, 1994.

———. *Narrative of the Life of Frederick Douglass, an American Slave.* 1845. Boston: Anti-Slavery Office. *Documenting the American South,* https://docsouth.unc.edu/neh/douglass/menu.html.

———. "Pictures and Progress." In *Picturing Frederick Douglass: An Illustrated Biography of the Nineteenth Century's Most Photographed American,* edited by John Stauffer, Zoe Trodd, and Celeste-Marie Bernier, 151–63. New York: Liveright Publishing, 2015.

Douglass-Chin, Richard J. *Preacher Woman Sings the Blues: The Autobiographies of Nineteenth-Century African American Evangelists.* Columbia: University of Missouri Press, 2001.

Driskell, David C. *Two Centuries of Black American Art*. Los Angeles County Museum of Art, New York: Knopf, 1976.

Elaw, Zilpha. "Memoirs of the Life, Religious Experience, Ministerial Travels and Labours of Mrs. Zilpha Elaw, An American Female of Colour." In *Sisters of the Spirit: Three Black Women's Autobiographies of the Nineteenth Century*, edited by William Andrews, 49–160. Bloomington, IN: Indiana University Press, 1986.

Equiano, Olaudah. *The Interesting Narrative of the Life of Olaudah Equiano, or Gustavus Vassa, Written by Himself.* 1789. Edited by Werner Sollors, New York: W. W. Norton, 2001.

Everett, Anna. "*Daughters of the Dust* (1991): Toward a Womanist/Diasporic Film Aesthetic." In *Film Analysis: A Norton Reader*, edited by Jeffrey Geiger and R. L. Rutsky, 850–71. New York: W. W. Norton, 2005.

Ferguson, Moira. *Nine Black Women: An Anthology of Nineteenth-Century Writers from the United States, Canada, Bermuda, and the Caribbean*. New York: Routledge, 1998.

Ferguson, SallyAnn H. "Christian Violence and the Slave Narrative." *American Literature: A Journal of Literary History, Criticism, and Bibliography* 68, no. 2 (June 1996): 297–320.

Fine, Elsa Hong. *The Afro-American Artist: A Search for Identity*. New York: Holt, Rinehart and Winston, 1973.

Fish, Cheryl J. *Black and White Women's Travel Narratives: Antebellum Explorations*. Gainesville: University Press of Florida, 2004.

———. "Journeys and Warnings: Nancy Prince's Travels as Cautionary Tales for African American Readers." In *Women at Sea: Travel Writing and the Margins of Caribbean Discourse*, edited by Lizabeth Paravisini-Gebert and Ivette Romero-Cesareo, 225–43. London: Palgrave, 2001.

Fitzpatrick, Kristin. "American National Identity Abroad: The Travels of Nancy Prince," In *Gender, Genre, and Identity in Women's Travel Writing*, edited by Kristi Siegel, 263–78. New York: P. Lang, 2004.

Foster, Amber. "Nancy Prince's Utopias: Re-imagining the African American Utopian Tradition." *Utopian Studies: Journal of the Society for Utopian Studies* 24, no. 2 (2013): 329–48.

Foster, Frances Smith. *Written by Herself: Literary Production by African American Women, 1746–1892*. Bloomington: Indiana University Press, 1993.

Fussell, Paul. *Abroad: British Literary Traveling between the Wars*. New York: Oxford University Press, 1980.

Gabler-Hover, Janet. *Dreaming Black/Writing White: The Hagar Myth in American Cultural History*. Lexington, KY: University Press of Kentucky, 2000.

Gafney, Wilda C. *Womanist Midrash: A Reintroduction to the Women of the Torah and the Throne*. Louisville, KY: Westminster John Knox Press, 2017.

Gaines, Kevin K. *American Africans in Ghana: Black Expatriates and the Civil Rights Era*. Chapel Hill: University of North Carolina Press, 2006.

Gates, Henry Louis Gates, Jr., ed. *"Race," Writing, and Difference*. Chicago: University of Chicago Press, 1986.

Ghose, Indira. *Women Travellers in Colonial India: The Power of the Female Gaze.* New York: Oxford University Press, 1998.

Giddings, Paula. *When and Where I Enter: The Impact of Black Women on Race and Sex in America.* New York: Bantam, 1985.

Gilroy, Paul. *The Black Atlantic: Modernity and Double Consciousness.* Cambridge: Harvard University Press, 1993.

Glancy, Jennifer A. "Early Christianity, Slavery, and Women's Bodies." In *Beyond Slavery: Overcoming Its Religious and Sexual Legacies,* edited by Bernadette Brooten, 143–58. New York: Palgrave Macmillan, 2010.

Grammer, Elizabeth Elkin. *Some Wild Visions: Autobiographies of Female Itinerant Evangelists in Nineteenth-Century America.* New York: Oxford University Press, 2003.

Greenberg, Kenneth S. Introduction. *The Confessions of Nat Turner and Related Documents* 1996, 2nd ed., edited by Greenberg, 1–33. New York: Bedford/St. Martin's, 2017.

Greene, J. Lee, *Blacks in Eden: The African American Novel's First Century.* Charlottesville: University Press of Virginia, 1996.

Griffin, Farah J., and Cheryl J. Fish. Introduction. *A Stranger in the Village: Two Centuries of African-American Travel Writing,* edited by Griffin and Fish, xiii–xvii. New York: Beacon, 1998.

Gronniosaw, Ukawsaw. *A Narrative of the Most Remarkable Particulars in the Life of James Albert Ukawsaw Gronniosaw, An African Prince, Written by Himself.* 1770. *Black Atlantic Writers of the 18th Century,* edited by Adam Potkay and Sandra Burr, 27–66. New York: St. Martin's, 1995.

Gruesser, John C. "Afro-American Travel Literature and Africanist Discourse." *Black American Literature Forum* 24, no. 1 (1990): 5–20.

———. *Black on Black: Twentieth-Century African American Writing about Africa.* Lexington: University Press of Kentucky, 2000.

Gunning, Sandra. "Nancy Prince and the Politics of Mobility, Home and Diasporic (Mis)Identification." *American Quarterly* 53, no. 1 (March 2001): 32–69.

Guy-Sheftall, Beverly. "The Body Politic: Black Female Sexuality and the Nineteenth-Century Euro-American Imagination." In *Skin Deep, Spirit Strong: The Black Female Body in American Culture,* edited by Kimberly Wallace-Sanders, 13–35. Ann Arbor: University of Michigan Press, 2002.

Hall, Timothy D. *Contested Boundaries: Itinerancy and the Reshaping of the Colonial American Religious World.* Durham: Duke University Press, 1994.

HarperCollins Study Bible, The. New Revised Standard Version. Edited by Wayne A. Meeks. New York: HarperCollins, 1993.

Harrell, Willie J., Jr. *Origins of the African American Jeremiad: The Rhetorical Strategies of Social Protest and Activism, 1760–1861.* Jefferson, NC: McFarland & Company, 2011.

Hartman, Saidiya V. *Lose Your Mother: A Journey along the Atlantic Slave Route.* New York: Farrar, Straus and Giroux, 2007.

———. *Scenes of Subjection: Terror, Slavery, and Self-making in Nineteenth-Century America.* New York: Oxford University Press, 1997.

———. "Seduction and the Ruses of Power." *Emerging Women Writers,* special issue of *Callaloo* 19, no. 2 (Spring 1996): 537–60.

———. "The Time of Slavery." *South Atlantic Quarterly,* vol. 101, no. 4, 2002, 757–77.

———. "Venus in Two Acts." *Small Axe,* no. 26 (vol. 12, no. 2), 2008, 1–14.

Hartman, Saidiya, et al. "Memoirs of Return." In *Rites of Return: Diaspora Poetics and the Politics of Memory,* edited by Marianne Hirsch and Nancy Miller, 107–23. New York: Columbia University Press, 2011.

Hasty, Jennifer. "Rites of Passage, Routes of Redemption: Emancipation Tourism and the Wealth of Culture." *Africa Today,* 49, no. 3 (2002): 47–76.

Hawkins, Anne Hunsaker. *Archetypes of Conversion: The Autobiographies of Augustine, Bunyan and Merton.* Lewisburg: Bucknell University Press, 1985.

Hayford, Casely. *The Truth about the West African Land Question.* New York: Negro Universities Press, 1969.

Haynes, Carolyn A. *Divine Destiny: Gender and Race in Nineteenth-Century Protestantism.* Jackson: University Press of Mississippi, 1998.

Haynes, Rosetta R. *Radical Spiritual Motherhood: Autobiography and Empowerment in Nineteenth-Century African American Women.* Baton Rouge: Louisiana State University Press, 2011.

Hirsch, Marianne and Nancy K. Miller, editors. *Rites of Return: Diaspora Poetics and the Politics of Memory.* New York: Columbia University Press, 2011.

Hobson, Janell. *Venus in the Dark: Blackness and Beauty in Popular Culture.* 2nd ed., New York: Routledge, 2018.

———. "Viewing in the Dark: Towards a Black Feminist Approach to Film." *Women's Studies Quarterly* 30, no. 1–2 (Spring–Summer 2002): 45–59.

Holt, Thomas. *The Problem of Freedom: Race, Labor, and Politics in Jamaica and Britain, 1832–1938.* Baltimore: John Hopkins University Press, 1992.

hooks, bell. *Black Looks: Race and Representation.* Boston: South End Press, 1992.

———. "Representing Whiteness in the Black Imagination," *Displacing Whiteness: Essays in Social and Cultural Criticism,* edited by Ruth Frankenberg, 165–79. Durham: Duke University Press, 1997.

———. *Talking Back: Thinking Feminist, Thinking Black.* Boston: South End Press, 1989.

hooks, bell, and Cornel West. *Breaking Bread: Insurgent Black Intellectual Life.* Boston: South End Press, 1991.

hooks, bell, and Julie Dash. "Dialogue between bell hooks and Julie Dash." In *Daughters of the Dust: The Making of an African American Woman's Film,* edited by Julie Dash, 27–67. New York: New Press, 1992.

Howard-Pitney, David. *The Afro-American Jeremiad: Appeals for Justice in America.* Philadelphia: Temple University Press, 1990.

Hucks, Tracey E. "'Burning with a Flame in America': African American Women in African-Derived Traditions." *Journal of Feminist Studies in Religion* 17, no. 2 (Fall 2001): 89–106.

Hudson, Larry E., Jr. "'All That Cash': Work and Status in the Slave Quarters." *Working Toward Freedom: Slave Society and Domestic Economy in the American South*, edited by Larry Hudson, 77–94. Rochester: University of Rochester Press, 1994.

Humez, Jean M. "'My Spirit Eye': Some Functions of Spiritual and Visionary Experience in the lives of Five Black Women Preachers, 1810–1880." *Women and the Structure of Society: Selected Research from the Fifth Berkshire Conference on the History of Women*, edited by Barbara J. Harris and Jo Ann McNamara, 129–43. Durham: Duke University Press, 1984.

Israel, Adrienne M. *Amanda Berry Smith: From Washerwoman to Evangelist*. Lanham: Scarecrow Press, 1998.

Jacobs, Harriet. *Incidents in the Life of a Slave Girl*. 1861. Edited by Jean Fagan Yellin. Cambridge: Harvard University Press, 2000.

Jacobs, Sylvia M., ed. *Black Americans and the Missionary Movement in Africa*. Westport: Greenwood Press, 1982.

———. "The Historical Role of Afro-Americans in American Missionary Efforts in Africa," edited by Sylvia Jacobs, 5–29. Westport: Greenwood Press, 1982.

Jahn, Janheinz. *Muntu: African Culture and the Western World*. New York: Grove Weidenfeld, 1990.

Jea, John. *The Life, History, and Unparalleled Sufferings of John Jea, the African Preacher*. 1811. Portsea, England. *Documenting the American South*, https://docsouth.unc.edu/neh/jeajohn/jeajohn.html.

Jones, Jacqueline. *American Work: Four Centuries of Black and White Labor*. New York: W. W. Norton, 1988.

———. *Labor of love, labor of sorrow: Black women, work, and the family from slavery to the present*. New York: Basic, 1985.

Jones-Rogers, Stephanie E. *They Were Her Property: White Women as Slave Owners in the American South*. New Haven: Yale University Press, 2019.

Jordan-Zachery, Julia S. *Shadow Bodies: Black Women, Ideology, Representation, and Politics*. New Brunswick: Rutgers University Press, 2017.

Junior, Nyasha. *Reimagining Hagar: Blackness and Bible*. Oxford: Oxford University Press, 2019.

Katz, Jonathan M. "Protester Arrested in Toppling of Confederate Statue in Durham." *The New York Times*, August 15, 2017. https://www.nytimes.com/2017/08/15/us/protester-arrested-in-toppling-of-confederate-statue-in-durham.html.

King, Debra Walker. *Deep Talk: Reading African-American Literary Names*. Charlottesville: University Press of Virginia, 1998.

King, Jeannine. "Memory and the Phantom South in African American Migration Film." *Mississippi Quarterly: The Journal of Southern Cultures*, 63, no. 3–4 (2010): 477–91.

King, Martin Luther, Jr. *Strength to Love.* Minneapolis: Fortress Press, 2010.

Lamming, George. "A Monster, a Child, a Slave." In *The Tempest,* edited by Peter Hulme and William H. Sherman, 148–68. New York: W. W. Norton, 2004.

Lee, Jarena. "The Life and Religious Experience of Jarena Lee, A Coloured Lady, Giving an Account of her Call to Preach the Gospel." In *Sisters of the Spirit: Three Black Women's Autobiographies of the Nineteenth Century,* edited by William Andrews, 25–48. Bloomington: Indiana University Press, 1986.

Levecq, Christine. "What Is Africa to Me Now? The Politics of Unhappy Returns," *Journeys,* 16, no. 2 (2015): 79–100.

Logan, Lisa. "Uncle Tom's Cabin and Conventional Nineteenth-Century Domestic Ideology." In *Approaches to Teaching Stowe's Uncle Tom's Cabin,* edited by Elizabeth Ammons and Susan Belasco, 46–56. New York: Modern Language Association, 2000.

Loomba, Ania. *Colonialism/Postcolonialism.* New York: Routledge, 1998.

Lynch, Hollis R. Introduction. *Black Spokesman: Selected Published Writing of Edward Wilmot Blyden,* edited by Hollis R. Lynch, xi–xxxvi. New York: Humanities Press, 1971.

M'Baye, Babacar. "The Image of Africa in the Travel Narratives of W. E. B. Du Bois, Richard Wright, James Baldwin, and Henry Louis Gates Jr." *BMa: The Sonia Sanchez Literary Review,* 9, no. 1 (2003): 153–77.

MacGonagle, Elizabeth. "From Dungeons to Dance Parties: Contested Histories of Ghana's Slave Forts." *Journal of Contemporary African Studies* 24, no. 2 (2006): 249–60.

Machiorlatti, Jennifer A. "Revisiting Julie Dash's *Daughters of the Dust:* Black Feminist Narrative and Diasporic Recollection." *South Atlantic Review,* 70, no. 1 (2005): 97–116.

Marshall, Paule. *Praisesong for the Widow.* New York: Plume, 1983.

Martin, Joan M. *More Than Chains and Toil: A Christian Work Ethic of Enslaved Women.* Louisville, KY: Westminster John Knox, 2000.

Martin, Michael T. "'I Do Exist': From 'Black Insurgent' to Negotiating the Hollywood Divide—A Conversation with Julie Dash," *Cinema Journal,* 49, no. 2 (Winter 2010): 1–16.

Martin, Sandy Dwayne. "Black Baptists, Foreign Missions, and African Colonization, 1814–1882." In *Black Americans and the Missionary Movement in Africa,* edited by Sylvia Jacobs, 63–76. Westport, CN: Greenwood.

Mason, Mary G. "Travel as Metaphor and Reality in Afro-American Women's Autobiography, 1850–1972," *Black American Literature Forum,* 24, no. 2 (Summer 1990): 337–56.

Mbiti, John S. *African Religions and Philosophy.* New York: Doubleday, 1970.

McDowell, Deborah E. "Afterword." *Recovery Missions: Imaging the Body Ideals,* edited by Michael Bennett and Vanessa D. Dickerson, 296–317. New Brunswick: Rutgers University Press, 2001.

McKay, Nellie Y. "Nineteenth-Century Black Women's Spiritual Autobiographies: Religious Faith and Self-Empowerment." In *Interpreting Women's Lives: Feminist*

Theory and Personal Narratives, edited by Personal Narratives Group, 139–54. Bloomington: Indiana University Press, 1989.

McKittrick, Katherine. *Demonic Grounds: Black Women and the Cartographies of Struggle.* Minneapolis: University of Minnesota Press, 2006.

McKoy, Sheila Smith. "The Limbo Context: Diaspora Temporality and Its Reflection in *Praisesong for the Widow* and *Daughters of the Dust.*" *Callaloo* 22, no. 1 (1999): 208–22.

Mills, Sara. *Discourses of Difference: An Analysis of Women's Travel Writing and Colonialism.* New York: Routledge, 1991.

Moody, Joycelyn K. *Sentimental Confessions: Spiritual Narratives of Nineteenth-Century African American Women.* Athens: University of Georgia Press, 2001.

Morgan, Jennifer L. "'Some Could Suckle over Their Shoulder': Male Travelers, Female Bodies, and the Gendering of Racial Ideology, 1500–1770." In *Laboring Women: Reproduction and Gender in New World Slavery,* edited by Jennifer Morgan, 12–49. Philadelphia: University of Pennsylvania Press, 2011.

Morris, Mary. Introduction. *Maiden Voyages: Writings of Women Travelers,* edited by Morris in collaboration with Larry O' Connor. New York: Vintage, 1993.

Morrison, Toni. *Beloved.* New York: Penguin, 1987.

———. "Home." In *The House That Race Built,* edited by Wahneema Lubiano, 3–12. New York: Vintage, 1998.

———. "On Beloved." In *The Source of Self-Regard: Selected Essays, Speeches, and Meditations,* edited by Toni Morrison, 280–84. New York: Knopf, 2019.

———. *Playing in the Dark: Whiteness and the Literary Imagination.* New York: Vintage, 1992.

———. "Rootedness: The Ancestor as Foundation." *What Moves at the Margin: Selected Nonfiction,* edited by Carolyn C. Denard, 56–64. Jackson: University Press of Mississippi, 2008.

———. "The Site of Memory." In *What Moves at the Margin: Selected Nonfiction,* edited by Carolyn C. Denard, 65–80. Jackson: University Press of Mississippi, 2008.

Moses, Wilson Jeremiah. *Black Messiahs and Uncle Toms: Social and Literary Manipulations of a Religious Myth.* University Park: Penn State University Press, 1982.

Nayar, Pramod K. "Mobility, Migrant Mnemonics and Memory Citizenship: Saidiya Hartman's *Lose Your Mother.*" *NJES: Nordic Journal of English Studies* 12, no. 2 (2013): 81–101.

Nelson, Charmaine A. *The Color of Stone: Sculpting the Black Female Subject in Nineteenth-Century America.* Minneapolis: University of Minnesota Press, 2007.

Neptune, Harvey. "Loving through Loss: Reading Saidiya Hartman's History of Black Hurt." *Anthurium: A Caribbean Studies Journal* 6, no. 1 (2008): article 6, scholarlyrepository.miami.edu/anthurium/vol6/iss1/6.

Ogunleye, Foluke. "Transcending the 'Dust': African American Filmmakers Preserving the 'Glimpse of the Eternal.'" *College Literature,* 34, no. 1 (Winter 2007): 156–74.

Olney, James. "'I Was Born': Slave Narratives, Their Status as Autobiography and as Literature." In *The Slave's Narrative,* edited by Charles T. Davis and Henry Louis Gates, 148–75. New York: Oxford University Press, 1985.

Omolade, Barbara. "Heart of Darkness." *Words of Fire: An Anthology of African-American Feminist Thought,* edited by Beverly Guy-Sheftall, 362–78. New York: New Press, 1995.

"One More Bishop Chosen." *New-York Tribune,* May 26, 1888. *Chronicling America: Historic American Newspapers.* Lib. of Congress. chroniclingamerica.loc.gov/lccn /sn83030214/1888-05-26/ed-1/seq-4/.

Page, Hugh R., Jr., ed. *The Africana Bible: Reading Israel's Scriptures from Africa and the African Diaspora.* Minneapolis: Fortress Press, 2010.

Palmer, D. J., ed. *Shakespeare The Tempest: A Casebook.* London: Macmillan, 1991.

Paravisini-Gebert, Lizabeth, and Ivette Romero-Cesareo. *Women at Sea: Travel Writing and the Margins of Caribbean Discourse.* New York: Palgrave Macmillan, 2001.

Paris, Peter J. *The Spirituality of African Peoples: The Search for a Common Moral Discourse.* Minneapolis: Fortress Press, 1989.

Patterson, Orlando. *Slavery and Social Death: A Comparative Study.* Cambridge: Harvard University Press, 1982.

Peterson, Carla L. *Doers of the Word: African-American Women Speakers and Writers in the North (1830–1880).* New York: Oxford University Press, 1995.

———. "Foreword: Eccentric Bodies," In *Recovering the Black Female Body: Self-representations by African American Women,* edited by Michael Bennett and Vanessa D. Dickerson, ix–xvi. New Brunswick: Rutgers University Press, 2001.

Pettinger, Alasdair. Introduction. *Always Elsewhere: Travels of the Black Atlantic,* edited by Alasdair Pettinger, viii–xix. London: Cassell, 1998.

Petty, Sheila J. *Contact Zones: Memory, Origin, and Discourses in Black Diasporic Cinema.* Detroit: Wayne State University Press, 2008.

Phillips, Abby. "Why Bree Newsome Took Down the Confederate Flag in S.C.: 'I Refuse to Be Ruled by Fear.'" *Washington Post.* June 29, 2015.

Pierce, Yolanda. *Hell without Fires: Slavery, Christianity, and the Antebellum Spiritual Narrative.* Gainesville: University Press of Florida, 2005.

Pierre, Jemima. "Beyond Heritage Tourism: Race and the Politics of African-Diasporic Interactions." *Social Text* 27, no. 1 (98) (2009): 59–81.

Potkay, Adam, and Sandra Burr, eds. *Black Writers of the 18th Century: Living the New Exodus in England and the Americas.* New York: St. Martin's, 1995.

Pratt, Mary Louise. *Imperial Eyes: Travel Writing and Transculturation.* New York: Routledge, 1992.

Prince, Nancy. *"A Narrative of the Life and Travels of Mrs. Nancy Prince, Written by Herself."* In *Collected Black Women's Narratives,* edited by Anthony Barthelemy. New York: Oxford University Press, 1988.

Raboteau, Albert J. *A Fire in the Bones: Reflections on African-American Religious History.* New York: Beacon, 1995.

———. *Slave Religion: The "Invisible Institution" in the Antebellum South.* New York: Oxford University Press, 1978.

Rediker, Marcus. *The Slave Ship: A Human History*. New York: Viking, 2007.

Reiss, Benjamin. *The Showman and the Slave: Race, Death, and Memory in Barnum's America*. Cambridge: Harvard University Press, 2001.

Richards, Sandra L. "What Is to Be Remembered? Tourism to Ghana's Slave Castle-Dungeons." *Theatre Journal* 57, no. 4 (Dec 2005): 617–37.

Roach, Joseph R. *Cities of the Dead: Circum-Atlantic Performance*. New York: Columbia University Press, 1996.

———. "Culture and Performance in the Circum-Atlantic World." In *Performance Studies,* edited by Erin Striff, 124–36. London: Palgrave Macmillan, 2003.

Robinson, Cedric J. *Black Marxism: The Making of the Black Radical Tradition*. Chapel Hill: University of North Carolina Press, 2000.

Ryan, Judylyn S. "Spirituality and/as Ideology in Black Women's Literature: The Preaching of Maria W. Stewart and Baby Suggs, Holy." *Women Preachers and Prophets through Two Millennia of Christianity,* edited by Beverly Mayne Kienzle and Pamela J. Walker, 267–87. Berkeley: University of California Press, 1998.

Sadler, Rodney S., Jr. "Genesis." In *The Africana Bible: Reading Israel's Scriptures from Africa and the African Diaspora,* edited by Hugh R. Page Jr., 70–79. Minneapolis: Fortress Press, 2010.

Said, Edward. *Orientalism*. New York: Vintage, 1978.

Samuelson, Meg. "'Lose Your Mother, Kill Your Child': The Passage of Slavery and Its Afterlife in Narratives by Yvette Christiansë and Saidiya Hartman." *English Studies in Africa: A Journal of the Humanities* 51, no. 2 (2008): 38–48.

Sawyer, John F. A. *Prophecy and the Biblical Prophets*. Rev. ed., New York: Oxford University Press, 1993.

Schueller, Malini Johar. Introduction. In *A Colored Man round the World*. 1858, edited by David Dorr, ix–xliii. Ann Arbor: University of Michigan Press, 1999.

———. *U.S. Orientalisms: Race, Nation, and Gender in Literature, 1790–1890*. Ann Arbor: University of Michigan Press, 1998.

Schriber, Mary Suzanne, ed. *Telling Travels: Selected Writings by Nineteenth-Century American Women Abroad*. Dekalb: Northern Illinois University Press, 1995.

Seed, David, ed. *American Travellers in Liverpool*. Liverpool: Liverpool University Press, 2008.

Shakespeare, William. *The Tempest*. 1611. Edited by Peter Hulme and William H. Sherman. New York: W. W. Norton, 2004.

Sharpe, Christina. *In the Wake: On Blackness and Being*. Durham: Duke University Press, 2016.

Sharpley-Whiting, T. Denean. *Black Venus: Sexualized Savages, Primal Fears, and Primitive Narratives in French*. Durham: Duke University Press, 1999.

Shaw-Thornburg, Angela. "Problems of Genre and Genealogy in African-American Literature of Travel." *Journeys: The International Journal of Travel and Travel Writing* 12, no. 1 (2011): 46–62.

Shea, Daniel B. *Spiritual Autobiography in Early America*. Princeton: Princeton University Press, 1968.

Shick, Tom W. "Rhetoric and Reality: Colonization and Afro-Americans Missionaries in Early Nineteenth-Century Liberia." In *Black Americans and the Missionary Movement in Africa,* edited by Sylvia M. Jacobs, 45–62. Westport: Greenwood Press, 1982.

Siegel, Kristi, ed. *Gender, Genre, and Identity in Women's Travel Writing.* New York: Peter Lang, 2004.

Skloot, Rebecca. *The Immortal Life of Henrietta Lacks.* New York: Broadway Books, 2010.

Smallwood, Stephanie E. *Saltwater Slavery: A Middle Passage from Africa to American Diaspora.* Cambridge: Harvard University Press, 2007.

Smith, Amanda. *An Autobiography: The Story of the Lord's Dealings with Mrs. Amanda Smith, the Colored Evangelist.* 1893. New York: Oxford University Press, 1988.

Smith, Virginia Whatley. "African American travel literature." In *The Cambridge Companion to American Travel Writing,* edited by Alfred Bendixen and Judith Hamera, 197–213. New York: Cambridge University Press.

Spillers, Hortense. "'Mama's Baby, Papa's Maybe': An American Grammar Book." In *Black, White, and in Color: Essays on American Literature and Culture,* edited by Hortense Spillers, 203–29. Chicago: University of Chicago Press, 2003.

Stanley, Susie C. *Holy Boldness: Women Preachers' Autobiographies and the Sanctified Self.* Knoxville: University of Tennessee Press, 2002.

Steadman, Jennifer Bernhardt. *Traveling Economies: American Women's Travel Writing.* Columbus: Ohio State University Press, 2007.

Sterling, Dorothy, ed. *We Are Your Sisters: Black Women in the Nineteenth Century.* New York: W. W. Norton, 1984.

Stewart, Maria W. *Productions of Mrs. Maria W. Stewart.* 1835. In *Spiritual Narratives,* edited by Sue Houchins. New York: Oxford University Press, 1988.

"Stories from a Ferguson Prison." *Pass the Mic* from The Witness, August 19, 2015. https://thewitnessbcc.com/pass-the-mic-stories-from-a-ferguson-prison/.

Stowe, William W. *Going Abroad: European Travel in Nineteenth-Century American Culture.* Princeton: Princeton University Press, 1994.

Tate, Shirley Anne. *Black Women's Bodies and the Nation: Race, Gender and Culture.* London: Palgrave Macmillan, 2015.

Teubal, Savina J. *Ancient Sisterhood: The Lost Traditions of Hagar and Sarah.* Athens: Ohio University Press, 1997.

Thoburn, J. M. Introduction. *An Autobiography: The Story of the Lord's Dealings with Mrs. Amanda Smith, the Colored Evangelist (1837–1915).* 1893, edited by Amanda Smith, v–x. Cary: Oxford University Press, 1988.

Tompkins, Jane. *Sensational Designs: The Cultural Work of American Fiction, 1790–1860.* Cary: Oxford University Press, 1986.

Totten, Gary. *African American Travel Narratives from Abroad: Mobility and Cultural Work in the Age of Jim Crow.* Amherst: University of Massachusetts Press, 2015.

Townes, Emilie M., ed. *A Troubling in My Soul: Womanist Perspectives on Evil and Suffering.* Maryknoll, NY: Orbis, 1993.

Trafton, Scott. *Egypt Land: Race and Nineteenth-Century American Egyptomania.* Durham: Duke University Press, 2004.

"Travel." *Black Folk Don't,* season 1, episode 3, Black Public Media, Public Broadcasting Service, 11 Mar. 2012, www.pbs.org/video/2250428204/.

Truth, Sojourner. *"Narrative of Sojourner Truth, a Northern Slave."* Documenting the American South. https://docsouth.unc.edu/neh/truth50/menu.html.

Ukadike, N. Frank. "Reclaiming Images of Women in Films from Africa and the Black Diaspora." *Frontiers: A Journal of Women Studies* 5, no. 1 (1994): 102–22.

Wade-Gayles, Gloria, ed. *My Soul Is a Witness: African American Women's Spirituality.* Boston: Beacon, 1996.

Walker, Alice. *In Search of Our Mothers' Gardens: Womanist Prose.* New York: Harcourt, 1983.

Walker, David. *Appeal to the Coloured Citizens of the World.* 1830. Edited by Peter P. Hinks. University Park: Penn State University Press, 2002.

Wall, Cheryl A. *Changing our Own Words: Essays on Criticism, Theory, and Writing by Black Women.* New Brunswick: Rutgers University Press, 1989.

Wallace-Sanders, Kimberly. Introduction. *Skin Deep, Spirit Strong: The Black Female Body in American Culture,* edited by Kimberly Wallace-Sanders, 1–10. Ann Arbor, MI: University of Michigan Press, 2002.

Wallace, Maurice O., and Shawn Michelle Smith. Introduction. *Pictures and Progress: Early Photography and the Making of African American Identity,* edited by Wallace and Smith, 1–17. Durham: Duke University Press, 2012.

Washington, Harriet A. *Medical Apartheid: The Dark History of Medical Experimentation on Black Americans from Colonial Times to the Present.* New York: Doubleday, 2006.

Watson, Julia, and Sidonie Smith. "De/Colonization and the Politics of Discourse in Women's Autobiographical Practices." In *De/Colonizing the Subject: The Politics of Gender in Women's Autobiography,* edited by Smith and Watson, xiii–xxxi. Minneapolis: University of Minnesota Press, 1992.

Weems, Renita J. *Just a Sister Away: A Womanist Vision of Women's Relationships in the Bible.* Philadelphia: Innisfree Press, 1988.

Weisenfeld, Judith. "'My Story Begins before I Was Born': Myth, History, and Power in Julie Dash's *Daughters of the Dust.*" In *Representing Religion in World Cinema: Filmmaking, Mythmaking, Culture Making,* edited by S. Brent Plate, 43–66. New York: Palgrave Macmillan, 2003.

Weisenfeld, Judith, and Richard Newman, eds. *This Far by Faith: Readings in African-American Women's Religious Biography.* New York: Routledge, 1996.

"Wilderness." *The Oxford English Dictionary.* 2nd ed. 1989.

Williams, Delores S. *Sisters in the Wilderness: The Challenge of Womanist God-Talk.* Maryknoll, NY: Orbis, 1993.

———. "Visions, Inner Voices, Apparitions, and Defiance in Nineteenth-Century Black Women's Narratives." *Women's Studies Quarterly* 21, no. 1–2 (1993): 81–90.

———. "Women's Oppression and Lifeline Politics in Black Women's Religious Narratives." *Journal of Feminist Studies in Religion* 1, no. 2, (Fall 1985): 59–71.

Wilmore, Gayraud S. *Black Religion and Black Radicalism: An Interpretation of the Religious History of African Americans.* 3rd ed. Marynoll, NY: Orbis Books, 1998.

Wilson, Harriet E., and Henry Louis Gates Jr. *Our Nig; or, Sketches from the Life of a Free Black,* 1859. New York: Vintage, 1983.

Wright, David P. "'She Shall Not Go Free as Male Slaves Do': Developing Views About Slavery and Gender in the Laws of the Hebrew Bible." In *Beyond Slavery,* edited by Bernadette Brooten, 125–42. New York: Palgrave Macmillan, 2010.

Youngs, Tim. "Pushing against the Black/White Limits of Maps: African American Writings of Travel." *English Studies in Africa: A Journal of the Humanities* 53, no. 2 (2010): 71–85.

Index

Italicized page numbers refer to illustrations.

Abraham (biblical figure), 13–21, 25–35, 41, 82, 173–74
ACS (American Colonization Society), 65–66, 106
activism: biblical, 221; political, 131; social, 71, 131, 230n3; spiritual, 111, 124, 131, 136–39, 143, 145. *See also* anti-slavery activism
Africa: adoption of children from, 101–2; at center of Christianity, 97–99; colonial travel to, 186, 187, 189; Dark Continent myth of, 188, 240n5; homeland view of, 185; indigenous medicine in, 101; Islam in colonization of, 238n2; missionary work in, 90; origins of civilization in, 96; Pan-Africanism, 189–92, 194, 212, 214, 215; traditional spiritual practice in, 103–5, 234n41. *See also specific countries*
African cosmology, 75, 104, 148–49, 152, 155, 161–62, 174
African Methodist Episcopal (AME) Church, 72, 81, 84
Alexander, M. Jacqui, 37, 115, 147, 184, 214–15, 224n11, 224n15
alienation: in biblical slavery, 18; of Black people in US, 120, 122, 126, 181, 209–10; body/spirit divide and, 8; of Ghanaian émigrés, 190; of Hagar, 18, 24; as shared human condition, 143; of slaveholders, 66; spiritual, 39, 129, 130

Allen, Richard, 106
AME (African Methodist Episcopal) Church, 72, 81, 84
American Colonization Society (ACS), 65–66, 106
Andrews, William L., 34, 45, 224n10, 230n31
Angelou, Maya, 185, 190
anti-slavery activism: alternative spiritual legacy of, 111; critiques of, 68–69, 131–32, 138; domestic spaces for, 144; by Prince, 109, 124, 131–32, 139; on slave ships, 112–16; white leadership of, 37
Arbery, Ahmaud, 220, 241n1
Atlantic slave trade, 16, 18, 25, 90, 125, 182. *See also* Middle Passage
autobiographies. *See* Black autobiographies; spiritual autobiographies
Autobiography: The Story of the Lord's Dealings with Mrs. Amanda Smith, An (Smith): on Black female bodies, 100–101; critique of imperialism in, 94–98; embodied spiritual practice in, 72–74, 77, 79–82, 86, 107; hybrid nature of, 2, 107–8; itinerancy in, 72–73, 82, 91, 105; negotiating colonial and missionary ideologies in Liberia, 100–107; preface by Thoburn, 72, 231n5; on reclaiming Blackness in Egypt, 94–98; rhetorical practices utilized in, 74, 91, 93, 98–100, 102; shifting discourse in India, 98–100;

Autobiography (continued)
   spectacle to spectator shift in, 91–94;
   spiritual work in, 10, 71, 73–78, 88; theological critique of slavery in, 78; unruly and disruptive body in, 87, 90; visionary experience in, 73, 77, 81

Baker, Houston, 148
Bambara, Toni Cade, 169–70
Barker, Francis, 156
Barnum, P. T., 73
Barrett, Lindon, 55, 56
Barthelemy, Anthony G., 145
Berry, Mariam, 71, 76, 78–80
Berry, Samuel, 71, 74–79
biblical activism, 221
biblical slavery, 16–18, 225n10
Birkle, Carmen, 124
Black autobiographies: challenges for authors of, 145; free telling as feature of, 34; legacy of violence in, 17; white responses to, 45. *See also* spiritual autobiographies; *specific works*
Black citizenship: advocacy for, 72; collective struggle for, 111, 112; colonization movement and, 66, 124; denial of, 120, 124, 138; Smith on, 106, 107
Black female bodies: as chattel, 13, 59, 74, 163; coerced movement of, 107, 120; cultural anxiety surrounding, 22, 226n19; as divinely empowered, 57–58, 63, 70; dominant representations of, 36, 90; Elaw's *Memoirs* as counterdiscourse on, 42–44; erasure of, 4, 202, 217; as made for freedom, 7, 24, 38, 89; marginalization of, 4, 217; misnaming of, 6, 18–19, 32–34, 206, 223n8, 225n11; patriarchal control and constructions of, 57, 60, 61; racist views of, 57–58, 60; sanctification of, 50–51; Smith's *Autobiography* on, 100–101; spiritual knowledge housed in, 8, 46, 58, 63; as unruly and disruptive, 32–36, 87, 90, 173–77; violation of, 4, 14, 119. *See also* commodification; embodied spiritual practice; exploitation; objectification; sexual violence

Black feminism, 19, 34, 37
Black Lives Matter movement, 220, 241n3
Blackness: colonial identifications of, 101; criminalization of, 60, 138; disruption of fixed definitions of, 151; erasure of, 23, 24; of Hagar, 16, 19, 22–24; master narrative of, 56, 57; othering of, 22, 92; reclaiming in Egypt, 94–98; sexuality and, 22–23; slavery associated with, 45, 75, 140; spiritual and cultural value of, 83; Western constructions of, 128
Black theology, 19, 50, 82, 225n12
Blockett, Kimberly, 40, 45, 112, 228n5
Blyden, Edward Wilmot, 96–97, 232n29
Boone, Sylvia, 190–91
Boym, Svetlana, 191
Brantlinger, Patrick, 240n5
Braxton, Joanne, 43
British Anti-Slavery Society, 68–69
Brouwer, Joel, 150, 169
Brown, William Wells, 68, 92, 93
Bruce, Dickson, 52
Brueggemann, Walter, 230n31
Bunyan, John, 43, 142
Busia, Abena, 173
Buzzard, James, 127

Campbell, James, 185
camp meetings, 51–52, 77
Cannon, Katie G., 5
Carby, Hazel, 32, 101
Christian, Barbara, 148
Christianity: colonization and, 103, 104, 153–55, 157–59, 161, 207; conversion to, 48–50, 53, 76, 82–83, 103–4, 106, 122; feminism and, 232n20; in Ghana, 207–8; hypocrisy of believers, 66–67, 77, 119–20; incompatibility with slavery, 66, 78; openness to all races and nations, 49; origins of, 79, 97–99; revisionist history of, 97; varying geographies of, 38; white imperialistic model of, 66–67. *See also* missionary work
Cima, Gay Gibson, 123
cinematic decolonization, 150, 152, 153, 157, 173, 178, 183

circum-Atlantic world, 7–8, 110, 160, 164, 232n29
citizenship. *See* Black citizenship
Clark, Adam, 225n14
Clegg, Claude, 106
coerced movement: of Black female bodies, 107, 120; divide between free movement and, 2, 3; in Hagar's narrative, 15, 26, 29, 38
Collier-Thomas, Bettye, 50
colonization: acculturated victims of, 154–55; American Colonization Society, 65–66, 106; Christianity and, 103, 104, 153–55, 157–59, 161, 207; critiques of, 134, 184; defined, 184, 188; enforced geographies of, 8; Islam and, 237–38n2; missionary work and, 100, 106; movement for Black emigration, 66, 124; power structures of, 136; transference of culture in, 102, 233n38; unequal resource distribution in, 99–100; violence of, 136, 156, 187. *See also* decolonization; imperialism
Colquitt, Martha, 75
commodification: exploitation within space of, 62; in Hagar's narrative, 36; patriarchal capitalistic values and, 121; in slave markets, 79; of spiritual practice, 135; threat of, 73, 138, 140, 145
co-narration technique, 150, 153, 169
contested spaces, 137, 193
Cooper, Anna Julia, 233n35
Copeland, M. Shawn, 5, 7, 48
courthouse, as site of domination, 59–60, 80
Craft, William and Ellen, 92
Cruikshank, Isaac, *200*
Crummell, Alexander, 67–68
Cucinella, Catherine, 155
cultural imperialism, 35, 99, 169
cultural stripping, 18, 113, 235n7
Curry, Renee, 155

Dark Continent myth, 188, 240n5
Dash, Julie: cinematic practice of, 10–11, 149–53, 170; diaspora time as used by, 159–60, 169, 171; on marginalization of Black female filmmakers, 238n3; multi-perspectival storytelling by, 114, 150, 197; reshaping of viewer's gaze by, 158. *See also Daughters of the Dust*
Daughters of the Dust (film): African cosmology in, 148–49, 152, 155, 161–62, 174; cinematic decolonization in, 150, 152, 153, 157, 173, 178, 183; co-narration technique in, 150, 153, 169–70; Ibo Landing myth in, 171–73, 197, 239n24; Islam in, 11, 148, 158–61; kaleidoscope and kaleidoscopic perspective in, 150–51, 157, 170–72, 238n4; mission of film, 151; opening montage of, 152–53; rape in, 37, 162–63, 166–67, 175–78; on resistance aboard slave ships, 114; spiritual geographies and, 10, 148, 150, 159, 161, 178; spiritual practice in, 149, 153, 158–68, 170–72, 175; spiritual work in, 149, 159, 163, 168, 173; synopsis of, 148–49; tableaux in, 150, 152, 159, 238n8. *See also* Muhammed, Bilal; Peazant, Eula; Peazant, Haagar; Peazant, Nana; Peazant, Viola; Peazant, Yellow Mary; Unborn Child
Decembrist Revolt (1825), 128
decolonization: cinematic, 150, 152, 153, 157, 173, 178, 183; free territory and, 193; literary, 183; as spiritual work, 184; storytelling and, 173, 197; of viewing practices, 188
Delany, Martin, 47, 106
Devine, Calvin, 81, 231n13
diaspora time, 159–60, 169, 171
diasporic movement, 3, 10, 11, 184
Díaz, Junot, 208, 241n17
dispossession: continuing threat of, 149; in Hagar's narrative, 14, 15, 18, 20–21, 24; as inheritance for Black people, 25, 117, 217, 218, 220; slavery and, 20, 148–50, 178, 197, 210; spiritual practice as challenge to legacy of, 116, 164
Dobroliubov, Nicholas, 236n21
domestic spaces: for anti-slavery activism, 144; captivity of Black women in, 1, 84, 120–21; disordering of, 177; in free territory, 121; in Hagar's narrative, 17, 27–29,

domestic spaces (*continued*)
  32, 35; power structure within, 17, 29, 35; terror within, 121–22; violation of Black bodies in, 61. *See also* domestic work
domestic work: Elaw in, 28, 39, 41–42, 227n28; exploitation in, 28, 84–85, 109, 119, 122; Prince in, 28, 109, 118–22, 227n28; Smith in, 28, 71, 81, 84–86, 227n28; violence in, 118–20
Dorr, David F., 95–96
Douglas, Kelly Brown, 210–11
Douglass, Frederick, 47, 68, 77, 92, 96, 106, 117, 119
Douglass-Chin, Richard, 3, 40, 49

economic exploitation, 102, 118, 135–36, 218, 236n25
economic mobility, 117, 123
Egypt: at center of Christianity, 79, 97; reclaiming of Blackness in, 94–98
Elaw, Zilpha: birth and early years, 39, 228n1; conversion to Christianity, 48–50, 53; as domestic worker, 28, 39, 41–42, 227n28; Hagar as spiritual and literary ancestor of, 15; missionary work of, 65–70; theological framework utilized by, 5; vulnerabilities of Black life for, 41–43, 58–59, 218. See also *Memoirs of the Life, Religious Experience, Ministerial Travels and Labours of Mrs. Zilpha Elaw*
embodied spiritual practice: activism and, 131, 139; acts of resistance as, 79, 89; characteristics of, 7; contextual considerations, 10; in *Daughters of the Dust*, 162, 163, 165–66, 170; divine healing as, 63; in Elaw's *Memoirs*, 39–55, 58, 61–66, 70; in Hagar's narrative, 24–30, 32–38; itinerancy as expression of, 26, 27, 30; in *Lose Your Mother*, 184; memory and, 114–16, 159, 164; of Methodist Church, 39–40; in Prince's *Narrative*, 131, 132, 134, 137–41; sanctification and, 86–87; in Smith's *Autobiography*, 72–74, 77, 79–82, 86, 107; spiritual work and, 74; visionary experience and, 24, 46–55, 64,

70, 73, 77, 81; visionary movement and, 41, 42, 47
England: comparative critique of US and, 91–93; missionary work in, 65–70
erasure: in Africanist discourse, 181, 185; of alternative perspectives, 173; of Black female bodies, 4, 202, 217; of Blackness, 23, 24; colonial violence of, 156, 186; of Hagar, 19–20, 23, 24, 33–35; of historical archive of slavery, 164, 181, 192, 196–97; utopian visions and, 190–92
ethics of care, 207
eunuchs, 48–50
evangelism. *See* itinerant preachers; missionary work
exploitation: in domestic work, 28, 84–85, 109, 119, 122; economic, 102, 118, 135–36, 218, 236n25; of Hagar, 14, 16, 17, 22, 218; physical, 16, 28, 62, 73; sexual, 16, 37, 62, 121, 175–76, 218; of slave labor, 75

feminism: appropriation of Hagar by white feminists, 22–23; Black, 19, 34, 37; Christianity and, 232n20; recovery of Hagar's narrative by, 17, 20, 35
Fish, Cheryl J., 93, 110, 129, 133–34, 136
Fitzpatrick, Kristin, 125, 137, 140, 142
Floyd, George, 220, 241n1
Foreman, P. Gabrielle, 217
Foster, Frances Smith, 45
Foucault, Michel, 201
Fourteenth Amendment, 80
freedom: Black female bodies as made for, 7, 24, 38, 89; communal practice of, 116, 143; conditionality of, 142, 231n8; in Hagar's narrative, 9, 14, 21, 28–31, 34; incomplete nature of, 6, 42, 109, 118, 196; mobility and, 21, 38, 41, 110–12, 116, 122–23, 176, 219; purchase by enslaved people, 71, 74, 76–78; spaces of, 118, 143, 148; struggles for, 19, 109–10, 116, 136, 144, 180, 235n6; to travel, 89, 109, 110
free telling, 33–34, 224n10
free territory: building, 193, 211–15; domestic spaces in, 121; search for, 125, 180, 189, 219

Fugitive Slave Law, 78, 144–45. *See also* runaway slaves
Fussell, Paul, 94

Gabler-Hover, Janet, 22–23
Gafney, Wilda, 19, 24, 224n3, 227n31
Gaines, Kevin, 190
Ghana: Christianity in, 207–8; critical vision of, 185–94; emigration to, 180, 189–94, 208; fugitive slave community in, 212–13; heritage tourism in, 192–93; slave trade in, 181, 182, 212–13
Giddings, Paula, 85
Gilroy, Paul, 8, 113
Gossage, Ned, 77–78
Greenberg, Kenneth, 205
Greene, J. Lee, 21
Gruesser, John, 185
Gunning, Sandra, 123, 125, 236n21
Guy-Sheftall, Beverly, 23, 51

Hagar and Hagar's narrative: alienation of, 18, 24; alternative legacy for, 15, 25–36, 175; Black women as daughters of, 24, 36–37, 175; coerced movement in, 15, 26, 29, 38; dispossession in, 14, 15, 18, 20–21, 24; embodied spiritual practice in, 24–30, 32–38; enslavement of, 13–21, 26–33; erasure of, 19–20, 23, 24, 33–35; exile of, 14, 15, 20, 21, 174; exploitation of, 14, 16, 17, 22, 218; familiarity to Black women, 16–19; freedom in, 9, 14, 21, 28–31, 34; Haagar compared to, 173–74; itinerancy in, 15, 25–31, 36, 38; legacy within American culture, 13–25; as literary spiritual foremother, 9, 15, 21, 24; marginalization of, 19–22, 35; misnaming of, 18, 19, 32–34, 225n11; nineteenth-century uses of, 22–25; objectification of, 18, 19, 27; physical and sexual labor of, 13, 15, 16, 19, 22; recovery work and, 15, 17, 19–21, 24, 35; transgressive movement in, 26–27, 33, 38; unruly and disruptive body in, 32–36, 87, 173; vulnerability of, 18, 33, 41, 218; in wilderness, 14, 20, 21, 27–30, 32–33, 36, 52; Yellow Mary compared to, 175–77

Hall, Timothy, 26, 226n24
Hartman, Saidiya: on afterlife of slavery, 11–12, 15, 181, 196, 210; on courtrooms of antebellum South, 59–60; on free territory, 125, 189, 193, 211–15; on rape of Black female slaves, 226n18. See also *Lose Your Mother: A Journey along the Atlantic Slave Route*
Hawkins, Anne Hunsaker, 43
Hayford, J. E. Casely, 103–4
Haynes, Caroline, 85, 232n20
Haynes, Rosetta, 3, 40
heritage tourism, 192–93
Heth, Joice, 73
Higgins, Michelle, 220–21
Hobson, Janell, 158
holiness. *See* sanctification
Holiness movement, 71
hooks, bell, 42, 155, 158, 163, 209–10
Hopkins, Pauline, 96
host body, 123, 124
Hucks, Tracey, 148
Hudson, Larry, 74–75
Hulme, Peter, 156
Humez, Jean, 50
hybrid texts, 2, 41, 43, 107–8, 110, 223n5

Ibo Landing myth, 171–73, 197, 239n24
imperialism: critiques of, 94–98, 131; cultural, 35, 99, 169; enforced geographies of, 8; language of, 102; missionary work and, 65–66, 70, 91, 103–6; ordering principles of, 103; religious, 99, 237n26; violence and, 104, 105, 136. *See also* colonization
incarnational theology, 48
India: missionary work in, 72, 90; shifting discourse in, 98–100
indigenous people: African medicine and, 101; conversion to Christianity by, 103–4; economic exploitation of, 102; enslavement of, 112, 155; representations of, 100, 105
Isaac (biblical figure), 14, 20, 21, 29, 35, 227n29
Ishmael (biblical figure), 14, 20, 21, 27–30, 35

Index • 263

Islam, 11, 38, 148, 158–61, 237–38n2
Israel, Adrienne, 78
itinerary: definitions of, 7, 26, 226n24; in Elaw's *Memoirs,* 40–42, 47, 51–64, 70; embodied spiritual practice and, 26, 27, 30; in Hagar's narrative, 15, 25–31, 36, 38; in Smith's *Autobiography,* 72–73, 82, 91, 105; spiritual, 8, 24, 40, 47, 73, 91, 225n14; of Yellow Mary, 175. *See also* itinerant preachers; mobility; movement; travel
itinerant preachers: biblical figures invoked by, 23; camp meetings held by, 51–52, 77; dangers faced by, 40, 42, 58–59, 63–64, 73; hostile receptions to, 55–63, 229n15; opposition from local ministers, 63; visionary experience and, 40, 47, 52–54

Jacobs, Harriet, 61, 77, 119
Jacobs, Sylvia, 104
Jahn, Janheinz, 165–66
Jamaica: African spirituality in, 237n26; colonial systems of power in, 136; emancipation in, 132, 135, 236n25; missionary work in, 111, 132–36, 237n27
jeremiads, 139–41
Jones, Jacqueline, 74–75
Jordan, Kimberleigh, 21

kaleidoscope and kaleidoscopic perspective, 150–51, 157, 170–72, 238n4
King, Jeannine, 177
King, Martin Luther, Jr., 241n17

Lee, Jarena, 40–42
Lewis, Edmonia, 226n16
Liberia, negotiating colonial and missionary ideologies in, 100–107
limbo time. *See* diaspora time
linguistic violence, 201–2
literary archaeology, 198–200, 203, 206
literary decolonization, 183
Logan, Lisa, 121
Lose Your Mother: A Journey along the Atlantic Slave Route (Hartman): on building free territory, 193, 211–15; critical vision of Ghana in, 185–94; ethics of care and, 207; on fugitive slave community in Ghana, 212–13; hybrid nature of, 2; literary decolonization in, 183; recovery work in, 11, 180–82, 191, 194–95, 199–207, 210, 217; spiritual practice in, 184, 210; spiritual work in, 180, 182, 184, 216; storytelling as critical practice in, 199, 202–5
lynching, 106, 107, 140, 161, 163, 177–78

MacGonagle, Elizabeth, 193
Marchiorlatti, Jennifer, 178
marginalization: of Black female bodies, 4, 217; of Black female filmmakers, 238n3; of Black travel writing, 2, 223n5; of eunuchs, 49; of Hagar's narrative, 19–22, 35; of visionary practice, 55
Marshall, Paule, 172, 176–77
Martin, Joan, 75–77
Martin, Sandy Dwayne, 103, 104
Mbiti, John S., 234n41
McDowell, Deborah, 12, 221
McKittrick, Katherine: on auction block as site of domination, 56; on Black female bodies, 7, 122; on respatialization, 60, 144; on ships as symbols of Middle Passage, 113; on slave trade landscape, 80; on space and geography, 7, 26, 57, 66; on spatial histories, 235n9
McKoy, Sheila Smith, 159, 160
Memoirs of the Life, Religious Experience, Ministerial Travels and Labours of Mrs. Zilpha Elaw (Elaw): as counterdiscourse on Black female bodies, 42–44; critique of human language in, 45–46; embodied spiritual practice in, 39–55, 58, 61–66, 70; epigraph and dedication, 43–46; hybrid nature of, 41, 43; itinerancy in, 40–42, 47, 51–64, 70; oppositional spiritual practice in, 65, 68; resistance and redefinition in, 55–64; transgressive movement in, 63, 70; visionary experience in, 40–41, 46–55, 64, 67, 70; visionary movement in, 41, 42, 46, 47, 55–57, 70; visionary practice in, 40, 43–44, 46–51, 55–64

memory: ancestral, 116, 156, 157, 159, 164, 172; cultural, 98; embodied, 114–16, 159, 164; geographical, 116; oral transmission of, 157, 164; as site of spiritual resistance, 157

Methodist Church: AME Church, 72, 81, 84; Elaw's preaching before leaders of, 46, 59; embodied spiritual practice of, 39–40; sanctification in, 50, 229n21; slaveholders as members of, 78

Middle Passage: breach caused by, 189, 191, 192; as circum-Atlantic passage, 160; colonization schemes as reversal of, 65; movement of the sacred during, 147; parallels with Hagar's enslavement, 27; resistance aboard slave ships, 112–16, 144

Mills, Sara, 98, 232n30

missionary work: by Elaw, 65–70; imperialism and, 65–66, 70, 91, 103–6; by Prince, 109, 111, 132–36, 237n27; racism in, 100, 105–6; by Smith, 72, 90–91

Mitchel, Pierson and Rebecca, 39

mobile subjectivity, 93–94, 105, 123

mobility: divine call to, 40, 61; economic, 117, 123; freedom and, 21, 38, 41, 110–12, 116, 122–23, 176, 219; in Hagar's narrative, 15, 27, 175; in literary analysis, 3; marriage as means to, 109, 123, 124; policing of, 220; social, 126, 148; spiritual practice and, 1, 21, 27, 71, 122, 178, 183; threat posed by, 218; unequal access to, 109; visionary practice and, 40. *See also* itinerancy; movement; travel

Moody, Joycelyn, 3–4, 40, 43, 110, 133, 134

Morrison, Toni: *Beloved,* 31; engagement with historical record, 197–98; literary archaeology of, 198–200, 206; *Playing in the Dark,* 57; "Rootedness: The Ancestor as Foundation," 4, 174; "The Site of Memory," 198

movement: diasporic, 3, 10, 11, 184; spirit-led, 2, 24, 30, 38, 61, 65, 73; transgressive, 8, 26–27, 33, 38, 63, 70; visionary, 41, 42, 46, 47, 55–57, 70. *See also* coerced movement; itinerancy; mobility

Muhammed, Bilal (film character): at "Hand" ceremony, 165; historical basis for, 159–60; on Ibo Landing myth, 172; in opening montage, 152, 153; spiritual practice of, 153, 159–61

multi-perspectival storytelling, 114, 150, 183, 197

Narrative of the Life and Travels of Mrs. Nancy Prince, A (Prince): on ancestral spiritual legacy, 114–16; embodied spiritual practice in, 131, 132, 134, 137–41; on geography and genealogy, 111–12, 116; hybrid nature of, 2, 110; on near-death experience, 129–30; oppositional spiritual practice in, 110, 116, 145; portrait of Russian society and politics in, 125–29; representation of Black Jamaicans in, 133–36; ship voyage from Jamaica to US, 137–41; spectacle to spectator shift in, 126–27; spiritual transformation in Russia, 122, 125, 129–31; spiritual work in, 130, 133; on US as space of terror, 111–22

Nelson, Charmaine, 22, 90, 187–88

Newsome, Bree, 220

Nommo, 165–67, 171, 239n21

objectification: in domestic spaces, 121; of Hagar, 18, 19, 27; methods of, 92; resistance to, 7, 60; in Russian society, 125; in slave markets, 79–80; threat of, 73, 93

Ogunleye, Foluke, 173

oppositional gaze, 158

oppositional spiritual practice, 65, 68, 110, 116, 145

orality, as oppositional practice, 55, 116

Pan-Africanism, 189–92, 194, 212, 214, 215

Paris, Peter, 104, 161

Peazant, Eula (film character): at "Hand" ceremony, 165; on Ibo Landing myth, 171–73; interactions with Unborn Child, 170; Nommo utilized by, 165–67, 171; in opening montage, 152, 153; as rape victim,

Peazant, Eula (film character) (*continued*) 37, 162–63, 166–67, 177; spiritual practice of, 149, 153, 165–68, 170, 172

Peazant, Haagar (film character): comparison with biblical Hagar, 173–74; at "Hand" ceremony, 158, 165, 173; interactions with Unborn Child, 170; rejection of community by, 174–76

Peazant, Nana (film character): as co-narrator, 153, 169, 170; "Hand" ceremony performed by, 159, 163–65; interactions with Unborn Child, 170; Nommo utilized by, 166; in opening montage, 152, 153; spiritual practice of, 149, 153, 161–65, 170

Peazant, Viola (film character): bodily and spiritual purity of, 176; colonizing rhetoric of, 158; in opening montage, 152, 153; photographer hired by, 150, 153–54; scholarly analysis of, 154–55; on slave trade, 156–57; spiritual practice of, 153, 158–59

Peazant, Yellow Mary (film character): comparison with Hagar, 175–77; at "Hand" ceremony, 176; itinerancy of, 175; in opening montage, 149, 152, 153; as rape victim, 166–67, 175–78; sexual past of, 37; spiritual practice of, 153, 175

Peterson, Carla, 3, 42, 110, 133, 134

Pettinger, Alasdair, 183

Petty, Sheila, 176

physical exploitation, 16, 28, 62, 73

physical violence, 6, 35, 92, 161, 167, 202

Pierce, Yolanda, 47, 50–51, 69

Pilgrim's Progress (Bunyan), 43, 142

political activism, 131

Pratt, Mary Louise, 186

preachers. *See* itinerant preachers

Prince, Nancy Gardner: birth and early years, 109, 111, 117–18; conversion to Christianity, 122; as domestic worker, 28, 109, 118–22, 227n28; emigration to Russia, 109–11, 122–31; Hagar as spiritual and literary ancestor of, 15; "The Hiding Place," 141–43; marriage of, 109, 123–24; missionary work of, 109, 111, 132–36, 237n27; mobile subjectivity of, 123; social and political activism of, 131; spiritual activism of, 111, 124, 131, 136–39, 143, 145; theological framework utilized by, 5; on treatment of Black people in US vs. overseas, 93; vulnerabilities of Black life for, 139, 218. *See also Narrative of the Life and Travels of Mrs. Nancy Prince, A*

Puritan spiritual narratives, 44, 142

Raboteau, Albert, 225n13

racism: Black female bodies and, 57–58, 60; critiques of, 91, 92; misrepresentations based on, 45; in missionary work, 100, 105–6; resistance to, 88, 89; in Western cinema, 149–50; in white imperialistic model of Christianity, 66–67

radical spiritual practice, 1, 2, 140–41, 145, 146

rape: in *Daughters of the Dust,* 37, 162–63, 166–67, 175–78; Hagar as victim of, 15, 17; interracial, 177; justifications within slavery, 22. *See also* sexual violence

Ray, John and Mary Ellen, 186, 208–10

recovery work: forms of, 8–9; Hagar's narrative and, 15, 17, 19–21, 24, 35; integration of body/spirit in, 12, 224n15; in *Lose Your Mother,* 11, 180–82, 191, 194–95, 199–207, 210, 217; reclaiming Blackness in Egypt, 94–98; spiritual geographies and, 10, 12; as spiritual work, 180, 182

Rediker, Marcus, 114

Reiss, Benjamin, 73

religious imperialism, 99, 237n26

respatialization, 60–61, 80, 144

Richards, Sandra, 193

Roach, Joseph, 8, 157, 160

runaway slaves, 77–78, 80, 138, 144–45, 212–13

Russia: Decembrist Revolt in, 128; emigration to, 109–11, 122–31; racial ideologies in, 125, 128, 236n21; society and politics in, 125–29; St. Petersburg flood of 1824 in, 129–30

Ryan, Judylyn, 148

Sadler, Rodney, Jr., 17, 224n5

sanctification, 50–51, 71, 85–88, 229n21

Sarah (biblical figure), 13–21, 25–35, 41, 82, 173–74, 227n32, 227n41
Sawyer, John F. A., 140
Schueller, Malini Johar, 91, 93, 96
sexual exploitation, 16, 37, 62, 121, 175–76, 218
sexual violence: burden of victims of, 35; powerlessness of victims of, 154; in slavery, 6, 15, 17, 22, 224n5, 226n18. *See also* rape
Sharpe, Christina, 207
Shaw-Thornburg, Angela, 183, 223n5
singular thinking, 184, 224n11
slave narratives: on Christian hypocrisy, 119–20; of escape, 112–16; legacy of violence in, 17, 225n7. *See also specific works*
slavery: afterlife of, 5, 11–12, 15–17, 41, 175, 181, 196–98, 210; alternative communal narrative about, 116; biblical, 16–18, 225n10; Black female bodies as chattel, 13, 59, 74, 163; Blackness associated with, 45, 75, 140; critiques of, 131, 134; cultural stripping in, 18, 113, 235n7; dispossession and, 20, 148–50, 178, 197, 210; erasure of historical archive of, 164, 181, 192, 196–97; exploitation of slave labor, 75; at foundation of Black travel writing, 38; incompatibility with Christianity, 66, 78; indigenous people in, 112, 155; intersection of spiritual practice and travel with, 11, 71; justifications for, 16, 21, 45, 66; legacy of violence in, 17, 80, 163, 175, 225n7; power structure within, 16, 17; purchase of freedom from, 71, 74, 76–78; reproduction across social spaces, 144; Russian opposition to, 128; sexual violence in, 6, 15, 17, 22, 224n5, 226n18; as source of terror, 23, 112–13, 115, 117; theological critique of, 78; wage slavery, 118, 119, 218; womanhood within institution of, 32. *See also* anti-slavery activism; runaway slaves; slave trade
slave trade: abolishment of, 90, 156; Atlantic, 16, 18, 25, 90, 125, 182; denial of personhood in, 128; enforced geographies of, 8; in Ghana, 181, 182, 212–13;

illegal practicing of, 156–57; marketplace and, 61–62, 79–80. *See also* Middle Passage
Smalls, Robert, 117
Smallwood, Stephanie, 114–15, 235n7
Smith, Amanda Berry: birth and early years, 71; children of, 71, 81, 84, 101–2, 231n16, 233–34nn38–40; conversion to Christianity, 82–83; as domestic worker, 28, 71, 81, 84–86, 227n28; Hagar as spiritual and literary ancestor of, 15; legacy of work and liberation inherited by, 74–81; marriages of, 71, 81, 83–86, 88–89, 231n13; missionary work of, 72, 90–91; mobile subjectivity of, 93–94, 105; in temperance movement, 72, 230n3; theological framework utilized by, 5; vulnerabilities of Black life for, 71, 218. *See also Autobiography: The Story of the Lord's Dealings with Mrs. Amanda Smith, An*
Smith, James, 81, 83–86, 88–89
social activism, 71, 131, 230n3
social constructions, 8, 17, 60, 61, 70, 80
social mobility, 126, 148
spatial histories, 116, 235n9
Spillers, Hortense, 18, 34
spirit-led movement, 2, 24, 30, 38, 61, 65, 73
spiritual activism, 111, 124, 131, 136–39, 143, 145
spiritual alienation, 39, 129, 130
spiritual autobiographies: beginnings of, 40; key features of, 43, 110; legacy of movement in, 26. *See also specific works*
spiritual geographies, 10, 12, 148, 150, 159, 161, 178
spiritual itinerancy, 8, 24, 40, 47, 73, 91, 225n14
spiritual knowledge: alternative, 59, 75, 78; ancestral, 152; in Black female bodies, 8, 46, 58, 63; oppositional, 62; womanist theology on, 5
spiritual narratives: absence of Hagar from, 23, 24; bodily illness in, 82; communal, 148, 161, 169; Puritan, 44, 142; travel writing and, 9. *See also* spiritual autobiographies; *specific works*

spiritual practice: African traditions of, 103–5, 234n41, 237n26; commodification of, 135; in *Daughters of the Dust*, 149, 153, 158–68, 170–72, 175; in literary analysis, 3–4; in *Lose Your Mother*, 184, 210; mobility and, 1, 21, 27, 71, 122, 178, 183; oppositional, 65, 68, 110, 116, 145; radical, 1, 2, 140–41, 145, 146; storytelling as, 150; travel and, 1, 9–11, 15, 110. *See also* embodied spiritual practice
spiritual violence, 6, 161, 202, 235n7
spiritual work: in *Daughters of the Dust*, 149, 153, 158–68, 170, 173; decolonization as, 184; diasporic movement and, 11; embodied spiritual practice and, 74; in *Lose Your Mother*, 180, 182, 184, 216; during Middle Passage, 115; in Prince's *Narrative*, 130, 133; recovery work as, 180, 182; in Smith's *Autobiography*, 10, 71, 73–78, 88. *See also* itinerant preachers; missionary work
Stewart, Maria, 47, 106, 139–40
storytelling: cinematic, 178; as critical practice, 199, 202–5; as decolonizing practice, 173, 197; of Ibo Landing myth, 171–73; memory construction through, 115; multi-perspectival, 114, 150, 183, 197; as spiritual practice, 150
St. Petersburg flood (1824), 129–30
syncretism, 104, 153, 158, 161, 165, 237n26

tableaux, 150, 152, 159, 238n8
talking back, 4, 39, 219
Tamez, Elsa, 29
Tate, Shirley Anne, 18–19, 92, 227n37
Taylor, Breonna, 220, 241n1
temperance movement, 72, 230n3
Tempest, The (Shakespeare), 154–56
terror: in domestic spaces, 121–22; of near-death experiences, 129–30; sexual violation as act of, 177–78; slavery as source of, 23, 112–13, 115, 117; of travel, 42, 44, 120, 130, 137; US as space of, 106, 111–22
Teubal, Savina, 20, 226n15

theology: Black, 19, 50, 82, 225n12; Euro-American, 24, 218; incarnational, 48; slaveholding, 138; womanist, 5, 19
Thoburn, J. M., 72, 230n5
Thompson, Takiya, 220
tourism: heritage tourism, 192–93; as leisure pursuit, 90, 93; performative nature of, 127; rhetoric of, 91, 93; shifting subjectivity and, 91–94, 126–27; visual practice of, 95, 96
transgressive movement, 8, 26–27, 33, 38, 63, 70
travel: circum-Atlantic, 7–8; freedom to, 89, 109, 110; missionary, 65–70; motivations for, 90, 109–11, 124; spiritual practice and, 1, 9–11, 15, 110; as terror, 42, 44, 120, 130, 137. *See also* itinerancy; mobility; tourism; *specific locations*
travel writing: legacy of movement in, 26, 90, 110; marginalization of Black authors, 2, 223n5; racial constructions in, 96, 97; rhetorical practices in, 74, 91, 93, 98–100, 102; slavery at foundation of, 38; spiritual narratives and, 9. *See also specific works*
Truth, Sojourner, 47

Ukadike, N. Frank, 150
Unborn Child (film character): communal and ancestral connection through, 149, 168; as co-narrator, 153, 169, 170; interactions with, 170; memories transferred to, 172; in opening montage, 152; as product of rape, 162–63; spiritual practice of, 171
Underground Railroad, 71, 78

violence: of abstraction, 199, 207; colonial, 136, 156, 187; cultural stripping as form of, 18, 113, 235n7; in domestic work, 118–20; of erasure, 156; imperialism and, 104, 105, 136; institutionalized, 128–29; linguistic, 201–2; physical, 6, 35, 92, 161, 167, 202; repetitions of, 117, 201, 202, 207; slavery's legacy of, 17, 80, 163, 175, 225n7; spiritual, 6, 161, 202, 235n7; transmission across social spaces, 144; visual

reproduction of acts of, *200*, 200–201. *See also* lynching; sexual violence
visionary experience: by daughters of Hagar, 36; in Elaw's *Memoirs*, 40–41, 46–55, 64, 67, 70; embodied spiritual practice and, 24, 46–55, 64, 70, 73, 77, 81; itinerant preachers and, 40, 47, 52–54; in Smith's *Autobiography*, 73, 77, 81
visionary movement, 41, 42, 46, 47, 55–57, 70
visionary practice, 34, 40, 43–44, 46–51, 55–64
Vose, Money, 112–17

wage slavery, 118, 119, 218
Walker, Alice, 4, 217
Walker, David, 47, 106
Wallace-Sanders, Kimberley, 6
Weems, Renita, 19, 224n3
Weisenfeld, Judith, 147, 151–52, 167
Weskett, John, 202
Western medicine, 101, 233n36
whiteness: Elaw on, 49–50, 66, 69; master narrative of, 57; power structures and, 23; as prerequisite for divine knowledge, 58; Smith's view of, 88; sociohistorical construction of, 83
white supremacy, 57, 66, 89, 106, 128, 163, 220
Wilberforce, William, 200–202, 205
wilderness: camp meetings in, 51–52, 77; Hagar's journey into, 14, 20, 21, 27–30, 32–33, 36, 52; as spiritual place of struggle, 30–31, 36, 51–52, 71, 77, 130, 141–42
Williams, Delores, 19–20, 24, 29, 30, 34–35, 46–47, 51–52, 224n3
Wilson, Harriet, 119–20
womanhood: characteristics of, 32, 101; domesticity and, 85; exclusivity of, 37; marriage in cult of, 124; pure/impure binary of, 167; self-sacrifice and, 85; socially prescribed definitions of, 42; transgressing bounds of, 23, 36
womanism: as framework for theological study, 5, 19; moving past sacred/secular divide through, 219; origins and definitions of term, 4; recovery of Hagar's narrative by, 15, 17, 19, 21, 35; on work ethic of enslaved community, 75, 76
work ethic, 75–77

Recent books in the series
Studies in Religion and Culture

In Search of Justice in Thailand's Deep South: Malay Muslim and Thai Buddhist Women's Narratives
Edited by John C. Holt, compiled by Soraya Jamjuree, and translated by Hara Shintaro

Precarious Balance: Sinhala Buddhism and the Forces of Pluralism
Bardwell L. Smith

Words Made Flesh: Formations of the Postsecular in British Romanticism
Sean Dempsey

A Language of Things: Emanuel Swedenborg and the American Environmental Imagination
Devin P. Zuber

The Pragmatist Turn: Religion, the Enlightenment, and the Formation of American Literature
Giles Gunn

Rethinking Sincerity and Authenticity: The Ethics of Theatricality in Kant, Kierkegaard, and Levinas
Howard Pickett

The Newark Earthworks: Enduring Monuments, Contested Meanings
Lindsay Jones and Richard D. Shiels, editors

Ideas to Live For: Toward a Global Ethics
Giles Gunn

The Pagan Writes Back: When World Religion Meets World Literature
Zhange Ni

Freud and Augustine in Dialogue: Psychoanalysis, Mysticism, and the Culture of Modern Spirituality
William B. Parsons

Vigilant Faith: Passionate Agnosticism in a Secular World
Daniel Boscaljon

Postmodernism and the Revolution in Religious Theory: Toward a Semiotics of the Event
Carl Raschke

Textual Intimacy: Autobiography and Religious Identities
Wesley A. Kort

When the Sun Danced: Myth, Miracles, and Modernity in Early Twentieth-Century Portugal
Jeffrey S. Bennett

Encountering the Secular: Philosophical Endeavors in Religion and Culture
J. Heath Atchley

Religion after Postmodernism: Retheorizing Myth and Literature
Victor E. Taylor

Mourning Religion
William B. Parsons, Diane Jonte-Pace, and Susan E. Henking, editors

Praise of the Secular
Gabriel Vahanian

Doing Justice to Mercy: Religion, Law, and Criminal Justice
Jonathan Rothchild, Matthew Myer Boulton, and Kevin Jung, editors

Bewildered Travel: The Sacred Quest for Confusion
Frederick J. Ruf

Sacred Claims: Repatriation and Living Tradition
Greg Johnson

Religion and Violence in a Secular World: Toward a New Political Theology
Clayton Crockett, editor

John Ruskin and the Ethics of Consumption
David M. Craig

Printed in the USA
CPSIA information can be obtained
at www.ICGtesting.com
CBHW071019150224
4340CB00013BA/110